Join the
CRAMMERS CLUB

Are you interested in an exclusive discount on books, special offers on third-party products and additional certification resources? Join our online certification community and become a member of The Crammers Club today!

Visit our site at **www.examcram2.com** and sign up to become a Crammers Club Member. By answering a few questions you will be eligible for some exciting benefits, including

- **Free practice exams**
- Special third-party offers and discounts
- Additional discounts on all book purchases
- The latest certification news
- Exclusive content
- Newsletters and daily exam questions
- Author articles and sample chapters
- Contests and prizes

Win a library of five Exam Cram 2 books of your choice!

Join The Crammers Club today and you will automatically be entered in our monthly drawing for a free five-book library.

Exam Cram 2 or Training Guide books only.
Random monthly drawing of all Crammers
Club Members, limitations may apply.

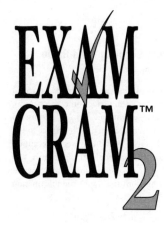

A+
PC Maintenance and Troubleshooting Field Guide

Charles Brooks

CERTIFICATION

Trademarks

All terms mentioned in this book that are known to be trademarks or service marks have been appropriately capitalized. Que Publishing cannot attest to the accuracy of this information. Use of a term in this book should not be regarded as affecting the validity of any trademark or service mark.

Warning and Disclaimer

Every effort has been made to make this book as complete and as accurate as possible, but no warranty or fitness is implied. The information provided is on an "as is" basis. The author and the publisher shall have neither liability nor responsibility to any person or entity with respect to any loss or damages arising from the information contained in this book.

Bulk Sales

Que Publishing offers excellent discounts on this book when ordered in quantity for bulk purchases or special sales. For more information, please contact

U.S. Corporate and Government Sales

1-800-382-3419

corpsales@pearsontechgroup.com

For sales outside the U.S., please contact

International Sales

international@pearsoned.com

Publisher
Paul Boger

Executive Editor
Jeff Riley

Acquisitions Editor
Jeff Riley

Development Editor
Steve Rowe

Managing Editor
Charlotte Clapp

Project Editor
Tonya Simpson

Copy Editor
Karen Annett

Indexer
Mandie Frank

Proofreader
Suzanne Thomas

Technical Editor
David Eytchison

Publishing Coordinator
Pamalee Nelson

Once again, I want to thank my wife, Robbie, for her support throughout another book campaign. Without her support and help, I'm sure there would be no books by Charles Brooks. I also want to mention Robert, Jamaica, Michael, and Joshua for adding to my life.

About the Author

Charles J. Brooks is currently the president of Marcraft International Corporation, located in Kennewick, Washington, and is in charge of research and development. He is the author of several books, including *Speech Synthesis, Pneumatic Instrumentation, The Complete Introductory Computer Course, Radio-Controlled Car Project Manual,* and *IBM PC Peripheral Troubleshooting and Repair.* A former electronics instructor and technical writer with the National Education Corporation, Charles has taught and written on post-secondary EET curriculum, including introductory electronics, transistor theory, linear integrated circuits, basic digital theory, industrial electronics, microprocessors, and computer peripherals.

Acknowledgments

There are so many people to thank for their efforts in preparing this book that I'm never sure where to start. But lots of folks worked very diligently to bring this book to market.

My staff at Marcraft has worked diligently to make certain that this is a quality product. I want to thank Cathy Boulay and Mike Hall for their artistic efforts, which are demonstrated throughout the book.

I also owe a big thanks to Grigoriy Ter-oganov, Yu Wen Ho, and Jason Ho of my Technical Services and Development staffs for many things, including turning my hands-on procedure ideas into working lab explorations, for their review and proofreading skills, and for their test-bank compilation work. Thanks also to Tony Tonda for all his work preparing user-support materials for the project.

I want to thank David Eytchison for his invaluable insight and excellent recommendations for improving this book.

As always, everyone I have worked with at Que Publishing has made this a pleasant experience. Jeff Riley, Steve Rowe, and Tonya Simpson, thanks again for another great life experience. Let's do another one sometime.

We Want to Hear from You!

As the reader of this book, *you* are our most important critic and commentator. We value your opinion and want to know what we're doing right, what we could do better, what areas you'd like to see us publish in, and any other words of wisdom you're willing to pass our way.

As an executive editor for Que Publishing, I welcome your comments. You can email or write me directly to let me know what you did or didn't like about this book—as well as what we can do to make our books better.

Please note that I cannot help you with technical problems related to the topic of this book. We do have a User Services group, however, where I will forward specific technical questions related to the book.

When you write, please be sure to include this book's title and author as well as your name, email address, and phone number. I will carefully review your comments and share them with the author and editors who worked on the book.

Email: feedback@quepublishing.com

Mail: Jeff Riley
Executive Editor
Que Publishing
800 East 96th Street
Indianapolis, IN 46240 USA

For more information about this book or another Que Certification title, visit our Web site at www.examcram2.com. Type the ISBN (excluding hyphens) or the title of a book in the Search field to find the page you're looking for.

Contents at a Glance

Table of Contents

. . . .

Part II Troubleshooting

Chapter 3
Hardware Troubleshooting Techniques......................................177

Part III Technical Data

Chapter 5

Introduction

I have wanted to create this book for some time. One of the things that seemed apparent during my work on various A+ and MCSA/MCSE certification books was the need for a simple book on important PC installation, configuration, and repair information. I want this book to be the tool that everyone in the PC administration and service environment keeps around.

This is not a certification prep book. Its only connection to certification is through the symptoms, procedures, and processes those certifications have highlighted as necessary for technicians and administrators to know.

How This Book Is Organized

The first two chapters of this book are dedicated to installing, configuring, and upgrading hardware components and operating system versions.

The second pair of chapters focuses on troubleshooting. Chapter 3, "Hardware Troubleshooting Techniques," deals with troubleshooting hardware failures, whereas Chapter 4, "Operating System Troubleshooting," deals with troubleshooting operating systems.

The final chapter is set aside for key technical data and reference sources. This book also contains a Quick Check crossover table that matches symptoms and error messages to troubleshooting processes in this book.

Elements in This Book

Along with the text of each chapter, you will also find notes, tips, cautions, figures, tables, and many lists. These elements are included to help enhance the book as well as to provide even more rich content.

Conclusion

Although I have attempted to bring together the key elements to which technicians and administrators need quick access, I do not pretend to think that I have single-handedly thought of everything. With that in mind, I invite my readers to share their ideas for key information that can be included in future revisions. However, this book needs to remain in a pocket-size format, so please don't send highly proprietary information that is specific only to a given model or manufacturer.

You can reach me directly with your comments, ideas for additional resources, and questions at

chuck@mic-inc.com

or at

Marcraft International
Chuck Brooks
100 N. Morain St., Suite 302
Kennewick, WA 99336

Please feel free to contact me at either of these addresses. I hope this product is very useful for you, and I want it to get better each time we update it. I feel the best way to do this is to stay in contact with you—my readers.

Thanks,

Charles J. Brooks

Troubleshooting Jump Table

Symptoms	Page Number
The system has detected unstable RAM at location x.	178
General failure error reading drive x.	179
Bad or missing command interpreter.	180, 235
Nonsystem disk or disk error.	180, 204
Bad file allocation table.	180
No indicator lights are visible, with no disk drive action and no display on the screen. Nothing works, and the system is dead.	187
The On/Off indicator lights are visible, but there is no disk drive action and no display on the monitor screen.	187
System produces a continuous beep tone.	187
Absence of lights.	187
Absence of the lights and the fan operation.	188
The On/Off indicator lights are visible and the display is visible on the monitor screen, but there is no disk drive action and no bootup occurs.	189
The On/Off indicator lights are visible and the hard drive spins up, but the system appears dead and there is no bootup.	189
System locks up during normal operation.	189
System does not hold the current date and time.	189
DMA error.	189
CMOS checksum failure.	189
Parity Check error.	189
CMOS is inoperational.	190

(continued)

Symptoms	Page Number
Speaker does not work.	190
Keyboard does not function.	190
Slow single beep from the speaker along with no display or other I/O operation.	191
System consistently locks up after being on for a few minutes.	191
Microprocessor is not running, but the power is on.	191
Infrequent and random glitches in the operation of applications and the system.	193
Permanent physical failures that generate NMI errors in the system.	193
Dead system board.	193
The bootup sequence automatically moves into the CMOS configuration display.	193
System refuses to maintain time and date information.	194
No characters appear onscreen.	194
KB/Interface Error—Keyboard Test Failure.	194
Unplugged keyboard.	195
Press F1 to continue.	195
Keyboard produces odd characters.	195
Cursor periodically freezes and jumps onscreen.	196
Mouse does not operate in safe mode.	197
No display.	198
Diagonal lines appear onscreen.	198
Display scrolls.	198
Monitor does not wake up early in the system's startup process.	199
Fuzzy characters appear on the display.	199
Monitor is showing poor colors, or only one color.	199
FDD Controller error message displays.	202
FDD activity light stays on constantly.	202
No boot record found.	202
System stops working while reading a disk.	202
Drive displays the same directory listing for every disk inserted in the drive.	202
System does not boot up to the floppy.	203
Computer boots up to a system disk in the A drive, but not to the hard drive.	204
Computer does not boot up.	204

Symptoms	Page Number
No motor sounds are produced by the HDD while the computer is running.	204
HDD Controller Failure message.	204
C: or D: Fixed Disk Drive error message.	204
Invalid media type.	204-205
No boot record found.	204
Nonsystem disk or disk error.	204
Invalid system disk.	204
Video display is active, but the HDD's activity light remains on and no bootup occurs.	204
Out of Disk Space message.	204
Missing operating system message.	180, 204
Hard drive boot failure.	204
Current drive no longer valid.	204
Drive Mismatch error.	205
Disk Boot Failure message.	205
Invalid Drive message.	206
Invalid Drive Specification message.	206
Buffer Underrun errors.	210
Tape drive cannot access secured files, or any files.	212
Device Manager cannot see the device after the proper driver has been loaded.	213, 219
Printer's Online light is on, but no characters are printed when print jobs are sent to the printer.	213
Device Not Found error.	213
USB controller does not appear in Device Manager.	217
Yellow warning icon appears next to the controller.	217-218
USB device does not install itself automatically.	217
FireWire bus runs particularly slow.	218
Failing infrared connection.	219
Modem does not dial out.	220
Modem does not connect after a number has been dialed.	220
Modem does not transmit after making connection with a remote unit.	220
Garbled messages are transmitted.	220

(continued)

Symptoms	Page Number
Modem connects, but cannot communicate.	223
Sound card operates correctly except when a printing operation is in progress.	224
PCMCIA adapter's icon shows an exclamation mark on a yellow background.	228
Device Manager displays the PCMCIA socket but no name for the card.	228
The names of the PCMCIA cards do not appear after the restart.	228
The names of other PCMCIA cards do appear in the Device Manager, but the card in question does not appear.	229
Nothing happens when you turn your portable computer on.	229
Warning messages appear about the battery not charging.	229
Intermittent system shutdowns when operating with only the battery.	229
Computer does not recognize its network connection when operating with only the battery.	229
Computer and input devices are slow when operating with only the battery.	230
Computer loses the time and date information when operating on battery power.	230
A single docking station connection does not work.	232
PS/2 mouse connection does not work.	232
Portable's touch pad works but the external mouse does not.	232
Operating system does not start (desktop does not load) after the Starting Windows message appears onscreen.	252
Computer stalls repeatedly for long periods of time.	252
User cannot print to a local printer after a complete troubleshooting sequence.	252
Computer has video display problems.	252
Computer slows down noticeably or does not work correctly.	252
System fails while loading the startup files.	253
System needs to load real-mode drivers.	253
Registry Failure error.	253
Cannot print to a remote printer.	253
Computer stalls during startup and cannot be started using a normal safe mode startup.	253
Corrupt CVF (Compressed Volume File) error.	254
Safe Mode and Safe Mode Command Prompt Only options fail to start the system.	254

Symptoms	Page Number
Disk boot failure.	235
HIMEM.SYS not loaded.	246
Swap file corrupt.	246
Damaged or missing core files.	246
Bad or missing **COMMAND.COM**.	246
Unable to initialize display adapter.	246-247
Device referenced in **WIN.INI** could not be found.	246
Device referenced in **SYSTEM.INI** could not be found.	246
HIMEM.SYS error.	247
Unable to initialize display adapter.	246-247
System disk invalid.	248
Invalid VxD Dynamic Link message.	248
Missing core file.	246, 249
System locks up and does not start.	250, 263
Error in **CONFIG.SYS** Line *XX* or Error in **AUTOEXEC.BAT** Line *XX*.	250
Unrecognized command in **CONFIG.SYS**.	250
Blue screen or Stop message.	248, 270, 272, 302, 305
Bootup stops after the POST.	271
Boot selection menu is never reached.	271
Missing operating system.	272
Disk Read error.	272
Invalid partition table.	272
Insert system disk message.	272
Error loading operating system.	272
Inaccessible boot device.	272
Kernel file is missing.	272
NTLDR could not be found.	272
Device or service has failed to start.	273
General Protection Faults.	237
This application has performed an illegal operation and is about to be shut down.	237
Out of memory.	262
Running out of resources.	264
User cannot log on.	294

(continued)

Symptoms	Page Number
User cannot recover an item that was deleted by another user.	294
User cannot recover any deleted items.	294
User cannot find key files using Windows utilities.	294
Users cannot gain access to folders.	296
User sends a print job to the printer, but cannot locate the document.	266, 303-304
User can see files in a folder, but cannot access any of the files.	296-297
Event log is full.	302
Printer is not producing anything in a Windows 9x/NT/2000 environment, even though print jobs have been sent to it.	266, 303
Printer operation stalls during the printing operation.	266
Local computer cannot see files and printers at the print server station.	268
Network cannot be seen in Network Neighborhood or My Network Places.	267
Network cannot be browsed.	267
User can browse the network but cannot access or use certain resources in remote locations.	267
User cannot see any other computers on the local network.	306
User cannot see other computers on different networks.	306
Clients cannot see the DHCP server, but do have an IP address.	307
Clients cannot obtain an IP address from a DHCP server that is on the other side of a router.	307
Users can see other local computers in a TCP/IP network, but cannot see remote systems on other networks.	307
Clients cannot obtain an IP address from a DHCP server that is located on the other side of a router.	307-308
When the user attempts to log on to the account, he is repeatedly asked to enter his account name and password until a predetermined number of failed attempts has been reached.	243-244
Disconnected message.	243
No Dial Tone message.	243
Port In Use message.	243
Can't Find Modem message.	243

PART I

Installing, Configuring, and Upgrading

Installing, Configuring, and Upgrading Hardware

Introduction

This chapter focuses on installing, configuring, and upgrading typical PC hardware components. It contains general procedures for installing most standard PC components.

Installing System Boards

Installing a system board is the most extensive hardware-related process in building or upgrading a PC system. The installation of most PC hardware components is a simple plug-and-play operation. However, the system board requires a more involved installation procedure that can be defined in six general steps:

1. Install the system board in the system unit.

2. Attach all internal cabling to the board (such as power connections, disk drive connections, and front panel connections).

3. Install option adapter cards in the appropriate expansion slot connectors (remove slot covers from the back panel of the chassis to accommodate new cards).

4. Install and configure all external I/O systems.

5. Test the system and reconfigure any CMOS settings required to bring the system up to its intended performance level.

6. Install the system unit's outer cover or side panels.

If you are upgrading to a new system board, you obviously need to remove the existing system board. This is a five-step process:

1. Disconnect and remove all external I/O systems.

2. Remove the system unit's outer cover.

3. Remove the option adapter cards.

4. Disconnect the cables from the system board.

5. Remove the system board.

Seating the System Board

Verify the positions of all jumper settings on the new system board. *This typically requires the use of the system board's installation/user's documentation.* Install the microprocessor and RAM on the board.

If possible, it is best to install the microprocessor and RAM on the system board and test it outside the system before installing it in the chassis.

Position the board over the floor of the system unit chassis and determine which screw holes match up between the case and the board, and note them. Install a brass standoff in each chassis hole that will be used to support (and ground) the system board. After all the standoffs are in place, align the system board with the standoffs.

In some case styles, you need to slide the system board behind power supplies and disk drive cages. In these situations, you should consider attaching any disk drive signal and auxiliary cabling to the board before sliding it under these obstacles.

If the hole pattern match is not good between the chassis and the board, you might need to install a couple of plastic clips or standoffs to support all areas of the system board.

With the system board in place, insert the grounding screws that secure the system board to the chassis.

Some cases employ plastic standoffs that drop into keyed holes in the floor of the system unit. To install system boards that use these, you must snap the plastic standoffs in the corresponding holes of the system board. Then, you drop the plastic standoffs in the system board slots and slide the board so that the feet lock into the keyed opening, as illustrated in Figure 1.1.

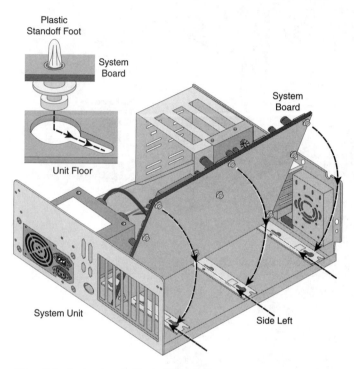

Figure 1.1   System board with plastic standoffs.

Connecting System Board Cables

Begin by connecting the power supply connections to the system board, as shown in Figure 1.2.

Then connect the floppy drive's signal cable (smaller signal cable) and the hard drive's signal cable (larger signal cable) to the disk drives and the system board, as depicted in Figure 1.3.

The system board provides an operator interface through a set of front panel indicator lights and switches. *Refer to the system board's installation documentation for the proper connection of these switches and indicators on the system board.* These indicators and switches connect to the system board through BERG connectors, as depicted in Figure 1.4.

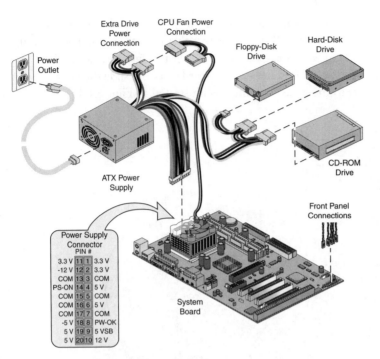

Figure 1.2 The ATX system board power connector.

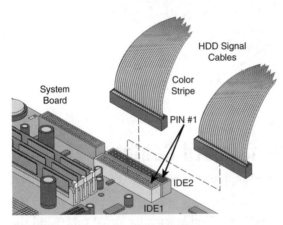

Figure 1.3 Connecting a drive's signal cable.

The connection pattern in the figure is representative of front panel connections; your connections might differ. Refer to the system board's installation documentation.

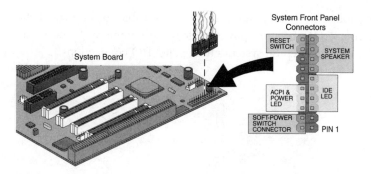

Figure 1.4   Front panel connections.

Installing Adapter Cards

The process used to install adapter cards is fairly simple:

1. Check the adapter card's installation information for any manual configuration settings that might need to be made.

2. Remove the expansion slot cover from the system unit's back panel. Align the adapter card with the appropriate expansion slot and firmly push it into the slot.

3. Secure the card to the back panel of the system unit with a single screw.

4. Attach any external connections to the card (that is, attach the phone line to the modem card or attach the network cable to the LAN adapter).

5. Install any device drivers required (PnP devices should be detected by the operating system and automatically configured for operation). Additional or updated drivers can be loaded from the operating system (for example, enhancing the operation of a video graphics adapter [VGA] card by loading a super video graphics adapter [SVGA] driver for the video display).

Connecting External I/O Systems

Connect all peripheral signal cables to the proper port or bus connector on the system unit. (These are typically found on the back panel of the system unit; however, many new case types place advanced I/O connectors on the front panel of the system.)

Connect the mouse, keyboard, and monitor signal cable to the rear of the unit. Finally, connect the monitor power cable to the commercial power outlet. Figure 1.5 depicts a typical system's back panel I/O connections.

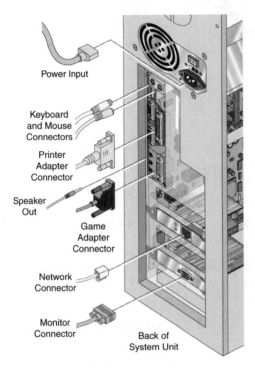

Power Input

Keyboard
and Mouse
Connectors

Printer
Adapter
Connector

Speaker
Out

Game
Adapter
Connector

Network
Connector

Monitor
Connector   Back of
                           System Unit

Figure 1.5   System unit back panel connections.

At this point, the system should be ready for testing. Plug all power cords into a commercial power outlet. Load the operating system and any applications onto the system's hard drive (if they are not installed already), and start the system. Check each application for functionality. This test is done before installing the system's outer cover so that any troubleshooting or updating that needs to be done can be performed in an efficient manner.

Installing the System Unit's Cover

Unplug the AC power cord from the system unit. Determine the type of case with which you are working. If the case is a desktop model, does the cover slide off the chassis in a forward direction, bringing the front panel with it, or does it raise off the chassis from the rear?

Check the back panel to determine how the outer cover is attached to the chassis. If screws go through the outer cover into the chassis, you need to remove them. Be certain not to remove the screws that hold the power supply to the chassis. In some tower cases, you need to remove the top cap from the chassis first. After this section has been removed, the other panels snap loose from the chassis. In other models, it is necessary to remove the plastic front cover from the unit first. This exposes screws that hold the panels to the chassis. Figure 1.6 shows typical techniques for installing the outer covers for different PC chassis styles.

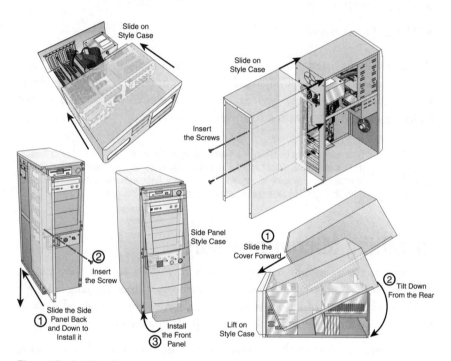

Figure 1.6 Installing the case.

Upgrading System Boards

In many situations, the best option for upgrading a PC system is to upgrade the entire system board. This is usually done to bring faster microprocessors and memory units together with newer chipsets and faster front side buses and I/O connections. In many cases, however, the components of the existing system board can be upgraded to provide additional performance at a lower cost than replacing the entire board.

The system board typically has five serviceable components. These include the following components:

➤ The microprocessor

➤ The RAM modules

➤ The CMOS backup battery

➤ The ROM BIOS IC

➤ The cache memory

Of the five items listed, three—the microprocessor, the RAM modules, and the ROM BIOS—can be exchanged (or updated) to increase the performance of the system. These devices are often mounted in sockets to make replacing or upgrading them a relatively easy task.

 Great care should be taken when exchanging these parts to avoid damage to the ICs from electrostatic discharge (ESD), which builds up on your body. Use approved antistatic wrist or ankle straps, work on antistatic floor and desk mats, and use room humidifiers to decrease the possibility of damaging discharges.

Installing Microprocessors

PC manufacturers mount microprocessors in sockets so that they can be replaced easily. This enables a failed microprocessor to be exchanged with a working unit. More often, though, the microprocessor is replaced with an improved version to upgrade the speed or performance of the system.

The notches and dots on the various ICs are important keys when replacing a microprocessor. They specify the location of the IC's pin 1. This pin must be lined up with the pin-1 notch of the socket for proper insertion.

Socket-mounted versions of microprocessors are installed in special *zero-insertion-force (ZIF)* sockets that permit the microprocessor to be placed in the socket without force and then be clamped in place. An arm-activated clamping mechanism in the socket shifts to the side, locking the pins in place. A ZIF socket and microprocessor arrangement is depicted in Figure 1.7.

To release the microprocessor from the socket, the lever arm beside the socket must be pressed down and away from the socket. When it comes free from the socket, the arm raises up to release the pressure on the microprocessor's pins.

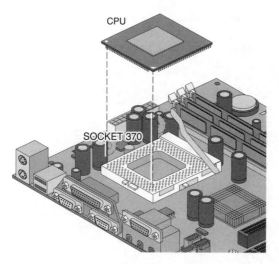

Figure 1.7 A microprocessor and ZIF socket.

A notch and dot in one corner of the CPU marks the position of the processor's pin 1. The dot and notch should be located at the free end of the socket's locking lever for proper installation. Both the CPU and the socket have one corner that does not have a pin (or pin hole) in it. This feature prevents the CPU from being inserted into the socket incorrectly.

Intel has offered several versions of Pentium microprocessors in a package type called *Single Edge Cartridges* (*SEC*). These processors mount vertically in an edge connector slot on the system board. The slot concept is very similar to the expansion slot connectors used with adapter cards. Because the cartridge mounts vertically on the system board, special mechanical supports must be installed on the system board to help hold it in place. These supports are normally preinstalled on the system board by its manufacturer.

The processor cartridge slides into the upright supports, as illustrated in Figure 1.8. It should be pressed firmly into the slot to ensure good contact.

As with other Pentium class processors, the cartridge-mounted Pentium processors require heat sinks and cooling systems to dissipate the tremendous amount of heat they generate. These processors employ special snap-on fan units that attach to the system board through special holes in the board. The fan is encased in a support structure that holds it in place. The fan unit receives power and speed control information from the system board through a two- or three-wire cable and connector.

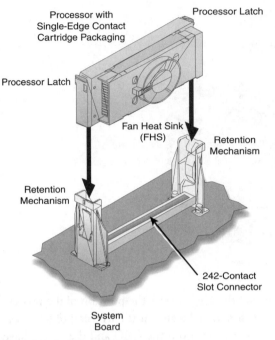

Processor with
Single-Edge Contact
Cartridge Packaging

Processor Latch

Processor Latch

Fan Heat Sink
(FHS)

Retention
Mechanism

Retention
Mechanism

242-Contact
Slot Connector

System
Board

Figure 1.8 Installing a cartridge processor.

Heat Sinks and Fans

Modern processors generate a considerable amount of heat. To prevent this heat from reaching a destructive level for the device, all Pentium processors require CPU cooling fans and heat sinks. These units are available in glue-on and snap-on models. A special heat conducting grease is typically used with snap-on heat sinks to provide good thermal transfer between the micro-processor and the heat sink.

This grease is normally applied to the heat sink by the supplier and appears as a thin pad on the bottom of the heat sink. When the processor heats up the compound, it becomes more liquidly and forms a seal between the heat sink and the processor. However, you can also obtain thermal grease for reapplication by contacting the heat sink manufacturer/supplier or from the Internet. Simply squeeze the grease from the tube onto the contact side of the heat sink. You only need to apply a thin layer of grease to the heat sink.

Power for the fans is normally obtained from one of the system's options power connectors or from a special jumper on the system board. These items must be installed before operating the microprocessor.

Installing Fans and Heat Sinks

The following steps will help you with installing fans and heat sinks:

1. Secure the microprocessor in its socket or slot.

2. Attach the fan unit to the heat sink. The fan and heat sink assemblies for most socket-mounted processors bolt together with the fan setting on top of the heat sink's cooling fans.

   Fan units for cartridge-style processors are typically mounted on the side of the cartridge by the manufacturer (some Pentium II and Pentium III Celeron processors did actually have removable fan units). These units clip directly to the processor package.

3. Check for the presence of thermal grease on the heat sink surface that makes contact with the microprocessor. If there is no grease present, apply a thin coating in the contact area.

4. For socket-mounted processors before Pentium 4, mount the fan/heat sink assembly squarely on top of the microprocessor, aligning the heat sink clips with the ears built in to the sides of the processor socket.

5. With Pentium 4 423-pin and 478-pin sockets, align the fan/heat sink unit with the special bracket installed on the system board. Slide the guides on the heat sink directly into the matching channels of the bracket and push down until the guides and channels on each side of the bracket lock. Finally, rotate the locking arms so that the cams push the fan assembly firmly down on the top of the processor.

Configuring the Microprocessor

Pentium microprocessors come in a number of speed ratings, and many use a dual-processor voltage arrangement. In addition, the processor might be a Pentium clone manufactured by someone other than Intel.

The microprocessor's internal core voltage supply is controlled through a *Voltage Regulator Module (VRM)* located on the system board.

Older Pentium system boards employed user-configured jumpers to establish the proper +3V and CPU core voltage settings for the particular type of microprocessor being installed. These settings are different for each system board model and can be found in the system board's documentation.

Most systems have the ability to autodetect the proper configuration settings for the new microprocessor. These microprocessors exchange information with the system's PnP BIOS during the configuration portion of the boot procedure to obtain the optimum settings.

Bus System Issues

Every system board has a defined set of communications paths, called *buses*, which run between its various components. These buses carry address, data, and control information between the microprocessor and the other components. In addition, different portions of the buses run at different speeds, so the chipset devices must act to synchronize the movement of information between the different buses.

When a new microprocessor is installed, coordinating it with the other system board devices requires that the timing relationships between all of the devices be recalculated. This process begins with the microprocessor and its main bus (called the *front side bus*). However, the other buses in the system run at predetermined speeds to maintain compatibility with the types of device they serve.

In some older systems, it is necessary to manually configure the relationship between the microprocessor and the system board's bus speeds to synchronize its operation with the other system board components. The jumpers are used to establish the microprocessor's external front side bus frequency. These settings can be found in the system board's documentation.

Most newer system boards feature autodetection functions as part of the PnP process that automatically detect the presence of the new processor on the board and synchronize the different bus speed configurations.

In the event of bus speed mismatches, the processor is usually limited to operating at all of the system board's lower capabilities.

Required Knowledge for Manually Configuring Processors

The following procedure provides a quick reference of the things you must do to manually configure a microprocessor on a Pentium system board:

1. Refer to the system board's documentation for the location and configuration of user-definable microprocessor configuration jumpers on the board. There should also be a table of settings that match acceptable microprocessors to the system board.

2. Physically install the microprocessor in the socket or slot.

3. Configure the system board jumpers responsible for setting the CPU type for the installed processor.

4. Configure the system board jumpers responsible for setting the Core/Bus Ratio (the clock synchronization between the microprocessor core and its bus interface units—often referred to as the multiplier setting).

5. Configure the system board jumpers responsible for setting the Bus Frequency (the front side bus speed).

6. You also need to properly set the CPU Core Voltage jumpers and 3V selector jumpers to finalize the configuration. This information must also be obtained from the system board documentation.

Upgrading Microprocessors

Physically upgrading a processor is a fairly easy operation after gaining access to the system board. Simply remove the microprocessor from its socket and replace it with the upgrade. Microprocessor manufacturers have devised upgrade versions for virtually every type of microprocessor on the market.

It is also common for clone microprocessors to be pin-for-pin compatible with older Intel socket designs. This strategy enables the end user to realize a speed increase by upgrading, along with an increase in processing power, for a potentially lower cost than with Intel chips.

You should always check the system board documentation before selecting an upgrade microprocessor for it. You must ensure that the system board will support the new processor in terms of the following when upgrading or exchanging a microprocessor:

➤ **Physical compatibility**—Ensure that the replacement microprocessor is hardware compatible (for example, pin configuration, socket versus slot or socket type A versus socket type B) with the original; otherwise, the system board will not support the new microprocessor type.

Be certain to properly orient the new processor in the socket or slot so that its pin 1 (usually identified by a notch in one corner of the socket) matches the socket's/slot's pin 1.

➤ **Speed/clocking ratings**—Be certain to configure the system board correctly for the new processor type (manually or automatically). There is no need to purchase a 2-GHz processor with a 400-MHz front side bus capability if the system only supports 1.2-GHz operation using a 133-MHz front side bus speed.

➤ **Technology**—Ensure the technology is compatible. For example, a 0.13 micron processor will not work in a socket system designed to support processors built with 0.18 micron technology.

➤ **Upgradable BIOS**—Verify that the existing BIOS can be upgraded to support the new microprocessor specifications.

As with a new installation, if you install an upgrade microprocessor in a system that does not have an Autodetect function for the microprocessor as part of the PnP process, you must manually ensure that the CPU Core Voltage, Front Side Bus Frequency, and Bus Ratio settings are properly configured for the new processor.

If these items are *not set correctly*, you might

➤ Burn up the new microprocessor

➤ Fail to start the system

➤ Encounter random errors during normal operations

➤ Fail to start the operating system

➤ See an incorrect processor type or incorrect processor speed during the power-on self test (POST) routines

Microprocessor Upgrade Paths

Table 1.1 shows the upgrade paths available to the major microprocessor types used in PCs.

Table 1.1 Microprocessor Upgrade Paths	
SOCKET TYPE	**MICROPROCESSORS**
Socket 7	Pentium (75 MHz–200 MHz)
Socket 8	Pentium Pro
Slot 1	Celeron, Pentium II, Pentium III
Slot 2	Xeon
Super Socket 7	AMD K6-2, K6-2+, K6-III, K6-III+, Pentium MMX
Socket 370	Cyrix III, Celeron, Pentium III
Slot A	AMD Athlon
Socket A	AMD Athlon, Duron
Socket 423	Pentium 4 (1.3 GHz–2.0 GHz)
Socket 478	Pentium 4 (1.4 GHz–2.2 GHz)
Socket 603	Pentium 4 Xeon (1.4 GHz–2.2 GHz)
Socket 418	Itanium/Intel (733 MHz–800 MHz)

Upgrading the BIOS

The physical microprocessor upgrade should also be accompanied by a logical upgrade. In particular, the system's BIOS version must support the parameters of the new microprocessor. If the BIOS code does not fully support the new processor, several error types can occur. For this reason, the capabilities of the system BIOS should always be examined when performing microprocessor upgrades.

Often, later BIOS versions are developed by the system board's manufacturer to permit installation of faster processors as they come on the market, or to support new operating system versions or service packs. Therefore, you should always check the manufacturer's Internet support site to determine whether the system board can support the processor type and speed to which you intend to upgrade.

Procedures for flashing the BIOS are covered in greater detail later in this chapter under the "Flashing BIOS" heading.

Testing the Upgrade

After the new processor has been installed, verify the operation of the upgrade. Simply boot up the system and see if error codes are generated. This simple step also enables you to verify that the system recognizes the newly installed processor.

Overclocking

With system boards on which the microprocessor parameters can be manually configured, it is possible to tweak the board to operate the microprocessor above its stated characteristics. In these systems, the microprocessor clock is set at a higher speed than the IC manufacturer suggests. This is referred to as *overclocking* the processor. This typically involves manually setting the processor configurations for higher microprocessor clock settings. Other actions that must be taken to overclock the processor include updating the BIOS to support the upgraded processor and improving the processor's cooling system.

In newer Pentium systems, the PnP process interrogates the processor during startup and configures it appropriately. This prevents the user from subjecting the processor to potentially destructive conditions, such as overclocking. However, the PnP process can be bypassed through the CMOS setup utility to produce overclocking situations.

Required Knowledge for Overclocking

The following procedure provides a quick reference for configuring over-clocking in a system:

1. Refer to the system board documentation to determine whether it has manual configuration jumpers for the processor, or whether it is con-figured automatically as part of the PnP process.

2. With older, manually configured system boards, you simply change the Bus Frequency configuration jumpers to provide between 15% and 20% additional bus speed (for stable operation). You can theoretically push the overclocking up to 50%, but the system becomes less stable as the percentage increases.

3. For overclocking past 15% or 20%, you also need to install improved cooling systems, such as case fans, liquid coolers, or refrigerant coolers to control the additional heat and protect the microprocessor.

4. Overclocking past 15% to 20% also requires additional microprocessor core voltage. This can be configured through the Core Voltage jumper. You might also need to install an upgraded VRM or voltage regulator IC to supply higher levels of voltage to the core of the processor.

5. The system's memory modules must be upgraded to work with the increased bus speed caused by overclocking. For example, boosting the front side bus speed of a microprocessor from 100MHz to 115MHz or higher requires that the memory modules be upgraded to 133-MHz operation.

6. For automatically configured system boards, overclocking must be established through the CMOS setup utility. In these systems, you must enter the CMOS setup and access the CPU Control or CPU Settings section to disable the autodetect default settings for the processor.

7. Some BIOS versions provide built-in overclocking options (such as from bus 100 to 110, 105, or 120 speeds). These settings can simply be selected from the screen. However, the overclocking capabilities are limited to those settings provided by the manufacturer.

8. Other BIOS versions provide a Manual option for setting the processor parameters. These BIOS provide more precise overclocking control and enable you to maximize the overclocking to the highest level the system will actually support (start and remain stable).

9. As with manually configured systems, you must upgrade the cooling systems and microprocessor core voltage capabilities to provide stable

operation and protection for the processor. When the processor is pushed to its highest levels of performance (such as running Windows with multiple, large applications open) the system might reboot itself, lock up, or produce random errors. When this happens, you must experiment with the core voltage level and the cooling systems.

Matching Processors to Incompatible Sockets

Several devices are available to match different processors to otherwise incompatible sockets and slots. These adapters include products to adapt socket-mounted processors to slotted system boards and to convert from one technology to another. Microprocessor conversion products can be found on the Internet by searching for the keywords "computer upgrade" or "microprocessor upgrade."

Installing Additional Processors

Some system boards provide multiple processor sockets or slots that permit additional processors to be added to distribute the processing load. You can use all, some, or just one of the available sockets by removing the terminator from the socket and installing the new processor. Adding additional processors represents the most effective means to upgrade the performance of the computer. However, you should take several steps before installing additional processors.

1. **Verify processor compatibility**—Ensure that the processor you are adding is compatible with the socket type on the board (preferably the same brand that is already on the board). You should also check the production run number of the processor to ensure that it is within one production run of its companion processors. In the case of Intel processors, this is referred to as a "stepping level." For example, if you have a Pentium III 750-MHz processor from stepping level 4, you should install additional processors that are defined as stepping level 3, 4, or 5.

   For optimum stability, you should install the same make, model, and clock speed for all processors. This includes using the same bus speed and multiplier settings and the same cache size to ensure there is no speed difference between cache feeds. Refer to the system board's manual or online documentation for detailed information about processor compatibility issues.

2. **Perform a BIOS upgrade**—Multiple processor system boards include a BIOS version with multiple processor support. This BIOS should be sufficient when installing directly compatible additional processors. However, for major upgrades, such as installing newer and faster processors, the BIOS might need to be upgraded. In many cases, newer BIOS versions are developed by the system board's manufacturer to permit the installation of faster processors as they enter the market. Therefore, check the manufacturer's Internet support site to determine whether your system board can support the processor type and speed you intend to use.

3. **Verify upgrade**—Verifying a processor upgrade is fairly simple. Boot up the system to see if an error code is generated and to verify that the system recognizes the newly installed processor.

 You should not interpret an automatic entry into the CMOS setup utility as an error when the system is initially booted after adding an additional processor. This is the process that systems often use to recognize new processors. You can use the system's CMOS setup utility (or their administrative tools package) to ensure that the system board is recognizing all the installed processors and that they are working properly.

Processor and Slot Specifications

Table 1.2 summarizes the characteristics of the most popular microprocessors from Intel and AMD.

Table 1.2	Microprocessor Characteristics						
MICROPROCESSOR	DIAMETER SIZE (mm)	VRM (VOLTS)	SPEED (MHz)	CACHE ON DIE (KB)	CACHE ON CARTRIDGE	CACHE ON BOARD (KB)	SOCKETS OR SLOT TYPES
Pentium	23.1x23.1	2.5—3.6	75—299	L1—8+8	-	L2—256/512	Socket 7
Pentium MMX AMD - K6-2 K6-3	25.4x25.4	2.0—3.5	166—550	L1—16+16 32+32	-	L2—255/1000	Socket Super 7
Pentium II/III Celeron (.25 micron)	25.4x25.4 18x62x140 Box	1.5—2.6	233—1000	L1—16+16	L2—256/512 128 KB	-	Slot 1
Xeon II/III (330) (.25 micron)	27.4x27.4 18x87x125 Box	1.5—2.6	500/550 700/900	L1—16+16	L2—512 KB 1 MB 2 M	-	Slot 2
Pentium III Celeron (.25 micron)	25.4x25.4 Slug 27.4x27.4 Opening	1.1—2.5	300—566	L1—16+16 L2—128/256	-	-	Socket 370 PPGA
Pentium III (Coppermine) Celeron (.18 micron)	9.3x11.3	1.1—2.5	566—1000	L1—16+16 L2—128/256	-	-	Socket 370 FC-PGA
Pentium III (Tualatin) Celeron (.13 micron)	31x31	1.1—2.5	800—1500	L1—16+16 L2—128/256/512	-	-	FC-PGA2
Pentium IV (.18 micron)	31x31	1.75	1300—2000	L1—12+8 L2—256	-	-	Socket 423 FC-PGA
Pentium IV (.18 micron) (.13 micron)	31x31 33x33	1.75 1.50	1400—2000 1800—2200	L1—12+8 L2—612	-	-	FC-PGA2
Pentium Xeon (.18 micron)	31x31	1.4—1.8 1.7	1400—2000	L1—12+8 L2—256	-	-	Socket 603 FC-BGA
Pentium Xeon (.13 micron)	35x35	1.4—1.8 1.475	1800—2200	L1—12+8 L2—612	-	-	Socket 603 FC-BGA2
Itanium (.18 micron) (266 MHz)*	71.6x127.7	1.7	733/600	L1—16+16 L2—612	L3—2 MB 4 MB	-	PAC-418
Athlon Duron	9.1x13.1	1.75	800—1400	L1—64+64	L2—256 KB	-	Slot A 242 CPGA
Athlon Duron	11.1x11.6	1.75	733—1800	L1—64+64	L2—256	-	Socket A 462 ORGA

Table 1.3 summarizes the characteristics of the Intel Pentium microprocessors.

Table 1.3	Characteristics of the Intel Pentium Microprocessors				
TYPE	ADDRESS BUSWIDTH	SPACE	INTERNAL CLOCK SPEED (MHz)	DATA BUSWIDTH	MATH CO-PROCESSOR
Pentium	32	4 GB	50 – 100	64	On-board
Pentium MMX	32	4 GB	166 – 233	64	On-board
Pentium Pro	36	4 GB x 4	150 – 200	64	On-board
Pentium II	36	64 GB	233 – 450	64	On-board
Pentium III	36	64 GB	450 – 1 GHz	64	On-board
Celeron	36	64 GB	266 – 766	64	On-board
Pentium 4	36	64 GB	1.4 – 1.5 GHz	128	On-board
Itanium	44	16 TB	733 – 800MHz	64	On-board

Table 1.4 shows the relationship between the various numbering systems. In addition to the 80×86 numbering system, Intel employed a "Px" identification up to the Pentium II. The Pentium II is identified as the Klamath processor. Subsequent, improved versions have been dubbed Deschutes, Covington, Mendocino, Katmai, Willamette, Flagstaff (P7), Merced, and Tahoe.

Table 1.4	Clone Processors		
INTEL	CYRIX	AMD	NEXTGEN
Pentium (P5/P54C)	M1 (6X86)	K5(5X86)	NX586/686
Pentium MMX (P55C)	M2 (6X86MX)	K6	
Pentium Pro (P6)	MXi	K6PLUS-3D	
Pentium II	M3	K7	
Pentium III	N/A	K75/Thunderbird	
Pentium Celeron	Cyrix III	Duron	

Intel created specifications for eight socket designs, designated Socket 1 through Socket 8. Intel also designed a Slot 1 specification for the Pentium II processor. This specification also serves its Celeron and Pentium III processor designs. Like Socket 7, the Slot 1 specification provides for variable processor core voltages (2.8 to 3.3) that permit faster operation and reduced power consumption. In addition, some suppliers have created daughter boards containing the Pentium Pro processor that can be plugged into the Slot 1 connector. This combination Socket 8/Slot 1 device is referred to as a slotkey processor.

The Slot 2 specification from Intel expands the Slot 1 SECC technology to a 330-contact (SECC-2) cartridge used with the Intel Xeon processor.

AMD produced a reversed version of the Slot 1 specification for its Athlon processor by turning the contacts of the Slot 1 design around. They titled the new design Slot-A. Although serving the same ends as the Slot 1 design, the Slot-A and Slot 1 microprocessor cartridges are not compatible.

In a departure from its proprietary slot connector development, Intel introduced a new ZIF socket standard, called Socket 370, for use with its Celeron processor. There are actually two versions of the Socket 370 specification. The first is the PPGA 370 variation intended for use with the Plastic Pin Grid Array (PPGA) version of the Celeron CPUs.

The other is the Flip Chip Pin Grid Array (FC-PGA) version. The processors in this category include the Cyrix III, Celeron, and Pentium III. Although the PPGA and FC-PGA processors both plug into the 370 socket, it does not mean they will work in system board designs for the other specifications.

AMD produced a 462-pin ZIF socket specification for the PGA versions of its Athlon and Duron processors. No other processors have been designed for this specification and only two chipsets have been produced to support it.

Table 1.5 summarizes the attributes of the various industry socket and slot specifications.

Table 1.5   Industry Socket/Slot Specifications

NUMBER	PINS	VOLTAGES	MICROPROCESSORS
Socket 1	169 PGA	5 V	80486 SX/DXx, DX4 Overdrive
Socket 2	238 PGA	5 V	80486 SX/DXx, Pentium Overdrive
Socket 3	237 PGA	5/3.3 V	80486 SX/DXx, Pentium Overdrive
Socket 4	237 PGA	5 V	Pentium 60/66, 60/66 Overdrive
Socket 5	320 SPGA	3.3 V	Pentium 75-133, Pentium Overdrive
Socket 6	235 PGA	3.3 V	Never Implemented
Socket 7	321 SPGA	VRM (2.5 V-3.6 V)	Pentium 75-200, Pentium Overdrive
Socket 8	387 SPGA	VRM (2.2 V-3.5 V)	Pentium Pro
Slot 1	242 SECC/SEPP	VRM (1.5 V-2.5 V)	Celeron, Pentium II, Pentium III
Slot 2	330 SECC-2	VRM (1.5 V-2.5 V)	Xeon
Super Socket 7	321 SPGA	VRM (2.0 V-3.5 V)	AMD K6-2, K6-2+, K6-III, K6-III+, Pentium MMX, Pentium Pro
Socket 370	370 SPGA	VRM (1.1 V-2.5 V)	Cyrix III, Celeron, Pentium III
Slot A	242 Slot A	VRM (1.2 V-2.2 V)	AMD Athlon
Socket A	462 SPGA	VRM (1.2 V-2.2 V)	AMD Athlon, Duron
Socket 423	423 FC-PGA	VRM (1.7 V)	Pentium IV (1.3 GHz – 2.0 GHz)
Socket 478	478 FC-PGA	VRM (1.5 V-1.7 V)	Pentium IV Xeon (1.4 GHz – 2.2 GHz)
Socket 603	603 INT-PGA	VRM (1.5 V-1.7 V)	Pentium IV (1.4 GHz – 2.2 GHz)
Socket 418	418 INT-PGA	VRM (1.7 V)	Itanium/Intel (733 MHz – 800 MHz)

Installing Memory Modules

Modern system boards typically provide one or more rows of dual inline memory module (DIMM) sockets. These sockets accept small, piggyback memory modules that can contain various combinations of dynamic RAM (DRAM) devices. Both single inline memory modules (SIMMs) and DIMMs use edge connectors that snap on to a retainer on the system board. The DIMMs used on Pentium boards are typically 168-pin, snap-on modules.

The DIMM module simply slides vertically into the socket and is locked in place by a tab at each end, as illustrated in Figure 1.9.

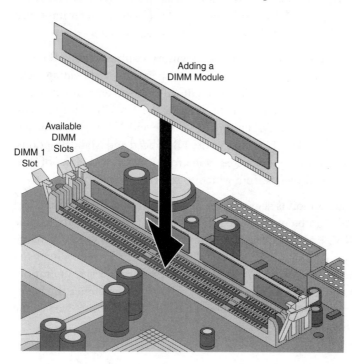

Figure 1.9 Installing DIMM modules.

Physically installing the RAM devices is all that is normally required. The system's PnP operation automatically detects the type of RAM installed and establishes proper settings for it during the boot process.

RAM Adjustments

Steps can be taken to optimize key RAM parameters through the CMOS setup utility. However, only technicians who are aware of the implications of these changes should adjust these parameters.

In older systems, you can manually configure DRAM timing for the installed RAM to optimize the timing between the front side bus and the speed of the RAM device actually installed. The Chipset Features section of the CMOS typically offers three memory configuration options—Normal, Auto, or Turbo operation. The Auto option permits the system to assign the Latency factor, whereas the Turbo option boosts the clocking and adjusts the voltage of the RAM modules to make them run faster.

It is also possible to change the CAS Latency timing (number of clock pulses required to access the internal buffers of the SDRAM devices). This is done to compensate for small access timing variations between similar RAM modules. Typical options here are 2 and 3 cycles (2 offers much improved speed over 3 cycles; however, the system might be less stable).

In Pentium 4 systems with dual-channel memory configurations, the system's RAM layout is designed to work with the special hyperthreading technology of the processor. Memory adjustments in these systems are also performed through the Chipset Features screen of the CMOS. Basically, two options are presented—DRAM Timing Selectable and Memory Frequency. The DRAM Timing Selectable option offers By Speed and Manual options. When the By Speed option is selected, you are presented with a list of supported RAM types and speeds from which to select.

When the Manual option is selected, the system activates RAM timing and delay options that can be manipulated individually. These normally include CAS Latency, RAS Precharge Delay, RAS to CAS Delay, and CAS Precharge Delay. All of these settings are speed-matching delays used to coordinate the various chip-level activities involved in a memory access operation. Remember that these are latency and delay settings, so the higher the latency selection or the more delay that is introduced, the slower that part of the memory operation occurs.

Upgrading Memory

Having more RAM onboard enables the system to access more data from extended or expanded memory, without needing to access the disk drive. This speeds up system operation considerably. Normally, upgrading memory is as simple as installing new memory modules in vacant SIMM or DIMM slots. If the slots are already populated, it is necessary to remove the existing memory modules to install faster or higher-capacity modules.

When upgrading memory in a newer PC, you must be aware of the following concerns:

➤ The types of memory that can be installed on the existing system board

➤ The makeup of the new modules (number and type of ICs on the modules)

➤ The speed rating of the memory module

Using the System Board Documentation

You should consult the system board's documentation to determine the speed at which the memory devices must be rated. You should be aware that RAM and other memory devices are rated in access time rather than clock speed. Therefore, a 70-nanosecond (ns) RAM device is faster than an 80-ns device.

Also consult the system board documentation to determine the maximum amount of RAM the board can handle. There is no need to buy 512MB of RAM if the system can only use 256MB. You should also consult the documentation to verify the types and arrangements of memory modules that can be used with the existing board.

Finally, the guide should be checked for any memory configuration settings that must be made to accept the new memory capacity.

Advanced SDRAM Technologies

Advanced versions of synchronous DRAM (SDRAM) include

➤ **Single Data Rate SDRAM (SDR-SDRAM)**—This version of SDRAM transfers data on one edge of the system clock signal.

➤ **Synchronous Graphics RAM (SGRAM)**—This type of SDRAM is designed to handle high-performance graphics operations. It features dual-bank operations that permit two memory pages to be open at the same time.

➤ **Enhanced SDRAM (ESDRAM)**—This advanced form of SDRAM employs small cache buffers to provide high data access rates. This type of SDRAM is used in L2 cache applications.

➤ **Virtual Channel Memory SDRAM (VCM-SDRAM)**—This memory design has onboard cache buffers to improve multiple access times and to provide I/O transfers on each clock cycle. VCM-SDRAM requires a special chipset to support it.

➤ **Double Data Rate SDRAM (DDR-SDRAM)**—This is a form of SDR-SDRAM that can transfer data on both the leading and falling edges of each clock cycle. This capability doubles the data transfer rate of traditional SDR-DRAM. It is available in a number of standard formats, including Small Outline DIMMs (SODIMMs) for portables.

➤ **Enhanced DDR SDRAM (EDDR-SDRAM)**—This is an advanced form of DDR-SDRAM that employs onboard cache registers to deliver improved performance.

➤ **Extended Data Out (EDO) DRAM**—EDO increases the speed at which RAM operations are conducted by cutting out the 10-ns wait time normally required between issuing memory addresses. This is accomplished by not disabling the data bus pins between bus cycles. The advantage of EDO DRAM is encountered when multiple sequential memory accesses are performed. By not turning off the data pin, each successive access after the first access is accomplished in two clock cycles rather than three.

Rambus DRAM

A company named Rambus has designed a proprietary DRAM memory technology that promises very high data delivery speeds. The technology has been given a variety of different names that include Rambus DRAM (RDRAM), Direct Rambus DRAM (DRDRAM), and RIMM. The RIMM reference applies to a special 184-pin memory module that is designed to hold the Rambus devices.

Figure 1.10 shows that RIMMs look similar to DIMMs. However, their high-speed transfer modes generate considerably more heat than normal DIMMs. Therefore, RIMM modules include an aluminum heat shield, referred to as a heat spreader, to protect the chips from overheating.

Static RAM (SRAM) Technologies

Like DRAM, static RAM (SRAM) is available in a number of different types. Many of the memory organization techniques described for DRAM are also implemented in SRAM.

➤ **Asynchronous SRAM**—Delivers data from the memory to the microprocessor and returns it to the cache in one clock cycle; standard SRAM.

➤ **Synchronous SRAM**—Uses special clock signals and buffer storage to deliver data to the CPU in one clock cycle after the first cycle. The first address is stored and used to retrieve the data while the next address is on its way to the cache.

➤ **Pipeline SRAM**—Uses three clock cycles to fetch the first data and then accesses addresses within the selected page on each clock cycle.

➤ **Burst-mode SRAM**—Loads a number of consecutive data locations from the cache, over several clock cycles, based on a single address from the microprocessor.

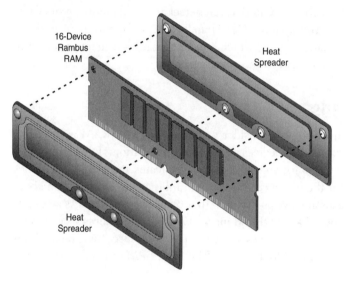

Figure 1.10   RIMM Modules.

Memory Overhead Terminology

When dealing with different memory types, you need to be familiar with some special terminology. Some RAM types come in registered (buffered) or unregistered (unbuffered) styles. Likewise, parity RAM and EC RAM devices have special functions that make them incompatible with other memory technologies.

In digital memory terms, a *buffer* or *register* is a temporary holding area for data shared by devices that operate at different speeds or have different priorities. These structures permit memory modules to operate without the delays that other devices impose. Some types of SDRAM memory modules contain buffer registers directly on the module. The buffer registers hold and retransmit the data signals through the memory chips.

Parity RAM is a special type of memory module that provides for parity checking to occur. Parity is a simple error-detection method used to detect single-bit errors in computer words when they are retrieved from memory. This involves adding an extra bit to the word when it is stored. When the word is read back from memory, a new parity bit is generated and compared to the original stored version to determine whether any change has occurred in the word. This requires the presence of an extra bit on the memory module for each storage location. You must specify that the system will use parity RAM or not use it.

Error Correction Code (ECC) SDRAM is a type of SDRAM that includes a fault detection/correction circuit that can detect and fix memory errors without shutting down the system. Occasionally, the information in a single memory bit can change states, which, in turn, causes a memory error to occur when the data is read from memory.

RAM Speeds

Another important factor to consider when dealing with RAM is its speed. Manufacturers mark RAM devices with speed information. DRAM modules are marked with a numbering system that indicates the number of clock cycles required for the initial read operation, followed by information about the number of reads and cycles required to move a burst of data. As an example, a fast page mode (FPM) DRAM marked as 6-3-3-3 requires six cycles for the initial read and three cycles for each of three successive reads. This moves an entire four-byte block of data. EDO and FPM can operate with bus speeds up to 66MHz.

SDRAM devices are marked a little differently. Because they are designed to run synchronously with the system clock and use no wait states, a marking of 3:3:3 at 100MHz on an SDRAM module specifies the following:

➤ The Column Address Strobe (CAS) signal setup time is three bus cycles.

➤ The Row Address Strobe (RAS) to CAS changeover time is three cycles.

➤ The RAS signal setup time is three clock cycles.

The bus speed is specified in MHz. These memory modules have been produced in the following specifications so far:

➤ PC66 (66MHz or 15ns)

➤ PC83 (83MHz or 12ns)

➤ PC100 (100MHz or 10ns)

➤ PC133 (133MHz or 8ns)

➤ PC150 (150MHz or 4.5ns)

➤ PC166 (166MHz or 4ns)

Continued advancements in memory module design have made the MHz and CAS setup time ratings obsolete. Onboard buffering and advanced access strategies have made these measurements inconsequential. Instead, memory performance is being measured by total data throughput (also referred to as bandwidth) and is being measured in terms of gigabytes per second (GBps). As an example, some of the new standard specifications include

➤ PC1600 (1.6GBps/200MHz/2:2:2)

➤ PC2100 (2.1GBps/266MHz/2:3:3)

➤ PC2600 (2.6GBps/333MHz/3:3:3)

➤ PC3200 (3.2GBps/400MHz/3:3:3)

When dealing with Rambus memory devices, you should be aware that they use special, proprietary, high-speed buses to interact with the microprocessor. Because the memory bus is proprietary to the Rambus design, other memory types cannot be substituted for them. These devices have existed in four different speed ratings. The original Rambus devices were rated for 400-MHz operation. As the following list indicates, newer Rambus devices can be used with even faster memory buses:

➤ PC-600 (600MHz RAMBUS/RDRAM/RIMM)

➤ PC-700 (700MHz RAMBUS/RDRAM/RIMM)

➤ PC-800 (800MHz RAMBUS/RDRAM/RIMM)

 The Rambus bank architecture is typically based on a two-slot arrangement. Both slots must be filled with matching memory modules for the memory system to work. For this reason, Rambus devices are typically sold as matching pairs.

The system BIOS on these boards has an Autodetect function built in that can be used to automatically detect the type of memory devices that are installed and configure the memory bus specifically for it. Mixing memory device types can cause assorted memory errors, including complete system failures, random lockups, and soft errors. If the autodetect setting is not selected in the BIOS, it is possible to set the system up to underclock or overclock the memory bus.

The system board's documentation provides information about the types of devices it can use and their speed ratings. It is important to install RAM that is compatible with the bus speed the system is running. Normally, installing RAM that is rated faster than the bus speed does not cause problems; however, installing slower RAM, or mixing RAM speed ratings within a system might cause it not to start, or to periodically lock up.

Optimizing Memory

You must ensure that the memory type and size you want to install is supported by the system board and that the system board does not already have the maximum amount of memory installed. The system board's documentation includes information on the type, configuration, and size of memory it accepts.

In addition, verify that the memory you want to install is compatible with the memory currently installed on the board. For example, if the memory currently installed in the machine is rated as PC133, you do not want to install an additional PC100-type memory module.

Normally, you should use the same type, brand, and speed of memory devices for RAM upgrades. Because the information detailing the RAM module's type and speed is rarely annotated on the device, you might need to check the signal-to-clock rate value (the CAS number) for comparison. For instance, if your current memory modules are described as CAS3 units, you should get CAS3 type memory for a compatible replacement, or for adding additional memory.

You should never mix memory types or speed ratings when upgrading a system board. If the new memory modules are not technically compatible with the existing memory, the old memory should be removed. Remember that just because the memory modules are physically compatible with the DIMM slot does not mean that they will work together in a system. Mismatched memory speeds and memory styles (registered/unregistered, buffered/unbuffered, ECC, and so on) can cause significant problems in the operation of the system. These problems can range from preventing bootup to creating simple soft memory errors.

Verifying the Memory Upgrade

To verify the memory upgrade, attempt to observe the memory test display during the POST process to ensure that the system sees the additional memory. Afterward, boot up to the operating system to verify that it also recognizes the installed memory.

Required Knowledge for Installing, Upgrading, Troubleshooting, and Performance Tuning Memory

The following list provides a set of quick references for installing, upgrading, troubleshooting, and tuning the installed RAM on a system:

1. Refer to the system board documentation to determine its total RAM capacity, its memory configuration options, and the RAM types that can be used with it.

2. Examine any installed memory to determine whether it is compatible with any additional memory that you want to install. (For example, can you add to it, or does it simply need to be replaced?)

3. Install only matching memory modules. (Do not mix RAM types or speeds.)

4. Verify that the speed of the DIMM modules is compatible with the speed that the system board is actually running. Slower memory modules can reduce the performance of the system by up to 25%. If the RAM is too slow, or has too much resistance for the system board's buses, the RAM modules will actually lock up the system.

5. Check the documentation for Split Bank configurations (some pre-Pentium 4 machines based on Celeron processors). These boards have very specific requirements for the construction of the DIMMs that can be installed. The DIMM module cannot use more than eight memory chips because the combined resistance of more devices adversely affects the operation of the memory unit. This is usually highlighted in the system board's documentation.

6. If the system is having stability problems, access the CMOS setup utility and check the DRAM configuration options (usually located under the Chipset Features option). Record the current settings for Bus Speed and RAM Type so that you can reset them to the Auto option. If this returns the system to stability, experiment with each setting to determine which setting (or settings) causes the instability.

7. If the system locks up or performs a memory dump (produces a Blue Screen error), check the installed RAM modules to ensure they are compatible with each other. These are failures typically produced by mismatched RAM devices.

8. For dual-channel DDR memory used with Pentium 4 systems, always purchase matched pairs of modules from the supplier. The manufacturer certifies that the matched modules have similar timing and load-resistance characteristics.

9. Remember that mismatched memory speeds and memory styles (registered/unregistered, buffered/unbuffered, ECC, and so on) can cause significant problems in the operation of the system. These problems can range from preventing bootup to creating simple soft memory errors.

Flashing BIOS

When the microprocessor is upgraded, the BIOS should also be upgraded to support it. In newer system boards, this can be accomplished by *flashing* (electrically altering) the information in the BIOS with the latest compatibility firmware. In these systems, new BIOS information is downloaded into the BIOS IC where it is permanently held until it is rewritten (even if power is removed from the IC).

When you flash firmware, you direct the system board to send electrical charges into a ROM chip that will rewrite its programming. To flash the ROM device, you must have a program from its vendor that can be downloaded into the IC. This program writes the updated information into the chip so that the physical device now holds the latest version of information.

The flash download operation can be conducted from a floppy disk, from the hard drive, or from a manufacturer's website. In each case, the system is rebooted and the flash download's executable file is run to transfer the new information into the BIOS IC. A graphical representation of this process is shown in Figure 1.11.

If the system BIOS doesn't possess the flash option and does not support the new microprocessor, it is necessary to obtain an updated BIOS IC that is compatible with the new processor (and with the system board's chipset). The old IC must be removed from the board and be replaced by the new IC. The upgraded BIOS can normally be obtained from the system board manufacturer. If not, the entire system board needs to be upgraded.

Required Knowledge for Flashing a BIOS

The same technique is used for flashing the system's ROM BIOS, as well as the various ROM BIOS extensions associated with video cards, network cards, modem, and RAID controllers. Each peripheral device has its own utility program for flashing their ROM devices.

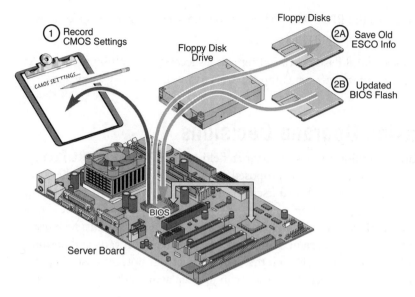

Figure 1.11 Flashing BIOS.

Although you can flash the BIOS of many different types of devices, the general process to do so remains the same:

1. Document the existing CMOS settings.

2. Obtain the correct flash program version for the chipset used on the system board. This is normally downloaded from the website of the system board manufacturer or the BIOS manufacturer. Two different files are downloaded as part of the flash ZIP file.

3. Unzip the flash file into its two components—the flash program (the .exe file) and the BIOS parameters to be loaded (the .bin file).

4. Use a startup disk to boot the system to a command prompt.

5. Execute the flash file. The program should recognize the BIOS information on the board. If the program is not compatible with the installed BIOS, an error message is produced.

6. If the flash is compatible, the program should next give you the option to back up the original BIOS program to a floppy disk. Simply specify a name for the old version to be saved under. In case the process fails, you can use the original BIOS program to attempt to restore the settings back to its original form.

7. The flash program next provides a request for confirmation about updating the BIOS settings. If you answer Yes, the flash program

updates the BIOS with the new program according to the directions of the device manufacturer.

8. A successful flash operation returns a successful operation message. At this point, restart the computer to activate the new BIOS settings.

Making Upgrade Decisions

Before upgrading the system board's field replaceable unit's (FRU) components, check the cost of the proposed component upgrade against the cost of upgrading the system board itself. In many cases, the RAM from the original board can be used on a newer, faster model that should include a more advanced microprocessor. Before finalizing the choice to install a new system board, however, be certain that the current adapters, software, and peripherals will function properly with the updated board. If not, the cost of upgrading might be unexpectedly higher than just replacing an FRU component.

HDD Installation

The hard disk drive (HDD) hardware installation process is similar to that of other storage devices; however, the configuration and preparation of a typical hard disk drive is more involved than that of a floppy drive. You should confirm an Integrated Drive Electronics (IDE) drive's Master/Slave/Cable Select, or a small computer system interface (SCSI) drive's ID configuration setting before installing the unit in the drive bay.

Most IDE drives come from the manufacturer configured for operation as a single drive, or as the *master drive* in a multidrive system. To install the drive as a second drive, or *slave drive*, you usually need to install, remove, or move a jumper block, as illustrated in Figure 1.12. Some hosts disable the interface's Cable Select pin for slave drives.

If a replacement hard drive is being installed for repair or upgrading purposes, the data on the original drive should be backed up to some other media before replacing it, if possible.

Slide the hard drive into one of the system unit's open drive bays, and install two screws on each side to secure the drive to the system unit, as illustrated in Figure 1.13. Then connect the signal and power cables to it.

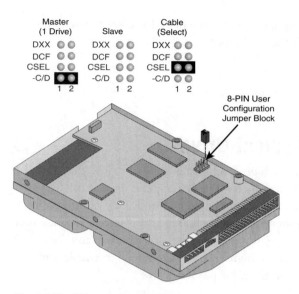

Figure 1.12   IDE master/slave settings.

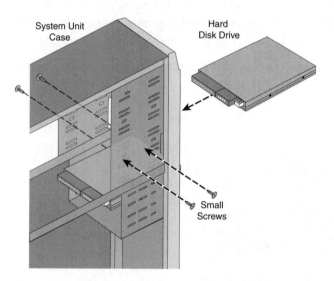

Figure 1.13   Securing the drive unit.

After completing the hardware installation process, the drive must be configured and formatted. Unlike floppy drives, which basically come in four accepted formats, hard disk drives are created in a wide variety of storage capacities. To prepare the hard disk for use by the system, three levels of preparation must take place. The order of these steps is as follows:

1. Set up the CMOS configuration for the drive (or allow the system to autodetect it through the PnP process).

2. Partition the drive.

3. Perform a high-level format on the drive.

Partitioning Physical Drives

Before a disk drive can have a high-level format applied to it so that it can be used to perform useful functions for the system, the drive must be partitioned. *Partitioning* is the practice of dividing a physical drive into multiple logical storage areas and then treating each area as if it were a separate disk drive. This is normally done for purposes of organization and increased access speeds. However, drives might also be partitioned to enable multiple operating systems to exist on the same physical drive.

Fortunately, disk operating systems already had the ability to partition large physical drives into multiple logical drives. When this is done in the Microsoft operating system environment, each logical drive is assigned a different drive letter (such as C, D, E, and so on) to identify it to the system.

Figure 1.14 illustrates the concept of creating multiple logical drives on a single physical hard drive.

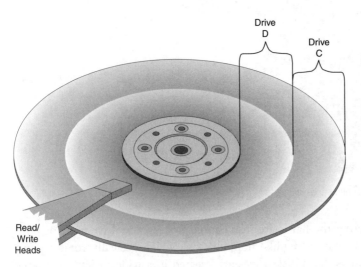

Figure 1.14 Partitions on an HDD.

Consumer-based Microsoft operating systems (that is, MS-DOS and Windows 3.x up through Windows Me) have provided for two partitions on a physical hard disk drive. The first partition is referred to as the *primary partition* and must be created on the disk first. After the primary partition has been established and properly configured, an additional partition referred to as an *extended partition* can be created on any unused disk space that remains. In addition, *the extended partition can be subdivided into 23 logical drives (the letters of the alphabet minus a, b, and c)*. These drives are dependent on the extended partition, so it cannot be deleted if logical drives have been defined within it.

When the primary partition is created on a hard disk, a special table is created in its master boot sector called the *partition table*. This table is used to store information about the partitions and logical drives on the disk. It includes information about where each partition and logical drive begins and ends on the physical drive. This is expressed in terms of beginning and ending track numbers.

Each time a logical drive is added to the system, a complete disk structure—including a boot sector and preliminary directory management structure—is created. Its beginning and ending locations are also recorded in the partition table when the new drive is created.

The table also includes a setting that identifies the partition or logical drive that is *active*. The active partition is the logical drive to which the system boots. On a partitioned drive, only one logical drive can be active at a time. When the system checks the drive's master boot sector looking for a Master Boot Record (MBR) during bootup, it encounters the partition table and checks it to determine which portion of the disk has been marked as active.

With this information, the system jumps to the first track of the active partition and checks its boot sector for a *partition boot record* (an MBR for that partition). If an operating system has been installed in this partition, the boot sector contains an MBR for it and the system uses it to boot up with. This arrangement enables a single physical disk to hold different operating systems to which the system can boot.

Partitioning with More Than One HDD

Most PCs can have multiple physical hard disk drive units installed in them. In a system using a Microsoft operating system, the primary partition on the first disk drive is designated as drive C. The system files must be located in this partition, and the partition must be set to Active for the system to boot up from the drive.

FDISK

The partitioning program for MS-DOS, Windows 9x, and Windows Me is named *FDISK*. The FDISK utility in MS-DOS version 4.0 raised the maximum size of a logical drive to 128MB, and version 5.0 raised it to 528MB. The FDISK utility in Windows 9x provided upgraded support for very large hard drives. The original version of Windows 95 set a size limit for logical drives at 2GB. The FDISK version in the upgraded OSR2 version of Windows 95 extended the maximum partition size to 8GB.

Partitioning in Windows NT 4.0, Windows 2000, and Windows XP

In Windows NT 4.0, the partitioning process is performed through the *Disk Administrator* utility. In Windows 2000 and Windows XP, partitioning is done through the *Disk Management* utility. These utilities perform all of the basic functions that the FDISK utility does. For instance, both utilities can be used to partition drives and both show you the basic layout of the system's disks, including the following:

➤ The size of each disk

➤ The size and file system type used in each logical drive

➤ The size and location of any unformatted (free) space on the drive

However, these advanced disk utilities can also provide many advanced functions associated with enterprise (large-scale business oriented) computing systems. The Disk Administrator and Disk Management utilities can be used to create both traditional primary and extended partitions for Windows NT, Windows 2000, and Windows XP systems. They can also be used to create volumes (partitions that involve space on multiple physical drives).

Utilizing Larger Partition Sizes with Enhanced Cylinder, Heads, Sectors (ECHS)

Modern BIOS includes enhanced disk drive handling modes that employ special *logical block addressing (LBA)* techniques to utilize the larger partition sizes available through newer operating systems. This technique—known as *Enhanced Cylinder, Heads, Sectors (ECHS)*—effectively increases the number of R/W heads the system can recognize from 16 to 256. The maximum allowable disk drive parameters of 1,024 cylinders, 63 sectors/track, and 512 bytes/sector remains unchanged.

The high-level format procedure is performed by the operating system and fills in or re-creates the preliminary logical structures on the logical drive during the partitioning process. These structures tell the system what files are in the logical disk and where they can be found. In Windows 9x and Windows Me systems, the format process creates *file allocation table (FAT)* and root directory structures for the partition. In the case of Windows NT, Windows 2000, and Windows XP systems, the format operation might produce FATs and root directories, or it might produce more flexible *Master File Table (MFT)* structures.

Disk Drive Subsystem Enhancements

If you are installing IDE hard drives, ensure that the jumper(s) are correctly configured and that the system board supports the type of IDE drives you are installing. For instance, if the IDE controller on the system board only supports up to ATA-66 drives, you have little reason to purchase ATA-100 drives, unless you plan to upgrade the system board in the near future.

When you upgrade a SCSI component, you must be aware that the SCSI controller and the devices have the ability to adapt to lower functionality. If you upgrade one or more SCSI devices in a system, but do not upgrade the SCSI host adapter, the devices will very likely operate, but they will only operate at the maximum performance level of the adapter.

If you update the adapter and one or more devices, but still have some older SCSI devices installed, those devices that can operate at higher performance levels attempt to do so, while the slower devices work at their level. However, the fact that the controller must slow down to work with the slower devices effectively slows down the operation of the entire SCSI system.

You might need to upgrade the BIOS to support the new hard drive installation if the current BIOS does not support the drive type or size you intend to install. The best place to determine the types and sizes of hard drives your current BIOS will support is the system board's documentation. The best place to determine whether there is an updated BIOS available to support the new hard drive (and to download the BIOS loader routine) is the system board manufacturer's support Internet site.

RAID Adapter Enhancements

Redundant Array of Independent Disks (RAID) systems are available in two basic varieties—IDE and SCSI RAID systems. In each case, the components of the system include a RAID controller (usually an adapter card) and the RAID drives. At the center of each system is the RAID controller card. Therefore, the speed and efficiency of the RAID system cannot be upgraded by upgrading the adapter card.

If you are working with an ATA66 IDE RAID adapter and you install new Enhanced Integrated Drive Electronics (EIDE) drives, the system is limited to the operating speed and characteristics of the controller card. Likewise, if the RAID system is built on Wide SCSI 2 devices and you upgrade the drives to Fast-Wide SCSI 2 devices, the system would still function as a Wide SCSI 2 system.

Required Knowledge for Installing Hard Disk Drives

The following procedure provides a quick reference of the things you must do to install an IDE or a SCSI hard disk drive in a system:

1. Configure the drive's Master/Slave or SCSI ID selection jumpers before installing the drive in the system. For SCSI drives, verify that the drive is properly terminated for its position in the system.

2. Attach the signal cable to the drive and verify that the pin 1 placement is correct. Omit this step if you are adding a new drive to a system that already has drives installed. You need to attach the signal cable to the drive after it is physically installed in the drive bay.

3. Thread the signal cable through the front of the drive bay opening and slide the drive into one of the available drive bays until it clears the front panel.

4. Install two screws through each side of the disk drive bay to hold the drive unit securely in the bay.

5. Attach one of the computer's free option power connectors to the drive. These connectors are keyed so that they cannot be reversed.

6. If a SCSI drive is being installed, insert the SCSI host adapter card in one of the available expansion slots.

7. Connect the drive's signal cable to the host adapter (either on the system board or on the host adapter card), ensuring that the pin 1 alignment is correct.

8. Turn on the system and observe the startup messages to ensure that system sees the new drive. If a message appears saying that the "System recognizes a new device" and then stops, enter the CMOS setup and change the IDE controller's mode from Manual to Auto so that the system automatically accepts the parameters of the new drive.

9. Check the boot sequence order in the CMOS to verify that the CD-ROM is selected as the first boot option.

10. Save the settings and exit the CMOS utility. This should cause the system to perform a reboot. Place the distribution CD with the operating system on it in the CD-ROM drive while the system starts up.

11. For newer operating systems (such as Windows 2000 and Windows XP), the system recognizes the new drive and brings you directly to the beginning of the OS installation process. With older operating systems (such as Windows 9x, Windows Me, or Windows NT), you are given the option to boot from the hard drive or from the CD-ROM.

12. For a new drive, the next option the operating system offers is to partition the drive. The tool used to do this is dependent on the operating system version being used—it could be FDISK, Disk Manager, or a third-party partitioning tool.

13. After the drive has been partitioned, the next step is to format the drive with a file management system and install the operating system. The installation process automatically reboots the system between the installation of the file system and the installation of the operating system files.

HDD Upgrading

One of the key components in keeping the system up to date is keeping the hard disk drive capabilities current. Many newer programs place high demands on the hard drive to feed information, such as large graphics files or digitized voice and video, to the system for processing. Invariably, the system begins to produce error messages stating that the hard drive is full. The first line of action is to use software disk utilities to optimize the organization of the drive. The second step is to remove unnecessary programs and files from the hard drive. Programs and information that are rarely, or never, used should be moved to an archival media, such as removable disks or tape.

Sometimes, you need to determine whether the existing hard drive needs to be replaced, or another drive needs to be added to optimize the performance of the system. One guideline suggests that the drive should be replaced if the percentage of unused disk space drops below 20%.

Another reason to consider upgrading the HDD involves its capability to deliver information to the system efficiently. If the system is constantly waiting for information from the hard drive, replacing it with a faster drive should be considered as an option. Not all system slowdowns are caused by the HDD, but many are. Remember that the HDD is the mechanical part of the memory system and that everything else is electronic.

As with the storage space issue, HDD speed can be optimized through software configurations, such as a disk cache. After it has been optimized in this manner, however, any further speed increases must be accomplished by upgrading the hardware.

Planning for an HDD Upgrade

When considering an HDD upgrade, determine the actual system needs for the hard drive. Multimedia-intensive applications can place heavy performance demands on the hard disk drive to operate correctly. Moving large image, audio, and video files into RAM on demand requires high performance from the drive. Critical HDD specifications associated with disk-drive performance include the following:

> **Access time**—The average time, expressed in milliseconds, required to position the drive's R/W heads over a specified track/cylinder and reach a specified sector on the track

> **Track seek time**—The amount of time required for the drive's R/W heads to move between cylinders and settle over a particular track following the seek command being issued by the system

> **Data transfer rate**—The speed, expressed in megabytes per second (MBps), at which data is transferred between the system and the drive

In contemporary systems, the choice of hard drives for high-performance applications is between IDE/EIDE drives and SCSI drives. The EIDE drives are competitive and relatively easy to install; the high-end SCSI specifications offer additional performance, but require additional setup effort and an additional host adapter card.

Finally, determine how much longer the unit in question is likely to be used before being replaced. If the decision to upgrade the HDD stands, ultimately, the best advice is to get the biggest, fastest hard drive possible. Don't forget to consider that a different I/O bus architecture might add to the performance increase.

Applying Correct Cabling to an HDD Upgrade

When upgrading the hard drive, be certain that the correct cabling is being used to connect the drive to the system.

You should know that installing a new ATA-66 or ATA-100 drive in a system using the old IDE cable causes the drive's operation to be diminished to the level of the old drive. Without the new cables, communications with the drives is limited to the lesser standard determined by the 40-conductor signal cable.

Upgrading SCSI Drives

When upgrading SCSI drives, ensure that the new drive is correctly configured and terminated for its position in the system. Verify that the SCSI host adapter will support the new drive type. For example, a standard SCSI-I host adapter does not support a Fast-Wide SCSI drive. The physical cable and the communication speed differences between the two specifications do not match.

If you have an older IDE system that does not support faster EIDE/ATA drive types, you might consider adding a SCSI adapter and drive to the system to upgrade it. Because the SCSI system is not limited by the system board capabilities, you can greatly enhance the system's disk drive performance by doing this.

Required Knowledge for Upgrading a Hard Drive

The following list provides a quick reference of things you must keep in mind and do when upgrading a hard drive unit:

1. Check the system board to determine the current HDD management capabilities of the system. There is no need to purchase a large hard disk drive if the BIOS will not support it. You might need to obtain a flash program for your BIOS so it will support the larger drive capacity. Likewise, there is no reason to install a very fast IDE drive if the controller will not support its maximum speed capabilities. (Consider using an external USB or IEEE-1394 drive in these systems.)

2. Configure the replacement drive's Master/Slave or SCSI configuration settings appropriately for where the drive will function in the system. This might be a good time to determine whether there is a more efficient configuration option than the one you are replacing (such as separating CD-ROM and DVD drives on different channels).

3. Back up any necessary data on a separate media so that it can be restored to the replacement drive after it has been installed. Typically, there is no need to back up the operating system in an upgrade situation.

4. Disconnect the signal cable and power supply connection from the disk drive unit. Make note of where the pin 1 connection stripe is. (If you are upgrading from an EIDE drive to an ATA-66, ATA-100, or ATA-133 drive, you also want to install the 80-conductor EIDE signal cable.)

5. Remove the retaining screws that secure the drive in the drive bay from each side of the bay.

6. Slide the old drive out of the disk drive bay and set it aside. Verify the location of the pin 1 position.

7. Verify the location of the pin 1 position on the new drive's signal cable connection. Insert the new drive in the vacant disk drive bay, and install the retaining screws on each side.

8. Attach the signal cable and power connection to the new drive unit. Observe the pin 1 orientation to ensure it is correct for the new drive.

9. Turn on the system and observe the startup messages to ensure that the system sees the new drive. If the system is not set up to autodetect the new drive, an error message should be produced saying "... drive not present." If so, enter the CMOS setup and change the IDE controller's mode from Manual to Auto so that the system automatically accepts the parameters of the new drive (or manually configure the drive in CMOS).

10. If the drive is the only hard drive or is replacing the C: drive, check the boot sequence order in the CMOS to be certain that the CD-ROM is selected as the first boot option. Save the settings and exit the CMOS utility.

11. If the system recognizes the full size of the drive, partition the drive as desired. If not, perform the flash operation so that the BIOS supports the full size of the drive.

12. Format the drive with the desired operating system.

13. Reinstall or copy your preexisting programs and data to the new drive.

Installing CD-ROM/DVD Devices

Before installing an internal CD-ROM drive, confirm its Master/Slave/Single, or SCSI ID configuration setting. Afterward, install the CD-ROM unit in one of the drive bays, connect the power and signal cables, and load the CD-ROM driver software. In a Windows system, the operating system should automatically detect the CD-ROM drive and install the correct drivers for it as a part of the process.

If the interface type is different than that of the HDD, it is necessary to install a controller card in one of the system's expansion slots. Finally, refer to the owner's manual regarding any necessary jumper or switch settings.

To connect the drive to the system, hook up the CD-ROM drive to the HDD signal cable, observing proper orientation. Connect the audio cable to the drive and to the sound card's CD Input connection (if a sound card is installed).

In a single HDD system, the CD-ROM drive can be set up as the slave drive on the primary interface. However, the operation of the drives is much cleaner if the CD-ROM is set up as the master drive on the secondary IDE interface. In this manner, each drive has access to a full IDE channel instead of sharing one.

Likewise, in a two-HDD system, the CD-ROM drive would most likely be configured as the master or single drive on the secondary interface. If the system also contains a sound card that has a built-in IDE interface, it should be disabled to prevent it from interfering with the primary or secondary interfaces.

Configuring CD-ROM/DVD Devices

The CD-ROM or DVD drive must be properly configured for the system in which it is being installed. In an IDE system, the Master/Slave setting must be confirmed. In a SCSI system, the ID setting must be correct. In a SCSI system, the only requirement is that a valid ID setting is configured. In an IDE system, however, some thought might be required as to how to configure the drive. The SCSI drive must also be appropriately terminated for its position in the system.

Consult the drive's documentation for instructions on software installation. Typically, all that is required is to insert the original equipment manufacturer (OEM) driver disk into the floppy drive, and follow the manufacturer's directions for installing the drivers. If the drive fails to operate at this point, reboot the system using single-step verification and check the information on the various boot screens for error messages associated with the CD-ROM drive.

Installing CD-RW and DVD-RW Drives

The hardware installation process involved with rewritable CD-ROM and DVD drives is identical to that used with standard CD-ROM and DVD drives. However, prior to the Windows XP operating system, rewritable CD-RW and DVD-RW drives required third-party application packages to perform their write and rewrite functions. These applications had to be installed from the OEM CD that was packaged with the drive or from a CD obtained from an independent supplier.

In the Windows XP environment, rewritable drives are supported directly from the operating system and don't require any third-party applications. When you insert a blank disc in one of these drives, the operating system detects it and opens a dialog box that asks you what you want to do with the disc. Most users still prefer to install a third-party program to manage all of the functions of these drives.

Required Knowledge for Installing CD-ROM and DVD Drives

The following procedure provides a quick reference of the things you must do to install a CD-ROM or DVD drive in a system:

1. Configure the drive's Master/Slave or SCSI ID selection jumpers before installing the drive in the system. Verify the orientation of the pin 1 position on the drive before installing it. If you are installing the drive on the secondary IDE channel, you might need to connect a new signal cable to the drive before you install it (if one is not already installed for this channel). If the drive is a SCSI drive, verify that it is properly terminated for its position in the system.

2. Slide the drive into one of the available drive bays until its faceplate is flush with the front panel of the chassis.

3. Install two screws through each side of the disk drive bay to hold the drive unit securely in the bay.

4. If not already installed, attach the signal cable to the drive. Observe proper connection orientation for the pin 1 indicator.

5. Attach one of the computer's free option power connectors to the drive. These connectors are keyed so that they cannot be reversed.

6. If a new cable is being installed, connect the drive's signal cable to the host adapter (either on the system board or on the host adapter card), ensuring that the pin 1 alignment is correct.

7. Turn on the system and observe the startup messages to ensure that the system sees the new drive. If the drive is missing, access the CMOS setup utility and verify that the channel is enabled.

8. Start up the operating system and install any support software required for the drive (such as CD or DVD writer programs).

Installing Tape Drives

Tape drive units are another popular type of information storage system. These systems can store large amounts of data on small tape cartridges. The original quarter-inch cartridge (QIC) standard was QIC-40. This standard called for a unit that could be connected to a floppy disk drive interface so that it acted like a large drive B.

Specifications that depart from the floppy disk drive interface and use the universal serial bus (USB), EIDE, or SCSI interfaces produce data storage potentials into the hundreds of gigabyte range.

Required Knowledge for Installing Tape Drives

The following procedures provide a quick reference of the things you must do to install a tape drive in a PC system.

The general steps for installing tape drives depend on whether they are internally or externally mounted. Physically installing internally mounted tape drives is very much like installing floppy disk drives or IDE and SCSI hard drives. General steps for physically installing tape drives that employ IDE and SCSI interfaces include the following:

1. Configure the tape drive's Master/Slave or SCSI ID selection jumpers before installing the drive in the system. If the drive is a SCSI drive, verify that the drive is properly terminated for its position in the system.

2. Verify the orientation of the pin 1 position on the drive before installing it. If you are installing the drive on the secondary IDE channel, you might need to connect a new signal cable to the drive before you install it (if one is not already installed for this channel).

3. Slide the tape drive into one of the available drive bays until its front panel is flush with the front panel opening.

4. Install two screws through each side of the disk drive bay to hold the drive unit securely in the bay.

5. If not already installed, attach the signal cable to the drive. Observe proper connection orientation for the pin 1 indicator.

6. Attach one of the computer's free option power connectors to the tape drive. These connectors are keyed so that they cannot be reversed.

7. If a new signal cable is being installed with the drive, connect the cable to the host adapter (either on the system board or on the host adapter card), ensuring that the pin 1 alignment is correct.

The installation of tape drives that use USB or FireWire interfaces can be treated as any other external peripheral. Normally, this involves the following steps:

1. For USB tape drives, enable the USB resources in the CMOS setup utility. In some cases, this involves enabling the port and reserving an IRQ resource for the device.

2. Plug the external power module into the tape drive and the commercial outlet.

3. Plug the device into an open USB or FireWire connector.

4. Wait for the operating system to recognize the device and configure it through the PnP process.

After the tape drive has been physically installed, you must install and configure its Application/Utilities program:

1. Turn the system on and access the Device Manager to verify that the system recognizes the new drive as a tape drive.

2. Place the tape drive's setup disc in the CD-ROM drive, and run its installation program to set up the tape drive application.

Installing Adapter Card-Based Peripherals

In addition to installing hard drives and peripheral devices that connect to standard I/O ports, technicians must be able to successfully install and configure peripheral devices (or systems) that connect to the system in other ways—such as through the system's expansion slots. The steps for installing these types of peripherals and systems are generally very similar from device to device:

1. Check the adapter card's installation information for any manual configuration settings that might need to be made and set the card up as required.

2. Remove the system unit's cover.

3. Remove an expansion slot cover from the system unit's back panel. Align the adapter card with the appropriate expansion slot and firmly push it into the slot.

4. Secure the card to the back panel of the system unit with a single screw.

5. Attach any external connections to the card (for example, attach the phone line to the modem card or attach the network cable to the LAN adapter). Also, make any external power supply connections to the peripheral device.

6. Install any device drivers required. (PnP devices should be detected by the operating system and automatically configured for operation. If not, you must load drivers for the device from its installation disk or CD.) Additional or updated drivers can be loaded from the operating system (for example, enhancing the operation of a VGA card by loading an SVGA driver for the video display).

7. Shut down the operating system, turn the computer off, and reinstall the system unit's outer cover.

This process can be used to install diverse I/O devices such as modems and LAN adapters, as well as scanners and other devices that use option adapter cards in expansion slots. However, for many devices, the advent of newer hot-swap I/O buses, such as USB and FireWire, has reduced this process to more or less just connecting the device to the bus.

Installing Sound Cards

Installing a sound card is similar to installing any other adapter card. Refer to the card's user guide to determine what hardware configuration settings might need to be made before inserting the card into the system. It might also be beneficial to run a diagnostic software package to check the system's available resources before configuring the card.

After the hardware configuration has been completed, simply install the card in one of the system's vacant expansion slots and secure it to the back panel of the system unit. Plug the microphone and speakers into the proper RCA mini jacks on the card's back plate. With the card installed in the system, load its software drivers according to the directions in the user guide. Figure 1.15 depicts the connectors located on the back of a typical sound card.

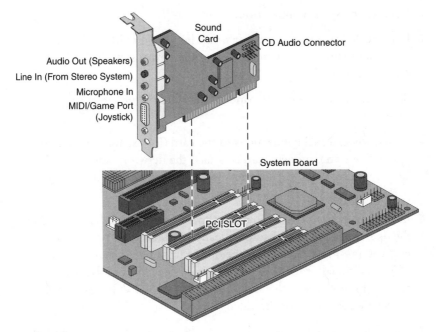

Figure 1.15 Sound-card connections.

Most sound cards support microphones through stereo RCA mini jacks. A very similar speaker jack is also normally present on the back of the card. Depending on the card, the jack might be designed for mono or stereo output. An onboard volume control wheel might also protrude through the card's back plate.

Installing Modems

A modem can be either an internal or an external device, as illustrated in Figure 1.16. An internal modem is installed in one of the computer's expansion slots, and has its own interfacing circuitry. The external modem is usually a box that resides outside the system unit and is connected to one of the computer's serial ports by an RS-232 serial cable. These units depend on the interfacing circuitry of the computer's serial ports. Most PC-compatible computers offer two serial-port connections. Of course, both types of modems connect to an outside telephone line through a standard RJ-11 connector. External modems also require a separate power source.

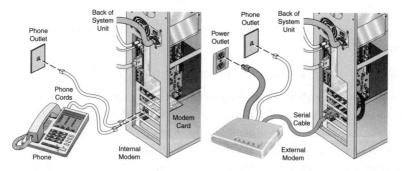

Figure 1.16 Internal and external modems.

Installing an Internal Modem

Use the following steps to install an internal modem.

1. Prepare the system for installation.

   a. Turn the system off.

   b. Remove the cover from the system unit.

   c. Locate a compatible empty expansion slot.

   d. Remove the expansion slot cover from the rear of the system unit.

2. In a non-PnP system, configure the modem's interrupt request (IRQ) and COM Port settings.

   a. Refer to the modem user's manual regarding any IRQ and COM jumper or switch settings.

   b. Record the card's default IRQ and COM settings.

   c. Set the modem's configuration to operate the modem as COM2.

3. Install the modem card in the system.

   a. Install the modem card in the expansion slot.

   b. Reinstall the screw to secure the modem card to the back panel of the system unit.

c. Connect the phone line to the appropriate connector on the modem.

d. Connect the other end of the phone line to the commercial phone jack.

4. Disable any competing COM ports (such as COM2 on the system board).

a. Disable COM2 in the CMOS setup utility.

5. Install any device drivers required. (PnP devices should be detected by the operating system and automatically configured for operation. If not, you must load drivers for the device from its installation disk or CD.) Additional or updated drivers can often be obtained from the modem manufacturer's website on the Internet.

6. Shut down the system.

7. Finish the hardware installation.

a. Replace the system unit's outer cover.

Installing External Dial-Up Modems

In most cases, the steps associated with installing a dial-up modem are identical to those involved with other peripheral devices. You should use the following steps to install an external modem:

1. Make the modem connections.

a. Connect the serial cable to the 9-pin serial port at the rear of the system.

b. Connect the opposite end of the cable to the serial port connector of the external modem unit.

c. Connect the phone line to the appropriate connector on the modem.

d. Connect the other end of the phone line to the phone system jack.

e. Optionally, connect a telephone handset to the appropriate connector on the modem.

f. Verify that the power switch or power supply is turned off.

g. Connect the AC adapter power supply to the external modem unit.

h. Verify the connection arrangement, as illustrated in Figure 1.17.

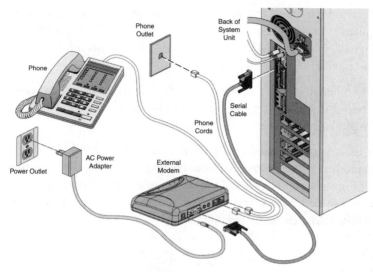

Figure 1.17   Installing an external modem.

2. Enable the system's internal support circuitry.

   a. Remove the cover from the system unit.

   b. Enable COM2 on the system board (through the CMOS setup utility).

   c. Replace the system unit cover.

Modem Configuration

With PCI-based internal modems, the installation and configuration process is fairly simple. These cards possess PnP capabilities that enable the system to automatically configure them with the system resources they need to operate.

Although all Windows operating systems since Windows 95 (excluding Windows NT) have provided PnP support for modems, if the PnP process does not recognize a given modem, the operating system requests that the OEM driver disk be inserted in the floppy or CD-ROM drive so that it can obtain the drivers required to support the modem. In some cases, these drivers might need to be loaded through the Windows Add/Remove Hardware applet in Control Panel.

Installing Digital Modems

Although dial-up modems continue to play a large part in the wide area networking field, they tend to be limited in their capability to move data.

However, several high-speed broadband communications technologies have become available to most users. These technologies include Integrated Services Digital Network (ISDN), Digital Subscriber Line (DSL), cable modems, and satellite communication links.

Each of these technologies is provided through a service provider that supplies the service for a fee. These technologies also all involve some type of specialized digital modem to make the connection.

Figure 1.18 illustrates a typical digital modem connection scheme. Although each digital modem type employs different connection media, the structure of the physical installation is identical for all the different technologies. The modem sits between the computer and the outside service media (such as telephone wires, CAT5 cable, or satellite dish).

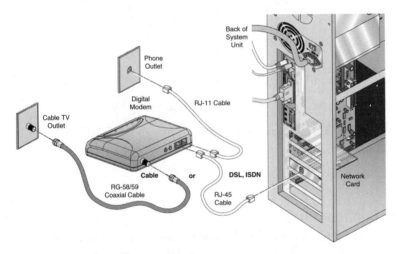

Figure 1.18 Installing digital modems.

The host system sees the digital modems in ISDN, DSL, and cable modem connections through a network adapter card, so the system must be configured for network operation. No OEM drivers need to be loaded for these devices to function. In the case of the satellite connection, the host computer's USB port is used. Because satellite modems are not typical connectivity devices, you might need to load OEM drivers supplied by the manufacturer for the system to work with the PC.

In residential installations, this connection scheme is normally direct. However, in business environments, one computer is typically used as a gateway between the internal LAN and the external network (that is, the Internet). Some LAN connection schemes include a router between the gateway computer and the outside network to represent the complete LAN as a single unit. This makes unauthorized access to the internal LAN harder for outsiders to accomplish.

Required Knowledge for Installing Digital Modems

The following procedure provides a quick reference of the things you must do to install a broadband cable modem or DSL modem:

1. Obtain the digital modem and support documentation from the service company. This equipment should come as part of the cable or DSL service agreement.

2. Install a network adapter card in the host computer.

3. For broadband DSL connections, the first step is to place filters on all phone and fax connections throughout the house—except for the one the DSL modem will use. Note: This must include telephone connections to satellite receivers, answering machines, and computer fax modems.

4. Connect the digital modem to the commercial connection (that is, the broadband interface for the cable or the telephone line) and power up the modem. For cable modems, connect the cable to the modem. Connect the DSL modem to the phone line.

5. Connect the digital modem to the network adapter or a router. In both cases, this involves connecting a CAT5 cable between the digital modem and NIC (or router). If a router is used, the host computer must be connected through the router.

6. Start the host computer and configure the network connection for DHCP operation. Verify that all of the status lights on the digital modem are active—typically, Power, Activity, and Link lights. (Power and Link should be on and solid, Activity might flicker depending on the activity level of the network.)

7. Configure authentication for the connection. Depending on the service provider's requirement, you might need to run their installation disk. Typical required information includes account number, username, and password (assigned by the service provider when the kit is delivered).

   You might encounter two different processes for configuring authentication for the connection—Point-to-Point Protocol over Ethernet (PPPoE) and non-PPPoE. If there is an installation CD, the authentication process is performed automatically as part of the setup. However, if no installation CD is provided, you must manually configure the router to perform the authentication process.

Under the PPPoE method, the authentication requires that a username and password (supplied by the service provider) be entered in the router's configuration table. Under the non-PPPoE method, the MAC address of the NIC or router connected directly to the digital modem must be supplied to the service provider (usually over the telephone).

8. Verify that you have received an IP address from the router (ipconfig /all). The IP address of the machine should be in the range supplied by the router (typically 192.168.1.X). You should also see a gateway address that should match the address of the router (typically 192.168.1.1).

9. PING the default gateway (router) to confirm connectivity.

10. Open a browser and attempt to access a website (www.mic-inc.com).

If you cannot access the Internet, obtain a known IP address from the Web and attempt to PING it. If this does not work, contact the technical support service of the service provider.

Upgrading Adapters

Normally, updating adapters in a PC involves installing additional network interface cards (NICs), modems, or other proprietary adapter cards. You should always use the following guidelines for upgrading adapter card-based peripherals in a system:

1. **Verify compatibility**—When you are installing adapter cards, you should verify their compatibility with the system board, its adapter slot, and the other cards installed in the system. For example, if you are upgrading a PCI card, you should ensure that the voltage is compatible with the available PCI slot. If your PCI slots only support 3.3v adapters, the card you are upgrading to also needs to be 3.3v.

   PCI cards that operate on 3.3v and those that use 5v are configured differently. Therefore, a 3.3v card only fits in a 3.3v slot, whereas 5v cards only fit in a 5v slot. On the other hand, some PCI cards support both 5v and 3.3v operation. There is less to worry about with such dual-voltage cards.

2. **Perform BIOS upgrade**—A system BIOS upgrade is not required when upgrading adapter cards, but some adapter cards contain their own specific BIOS. These BIOS might need to be upgraded to permit the adapter to work with the other components in the system. If in

doubt, refer to the installation documentation and the associated manufacturer's websites for specific information pertaining to the adapters you are using.

3. **Obtain the latest drivers**—In most cases, the drivers that came with an adapter card include the necessary drivers for the operating system you are using. However, the latest driver on the CD-ROM or floppy disk supplied with the component is often not the latest driver available for the noted operating system. Check the manufacturer's website for newer versions.

4. **Implement ESD best practices**—To prevent the adapter from being damaged, ensure that it is enclosed in an antistatic bag when not in use. Be certain to wear an antistatic device when handling the adapter. Most adapters include static sensitive components that can be damaged by very small electromagnetic shocks, so take extra care when handling or installing your adapter cards.

5. **Verify upgrade**—Some specific attributes are common when verifying proper installation of a wide variety of adapter cards. For instance, all adapters use resources, such as IRQ, I/O memory, and/or base memory address. You must ensure that none of these settings are conflicting with those of other hardware devices in the system.

You can check this in Windows by checking the system properties in Control Panel, and looking at the Hardware tab for hardware errors. Although some adapter cards require jumper settings to be preset for these attributes, others do not require jumpers, or include jumperless BIOS. The newer plug-and-play operating systems in use today normally automatically set up your adapter to preclude conflicts.

Specialized Video Cards

If you are designing a high-end computer, such as a computer to produce multimedia presentations (or view them), a high-end video display card is normally required. This type of video adapter card normally includes a heat sink and possibly a bolt-on or snap-on fan unit to cool its video controller IC. The operating speeds and complexity of these devices have increased to the point where active cooling methods are required. Cooling units that include fans require a power connection to drive the fan. This connection can be made on a special connector on the video card or to the system board, as illustrated in Figure 1.19.

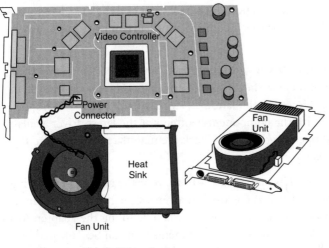

High-End Video Card

Figure 1.19   Advanced cooling on high-end video cards.

Optimizing Network Adapters

In a networked system, by design all the nodes in the network run at the same speed. That means that the performance of the network is limited by its slowest component. If the system is using mostly adapter cards and devices rated for 100-MHz operation but one or more of the cards are only rated for 10-MHz operation, the system is limited to 10-MHz operation. Therefore, all of the adapters in the system should be updated to use the highest speed to realize the maximum performance available.

Installing and Upgrading Peripherals

To successfully add peripheral devices to a PC-compatible system, you must be able to recognize the type of port the device requires, locate standard I/O port connections, and determine what type of cabling is required to successfully connect the port and the device.

Ports

Although many different methods have been developed to connect devices to the PC-compatible system, the following three ports have been standard since the original PCs were introduced:

➤ The RS-232C serial port

➤ The IBM game port

➤ The IBM versions of the Centronics parallel port

The following two connection types have become standards for connecting networked computers together:

➤ RJ-45 (Registered Jack) Ethernet connectors

➤ BNC (British Naval Connector) coaxial connectors

ATX Ports

In an ATX system, the I/O port connections have been integrated into a vertical stack form factor located at the rear of the board. Figure 1.20 illustrates typical connectors located on the back of an ATX-style system.

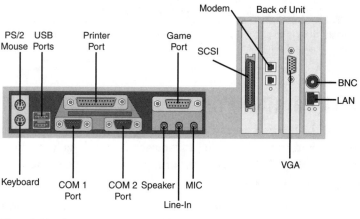

Figure 1.20 ATX back panel connections.

The ATX specification employs two 6-pin mini-DIN connectors (also referred to as *PS/2 connectors*) for the mouse and keyboard. Of course, the fact that both connections use the same type of connector can lead to problems if they are reversed. The standard also provides for two USB port connections, a DB-25F D-shell parallel printer port connector, two RS-232 serial COM ports implemented in a pair of DB-9M D-shell connectors, a

DB-15F D-shell game port, and an RCA mini jack audio port. Unlike the AT-style integrated I/O connections, these port connections require no system board connecting cables that can become defective.

Table 1.6 summarizes the types of connectors typically found on the back panel of both AT and ATX system units, along with their connector and pin count information.

Table 1.6 Typical I/O Ports		
Port	**AT**	**ATX**
Keyboard	5-pin DIN	PS/2 6-pin mini-DIN
Mouse	(See note)	PS/2 6-pin mini-DIN
COM1	DB-9M	DB-9M
COM2	DB-25M	DB-9M
LPT	DB-25F	DB-25F
VGA	DB-15F (3 row)	DB-15F (3 row)
Game	DB-15F (2 row)	DB-15F (2 row)
Modem	RJ-11	RJ-11
LAN	BNC/RJ-45	BNC/RJ-45
Sound	RCA mini jacks	RCA mini jacks
SCSI	Centronics 50-pin	Centronics 50-pin

In AT class computers, there is no port dedicated to the mouse. In these systems, the mouse typically uses the COM1 serial port connector.

IEEE-1284 Parallel Port Devices

The least difficult I/O devices to add to a PC system are those that use the system's parallel printer port. Installing this device is easy largely because, from the beginning of the PC era, a parallel printer has been one of the standard pieces of equipment to add to a system.

This standardization has led to fairly direct installation procedures for most devices. Obtain an *IEEE-1284*–compliant cable and plug it into the appropriate LPT port on the back of the computer. Connect the Centronic-compatible end of the cable to the device, plug the power cord into the device, load a device driver to configure the software for the correct printer, and print.

One note of caution concerning parallel printer cables: The Institute of Electrical and Electronics Engineers (IEEE) has established specifications for bidirectional parallel printer cables (IEEE-1284). These cables affect the operation of Enhanced Parallel Port (EPP) andEnhanced Capabilities Port (ECP) parallel devices. Using an older, noncompliant unidirectional cable with a bidirectional parallel device prevents the device from communicating properly with the system and might prevent it from operating.

Be aware that using an older, noncompliant unidirectional cable with a bidirectional parallel device prevents the device from communicating properly with the system and might prevent it from operating.

Regardless of the type of device being installed, the steps for adding an IEEE-1284 device to a system are basically the same. Connect the device to the correct I/O port at the computer system. Be certain the port is enabled for EPP or ECP operation in the CMOS setup utility. Then set up the appropriate device drivers. Figure 1.21 summarizes these steps.

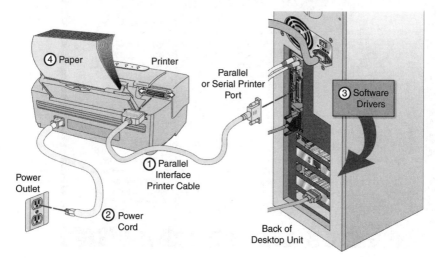

Figure 1.21   Printer installation steps.

Installing Devices Using Advanced Buses and Ports

Most new I/O ports and buses (for example, USB, IEEE-1394, PCMCIA, *Infrared Data Association [IrDA]*) feature hot insertion and removal capabilities for their devices. This is in addition to the traditional PnP operation. The devices that connect to these ports and buses are designed to be plugged in and removed as needed. Installing these devices is practically a hands-off operation.

Installing a USB or FireWire Device

Installing a USB or FireWire device normally involves the following steps:

1. Enable the USB resources in the CMOS setup screen, as illustrated in Figure 1.22. In some cases, this involves enabling the port and reserving an IRQ resource for the device.

2. Plug the device in to an open USB connector.

3. Wait for the operating system to recognize the device and configure it through the PnP process.

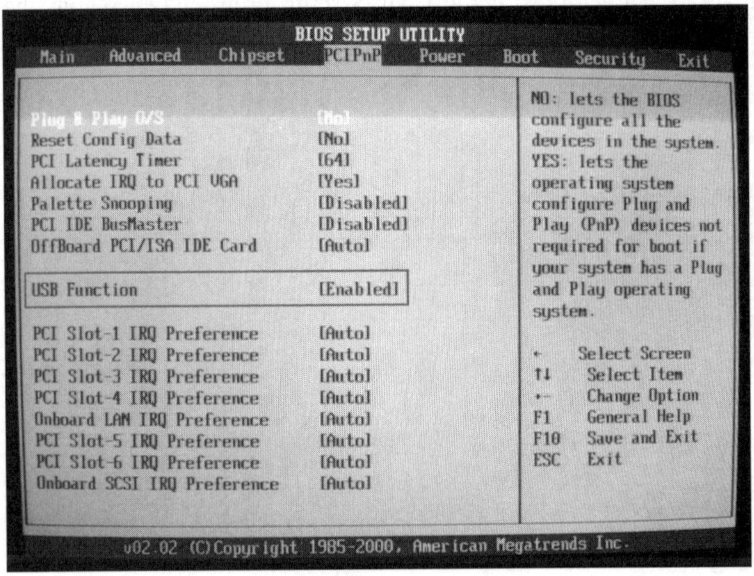

Figure 1.22 Enabling the USB resources.

Microsoft Windows 98, Windows 2000, or Windows XP operating systems detect the presence of the USB or FireWire device and start their Found New Hardware Wizard program, depicted in Figure 1.23, to guide the installation process. Simply follow the instructions provided by the wizard to set up the new device—there is no need to shut down or turn off the computer.

Figure 1.23   The Windows Found New Hardware Wizard.

Installing IrDA Devices

Installing an IrDA device in an infrared-enabled system is a fairly simple process. When an IrDA device is installed in the system, a Wireless Link icon appears in the Windows Control Panel. (Remember, infrared port operations must first be enabled through the CMOS setup utility.) When another IrDA device comes within range of the host port, the *Infrared* icon appears on the Windows desktop, as depicted in Figure 1.24, and in the taskbar. In the case of an IrDA printer, a printer icon appears in the Printer folder.

Right-click the Infrared icon on the taskbar to turn on the infrared communication function. Be certain that the *Enable Infrared* communication check box is checked. To turn off infrared communications, ensure that this item is not checked. When infrared communication has been turned off, the Search for Devices Within Range and Enable Plug and Play functions are also turned off. To engage support for infrared plug-and-play devices, right-click the Infrared icon on the taskbar.

Ensure that the Enable Plug and Play option is checked. Conversely, to turn off support for plug-and-play device installation, ensure that this item is not checked. It is only available if the infrared and searching functions are enabled. If the taskbar icon is not visible, click the Related Topics option.

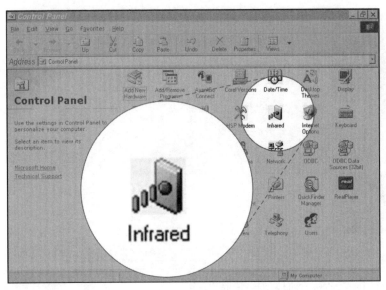

Figure 1.24 The Windows Wireless Link icon.

Simply right-click the Infrared icon on the taskbar to install software for an infrared device. Be certain that the Enable Plug and Play check box is checked and verify that the new device is within range. If you are not sure whether the device you are installing is plug-and-play capable, check its user's guide. If it is not a plug-and-play device, install its drivers by accessing the Add New Hardware icon in Control Panel.

Installing Digital Cameras

Digital cameras are mobile devices that are mostly plugged in to the computer simply to download pictures. Therefore, most digital cameras feature the capability of being connected to parallel ports, serial ports, and USB ports. Some cameras can also communicate through IEEE-1394 FireWire ports. USB and FireWire ports feature hot-swap capabilities that permit the camera to be plugged in to the system and removed while power is still applied. Figure 1.25 shows a typical digital camera connection scheme.

With operating systems prior to Windows XP, software applications for downloading the pictures from the camera must be loaded on the PC before any transfers can be conducted. The camera manufacturer typically furnishes these applications as part of the camera package. Likewise, the software supplied with the camera can be used to display the images and typically offers a limited number of graphic manipulation features (for example, rotate, color balance, crop, resize). Most digital cameras deliver the images to the PC in a JPEG format. This format is compact, but it can be manipulated with virtually any commercial graphic design software.

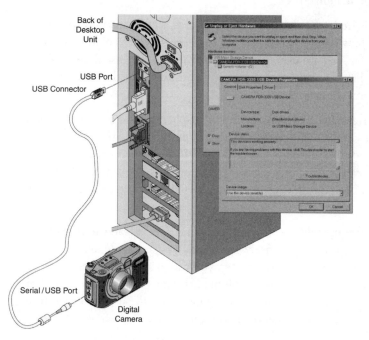

Figure 1.25 Digital camera connections.

Upgrading Peripheral Devices

Devices that come under this category include printers, external modems, external CD devices, and input devices, such as the keyboard and mouse. The steps involved in this process are similar to those listed for upgrading adapter cards presented earlier in this chapter. You should use the general procedure that follows when you are upgrading a system's peripheral devices:

1. **Verify compatibility**—Because peripheral devices can vary greatly in their configuration and use, you should always refer to the device's documentation to ensure that it will work properly with your system. Because external devices must connect to the computer through its interface ports (that is, serial and parallel ports, USB, FireWire, and, in some cases, external SCSI connectors), you must ensure that the proper port is available for the device to be installed.

2. **Perform firmware upgrade**—Prior to installing a peripheral, consult the manufacturer's website for any updates that might exist for its

firmware, or any updated device drivers that might be available. To apply firmware updates, you must first obtain the firmware update tool from the manufacturer.

3. **Obtain the latest drivers**—In most cases, the installation software that came with the peripheral has the necessary drivers for the operating system you are using. The latest driver on the installation CD or floppy disk is normally the latest driver available at the time the peripheral shipped.

4. **Implement ESD best practices**—Peripherals tend to be less sensitive to electrostatic damage than PC board devices and are often directly grounded through their power cords. However, because peripheral devices can tend to be expensive, you should still properly ground yourself before working with them. It is always better to be safe than sorry.

5. **Verify the upgrade**—Because peripheral devices can vary greatly in their configuration and use, you can test your upgrade in a variety of ways. For instance, with a printer, you can print a test page, print a page from a client, or print multiple print jobs to test the queue. For a Zip disk, this might include moving data onto the disk and then trying to examine the data on another computer later.

6. **Check system resources**—Normally, peripherals use the resources associated with the port to which they are attached. If the peripheral tests OK, you normally do not have to verify system resources.

Implementing Ports

Most Pentium-based systems integrate the standard AT-compatible I/O functions into the system board. In these systems, the BIOS's Integrated Peripherals screen provides configuration and enabling settings for the system board's IDE drive connections, floppy-disk drive controller, onboard universal asynchronous receiver-transmitters (UARTs), and onboard parallel port. Figure 1.26 shows a typical Integrated Peripherals screen.

The parallel printer port can be configured for normal PC-AT–compatible Standard Parallel Port (SPP) operation; for extended bidirectional operation (EPP); for fast, buffered bidirectional operation (ECP); or for combined ECP+EPP operation. The normal CMOS setting should be selected unless both the port hardware and driver software support EPP and/or ECP operation.

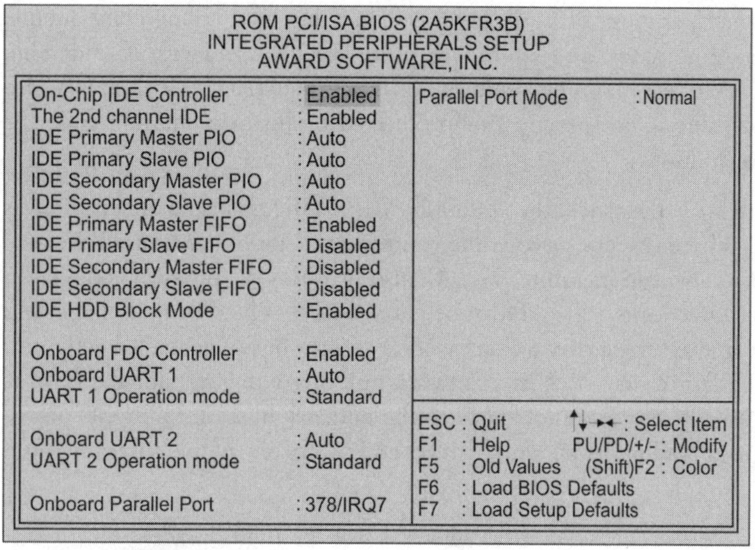

```
                    ROM PCI/ISA BIOS (2A5KFR3B)
                    INTEGRATED PERIPHERALS SETUP
                       AWARD SOFTWARE, INC.

On-Chip IDE Controller      : Enabled    Parallel Port Mode        : Normal
The 2nd channel IDE         : Enabled
IDE Primary Master PIO      : Auto
IDE Primary Slave PIO       : Auto
IDE Secondary Master PIO    : Auto
IDE Secondary Slave PIO     : Auto
IDE Primary Master FIFO     : Enabled
IDE Primary Slave FIFO      : Disabled
IDE Secondary Master FIFO   : Disabled
IDE Secondary Slave FIFO    : Disabled
IDE HDD Block Mode          : Enabled

Onboard FDC Controller      : Enabled
Onboard UART 1              : Auto
UART 1 Operation mode       : Standard
                                          ESC : Quit         ↑↓ ←→ : Select Item
Onboard UART 2              : Auto        F1  : Help         PU/PD/+/- : Modify
UART 2 Operation mode       : Standard    F5  : Old Values   (Shift)F2 : Color
                                          F6  : Load BIOS Defaults
Onboard Parallel Port       : 378/IRQ7    F7  : Load Setup Defaults
```

Figure 1.26 Integrated Peripherals screen.

IrDA ports provide short-distance wireless connections for different IrDA-compliant devices, such as printers and personal digital assistants. Because the IrDA port communicates by sending and receiving a serial stream of light pulses, it is normally configured to work with the UART of the system's second serial port. This arrangement is established through the Integrated Peripherals screen of the CMOS setup utility. In this manner, the infrared port is assigned the same system resources normally reserved for the COM2/COM4 serial ports.

To enable the IrDA port, the mode for the COM2 UART must be set to automatic and one of the infrared protocol settings (HPSIR or ASKIR) must be selected. In addition, the transmission duplex mode must be selected (normally half-duplex). The operation of the infrared port and the second serial port is mutually exclusive. When the infrared option is enabled in CMOS, the second serial port is disabled.

Installing Wireless LAN Components

Wireless local area networks (*WLANs*) are becoming a popular option for connecting devices in residential and small office environments, airports, coffee bars, and restaurants, as well as large corporations. Wireless LANs provide the maximum amount of flexibility for connecting networking components, and because no wires are required, they provide the users with considerable mobility. Wireless is also becoming an economical choice for locations where installing cable is not practical or prohibited by historic building codes or other restrictions.

As Figure 1.27 illustrates, the *access point (AP)* is the mainstay of the wireless network. These devices serve as the central connection point for all the network devices within its range. The AP also provides the physical connection with wired networks. The AP can be connected to a host computer that is a node on an existing hard-wired network, or it can be connected directly into a connectivity device, such as a network hub or router. Installing the AP is normally a matter of connecting it to the network host, installing its power adapter, and loading its network drivers and protocols on the host computer.

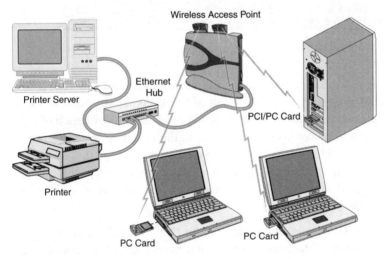

Figure 1.27 Wireless network components.

The antennas in the AP establish a range of transmission around the AP called a *hotspot*. Other wireless computing devices (clients) can access the network throughout the hotspot as long as they are within range of other wireless terminals or the AP.

A wireless client can be any type of computer or peripheral designed to use the same wireless protocol that the AP is using. Such devices include desktop computers with wireless PCI cards, laptop computers using PCMCIA cards, and wireless peripheral equipment using built-in wireless interfaces. For most computers, all that is necessary to start sharing data and resources wirelessly is to install the proper wireless adapter cards and network software.

Required Knowledge for Installing Wireless LANs

The following procedure provides a quick reference of the things you must do to install a wireless network:

1. Review the documentation for installing your wireless AP, and determine any restriction in the area where you will be installing the network. Also, obtain the IP address of the wireless access point from the documentation.

2. Connect the AP (or wireless router) to the NIC card in the host computer (or into a hard-wired hub) using a standard CAT5 cable.

3. Start the host computer, open a web browser, and enter the designated IP address obtained from the AP's documentation. This should produce the AP's web-based configuration tool.

4. Enable and configure the security or encryption settings for the AP. Determine the type of authentication and encryption methods that you want to establish. Typical settings include selecting the *Wired Equivalent Privacy (WEP)* protocol to minimize the risk of security compromise on the wireless LAN (because unauthorized computers with wireless receivers can pick up the transmission).

5. You must first associate the AP with the network and then authenticate with the network second. Required values include an encryption key that can be 64 or 128 bits in length (the encryption key must be the same for all devices that want to communicate with the AP). Record the (normally hex) encryption key value so that you can implement it on all the client computers. This completes the association component of establishing a wireless network.

6. For an additional security measure, you must establish authentication and encryption. This process can vary from AP to AP. Key points to remember are to record the encryption key values so they can be entered in the client computers.

When troubleshooting association and authentication problems, only change one value at a time. If you change settings for both options at the same time, you will never figure out which function is not working properly.

7. Install wireless networking cards in the wireless LAN's client computers.

8. Install drivers for the wireless cards in the client computers.

9. Open the wireless card utility on each client computer to configure the association encryption first, followed by setting the authentication encryption key.

> When troubleshooting these systems, you should turn off the authentication encryption on the AP first and attempt to connect. If this is unsuccessful, check the association encryption keys.

> Some older wireless cards might not support 128-bit encryption. In these cases, you must force the AP to use 64-bit encryption if possible (or upgrade the wireless card on the clients).
>
> A very good shareware utility called *Netstumbler* can be used to check APs. This utility is free and can be obtained at http://www.Tucows.com or http://www.download.com.

Loading and Adding Device Drivers

One of the reasons for the success of the PC-compatible system is its versatility. This versatility is the result of an open architecture that permits all types of devices to be added to it. This is accomplished through the use of software device drivers that interface diverse equipment to the basic system. Although the process for installing equipment and their drivers in a PC has become increasingly easy, the technician must still be able to install whatever drivers are necessary in the event a manual install is the only way to get a piece of hardware working.

Windows 9x Device Drivers

The PnP-compliant design of Windows 9x and Windows Me makes installing most new hardware nearly automatic (as long as the new device is also PnP compliant). The PnP function automatically detects the presence of any new PnP-compliant hardware when the system is started. If the device is PnP compliant, the operating system attempts to load drivers for it from its own list of drivers. If the system cannot find a suitable driver for the device, it stops and asks for a location where the driver files can be found. If Windows does not detect a new plug-and-play device, either the device is not working properly or it is not installed correctly.

Manually Installing Drivers on Windows 9x and Windows Me Machines

If the device is not PnP compliant, or the system just can't detect it for some reason, it is necessary to use the Windows 9x *Add New Hardware Wizard*. The Add New Hardware Wizard is a series of screens that guide the installation process for the new device. The new card or device should already be physically installed in the system before running this procedure. The Add New Hardware icon can be found under the Control Panel option of the Settings menu. It can also be accessed through the Hardware tab of the System Properties window.

If the wizard does not detect the hardware, you can attempt to locate the device in the wizard's list of supported devices. The only other option for installing hardware devices is to obtain an OEM disk or CD for the device that has Windows 9x or Windows Me drivers and manually install the drivers. If the driver disk does not have an AutoStart function, it is necessary to click the Have Disk button in the Update Device Driver Wizard page and supply the file's location to complete the installation process.

Windows NT, Windows 2000, and Windows XP Device Drivers

As mentioned earlier, Windows NT does not support as many hardware devices as the Windows 9x platforms do. However, Windows 2000 and Windows XP still offer support for a fairly wide range of disk drive types, VGA video cards, NICs, tape drives, and printers. To determine what devices Windows NT, Windows 2000, or Windows XP supports, it is necessary to consult the Hardware Compatibility List (HCL) for the version of Windows being used.

 The Hardware Compatibility List information for the version of Windows being used can be obtained from the Microsoft website (https://winqual.microsoft.com/download/default.asp).

If drivers for the device being installed are not listed on the HCL, there is a good chance the device will not operate or will not operate well in the Windows NT environment. If this is the case, the only recourse is to contact the device's manufacturer for Windows NT drivers. It is a good idea to check the manufacturer's website for updated drivers that can simply be downloaded.

Adding Devices to a Windows NT 4.0 Machine

Windows NT 4.0 does not possess plug-and-play capabilities, although it does feature some autodetection capabilities. It also has no Add New Hardware Wizard. Under Windows NT 4.0, devices must be installed manually either through the icons in Control Panel or through installation routines provided by the equipment manufacturer.

Adding Devices to a Windows 2000 or Windows XP Machine

Adding new devices to Windows 2000 or Windows XP is typically performed automatically through the system's plug-and-play process. However, devices can be manually added to a Windows 2000 system through the Add/Remove Hardware icon located in Control Panel. In Windows XP, the icon is simply labeled *Add Hardware*. Double-clicking this icon produces the Add/Remove Hardware (Add Hardware) Installation Wizard that guides the installation process or aids in troubleshooting problems with the new hardware component. In cases in which the device came with an installation CD, Microsoft recommends that you use the CD instead of the Add Hardware Wizard.

Double-clicking on a device icon in Control Panel produces a Properties dialog box for that device. The dialog box holds configuration information specific to that device. The tabs located in the dialog boxes can be used to review and change settings and drivers for the device.

Finding Updated Device Drivers

Device manufacturers often continue to develop improved device drivers for their products after they have been released into the market. In addition, there is relatively little cooperation between hardware manufacturers and operating system companies. Therefore, you might need to locate new drivers for existing equipment that is not included in an early release of an operating system such as Windows 2000 or Windows XP.

To find new or updated drivers for a specific device, you should contact the product vendor's website and search for your specific network operating system. Typically, you need to know the specific make and model of your device. In most cases, the appropriate device drivers can be downloaded directly from the vendor's website or obtained through mail. However, some vendors only supply their drivers by shipping them to the user on CD.

In addition, device drivers can be obtained for various pieces of hardware at several third-party websites on the Internet. These sites tend to be especially useful for finding device drivers for older pieces of hardware, when original copies of drivers have been lost.

Driver Signing

Windows 2000 and Windows XP support a relatively wide array of newer hardware devices. These devices include DVD, USB, and IEEE 1394 devices. Microsoft works with hardware vendors to certify their drivers. These drivers are *digitally signed* so that they can be loaded automatically by the system.

Because poorly written device drivers had traditionally been a third-party problem for Microsoft, they created a Windows Hardware Quality Labs (WHQL) approval system for hardware manufacturers. Manufacturers who want to assure their customers that their products work with Windows 2000 and Windows XP operating systems can submit their equipment and drivers to Microsoft for certification. Microsoft grants tested drivers a digital signature that is embedded in the driver to show that it has been approved. When Windows 2000 or Windows XP loads the driver, it checks for the signature.

Driver signing is controlled through the Windows 2000 and Windows XP System icon located in Control Panel. In the System applet, select the Hardware tab, and click the Driver Signing button. The Driver Signing Options page appears. On this page, you can establish how the system should react when it detects an unsigned driver. The options are

➤ **Warn**—This setting causes Windows to notify the user when an unsigned driver has been detected. It also produces an option to load or not to load the driver.

➤ **Block**—As its title implies, this option does not permit any unsigned drivers to be loaded into the system.

➤ **Disable (Ignore in Windows XP)**—This option disables the digital signature check and automatically loads any driver without providing a warning to the user.

If you check the Apply Setting as System Default check box, the signature verification setting is applied to anyone who logs on to the system. Otherwise, only the currently logged-on user is affected.

Because Windows 2000 and Windows XP are designed with centralized network security in mind, some administrative control issues might be encountered when loading device drivers into one of these systems. If the system detects a valid digital signature, or the *Designed for Windows Logo*, when it checks the driver, it normally accepts the driver without any problems. However, if there is no digital signature or logo, administrative privileges are required to load the driver into the system.

You must also be a member of the Administrators group to install drivers using the Add Hardware Wizard or when a network policy setting has been established to restrict who can install devices.

Power Supply Upgrade Considerations

One consideration that might not be apparent when system components are being upgraded is the power supply. The power supply unit in a computer comes with a given power rating (in watts). The voltage level for a given location in the world is fixed (that is, 120 or 220 Vac) and the power required can be calculated by multiplying the voltage level by the maximum current rating (in amperes) of all the devices in the system.

In the field, it is difficult to accumulate the current values for all the devices in the system. Therefore, each time a new drive or device is added to the system, more current is required. For example, upgrading the processor can easily increase the power consumption in the system by more than 20 watts. A typical Pentium processor might require 65 watts of power to operate. Advanced Pentium processors have increased their power consumption to over 80 watts.

Likewise, replacing RAM with faster or bigger RAM devices tends to increase power consumption as well. Simply increasing the installed memory from 128MB to 256MB by adding an additional DIMM almost doubles the power consumption of the system's memory (for example, from 6 watts to 12 watts).

Adding adapter cards to the system also significantly increases the amount of power the power supply must deliver to the system board. A typical adapter card might require 12 to 15 watts with good connections to the slot. A high-end video adapter used for games might consume up to 100 watts.

However, disk drive devices tend to consume more power than most other system devices, simply because they use motors to spin the disk or disc and to position the read/write mechanism. A typical hard disk drive can require up to 20 or 30 watts each.

It is relatively easy to consume hundreds of watts of power for a normal system. The typical power supply used with basic Pentium desktop systems is 300 watts. One third of this value must be reserved simply for startup of the computer. During this time, the system requires more power than it does when it is running. For systems using the high-end video card mentioned earlier, the power supply might need to be capable of delivering 500 watts of power.

You can determine whether the system needs a power supply upgrade in two ways. The first is to approximate how much each device requires and double that value to provide for operating safety and the startup surge. The second method involves purchasing all of the upgrade items and turning on the system to discover that it does not start.

Required Knowledge for Upgrading the Power Supply

The following procedure provides a quick reference of the things you must do to upgrade the power supply:

1. Use the information in the preceding section to assess the power requirements of your system. If available, examine the electrical specification in all component documentation to determine electrical power usage more closely.

2. Multiply electrical current requirements of components by 120 to produce the device's power consumption rate in watts.

3. Add all of the power consumption figures together and double this value to arrive at the power rating necessary for the replacement power supply.

4. Obtain a power supply unit that has both the correct wattage rating and the correct form factor (that is, ATX) for your computer.

5. Disconnect the exterior power connections from the system unit. Unplug the power cable from the commercial receptacle.

6. Disconnect the interior power connections. Disconnect the power supply connections from the system board, and disconnect the options power supply connectors from the floppy disk drive, the hard disk drive, and from the CD-ROM/DVD drive. Finally, disconnect the power supply connector to the front panel switches.

7. Remove the four retaining screws that secure the power supply unit to the rear of the system unit. (Note: In some AT style cases, an additional pair of screws are used along the front edge of the power supply to secure it to the metal bracket on which it is mounted.) Store the screws properly.

8. Remove the power supply from the system unit by lifting it out of the chassis.

9. Position the new power supply in the chassis and secure it to the chassis using the screws removed from the old unit.

10. Reconnect the FDD, HDD, and CD-ROM/DVD drive power connections to the devices.

Installing, Configuring, and Upgrading Operating Systems

Introduction

This chapter contains procedures for installing, configuring, and upgrading operating systems. It also includes information and procedures for installing applications and printers, as well as for configuring local area and wide area network connections within different operating systems.

Disk Preparation

Installing an operating system on a new hard drive has evolved into a basic, four-step process:

1. Partition the drive for use with the operating system. As part of the install process, this operation can be performed with the FDISK utility in Windows 9x and Windows Me, or as an integral part of the installation process in Windows 2000 or Windows XP.

2. Format the drive with the basic operating system files. This operation is performed by the operating system. In Windows 2000 and Windows XP, you are given an option to select the file management system type with which to format the disk or partition.

3. Run the appropriate setup utility to install the complete operating system.

4. Load all the drivers necessary to enable the operating system to work with the system's installed hardware devices.

Installing Windows 95

Although Windows 95 is becoming antiquated as an operating system, in terms of Microsoft's view of current operating systems, many desktops still run this OS. As a result of this reality, we cover the installation of Windows 95 in the event that you are required to perform this task.

The Windows 95 operating system must be installed over an existing FAT16 partition on the drive. This prevents it from being installed over some other type of operating system, such as Windows NT or a Novell NetWare operating system.

The Windows 95 system must be at least an 80386DX or higher machine, operating with at least 4MB of RAM (8MB is recommended). Although the 80386DX is the listed minimum microprocessor for running Windows 95, the recommended processor is the 80486DX, and the Pentium processors are the preferred microprocessor for running Windows 95. Likewise, 4MB might be the minimum RAM option, with 8MB being the recommended option, but 16MB, 32MB, or 64MB are preferred for running Windows 95.

The system should also possess a mouse, a keyboard, and a VGA or better monitor. The system's hard drive should have at least 40MB of free space available to successfully install Windows 95.

In addition, the Windows 95 setup routine provides for different types of installations to be established, including *Typical*, *Portable*, *Compact*, and *Custom*. All these options install different combinations of the possible Windows 9x system. Therefore, they all have different system requirements for proper installation.

Performing a Typical installation in an MS-DOS system requires a minimum of 40MB of free drive space. Conversely, conducting a Compact installation on the same system requires only 30MB.

To run the Windows 95 setup program from the command line, follow these steps:

1. Boot the computer.

2. Insert the Windows 95 Start Disk (Disk 1) in the A drive, or place the Windows 95 CD in the CD-ROM drive.

3. Move to the drive that contains the Windows 95 installation files.

4. At the command prompt, type setup, and press the Enter key.

5. Follow the onscreen directions and enter the information requested by the program for the type of installation being performed.

Installing Windows 98

Unlike Windows 95, only the Upgrade version of Windows 98 requires an existing operating system such as MS-DOS, Windows 3.x, or Windows 95 for installation. The distribution CD for the full version of Windows 98 can be used to boot the system and provide options to partition and format the drive.

To install Windows 98, the system hardware must be at least an 80486DX/66 or higher machine, operating with at least 16MB of RAM. The system should also possess a keyboard, a mouse, and a 16-color VGA or better monitor. The system's hard drive should have between 120MB and 355MB of free space available to successfully install Windows 98. The actual amount of disk space used depends on the type of installation being performed (*Typical, Custom, Portable, Compact, New, Upgrade*, and so on). Typical installations use between 170MB and 225MB of disk space.

The installation is carried out in a five-step procedure as follows:

1. **Preparing to run Windows 98 setup**—During this part of the procedure, the setup program performs several steps to prepare the Windows 98 Setup Wizard to guide you through the installation process. These include displaying the Windows 98 Setup dialog box, creating a Setuplog.txt file, identifying the source drive and the drive where the install will occur, creating a directory for a mini-install version of Windows, and extracting the files necessary to run the Setup Wizard.

2. **Collecting information about your computer**—After the setup files have been extracted to the hard drive, the Windows 98 Setup Wizard begins operation by presenting the Microsoft Licensing Agreement and asking you to enter the product key number, as illustrated in Figure 2.1. The product key can be found on the software's Certificate of Authenticity or on the CD's liner. On standalone machines, this

number must be entered correctly to continue the installation. Conversely, there is no product key request when Windows 98 is being installed across a network.

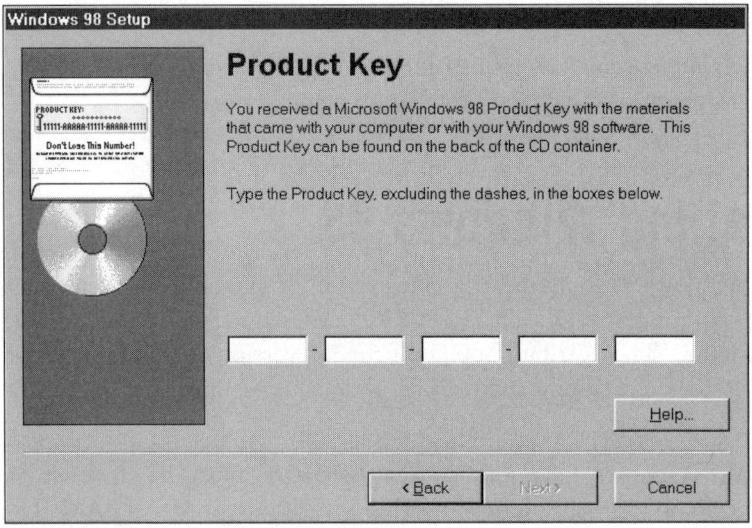

Figure 2.1 Windows 98 Setup Wizard Product Key dialog box.

After the registration information has been gathered, the setup program begins to collect information about the system. This information includes

a. The location of the installation directory into which Windows 98 files should be moved

b. Verification that the selected drive has enough space to hold the Windows 98 installation

c. The type of installation desired (that is, Typical, Portable, Compact, or Custom)

d. The user's company and usernames

e. The Windows 98 components that should be installed

f. The computer's network identification (if installing in a network environment)

g. The Internet location from which the system can receive regional update information

After gathering this information, the setup routine stops to prompt you to create an emergency start disk and then begins installing Windows 98 files to the selected drive.

3. **Copying Windows 98 files to your computer**—This portion of the operation begins when the Start Copying Files window appears on the screen. The complete operation of this phase is automated, so no external input is required. However, any interruption of the setup operation during this period might prevent the system from starting up again. In this event, it is necessary to rerun the setup routine from the beginning.

4. **Restarting your computer**—After the setup routine copies the Windows 98 files into their proper locations, it presents a prompt to restart the system. Doing so enables the newly installed Windows 98 functions to become active. The restart is conducted automatically if no entry is detected within 15 seconds.

5. **Setting up hardware and finalizing settings**—After the system is restarted, the setup program finalizes the installation of the operating system.

Upon completion of these steps, the setup program again restarts the system and presents a logon prompt. After the logon process, the setup program establishes a database of system driver information, updates the system's settings, establishes personalized system options, and presents a Welcome to Windows 98 window.

Installing Windows 98 from a Network Server

In medium and large organizations, it is not practical to visit each computer to manually install the operating system. For these situations, it is preferable to automate the installation process by placing the distribution files on a server and using installation *scripts* to conduct a remote install operation.

Arguably, there probably aren't too many remote installs of Windows 98 occurring anymore. However, this operation is still being performed and uses the same procedures discussed later for the Windows NT line of operating systems.

1. To perform server-based automated installs, you need to have the Windows 98 files and the setup script files located on the server.

2. Boot the local machine up to a startup disk with network support.

3. At the command prompt, run the setup program across the network by specifying the location of the batch file that contains the setup script. The general format for doing this is as follows:

```
\\servername\remote_windowsdirectoryname\Setup.exe script.inf
```

After installing Windows 98 from a server, the local copy of the Registry retains the path information for the install and automatically attempts to perform any hardware or software upgrade support functions from that location.

Installing Windows Me

The Windows Me operating system can be installed on any computer using a Pentium 150MHz or equivalent microprocessor, with at least 32MB of RAM installed. The system should also possess a keyboard, a mouse, a CD-ROM or DVD drive, and a 16-color VGA monitor or better. The system's hard drive should have 200MB of free space available to successfully install Windows Me. The actual amount of disk space used depends on the type of installation being performed (Typical, Custom, Portable, Compact, New, Upgrade, and so on). Typical installations use 320MB of disk space. A Custom installation that includes all available Windows components requires up to 400MB of space.

To install Windows Me, follow these steps:

1. Like Windows 98, the distribution CD for the full version of Windows Me can be used to boot the system and provide options to partition and format the drive. The first step in this installation process is to ensure that the system will check the CD-ROM drive for a bootable disc. You can accomplish this through the Boot Sequence setting in the CMOS setup utility.

2. After verifying the boot sequence, the next step is typically to partition the drive for the operating system. At the command prompt, type FDISK to open the FDISK utility, and press the Enter key to enable large disk support. From the FDISK menu screen, depicted in Figure 2.2, select the options to create a partition, set the active partition, exit the FDISK utility, and restart the computer.

3. If the system does not autostart the Windows Me CD, restart the computer. At this point, you should insert the Windows Me CD-ROM in the appropriate drive and boot the computer to the CD-ROM. From the Startup menu, select the Start Computer with CD-ROM Support option, and press the Enter key.

```
                    Microsoft Windows Millennium
                       Fixed Disk Setup Program
                 (C) Copyright Microsoft Corp.  1983 - 2000


                            FDISK Options

Current fixed disk drive: 1

Choose one of the following:

1. Create DOS partition or Logical DOS Drive
2. Set active partition
3. Delete partition or Logical DOS Drive
4. Display partition information

Enter choice: [1]

Press Esc to exit FDISK
```

Figure 2.2   The FDISK main screen display.

4. Run the Windows Millennium setup program. Reboot the computer to the CD-ROM, select the Start Setup from CD-ROM option, and press the Enter key. At the Windows Me Setup window, press Enter. The setup program prompts you to format the hard disk drive. Press Enter again to begin the formatting process.

5. The setup process then performs some routine system checks. Press Enter to continue the installation.

6. Click the Next button on the Welcome to Windows Me Setup window, as depicted in Figure 2.3, to start the Windows Me installation process.

7. When prompted, select a directory where the Windows Me operating system should be installed. It is strongly recommended that you use the Windows default selection (click the Next button to accept the default c:\Windows directory for the install).

In the case of a dual-boot situation, you should create a new folder specifically for each operating system. Therefore, you should create a folder for Windows 98 at this point in the setup operation. Clicking the Other Directory option followed by the Next button opens the Change Directory dialog box. From this point, you simply provide the name of the new directory and the wizard creates it if it does not already exist.

8. The Setup Option window lists four types of installations from which to choose. Select the appropriate installation type, and click the Next button.

Figure 2.3 The Welcome to Windows Me Setup window.

9. In the Windows Components Setup window, click the Install the Most Common Components option, and click the Next button.

10. When prompted at the Network Identification window, enter the computer name and accept the default workgroup name (or enter the appropriate name). Click the Next button to proceed.

11. Establish the country/region where the computer is located, and click the Next button.

12. Establish the time zone setting for the computer system, and click the Next button. You should now be prompted that Windows Me is ready to begin copying files. Click the Finish button to begin copying files. After the system reboots and installs drivers, you are prompted to enter user information. When ready, click the Next button to move forward.

13. When the License Agreement window appears, click the I Accept the Agreement radio button, and then click the Next button.

14. On the Product Key window, enter the product key number, and then click the Next button.

The product key can generally be found either on the CD-ROM sleeve or on the CD itself.

15. Click the Finish button to complete the Windows Millennium Edition setup. The computer reboots at this point. When Windows restarts, it resumes the setup and begins checking and setting up the hardware and then automatically restarts the system again.

16. Windows continues its setup process and configures the system software. When the Restart timer appears, click the Restart Now button or let Windows restart the system again to complete the installation.

17. When the system restarts, an Enter Windows Password window might appear. Enter the username and, if desired, enter a password. Otherwise, click the OK button.

After the Windows Me operating system installation is complete, the setup utility installs any hardware it found and personalizes the system. The operating system is now installed and ready for you to investigate some of its basic features.

Adding CAB Files to the Installation

The Windows operating system files are stored in the form of special compressed Cabinet (.CAB) files on the distribution CD. This includes the many device driver files that the operating system contains to support peripheral devices. Many technicians copy these files over to the hard disk drives of Windows 9x and Windows Me machines after completing the installation process.

The files can be stored anywhere on the drive, but placing them in a \Windows\Cab folder makes them easy to find. The process is as simple as performing a copy operation from the distribution CD to the folder.

Doing this throughout a controlled environment enables the technician to perform routine hardware and software additions without needing a Windows CD to carry them out. There is nothing more irritating than to install a new hardware device or software package and then to encounter the "You Need the Windows CD" type message because the system is looking for Cabinet files from which to pull drivers.

This practice is not typically performed in the Windows 2000 and Windows XP environments because the CAB files are automatically copied over to the

\Winnt\System32\Driver\Cab folder. However, you can add the CAB files to disk images so that they are present when the image CD is being used to perform clone installations. This is convenient in that you do not need to have a Windows distribution CD around to troubleshoot CAB and DLL file problems that occur in Windows setup procedures.

Installing Windows NT, Windows 2000, and Windows XP Operating Systems

The installation process for Windows NT versions, including Windows NT, Windows 2000, and Windows XP, can be a little more difficult than that of the Windows 9x and Windows Me versions.

The first issue to deal with is the hardware compatibility issue. Windows NT, Windows 2000, and Windows XP make no claims to maintaining compatibility with a wide variety of hardware devices. If your current hardware does not appear in the Microsoft *Hardware Compatibility List* (HCL), you are on your own for technical support.

The second factor to sort out is which file management system should be used. Windows NT, Windows 2000, and Windows XP can be configured to use either a typical FAT-based file system, or its own proprietary NTFS file system.

Installation Methods

Windows NT, Windows 2000, and Windows XP operating systems can be installed using the following two different methods:

➤ Install from the Windows distribution CD.

➤ Install across a network connection using a copy of the installation files obtained from a network server.

Installing from CD

In both cases, the installer must have access to the operating system's installation files. This primarily means the equivalent of the \I386 folder on the distribution CD. If the local unit has a bootable CD-ROM drive, you can simply insert the CD in the drive and boot directly to it. When the system starts, it autostarts the CD, and the installation can take place directly from the CD. If the system does not support a bootable CD, you need to start the system using a boot floppy, load the CD-ROM drivers, and run the setup utility from the CD. This requires running the *Winnt.exe* or *Winnt32.exe* files from the Windows CD's \I386 folder.

Installing from a Network Location

As mentioned earlier, in a network environment, it is possible to perform installs from a network server. This is particularly efficient when you need to perform multiple installations of the operating system around the network (such as when a new operating system version is rolled out across a business or office environment). In these settings, the operating system files are placed on a *distribution server* and executed from the *destination* (receiving) *computer*.

Simply boot the destination computer to a start disk that has the *MS-DOS Client for Microsoft Networks* utility on it, connect to the shared folder on the server that holds the setup files, and execute the Winnt.exe or Winnt32.exe file. Of course, the disk drive of the destination drive must be partitioned and formatted before engaging the installation routine.

A utility for generating the MS-DOS client is distributed with Windows NT, Windows 2000, and Windows XP operating systems. The client is also available as an FTP download from the following site:

ftp://ftp.microsoft.com/bussys/clients/msclient/

To perform the download, an FTP utility is required.

Unattended Installations and Disk Images

In a large corporate network, it could literally take weeks to perform a network operating system upgrade for all the systems on the network. For these environments, network operating system manufacturers have provided options for automating the installation process using the network and one or more *distribution servers*. Two automation methods are offered for Windows NT 4.0, Windows 2000, and Windows XP networks:

➤ Unattended automated installations using answer files

➤ Disk cloning using disk images

Using Answer Files

In an unattended installation using *answer files*, administrators run scripted answer files that have been created to provide automatic answers to all the questions normally asked by the setup/install routine. An administrator can run multiple installations across the network at one time.

If there are circumstances that require different answers for different computers on the network, a *Uniqueness Database File* (*UDF*) must also be created to supply the unique settings required for those computers.

The Windows 2000 and Windows XP *Setup Manager Wizards* can be used to create answer files for unattended Windows installations and for Sysprep disk image cloning. This wizard can also be used to create answer files for Windows *Remote Installation Services* (*RIS*) servers to conduct RIS image-based installations across the network. It can only be used to deploy Windows 2000 Professional and Windows XP Professional operating systems.

This book deals primarily with attended, local installations of the Windows 2000 and Windows XP operating systems. Automated installations are normally the responsibility of the network administrator. However, even newer technicians might be asked to create images for different types of computers and roll them out on an as-needed basis.

Disk Cloning

The second high-volume automated installation method employs clone copies of a given installation and simply re-creates that exact installation on multiple computers across the network. *Disk cloning* requires that a disk image be created of a *reference computer*. This computer must be an exact copy of the hardware and software that you want to clone.

Remote Installation Services Images

You must establish a RIS server on the network and then boot up systems as RIS clients that can download the image from the server. The images can be *CD-based* images or *Remote Installation Preparation* (*RIPrep*) images created with the Windows Remote Installation Preparation Wizard.

The general procedure for creating RIPrep images is as follows:

1. Install and configure RIS on a Windows server using the Windows Components option found using the Add/Remove Programs icon in Control Panel.

2. Execute the command Risetup.exe from the Run option of the Start menu on the RIS server. The RIS Wizard installs the RIS software, creates an initial CD-based image of the system, creates RIS answer files in the form of setup information (.SIF) files, and configures the Client Installation menu required for remote installation operations.

3. Authorize the RIS server. This is performed through the server's Administrative Tools and requires that the DHCP administrative utility be configured to *authorize* the server.

4. Create a reference computer as a template for the clone image. Configure this system with "most common denominator" user and system settings. Also, install and configure any application programs that will be part of the disk image.

5. Copy the Administrator profile into the Default User profile to ensure that everyone will be able to use the settings applied in the previous step.

6. From the command prompt, run RIPrep to prepare the system for duplication and create a disk clone image. This creates an exact snapshot of the reference system that can be stored on the RIS server and can be copied to as many different computers as desired.

7. On the RIS client end, you must boot the system to an RIS boot disk containing the PXE protocol and network adapter card. The RIS boot disk is created using the Remote Boot Floppy Generator (`Rbfg.exe`) utility under the `\Remoteinstall\Admin` folder of the RIS server. The network adapter card automatically requests an IP address from the network's DHCP server and attempts to locate the RIS server in the network.

8. When the client machine locates the RIS server and connects to it, it automatically downloads the image—provided the administrator has signified that the computer should receive that image.

Creating Disk Images

The *Sysprep* tool is used to prepare the reference computer for cloning. Third-party cloning software is required to actually create and distribute the *disk image* file that is used to clone the installation process on the remote computers.

The basic steps for creating a disk image include

1. Install the Windows 2000 or Windows XP operating system on the reference computer and log on as Administrator.

2. Install and configure any application packages that are to be part of the disk image.

3. Configure a default set of User settings and Windows components that can be applied to everyone who will use the computers being cloned (for example, Start menu, Desktop, and so on).

4. Under the System icon (found in Control Panel), copy the Administrator profile to the Default User profile to ensure that everyone who logs on to one of the clone computers will receive the proper settings.

5. Copy the `Sysprep.exe`, `Setupcl.exe`, and `Sysprpe.inf` files into the Sysprep directory of the reference computer (or on a floppy disk).

6. From the command prompt, run the Sysprep utility to prepare the system for cloning.

7. Run a disk-cloning utility (such as Norton Ghost from Symantec or Casper XP from Future Systems Solutions) to create an exact snapshot of the system. This snapshot can be stored on a distribution server and then can be copied to as many different computers as desired.

   Because the snapshot contains an exact picture of the reference system, including its Registry and configuration files, the copies must be installed on systems that either have the same or very similar hardware configurations. It is particularly important that the hardware abstraction layers (HALs) and disk controller types match. Differences in plug-and-play devices are automatically detected and corrected during the first startup.

8. When the clone system is started for the first time, the system requests information about several user and computer-specific settings, such as licensing, user and company names, computer name and administrator password, product key, regional options, and time zone settings.

The general steps for using a third-party, disk-cloning program to make disk images is as follows:

1. Install the disk-cloning software on a computer system.

2. As part of the installation process, the disk-imaging software provides for making a boot floppy that can be used to run the software on the reference and target computers.

3. Prepare a reference computer with the exact installation that you want to clone.

4. Boot the reference computer using the disk-imaging boot disk.

5. Follow the instructions presented by the imaging software to create the bit-by-bit clone image of the system. This is typically a menu selection to create an image for the system. You must inform the cloning software where to store the image after it is completed (for example, on a CD-ROM or remote network drive).

6. Allow the image to be copied to the destination (CD or network drive). This might take a few minutes.

7. Boot the target computer using the boot disk and create a new partition on the drive.

8. Tell the disk-cloning client where to get the image and tell it where to write the image on the target. This is normally a menu function as well.

9. Configure the target computer after the cloning process has concluded.

Installing Windows 2000 Professional

The minimum hardware requirements for installing Windows 2000 Professional on a PC-compatible system are

➤ **Microprocessor**—133MHz Pentium (P5 equivalent or better)

➤ **RAM**—64MB (4GB maximum)

➤ **HDD space**—650MB or more free on a 2GB drive

➤ **Monitor**—A standard VGA monitor is a minimum

For installation from a CD-ROM, a 12x drive is required. If the CD-ROM drive is not bootable, a high-density, 3.5-inch floppy drive is also required.

Before installing Windows 2000 Professional from the distribution CD, it is recommended that you run the file *checkupgradeonly*. This file is located on the installation CD under **\I386\winnt32** and checks the system for possible hardware compatibility problems. The program generates a text file report named **upgrade.txt** that can be found under the **\Windows** folder. It contains Windows 2000 compatibility information about the system, along with a list of potential complications.

For systems with hardware devices not on the Windows 2000 HCL, you should contact the manufacturer of the device for new, updated Windows 2000 drivers for their device. Many peripheral makers post their latest drivers and product compatibility information on their Internet websites, where customers can download them. You can also try the device with Windows NT or Windows 9x drivers to see if they will work. The final option is to obtain a device that is listed on the Windows 2000 HCL.

Conducting a new Windows 2000 Professional installation requires a Windows 2000 Professional *distribution disc*. If the system cannot boot to a CD-ROM drive, you also need Windows 2000 Professional setup disks.

First, determine whether the installation is a *clean install* or an *upgrade*. If a new installation is being performed, the setup program installs the Windows 2000 files in the \WINNT folder.

For a CD-ROM install, boot the system to the existing operating system, and then insert the Windows 2000 Professional distribution CD into the CD-ROM drive. If the system detects the CD in the drive, click the Install Windows 2000 option. If not, start the setup program through the Run dialog box.

To install Windows 2000 from a Windows 9x or Windows NT 4.0 system, click the Start button, and then click Run from the menu. At the prompt, enter the location of the Windows 2000 start file (Winnt.exe or Winnt32.exe) on the distribution CD (for example, d:\I386\Winnt32.exe).

In the case of 16-bit operating systems, such as MS-DOS or Windows 3.x, the Winnt.exe option should be used. Winnt32.exe is used with 32-bit operating systems.

To install Windows 2000 Professional across a network, first establish a shared connection between the local unit and the system containing the Windows 2000 Professional setup files. This requires a Windows 2000 Professional-compatible network interface card (NIC). At the command prompt, enter the path to the remote Winnt32.exe file (or Winnt.exe file).

Attended Windows 2000 Professional Installations

The attended Windows 2000 setup process covers three distinct phases:

➤ A text-mode phase

➤ A GUI phase (controlled by the Setup Wizard)

➤ A network phase, in which the Windows network components are installed

The basic procedure for performing an attended installation of Windows 2000 includes

1. Place the Windows 2000 Professional distribution CD in the drive and start the system. If the system does not boot to the CD, restart the system and check the CMOS setup utility to verify that the CD-ROM drive is selected first in the boot sequence.

2. Unless you need to install a third-party SCSI or RAID driver, the system should automatically advance to the Welcome to Setup screen. Press the Enter key to advance to the End User Licensing Agreement.

3. When you accept the agreement, the setup procedure moves into the Setup Partitioning screen. Select the appropriate option for the current system (that is, Set Up Windows 2000, Create a Partition in Unpartitioned Space, or Delete the Selected Partition).

4. When the partitioning process is completed, select the desired partition where Windows 2000 should be installed. Normally, you should use the default setting of \WINNT under the root directory in the highlighted partition.

5. Select the file system to be used on the partition (FAT or NTFS). FAT partitions larger than 2GB are automatically formatted as FAT32. If the partition is already FAT or FAT32, you are asked whether you want to convert it to NTFS.

6. Next, you are asked whether you want to perform a thorough exam of the partition. Click Yes to conduct the examination or press Esc to bypass it.

7. At this point, the system restarts, after which the setup routine loads the files required for the graphically based portion of the installation process, and the Setup Wizard appears.

8. The first operation performed by the Setup Wizard is the hardware detection process. This process is designed to determine which devices are installed in the system.

9. Next, the GUI portion of the install presents the Regional Settings window, where you can configure locale and keyboard settings. Click Next to select the default values.

10. After this, the Personalize Your Software window appears so that you can identify yourself and your organization. This name creates the initial user account.

11. Next, you are asked to input the product key from the CD case in which the distribution disc ships. This is the complete default licensing activity for Windows 2000 Professional, which enables up to 10 simultaneous inbound connections to be established.

12. The Computer Name and Administrator Password window appears. The computer name entered here defines the computer for the network and can be up to 63 characters in length. The password for the administrator's account can be up to 14 characters in length.

13. The final step in the GUI portion of the install is the Date and Time Settings window. Establish the local time and date for the system.

14. If the system has detected a network connection, the Network Settings window appears. If you select the Typical option from this window, setup automatically configures Client for Microsoft Networks, File and Print Sharing for Microsoft Networks, and TCP/IP. You can choose the Custom option if you need to manually configure IP settings or install additional services.

15. If the Custom option is selected, you are presented with the Network Components window, where additional networking components can be selected and configured.

16. Finally, you are asked to join a workgroup or computer domain. You must also enter the name of the workgroup or domain to be joined.

Installing Windows XP Professional

The installation process for Windows XP is considerably different from previous Windows installation processes in that Windows XP requires you to *activate* your copy of the operating system within 30 days after installing it. This process is electronic and is meant to ensure that the copy of XP being used is legitimate and that it is only being used on one computer. If you attempt to install it on a second computer and activate it, an error message is generated notifying you that the registration is already active.

If you have not had to register new software with Microsoft yet, simply follow the instructions Windows XP provides and you will be able to quickly and efficiently register the software. This is especially efficient if the machine on which you are installing XP happens to be connected to the Internet.

If you are adding XP across a corporate environment, be certain that you have enough licenses to cover all machines. The last thing you want is to have a software audit on your corporation's computers and not have enough licenses to cover all of your machines. Stay in close contact with Microsoft's licensing department if you have questions.

If you exceed the 30-day window of the *Windows Product Activation* (*WPA*) period without activating the operating system, it simply locks you out of the system. Even if you log on as an Administrator, you are presented with the following message instead of a normal desktop display:

"This copy of Windows must be activated with Microsoft before you can log on. Do you want to activate Windows now? (Yes/No)"

If you select the Yes option, the system immediately enters the activation process. If the system successfully completes this process, the operating system resumes normal operation. However, if you answer No, or your machine cannot complete the activation process, the system does not let you continue. You are completely locked out of the operating system and cannot do anything until you successfully complete the activation process.

For technicians, activation does not normally become a problem until an extensive system upgrade is performed (such as changing three major components) or a hard drive must be replaced. When these events occur, it is necessary to deal with Microsoft's licensing department to reactive the license.

Windows XP Installation Requirements

The minimum hardware requirements for installing Windows XP Professional on a PC-compatible system are

➤ **Microprocessor**—Pentium II 233MHz or higher or compatible processor required/Pentium II 300MHz or compatible processor recommended. Dual-processor configurations are also supported with Windows XP.

➤ **RAM**—64MB required/128MB recommended. The more memory installed, the better. Maximum supported RAM is 4GB.

➤ **HDD space**—2GB with 650MB of free space required/2GB of free hard disk space recommended. A 1.5-GB partition size is required, with 2GB recommended. Additional disk space is required for installing over a network. The maximum hard disk space supported for a partition is 2TB.

➤ **Display device**—A VGA-compatible or higher display adapter with a monitor capable of 800 × 600 resolution required/SVGA-compatible display adapter recommended.

➤ **Input devices**—Keyboard and mouse (or other pointing device) required.

➤ **CD-ROM**—A 12x or faster CD-ROM drive recommended (this item is required to perform the setup operation from the CD-ROM). If the CD-ROM drive is not bootable, a high-density, 3.5-inch floppy drive is also required.

Other installation hardware requirements associated with network installations include a high-density, 3.5-inch drive for performing the setup operation across the network using a network client or boot disk along with an appropriate network adapter card.

As with the Windows NT and Windows 2000 systems, all hardware devices included in a Windows XP Professional system must be listed on the *Windows XP HCL*. These devices have been tested and are supported by Microsoft. As with Windows NT and 2000, copies of the Windows XP HCL can be obtained at two locations:

➤ On the Windows XP Professional distribution CD in a file named Hcl.txt in the \Support folder.

➤ On the Microsoft website at http://www.microsoft.com/hcl. The HCL version on the Microsoft website typically represents the most up-to-date listing.

Windows XP Preinstallation Steps

Before installing Windows XP Professional from the CD, run the Windows XP version of the checkupgradeonly utility. This file is located on the installation CD under \I386\Winnt32. It checks the system for possible hardware compatibility conflicts and generates a text file report named upgrade.txt that contains Windows XP compatibility information, along with potential complications for the system. The report can be accessed in the \Windows folder.

If the system has hardware devices not on the Windows XP HCL, Microsoft has not tested or approved those devices and does not support them. Contact the device manufacturer to determine whether any new or updated Windows XP drivers are available for their device. Most peripheral makers post their latest drivers and product compatibility information on their corporate Internet websites.

Note that most peripheral makers post their latest drivers and product compatibility information on their corporate Internet websites.

Attended Windows XP Installations

Like Windows 2000, the attended Windows XP setup process consists of a text-mode phase, a graphical Setup Wizard phase, and a network phase, in which the Windows network components are installed.

The basic procedure for performing an attended installation of Windows XP includes

1. Place the Windows XP distribution CD in the drive and start the system. If the system does not boot to the CD, restart the system and

check the CMOS setup utility to verify that the CD-ROM drive is selected first in the boot sequence.

2. If the system detects the CD in the drive, simply click the Install Windows XP option. If not, start setup through the Run command. (In Windows 9x and Windows NT 4.0, click Start and then Run. In Windows 3.x and NT 3.51, click File and then Run.)

3. At the prompt, enter the location on the Windows 2000 start file (`Winnt.exe` or `Winnt32.exe`) on the distribution CD; for example, `d:\I386\Winnt32.exe`. (In Windows 3.x, the `Winnt.exe` option should be used.)

4. Choose whether the installation is a New Install or an Upgrade. Unless you need to install a third-party SCSI or RAID driver, the system should automatically advance to the Welcome to Setup screen. Press the Enter key to advance to the End User Licensing Agreement.

5. When you accept the agreement, the setup procedure moves into the Setup Partitioning window. Select the appropriate option for the current system (that is, Set Up Windows XP, Create a Partition in Unpartitioned Space, or Delete the Selected Partition).

6. When the partitioning process is completed, select the desired partition where Windows XP should be installed. Normally, you should use the default setting of the root directory in the highlighted partition.

7. Select the file system to be used on the partition (FAT or NTFS). If either of the Quick Formatting options are selected, the system skips over performing a thorough examination of the disk and proceeds directly to installing the file system.

8. At this point, the setup routine loads the files required for the graphically based portion of the installation process, and the Setup Wizard appears.

9. The first stopping point in the GUI process is the Regional and Language Options window. Click Next to select the default values.

10. The next window enables you to personalize your software by inputting your personal and organization names.

11. Next, you are asked to input the product key from the CD case in which the distribution disc ships. This is the complete default licensing activity, which enables up to 10 simultaneous inbound connections to be established.

12. The Computer Name and Administrator Password window appears. The computer name entered here defines the computer for the network and can be up to 63 characters in length. The password for the administrator's account can be up to 14 characters in length.

13. The final step in the GUI portion of the install is the Date and Time Settings window. Establish the local time and date for the system.

14. If setup has detected a network adapter in the system, the Network Settings window appears. If you select the Typical option from this window, setup automatically configures Client for Microsoft Networks, File and Print Sharing for Microsoft Networks, and TCP/IP. You can choose the Custom option if you need to manually configure IP settings or install additional services.

15. If the Custom option is selected, you are presented with the Network Components window, where additional networking components can be selected and configured.

16. Next, you are asked to join a workgroup or computer domain. You must also enter the name of the workgroup or domain to be joined.

17. Finally, the Setup Wizard installs and configures the options selected through the setup process. This might take up to an hour to finalize, depending on the installed hardware.

Patches and Service Packs

In the Windows environment, you must address three parts of the operating system when installing a new version or upgrade:

➤ Operating system release version

➤ Operating system patches and service packs

➤ Third-party device drivers

The *operating system release* is the version of the installation media produced and distributed as a complete unit. However, due to the nature of product development and the pressures on software producers to bring new products to the market, new releases never seem to be complete or perfect. Therefore, the manufacturers continue to develop and upgrade their operating systems after they have been released.

Rather than providing customers with new versions of the operating system when new features are added or major problems are corrected, software manufacturers provide *OEM patches* for their products. Microsoft typically releases patches in the form of updates, or in collections that include additional functionality or new device drivers, referred to as *service packs*. Patches and service packs are not typically required to run an operating system release. The fact that it exists as a release means that it is a complete operating system.

When you install a fresh copy of an operating system that has been on the market for some time, or when you upgrade an existing operating system to a new version, you must install the new components in a definite order:

1. Install the operating system release.

2. Install the original equipment manufacturer (OEM) patches or the latest service pack.

3. Install the best device driver choices.

When the new version or the upgrade is installed, it should automatically install its own drivers for the devices it detects. In most cases, these drivers are the best choice for the installed devices because they have been tested to work with the operating system and should provide the least amount of problems. OEM drivers might not be written as well and tested as thoroughly as those supplied with the operating system.

If the device is not listed in the operating system's HCL, the device manufacturer's driver offers the only choice for operating the device. The other condition that calls for using the equipment manufacturer's driver occurs when the device does not operate correctly with the Windows-supplied drivers. New drivers delivered in service packs might offer a better choice than using the original operating system drivers. However, if they do not produce the operation desired, the OEM drivers must be reinstalled.

Service Packs

As mentioned in the previous section, *service packs* are collections of updates that repair problems with an existing operating system installation. You can use several methods to obtain service packs:

➤ **Download for a standalone computer**—Use the Windows Update feature to obtain a service pack for a single computer.

➤ **Download for multiple computer deployments**—Download the service pack from Windows Update in the form of a self-extracting executable file. These files can be very large and require sufficient bandwidth and storage space in the system. Run the executable file from the computer that needs an update.

➤ **Order a service pack**—You can obtain a CD-based version of a service pack from Microsoft. Unlike the downloaded versions, there is a small fee for the CD-based version.

➤ **Through Microsoft subscription services**—There are several subscription services, such as TechNet, that automatically include new service packs with new issues of the subscription service.

After you have obtained the service pack, you need to install it in the system or systems. To update an existing operating system installation locally or across a network, launch the executable file through the Windows Update utility.

You can also apply the service pack to the installation files on a distribution server. This requires that the executable file be run with a -s switch. Integrating the service pack with the installation files removes the need to apply the service pack through a second operation.

 If you must install new operating system components after installing the service pack, you need to have both the operating system and service pack files available for the install process.

The service pack install automatically creates an Uninstall utility by default. The uninstall folder consumes a majority of the space used by the service pack. You can save this disk space by using a -n switch when you perform the update. However, you cannot use the Uninstall feature to remove the service pack later (for example, when you discover that it has not reacted well with your system).

This brings up an important consideration when downloading and installing service packs and updates. You should always back up your system before installing these items. There is always a chance that the new files will not play well with your existing system (in some cases, it might make the system unusable).

Windows Update

Windows has built-in services for obtaining service packs, device drivers, and other updates. The Windows Update utility is a web-based utility that connects to the Microsoft website and analyzes the current condition and configuration of your operating system. Based on the analysis, the service recommends services and patches that apply to your system and its operating system. You can scroll through the offering and select the options that you want to add to your system.

You can access the Windows Update feature in multiple ways:

➤ Through Internet Explorer

➤ Through any web browser using http://microsoft.com/windowsupdate

➤ Through the Windows XP Help and Support Center

➤ Through the Start menu

➤ Through Device Manager

The Windows Update feature can also be configured to run automatically. Under this setting, users are notified automatically when new updates become available. This feature enables technicians to keep their systems fully patched with the latest fixes and security upgrades.

Operating System Upgrading

As mentioned earlier, it is not uncommon for a computer to have its operating system upgraded several times during its life span. The following sections of this chapter cover upgrading from Windows 9x environments to the Windows Me, Windows 2000, or Windows XP operating systems.

Upgrading to Windows 2000

Systems can be upgraded directly to Windows 2000 Professional from Windows 9x operating systems, as well as from Windows NT 3.51 and 4.0 workstations. This includes older NTFS, FAT16, and FAT32 installations. When you install Windows 2000, it can recognize all three of these file system types. If the computer is running an older Microsoft operating system, that OS version must be upgraded to one of these versions before it can be upgraded to Windows 2000. Otherwise, a clean install must be performed from a full version of the operating system. Table 2.1 lists the acceptable Windows 2000 upgrade routes.

Table 2.1   Windows 2000 Upgrade Routes

CURRENT OPERATING SYSTEM	UPGRADE PATH
Windows 95 and Windows 98	Windows 2000 Professional only
Windows NT 3.51 and 4.0 Workstation	Windows 2000 Professional only
Windows NT 3.51 and 4.0 Server	Any Windows 2000 product
Windows NT 3.1 and 3.5	Must be upgraded to NT 3.51 or 4.0 first and then to Windows 2000
Windows 3.x	Must be upgraded to Windows 95 or 98 first then to Windows 2000 Professional

The easiest upgrade path to Windows 2000 is from the Windows NT 4.0 operating system. Upgrading from Windows 9x is potentially more difficult.

As with previous Windows NT products, Windows 2000 does not attempt to remain compatible with older hardware and software. Therefore, some applications might not be compatible with Windows 2000 and might run poorly, or fail completely after an upgrade.

Upgrading to Windows 2000 is suggested for users who have an existing Windows operating system that is compatible with Windows 2000 and who want to maintain the existing data and preference settings.

Upgrading a System to Windows 2000 from a Previous Operation System Using a CD

The following steps help you upgrade a system to Windows 2000 using a CD. It is assumed that you have a currently installed OS that will accept a direct upgrade to Windows 2000.

1. To upgrade a system to Windows 2000 from a previous operating system using a CD-ROM install, boot the system to the existing operating system and then insert the Windows 2000 Professional distribution CD in the CD-ROM drive.

2. If the system detects the CD in the drive, simply click the Install Windows 2000 option. If not, start the setup operation through the Run command. (In Windows 9x and NT 4.0, click Start, and then click Run from the menu. In Windows 3.x and NT 3.51, click File, and then click Run.)

3. At the prompt, enter the location of the Windows 2000 start file (`Winnt.exe` or `Winnt32.exe`) on the distribution CD; for example, `d:\I386\Winnt32.exe`. (In the case of Windows 3.x, the `Winnt.exe` option should be used.)

4. On the initial window of the Setup Wizard, specify whether the installation is a clean install or an upgrade.

5. Follow the instructions the Setup Wizard places on the screen, entering any information required.

Upgrading a System to Windows 2000 from a Previous Operation System Using a Network Location

The following steps help you upgrade a system to Windows 2000 using a network location. As with the preceding CD install, it is assumed that you have a currently installed OS that will accept a direct upgrade to Windows 2000.

To upgrade Windows 2000 Professional from a previous operating system across a network, it is necessary to establish a shared connection between the local unit and the system containing the Windows 2000 Professional setup files.

1. Boot the local unit to the existing operating system and establish a connection with the remote unit.

2. At the command prompt, enter the path to the remote Winnt32.exe file (use the Winnt.exe file if an older 16-bit operating system is being used on the local unit). The Winnt command is used with 16-bit operating systems, such as DOS or Windows 3.x. The Winnt32 version is used with 32-bit operating systems, including Windows 95, 98, NT 3.5, and NT 4.0.

3. Choose the Upgrade Your Computer to Windows 2000 option.

4. Follow the instructions the Setup Wizard places on the screen, entering any information required.

Upgrading to Windows XP

Systems can be upgraded directly to Windows XP Professional from Windows 98, Windows Me, Windows NT 4.0 (with Service Pack 5 or higher) workstations, and Windows 2000 Professional. This includes older NTFS, FAT16, FAT32, and NTFS systems. As was the case with Windows 2000, the Windows XP operating system can recognize all three file system types when it is installed. Upgrading is preferable in many situations because it provides for the preservation of existing users and groups, user settings, data, and installed applications.

However, systems running Windows 95 or Windows NT Workstation 3.51 operating systems cannot upgrade directly to XP. Instead, they must have intermediate upgrades to bring them up to a Windows version that does support direct upgrading to Windows XP.

 Although older Windows operating systems can be upgraded using interim upgrades, the computer hardware on which they are running probably does not satisfy the minimum hardware requirements for Windows XP Professional.

Using the Checkupgradeonly or Check System Compatibility Option for Hardware Compatibility Issues with Windows XP

You should generate a system compatibility report prior to running the upgrade process. This permits potential problems to be detected and analyzed and allows solutions to be implemented. The report can be generated by running the WINNT32 /checkupgradeonly command from the \I386 folder on the Windows XP distribution CD, or by selecting the *Check System Compatibility* option on the Setup menu. Either actions launch the setup program for the sole purpose of generating the compatibility report (saved as the Upgrade.txt file)—the computer is not modified in any way by using either of these options.

Some portions of upgrading from Windows 98 to Windows XP Professional can be difficult. Although most operating system and user configuration settings upgrade easily, other items, such as applications and device drivers, might create problems. The majority of these issues show up when the compatibility report is generated.

If hardware or software incompatibilities are detected, the proper updates should be obtained and applied before proceeding with the upgrade. Uninstall any incompatible software detected until new compatible replacements can be loaded. Also, check the system BIOS version to verify that it is the latest revision available.

NOTE

As with Windows 2000 upgrades, remember to verify that BIOS-based virus protection is disabled before performing the Windows XP upgrade. This BIOS feature causes the setup process to fail because it interprets the setup routine's attempts to modify the boot sector as a virus activity.

Back up any important files and data before performing an upgrade to avoid losing them. Also scan for viruses and remove them from the system before conducting an upgrade. Finally, decompress any drive compressed with anything other than NTFS compression before performing the upgrade. Third-party compression formats are not supported.

Performing Local Upgrades

To initiate a local upgrade from a bootable CD-ROM drive, insert the Windows XP Professional distribution CD in the drive, and select the *Install Windows XP* option from the Setup menu, as illustrated in Figure 2.4. If the menu is not displayed automatically, run the setup utility from the Windows XP CD.

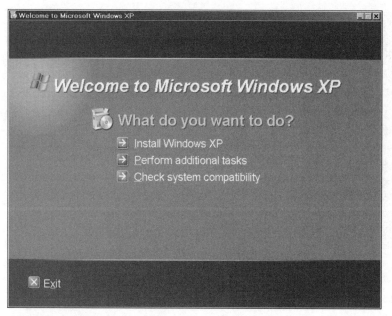

Figure 2.4   Windows XP Setup menu.

The opening Windows Setup Wizard window, depicted in Figure 2.5, asks for verification of whether an upgrade of the existing operating system is being conducted, or a new version of Windows XP is being installed. If the new installation option is specified, the existing operating system settings are overwritten along with any existing applications. The applications must be reinstalled to retain their use.

Two types of upgrades are available—*express* and *custom*. An express upgrade automatically upgrades the existing Windows installation and maintains all current settings. A custom upgrade enables you to change the following:

➤ Installation partition

➤ Installation folder

➤ Language options

➤ File system type (NTFS conversions allowed)

Upgrading to Windows XP requires a minimum of administrative intervention, and can be fully automated using answer files as previously discussed in this chapter. The information required to perform a standard upgrade is very similar to that involved with the standard setup process.

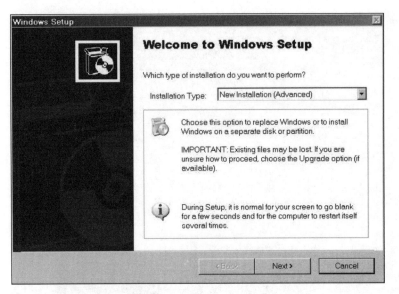

Figure 2.5 Windows Setup Wizard.

Administrators can use the Windows XP *User State Migration Tools* (*USMT*) to transfer user configuration settings and files from systems running Windows 9x and NT systems to a clean Windows XP installation. This preserves existing user information through the upgrade process. In this operation, user state information is backed up from the old operating system to a network server and then restored to the new Windows XP system. The following list describes the default settings transferred from the older system to the new Windows XP system by the USMT utility:

➤ The contents of all the My Documents, My Pictures, Desktop, and Favorites folders

➤ Most user interface settings, including display properties, fonts, mapped network drives, network printers, browser settings, folder options, taskbar options, and files and settings associated with the Microsoft Office applications

➤ Files with industry standard extensions, such as .DOC, .PPT, .TXT, and .XLS

Installing Dual-Booting Operating Systems

In a dual-boot system, a Startup menu is established that can be used to boot the system into different operating systems on the disk. Depending on which operating system option the user selects from the menu, the system retrieves the correct set of files and then uses them to boot the system.

Windows NT can be set up to dual boot with MS-DOS or Windows 9x operating systems. This option provides a method for the system to boot up into a Windows NT environment, or into an MS-DOS/Windows 9x environment. In such cases, a Startup menu appears on the display that asks which operating system should be used. Establishing either of these dual-boot conditions with Windows NT requires that the MS-DOS or Windows 9x operating systems be installed first. Be certain to install the Windows 2000 or Windows XP version in a new folder so that it does not overwrite the original operating system.

Although it is possible for Windows 2000 or Windows XP to share a partition with Windows 9x or Windows NT 4.0, this produces some potentially undesirable situations. Normally, you should install Windows 2000 or Windows XP and the other operating system in separate partitions.

The major drawback of dual booting with Windows NT or Windows 2000 is that the other operating systems are not capable of using applications installed in the other operating system's partition. Therefore, software to be used by both operating systems must be installed in the system twice, once for each operating system partition. Even when you permit Windows 2000 or Windows XP to share the same partition with a Windows 9x or Windows NT operating system, you need to reinstall the system's applications so that their install routines can modify the Windows 2000 or Windows XP Registry.

The native file management formats of Windows NT, Windows 2000, Windows XP, and other operating systems are not compatible. If the disk is formatted with NTFS, the MS-DOS or Windows 9x operating systems are not able to read the files in the NTFS partition. These operating systems are not "NTFS aware."

Windows NT and Windows 2000 can both operate with the FAT file systems used by MS-DOS and Windows 3.x/9x. Windows 2000 and Windows XP can be installed on FAT16, FAT32, or NTFS partitions. Windows 2000 and Windows XP also support the CD-ROM File System (CDFS) used with

CD-ROM drives in PCs. It is recommended that logical drives in a dual-boot system be formatted with the FAT system.

You should consider a few items when dual booting. Be aware that the system's *active partition* must be formatted with a file system that all the operating systems in the system can use. For example, Windows NT 4.0 does not support the FAT32 file system and cannot boot from a FAT32 partition. Likewise, Windows 98 does not support NTFS and cannot boot from an NTFS partition.

If you want to establish a dual-boot configuration with your current operating system, you must select the new installation option to preserve the existing operating system.

If drive C is formatted as NTFS, it is impossible to dual boot with any other operating system without employing a third-party boot manager utility. Therefore, Windows XP Professional should be the last operating system installed. The Windows XP boot manager is backward compatible with previous Microsoft operating systems; however, their boot managers are not compatible with Windows XP. For example, if you install Windows NT 4.0 as a second operating system in a dual-boot scenario after Windows XP Professional has been installed, the Windows NT 4.0 boot manager overwrites the Windows XP boot manager, making it unbootable.

You should ensure that each operating system is installed in a different folder. If possible, they should even be placed in different volumes (drive letters). For example, if you install Windows XP in a folder where another operating system exists, the XP files overwrite the previous operating system so that it does not boot. However, if you install Windows XP in a different folder on the same volume as an existing operating system, all the operating systems function.

Required Knowledge for Establishing a Dual-Boot System

The following list provides key information you need to have when you are establishing a dual-booting system:

1. Install the oldest operating system first. No matter which pair of operating systems you are bringing together, the oldest one should be installed first (9X/2000, 2000/XP, and so on).

2. Install the second operating system from bootup (not as an upgrade from a running operating system). The second install is also conducted as a clean install (start the install from the distribution media).

3. Install the second operating system in a different folder (a different partition is better). For example, allow the first operating system to install naturally, for example in the c:\Windows folder, and force the other operating system to install in the c:\WINNT folder.

4. When you install the second operating system, it detects that a dual-booting situation is being established and automatically upgrades the boot.ini file to reflect this.

5. After the second install has been completed, restart the system and choose an operating system to boot into from the Advanced Options menu.

Troubleshooting Operating Systems Install Failures

One of the three major categories of operating system problems is setup problems (those that occur during installation or upgrading). This category of problems typically involves failure to complete an OS installation or upgrade operation. In some cases, this can leave the system stranded between an older OS version and a newer OS version, making the system unusable.

The other two categories of general operating system problems are startup problems and operational problems. These categories happen at different places in the operation of the system and produce distinct types of errors.

Setup problems are errors that occur during the installation of the operating system on the hard disk drive. One of the most common OS setup problems occurs when the system's hard drive does not have enough free space to carry out the installation process. When this occurs, you must remove files from the disk until you have cleared enough room to perform the installation.

Setup problems also occur when the system's hardware does not support the operating system that is being installed. These errors can include the following:

➤ Microprocessor requirements

➤ Memory speed mismatches

➤ Insufficient memory

➤ Incompatible device drivers

The memory speed mismatch or mixed RAM-type problem might produce a Windows Protection error message during the installation process. This error indicates that the operating system is having timing problems that originate from the RAM memory used in the system. Correcting this problem involves swapping the system's RAM for devices that meet the system's timing requirements.

It is not uncommon for mouse or video drivers to fail during the installation of an operating system. If the video driver fails, you must normally turn off the system and attempt to reinstall the operating system from scratch. Conversely, if the mouse driver fails during the install, it is possible to continue the process using the keyboard. This problem is normally self-correcting after the system reboots.

A similar problem occurs when the operating system is looking for a PS/2 mouse and the system is using a serial mouse. It does not detect the serial mouse, and you have to complete the installation process using the keyboard. Afterward, you can check the CMOS Port Settings for the serial port to which the mouse is connected and install the correct driver for the serial mouse, if necessary.

The best way to avoid hardware-compatibility problems is to consult the Microsoft website to ensure that the hardware you are using is compatible with the operating system version you are installing.

Windows 9x Setup Problems

Windows 9x draws from the existing FAT structure when it is being installed. Therefore, an interruption or a crash during the installation process might leave the system with no workable operating system in place. If this occurs, you must boot the system from a bootable floppy disk and reinstall Windows 9x from that point.

If the system crashes during the hardware detection phase of a Windows 9x install, Microsoft recommends that you simply reboot the system until the installation process is successful. The Windows Setup Wizard marks startup steps that have failed and bypasses them the next time you attempt to install the operating system. The failed steps are recorded in the *Setuplog* text file.

The Windows 9x installation files are stored on the installation disk in a compressed Cabinet (CAB) file format. Therefore, they cannot just be copied over to the hard drive to repair files damaged in an aborted installation. The best recovery method for this situation is described in the following list:

1. Boot the system to a floppy disk.

2. Run FDISK to repartition the drive.

3. Format the drive.

4. Run the Windows 9x setup utility (provided your data was backed up beforehand).

If programs or hardware options fail to run properly after a system has been upgraded to a Windows 9x operating system, you should determine whether they require specific real-mode drivers to be retained in the CONFIG.SYS and AUTOEXEC.BAT files. Recall that during the restart phase of the installation process, Windows 9x deactivates entries that it perceives as incompatible or unnecessary by placing a remark (REM) statement at the beginning of the line. This might cause different applications or hardware to fail if they require these specific entries for operation. Be aware that restoring a driver can cause other problems within Windows 9x. The best choice is always to contact the software or hardware manufacturer for a Windows 9x driver.

Windows NT, Windows 2000, and Windows XP Setup Problems

When an attempt to install Windows NT, Windows 2000, or Windows XP fails, a *Stop error* normally results. Stop errors occur when Windows NT or Windows 2000 detects a condition from which it cannot recover. The system stops responding, and a screen of information with a blue or black background displays. Stop errors are also known as *Blue Screen errors* or as the *Blue Screen of Death (BSOD)*.

Other problems can typically occur during the Windows 2000 installation process. These problems include items such as the following:

➤ Noncompliant hardware failures

➤ Insufficient resources

➤ File system type choices

➤ WINNT32.EXE Will Not Run from the Command Prompt errors

Ways to correct these particular installation-related problems include the following:

➤ **Verify hardware compatibility**—The hardware-compatibility requirements of Windows NT, Windows 2000, and Windows XP are more stringent than those of the Windows 9x and Windows Me platforms. When either of these operating systems encounters hardware that is not compatible during the setup phase, it fails.

Be certain to check the appropriate HCL to ensure that your hardware is compatible with Windows 2000 or Windows XP. If the hardware is not listed, contact the hardware vendor to determine whether they support Windows 2000 before starting the installation. Check hardware manufacturers' websites for updated device drivers before installing the operating system.

➤ **Verify minimum system resource requirements**—Be certain that your hardware meets the minimum hardware requirements, including the memory, free disk space, and video requirements. When the Windows NT, Windows 2000, or Windows XP setup routine detects insufficient resources (that is, processor, memory, or disk space), it either informs you that an error has occurred and halts or just hangs up and refuses to continue the install.

➤ **Establish the file system type**—Determine the file system you are going to use. If you plan to dual boot to Windows 98 and have a drive that is larger than 2GB, you must choose FAT32. Choosing NTFS for a dual-boot system renders the NTFS partition unavailable when you boot into Windows 98. FAT16 does not support drives larger than 2GB. You can upgrade from FAT16 to FAT32, or from FAT32 to NTFS; however, you can never revert to the older file system after you have converted it without potentially losing data. You should also be aware that Windows NT does not support FAT32 partitions. Therefore, Windows NT 4.0 or earlier cannot be used on a Windows 9x drive. Consider using the lowest common file system during installation and upgrade later.

➤ **Verify that the** WINNT32 **startup file is being used properly**—The WINNT32.EXE program is designed to run under a 32-bit operating system and does not run from the command line. It is used to initiate upgrades from Windows 9x or Windows NT to Windows 2000 or Windows XP. From a 16-bit operating system, such as MS-DOS or Windows 95a, you must run the WINNT.EXE program from the command line to initiate the installation of Windows 2000 or Windows XP.

In most cases, a failure during the Windows NT, Windows 2000, or Windows XP setup process produces an unusable system. When this occurs, you should usually reformat the disk and reinstall the system files from the Windows setup (boot) disks.

Windows XP Setup Problems

If a setup attempt fails during the installation process, you will probably be left with a system that has no workable operating system in place. If this occurs, try the following steps:

1. You must first determine whether there are any hardware/software application conflict problems that could keep the system from starting.

2. If not, start the system from some type of bootable media and attempt to determine what might be happening that would keep Windows XP from installing.

3. Finally, if nothing appears as a likely cause of the problem, attempt to reinstall the Windows XP operating system from scratch.

Issues with Hard Drives and Windows XP Installations

If the Windows Setup Wizard does not detect sufficient hard disk space on the drive, a Stop error is created. When this occurs, remove files and programs to free up the needed disk space. You can also create an additional partition to hold Windows XP, or delete the existing partition and create a larger partition.

You should also verify that the system's hard drive and CD-ROM drives are on the Windows XP HCL. If the drives are not acceptable to the system, it is difficult to conduct the install. You should receive errors during the text-based portion of the Windows XP setup routine. If the drives are not on the HCL, you can attempt to load OEM drivers for the devices from an OEM CD-ROM or floppy, by pressing the F6 key when prompted and accessing the drivers on the disk.

Installation Problems from BIOS-Based Antivirus Utilities

BIOS-based antivirus utilities can prevent operating systems from being installed or upgraded. When the setup utility attempts to make the hard disk Windows XP bootable, a BIOS-based virus scanner interprets this action as an attempt by a virus to infect the system. In these cases, the system produces an error message indicating that a virus is attempting to infect the boot sector. To prevent this from happening

1. Disable the virus protection through the CMOS setup utility.

2. Enable the virus protection again after the operating system has been installed.

Generally, most other failures during the installation process involve hardware detection problems or component installation errors. If the Windows XP installation process fails during the hardware detection phase of the process, check the system for devices that are not listed on the Windows XP HCL. Because of Windows NT/2000/XP's relative intolerance for unapproved devices, you should verify that all the system's hardware components are listed on the HCL. If any component is not on the list, remove it, restart the installation process, and see whether the process advances past the error.

Troubleshooting OS Upgrade Failures

You will encounter many of the same problems performing an operating system upgrade that you do when performing a clean install. To review, these problems are normally related to the following:

➤ Insufficient hard drive or partition sizes

➤ Memory speed mismatches

➤ Insufficient memory problems

➤ Incompatible device drivers

While performing upgrade operations, you can also encounter problems created by version incompatibilities. New versions of operating systems are typically produced in two styles: *full versions* and *upgrade versions*.

Normally, you cannot use a full version of the operating system to upgrade an existing operating system. Doing so produces an *Incompatible Version error message* telling you that you cannot use this version to upgrade. You must either obtain an upgrade version of the operating system, or partition the drive and perform a new installation (losing your existing data).

You must have the appropriate version of the upgrade for the existing operating system. (For example, Windows 98SE comes in two versions—one upgrades both Windows 95 and Windows 98, whereas the other version upgrades only Windows 98.)

To determine the current version of a Windows operating system running on a computer, right-click the My Computer icon, click Properties from the shortcut menu, and, if necessary, click the General tab of the System Properties window. Another way to obtain the version of Windows is to open Windows Explorer, click the Help menu, and then click About Windows.

Adding Applications

In Windows 9x and Windows Me systems, the Add/Remove Programs icon in Control Panel is used to install new programs automatically. The main page of the Add/Remove window is the Install/Uninstall tab, depicted in Figure 2.6, used to add and remove the desired software package. The upper half of the tab contains the Install button that you click to start the software installation process.

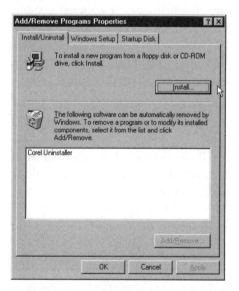

Figure 2.6 The Windows 9x Add/Remove Programs/Install/Uninstall tab.

Some Windows 9x applications might share support files (such as dynamic link libraries [DLLs]) with other applications. In these instances, the Uninstall utility produces a dialog box asking about deleting the shared files. The best response is to keep the file to avoid disabling the other application.

If the files are to be deleted, a backup should be made before running the Uninstall utility so that the files can be replaced if needed.

Most software manufacturers include a proprietary setup program for their Windows 9x and Windows Me applications. These programs normally run directly from the CD-ROM when they are inserted into the drive for the first time (unless the AutoPlay function is disabled).

For applications that don't feature the automatic installation function, or if the AutoPlay function is disabled, the software must be installed manually. This is accomplished through the Have Disk button. In Windows 2000 and Windows XP, the button name has been changed to CD or Floppy after you select the Add New Programs option. Clicking this button produces a dialog box asking for the name and location of the application's installation file. Most software suppliers provide a SETUP.EXE or INSTALL.EXE file to handle the actual installation and configuration process for their software.

Installing Additional Windows 9x and Windows Me Components

When Windows operating systems are installed, several optional components are not installed as part of the process. These optional components can be added to the system through the *Add/Remove Windows Components* utility. This utility permits different optional Windows components to be added to or removed from the system. Windows configuration settings can be changed through its dialog boxes.

In Windows 9x and Windows Me, this operation is performed through the Windows Setup tab, depicted in Figure 2.7, which is located under the Add/Remove Programs icon in Control Panel. The window in the center of the Setup tab provides a list of the standard Windows optional groups, along with their total sizes. You can double-click on the groups in this window to view a breakdown of the different components that make up the group. You can also select that only certain components of the group be selected for addition to the system, without installing the entire group.

One of the groups of options that you might typically leave out in Windows 9x and Windows Me is the *Accessibility options*. This group contains programs that modify the operations of the Windows keyboard, audio, and video for use by those who have physical conditions that inhibit their use of the computer. If you require visual warning messages for hearing disabilities or special color controls for visual difficulties, install this component and select the options to which you need access.

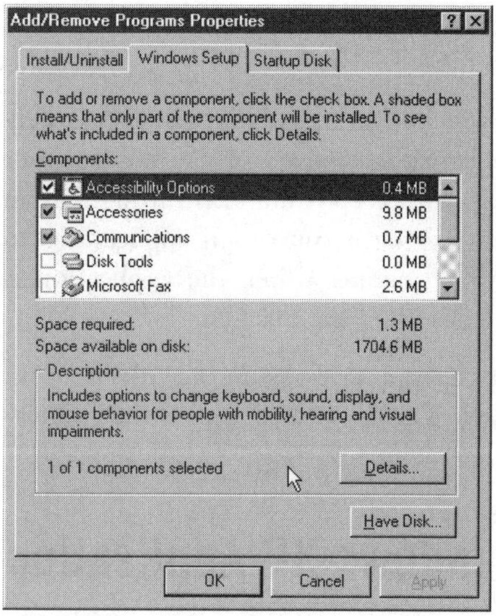

Figure 2.7 The Windows 9x Setup tab.

When the Accessibility options are installed, the icon appears in Control Panel, and when they're removed, it disappears. This option uses an additional 4.6MB of disk space in a Windows 98 system when it is installed.

Windows 2000 and Windows XP Applications

The Windows 2000 and Windows XP environments employ an Add/Remove Programs Wizard (actually *Add or Remove Programs* in Windows XP) to assist users in installing new applications. The Windows 2000 and Windows XP Add/Remove Programs icon is located in Control Panel.

Double-clicking the Add/Remove Programs icon produces the Add/Remove Programs dialog box. Any application that employs a SETUP.EXE or INSTALL.EXE installation routine can be installed through this window. Clicking the Install button causes the system to request the location of the installation program.

In addition to third-party applications, the Add/Remove Programs Wizard can be used to install or remove optional components of the Windows 2000 and Windows XP operating systems. Clicking the Windows 2000 or Windows XP Setup tab under the Properties dialog box produces a list of components that can be selected for inclusion or removal in Windows 2000 or Windows XP systems. To access this utility in Windows 2000, you select Control Panel, Add/Remove Programs, Add/Remove Windows Components.

In Windows XP systems, you select Control Panel, Add or Remove Programs, and Add/Remove Windows Components.

In Windows 2000 networks, application software can be installed remotely across the network. This way, the network administrator can control user application software across the network and keep it uniform throughout an enterprise. Likewise, the network administrator can assign applications to users so that they appear on their Start menus. When the application is selected for the first time, it is installed on the local machine.

The administrator can also place optional applications on the Add/Remove Programs dialog box in Control Panel. The user can install these applications from this location at any time.

Windows 2000 and Windows XP Application Installer

Windows 2000 and Windows XP both feature a versatile *Microsoft Installer (MSI)* applications installer called the *Windows Application Installer*. This program is designed to better handle DLL files in the Windows 2000 and Windows XP environments. In previous versions of Windows, applications copied similar versions of shared DLL files, and other support files, into the \Windows folder. When a new application overwrites a particular DLL file that another application requires for proper operation, a problem is likely to occur with the original software package.

The Windows 2000 and Windows XP *Application Installer* enables applications to check the system before introducing new DLLs to the system. Software designers who want their products to carry the Windows 2000 or Windows XP logo must write code that does not place proprietary support files in the \Windows directory—including DLL files. Instead, the DLL files are located in the application's folder.

Windows Installer-compatible applications can repair themselves if they become corrupted. When the application is started, the operating system checks the properties of its key files. If a key file is missing, or appears to be damaged, it invokes the Installer and prompts the user to insert the application distribution CD. After the CD is inserted, the Installer automatically reinstalls the file in question.

Launching Windows Applications

In the command-line environment, starting or launching an application is a simple matter of typing the name of its executable file at the command prompt of the directory in which it was installed. In the Windows environment, however, starting an application is as simple as double-clicking its icon or selecting it from the Start, Programs menu.

Actually, several acceptable methods are available to launch an application in the Windows environment. They include the following:

➤ From the Start menu, point to Programs, point to the folder where the desired application is located, and click the application name.

➤ From the Start menu, click Run, enter the full path and filename for the desired executable file, and then click the OK button.

➤ Double-click the application's filename in Windows Explorer or in My Computer.

➤ In My Computer or Windows Explorer, select the desired application file, and then click File on the menu bar. From the submenu, click the Open option. (You can also right-click, or alternate-click, on the application and choose Open.)

➤ Create a shortcut icon on the desktop for the application so that it can be started directly from the desktop by simply double-clicking its icon.

File Associations with Applications

In Windows, an application can be set up to run by association. The application is called into action any time an associated file (such as a document and its related word processor) is double-clicked. This is accomplished by defining the file's type in the Registry.

Because the Registry is a delicate place to operate, you can also associate an application program with a given file. In Windows NT, Windows 2000, and Windows XP, this is accomplished by defining the file's type in the *Open With* dialog box. The first time you attempt to open an application, the Open With dialog box appears.

1. Access the Open With dialog box by right-clicking the file's Properties/General tab and then selecting the Change option.

2. To associate a file with a particular application in Windows XP, access the file through My Computer or Windows Explorer and then right-click on it.

3. Then select the Open With (or Open) option from the menu. This produces the Open With dialog box, depicted in Figure 2.8. Select the application that you want to use to open the file.

Figure 2.8 The Windows XP Open With dialog box.

Installing Printers

After the physical connections have been made between the printer and host computer, the printer must then be installed in the operating system. The Windows environment supplies the printing function for all its applications. Installing the printer in Windows is normally a very straightforward process. Most printers support PnP operations and automatically initiate the installation process when they are first attached to a Windows 2000 or Windows XP computer. If a printer is not PnP compliant, you must use the *Add Print Wizard* to install it.

Installing Printers in Windows 9x and Windows Me

Windows 9x and Windows Me automatically adopt any printers that have been established prior to installation. If no printers are installed, the setup program automatically runs the *Add Printer Wizard* to enable a printer to be installed. Each printer in the system has its own print window and icon from which to work. The wizard can be accessed at any time through the My Computer icon or Start menu. From the Start menu, point to Settings, and click Printers. Likewise, through the My Computer or the Control Panel window, double-click the Printers folder or icon.

To install a printer in Windows 9x and Windows Me, complete the following steps:

1. Open the Printers folder and double-click the Add Printers icon.

2. From this point, the Add Printer Wizard guides the installation process. You simply need to answer the questions posed to you.

Because Windows 9x and Windows Me have built-in networking support, the printer can be a local unit (connected to the computer) or a remote unit located somewhere on the network. If the physical printer is connected to a remote computer, referred to as a *print server*, the remote unit must supply the printer drivers and settings to control the printer. Likewise, the print server must be set up to share the printer with the other users on the network.

To install a network printer, complete the following steps:

1. Access the Network Neighborhood icon on the desktop.

2. Locate and select the icon for the remote computer's network, and then locate the icon for the remote unit's printer.

3. Right-click the printer icon and choose the Install option from the shortcut menu, as illustrated in Figure 2.9.

4. After the remote printer has been installed, the local computer can access it through the Network Neighborhood icon.

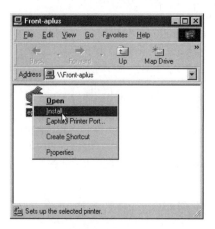

Figure 2.9   Installing a network printer in Windows 9x.

If the printer is not a model supported by the Windows 9x or Windows Me drivers list, OEM drivers can be installed from the device manufacturer's installation disk, which contains the OEMSETUP.INF file. After locating the appropriate .INF file, simply right-click the file and click Install from the context-sensitive menu.

Establishing Printers in Windows 2000 and Windows XP

Like Windows 9x, Windows 2000 and Windows XP automatically adopt any printers that have been established prior to their installation in the system. If no printers have been installed, the setup routine runs its *Add Printer Wizard* to enable a printer to be installed. The wizard can be accessed at any time through the My Computer icon or through the Start menu.

To install a printer from the Start menu in Windows 2000, navigate the Start, Settings, Printers path and open the Printers folder. In Windows XP, the Add Printer Wizard is accessed through the Start, Printers and Faxes, Add a Printer option.

Installing Local Printers on Windows 2000 and Windows XP Machines

To install local printers, complete the following steps:

1. Double-click the Add Printer icon (or in Windows XP, select the *Add a Printer* option from the *Printer Tasks* window). This produces the Add Printer Wizard to guide the installation process. Because Windows 2000 and Windows XP both have built-in networking support, the printer can be a local unit (connected to the computer), or a remote unit located somewhere on the network, as illustrated in Figure 2.10.

2. To install local printers, choose the Local Printer (Local Printer Attached to This Computer in XP) option. You should also have the Automatically Detect and Install My Plug and Play Printer option checked. This is the default setting that enables Windows to automatically discover and install the printer. When this option is checked, the system prompts you for driver information when you click the Next button.

3. If the Automatically Detect and Install My Plug and Play Printer option is not checked, or if Windows can't detect the printer, the procedure continues with a manual install process and the next window to appear is the Select the Printer Port window. Normally, the LPT1 options should be selected from the list of printer port options. Click Next to continue.

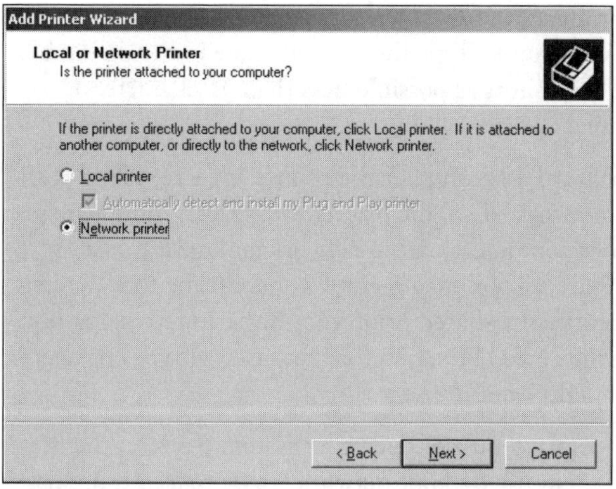

Figure 2.10 Selecting a local or network printer installation.

4. Next, the Add Printer Wizard produces a list of manufacturers and models from which to choose. In Windows XP, the window is titled Install Printer Software. A sample of this list is depicted in Figure 2.11. Simply select the correct manufacturer on the left, choose the desired printer model on the right, and then click the Next button.

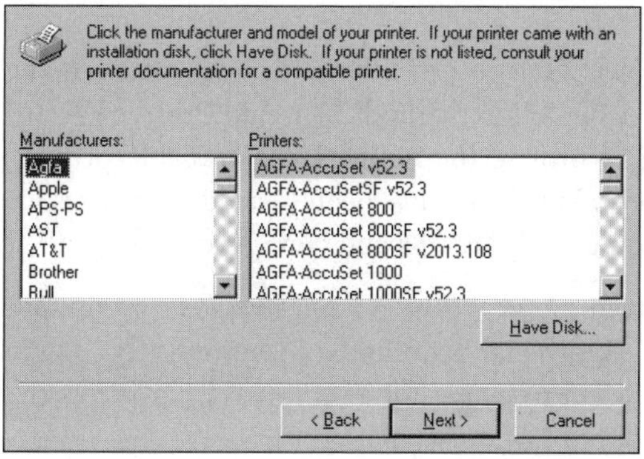

Figure 2.11 Selecting printer manufacturers and models.

If your printer does not appear in the list or you have a newer printer driver than those that shipped with Windows, you can click on the *Have Disk* button to specify where the printer driver can be located. Windows NT/2000/XP OEM drivers can be installed from a disk containing the OEMSETUP.INF file. In Windows XP, you can also select the Windows Update option to search for newer drivers.

5. Next, the wizard produces the *Name Your Printer* window asking you to supply a name for the printer. Type the desired name in the dialog box. This name should be as short as possible (less than 31 characters). Click Next to advance.

6. The Add Printer Wizard asks whether the printer is to be shared with other units on the network. If so, the printer must have a unique name to identify it to other computers on the network and must be set as *Shared*. Click the Share As option and enter a share name that the network will use to identify the shared printer in the activated dialog box. The shared printer must also be set up for the different types of operating systems that might want to use it.

7. Finally, the wizard displays a list of operating system types on the network. Select the types in use on your network (any, or all of those listed). Click the Finish button to complete the installation process.

Adding a Network Printer to Windows 2000 and Windows XP Computers

If you choose the *Network Printer* option from the Local or Network Printer window of the Add Printer Wizard, it provides you with options to install a network printer or a printer attached to a remote computer on the local machine.

In Windows 2000 and Windows XP, you can add network printers to the local computer using a PnP-like detection method. The Add Printer Wizard provides you with the option to browse the network for available printers (Find a Printer in the Directory). When one has been located, you can simply select it and Windows automatically installs and configures it for you.

As illustrated in Figure 2.12, from the Windows XP *Specify a Printer* window, you can also select to enter the Universal Naming Convention (UNC) path to a known remote printer, or select to search for a remote printer across the Internet using a Uniform Resource Locator (URL).

You can also manually configure a remote printer for operation with a local computer. To do this, select the *Create a New Port* option on the Select a Printer Port window. In most cases, you select the *Standard TCP/IP Port* option from the drop-down list and provide the printer name or an IP address for the printer so that a connection can be established with it.

Figure 2.12   Specifying a printer.

Printer Properties

Printer properties are all of the defining features about a selected printer and include information that ranges from which port it uses to what security features have been implemented with it. To examine or change the properties of a printer in Windows 2000 or Windows XP, perform the following steps:

1. Select the *Printers* option from the Start, Settings menu (or the Printers and Faxes option from the Start menu in Windows XP).

2. Inside the Printers (or Printers and Faxes) window, single click the desired printer to select it.

3. Click File from the menu bar, and then click Properties to display the printer's Properties dialog box, as depicted in Figure 2.13.

The *General* tab provides general information about the printer. This includes such information as its description, physical location, and installed driver name. The *Ports* tab lists the system's physical and logical local and network port settings, and the *Scheduling* tab displays the printer's availability, priority level, and spooling options. The *Sharing* tab shows the printer's share status and share name.

The *Advanced* tab can be used to configure the way documents are handled by the printer. These settings include options to define when a printer will be available, different priority queues for a single printer, and print spooling activities.

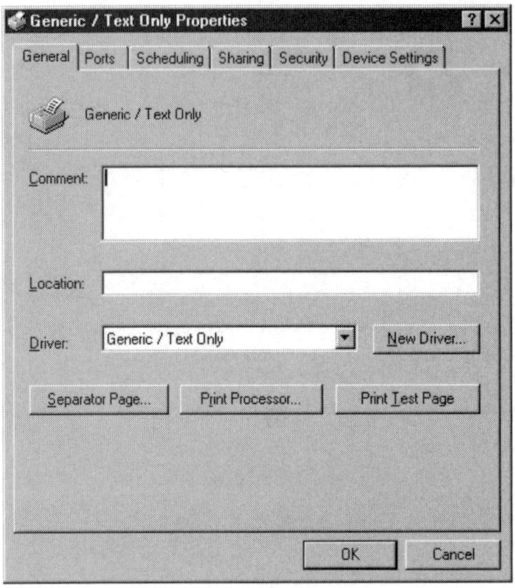

Figure 2.13 Printer Properties dialog box.

This last option is particularly important for troubleshooting printer problems because it enables you to bypass the Windows print spooler and print directly to the printer port. When a printer is not printing anything in a Windows system, even though print jobs are being sent to it, you should check the print spooler by selecting the option to Print Directly to the Printer. This bypasses any errors that might have occurred in the print spooling operation—such as failed print jobs. If the print job goes through, there is a problem in the spooler and it should be cleared.

The *Security* tab provides access to three major components—the Permissions button, the Auditing button, and the Ownership button. The Permissions button enables the system administrator to establish the level of access for different users in the system. The Auditing button provides user and event tracking capabilities for the administrator. Finally, the Ownership button displays the name of the printer's owner.

The *Device Settings* tab provides information about the printer, including such items as paper tray sizes and its font substitution tables. This feature is used to import downloadable font sets, install font cartridges, and increase the printer's virtual memory settings. The Device Settings tab, depicted in Figure 2.14, is one of the most important tabs in the Printer Properties dialog box.

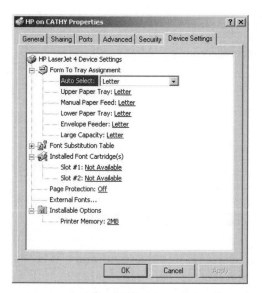

Figure 2.14 Windows 2000 Printer Properties, Device Settings tab.

Configuring LAN Connections

After the Windows operating system has been installed, it might be necessary to configure its LAN settings to make the computer a useful part of a networked environment. The process for doing this is slightly different for each Windows version.

Networking with Windows 9X

In Windows 9x and Windows Me, the peer-to-peer local area networking function is an integral part of the system. The heart of the Windows 9x and Windows Me networking system is contained in the desktop's Network Neighborhood applet and the Network applet in Control Panel.

Network Neighborhood

The *Network Neighborhood* window, depicted in Figure 2.15, is the primary network user interface for Windows 9x and Windows Me. It is used to browse and access shared resources on the LAN in a method similar to that used with Windows Explorer for a local hard drive. Most directory- and file-level activities, such as opening and saving files, can be performed through the Network Neighborhood (or My Network Places in Windows 2000 and Windows XP) window.

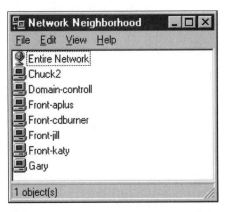

Figure 2.15 The Network Neighborhood window.

Microsoft networks group logically related computers together in work-groups for convenient browsing of resources. The local computer is part of a workgroup. Double-clicking the Network Neighborhood icon displays the printers and folders available in the workgroup. If the desired computer is not displayed, double-click the Entire Network icon. This action displays any other workgroups in the system along with any additional printers and folders that are available.

If the Network Neighborhood window is empty or its icon is missing, net-working connections have not been established. If this is the case, you must correctly configure networking on the local unit to connect to any other computers on the network. You accomplish this task through the Network applet in Control Panel.

The Network Applet in Windows 9X Control Panel

The Network applet in Control Panel, shown in Figure 2.16, provides con-figuration and properties information about the system's networks. The sys-tem's installed network components are listed on the Configuration tab.

Double-clicking an installed adapter's driver or clicking on the Properties button when the driver is highlighted produces its Configuration tab. The Add and Remove buttons on this dialog box are used to install and remove network drivers from the system.

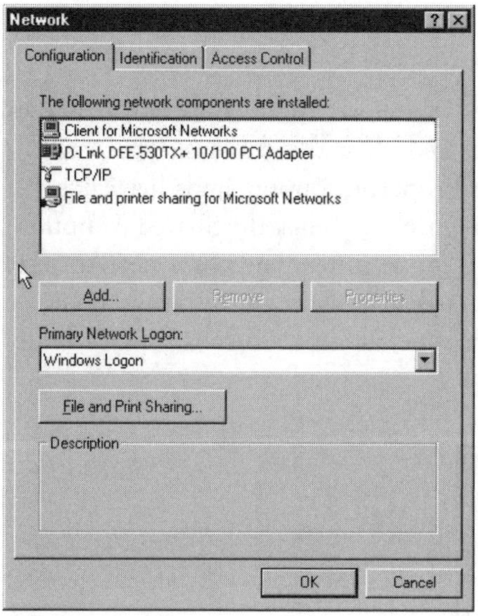

Figure 2.16   The Network dialog box.

The *Primary Network Logon* drop-down box is used to establish which type of network Windows 9x will enter when it starts up. This proves particularly helpful on systems that might be working in multiple network environments (such as a computer that might need to access Microsoft network resources in some situations and Novell network resources at other times).

The *File and Print Sharing* button is used to select the first level of resource sharing for the local unit. Sharing can be individually enabled or disabled for file and printer accesses from remote computers.

The *Identification tab* is used to establish a network identity for the local computer. This dialog box establishes the local computer's share name and workgroup association.

Similarly, the *Access Control tab* enables the local user to set the level of access control that is applied to remote accesses. The possible options include assigning a password requirement for each access or granting access to selected groups or users.

Windows 9x and Windows Me Resource Sharing

In Windows 9x and Windows Me peer-to-peer networks, resource sharing on the local computer is performed at the user level through the File and Print Sharing button on the Configuration tab of the Network applet. This option enables the user to grant other network users access to files, printers, or both. After sharing is enabled, the user can set sharing on several levels—the entire computer, complete disk drives, and folders.

To share a folder in Windows 9x and Windows Me, access the Windows Explorer or My Computer interface, and click the resource you want to share. From the File menu, click the Properties option, and then click the Sharing tab. On this tab, depicted in Figure 2.17, click the Shared As option, and then select the access type you want to implement. In a peer-to-peer environment, you are given the option to share, share in read-only mode, or share with password protection. There is no additional mechanism for limiting access by individual users.

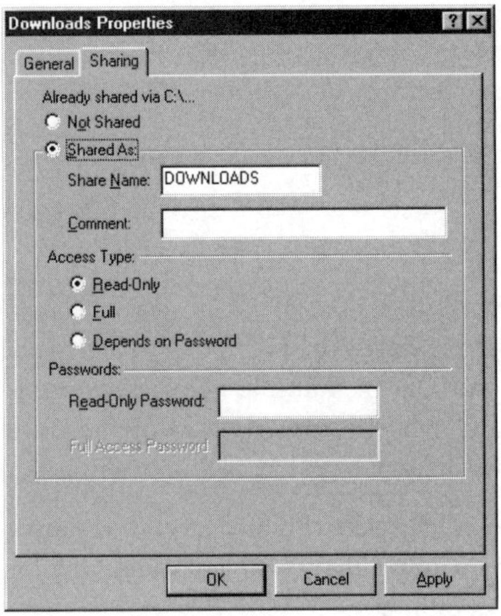

Figure 2.17   Sharing file and folder resources.

To *share a local printer* resource in the Windows 9x and Windows Me environment, click Start, point to Settings, and then click the Printers entry. From the Printers dialog box, select the printer you want to share, open the File menu, and then click Properties. From the printer's Properties dialog box, click the Sharing tab and then click the Shared As button.

Installing Windows 9x and Windows Me Network Components

The first step in establishing networking on a computer is to perform the physical installation. This typically involves installing a network adapter card and connecting the network cabling to it (although wireless connectivity is becoming quite widespread). The general procedure for installing adapter cards was presented in Chapter 1. After the network adapter card and cabling has been installed, the next step is to load and configure its drivers, protocols, and services for the connection. In most Windows 9x and Windows Me installations, most of these steps can be accomplished by simply rebooting the computer so that Windows can detect the network adapter.

The Windows networking utilities should produce an adapter driver, a *Microsoft Client protocol*, and a *Novell NetWare Client protocol* in the Network Configuration window in a typical installation. A default set of File and Print Sharing services is also loaded. The only items that must be installed manually are the protocols for the particular type of network being used. Clicking the Add button on the Network Configuration tab brings up the Select Network Component Type dialog box, depicted in Figure 2.18.

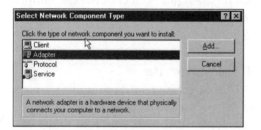

Figure 2.18 The Select Network Component Type dialog box.

The types of networking components include four categories:

➤ **Clients**—Software that enables the system to use files and printers shared on other computers

➤ **Adapters**—Drivers that control the physical hardware connected to the network

➤ **Protocols**—Rules that computers use to govern the exchange of information across the network

➤ **Services**—Utilities that enable resources and provide support services, such as automated backup, remote Registry, and network monitoring facilities

Selecting a component category and then clicking the Add button produces a listing of standard components included in the operating system. If a particular component is not supported in the standard listings, the Have Disk button enables the system to upload Windows-compatible drivers and protocols from a manufacturer's disk.

Configuring Clients in Windows 9x and Windows Me

Any network computer that uses the resources of another computer in the network is acting as its *client*. To use these resources, the local computer must have client software installed that enables it to work with the other computer. In some networks, this might mean working with computers that are using other types of operating systems. Windows 9x and Windows Me systems offer Microsoft and Novell clients that enable the computer to use resources that belong to these types of systems.

To add a new client to the computer, click the Add button on the Network Configuration tab, highlight the Client option in the Select Network Component Type dialog box, click the Add button, double-click the manufacturer in the Manufacturers list on the left, and then select the desired client from the Network Clients list on the right. Next click the OK button, and the new client appears in the Installed Network Components window of the Network page.

Configuring Adapters in Windows 9x and Windows Me

The Adapters portion of the TCP/IP configuration refers to loading drivers for the LAN and dial-up hardware devices used to connect to the communication media. As with the client components, adapters are added to the system and configured through the Select Network Component Type dialog box. From this dialog box, select the Adapters option, and click the Add button to produce the Select Network Adapters dialog box.

In this dialog box, you can select the manufacturer of the device and then select the specified adapter type. If the device does not appear in the listing, you can click the Have Disk button to load OEM drivers for the device from a manufacturer's disk.

Configuring Protocols in Windows 9x and Windows Me

Most installation procedures require only that the appropriate protocols be loaded for the network type. In Windows-based client/server LANs, TCP/IP is the leading choice of networking protocols. Therefore, the TCP/IP protocol must be activated and configured properly for the computer to function on the LAN.

You might need to add the NetBEUI, AppleTalk, and IPX/SPX (also known as *NWLink*) protocols, however, if the LAN contains computers with older Windows operating systems, Apple/Mac computers, or computers running Novell operating systems. You should also be aware that Microsoft offers separate TCP/IP protocols for local area and wide area networking. The additional TCP/IP protocol is used for dial-up Internet support.

The procedure for adding protocols is the same as that described for adding clients.

Configuring TCP/IP in Windows 9x and Windows Me LANs

In a simple local area network, only an IP address and a subnet mask setting are required. However, in larger networks, you might also be required to provide a default gateway (router) address, as well as an IP address for a DNS or WINS server.

To configure these TCP/IP values, select the TCP/IP protocol for the LAN from the listing in the Network applet and click the Properties button. This selection produces the IP Address tab of the TCP/IP Properties dialog box, as illustrated in Figure 2.19. You might also need to fill out several other tabs in this dialog box, as described in the following list:

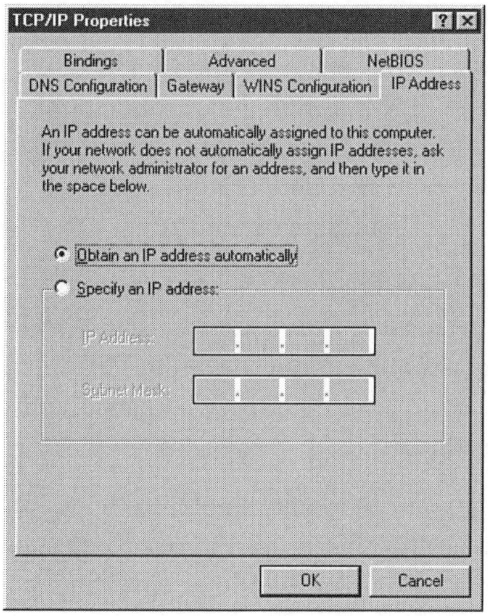

Figure 2.19 The TCP/IP Properties dialog box.

➤ **IP Address**—On this tab, you can configure the computer to obtain an IP address through an automatic service, such as DHCP, or you can manually configure a static address for the computer. Every computer on a network must have a unique IP address that identifies it.

Each computer must have a subnet mask entry to limit the mobility of the transmission to those nodes within the subnet (without subnets, every TCP/IP communication could range across every connected network link in the world; the traffic would be unbelievable). On a given subnet, every client on a subnet requires a unique IP address and every host also shares a common subnet mask and default gateway.

If the Obtain an IP Address Automatically option is selected, the computer attempts to locate a DHCP server when it boots onto the network. The DHCP server can provide it with all the TCP/IP configuration information it needs.

If no DHCP server is found, Windows computers default to a random IP address in the range of 169.254.XX.XX with a subnet mask of 255.255.0.0. This process is referred to as *Automatic Private IP Addressing (APIPA)*. This feature is useful in smaller, single-segment networks because it effectively autoconfigures such networks. APIPA is not available in Windows 95 or Windows NT 4.0.

To use the manual configuration option, you must know the IP address and subnet mask settings you want to use.

➤ **DNS Configuration**—This tab enables you to specify the IP addresses of Domain Name System servers that are responsible for reconciling DNS computer names to actual IP addresses. In a LAN, this is typically a specified server in the network. In a wide area network environment, such as the Internet, this is typically the IP address of the ISP.

Various *DNS suffixes* can be attached to enable the DNS system to attempt to resolve incomplete domain names. This listing attaches specified domain suffixes (such as mic-inc.net, mic-inc.com, and so on) to names it receives. These suffixes are attached to the received names and tried in the order they are entered in the list.

➤ **WINS Configuration**—On this tab, you can specify the IP addresses of a Windows Internet Naming Service server that is used to resolve the NetBIOS/NetBEUI names associated with older Windows operating systems to IP addresses.

➤ **Gateway**—On this tab, which is the default, you can specify the IP address of the router (or other gateway device) that separates your network segment from other segments. The computer uses this address to communicate with IP addresses outside the local segment.

Networking with Windows 2000 and Windows XP

During the Windows 2000 and Windows XP installation process, the network portion of the operating system must be configured to function as a workgroup node or as part of a domain.

If the system has been upgraded from an existing Windows NT version, Windows 2000 adopts the current computer account information. If the installation is new, the setup utility requests that a new computer account be established. This account is normally assigned by the network administrator prior to running the setup utility. Joining the domain during setup requires a username and password.

My Network Places

In Windows 2000 and Windows XP systems, the Network Neighborhood folder has become a more powerful *My Network Places* applet, shown in Figure 2.20. The new applet includes new *Recently Visited Places* and *Computers Near Me* views. The Add Network Place options enable the user to more easily establish connections to other servers on the network. The user can establish shortcuts to virtually every server on the network.

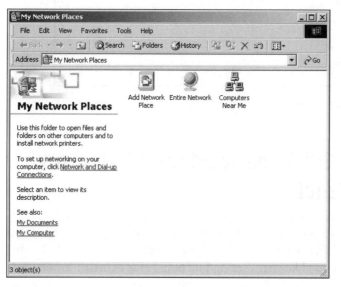

Figure 2.20 My Network Places.

In the Windows XP operating system, the My Network Places icon opens to a display of the My Network Places window, as depicted in Figure 2.21. As the figure illustrates, the Network Tasks pane offers options to add a network place, view network connections, set up a home or small office network, and view workgroup computers. This list of options varies with the type of network that has been established. For instance, in larger domain-based networks, the list would include an option to search Active Directory (if the system is being used in a Windows 2000 Active Directory-based network). The Local Network pane contains icons for each of the network connections the local computer has available.

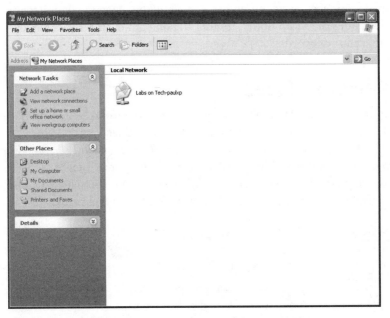

Figure 2.21   The Windows XP My Network Places window.

Windows 2000 and Windows XP Network Control Panel

The Network icon under the Windows 2000 Control Panel has been changed to the *Network and Dial-Up Connections* folder. It provides access to the Network and Dial-Up Connections applet, depicted in Figure 2.22. This applet provides several key networking functions, such as installing new network adapter cards and changing their settings, changing network component settings, and installing TCP/IP.

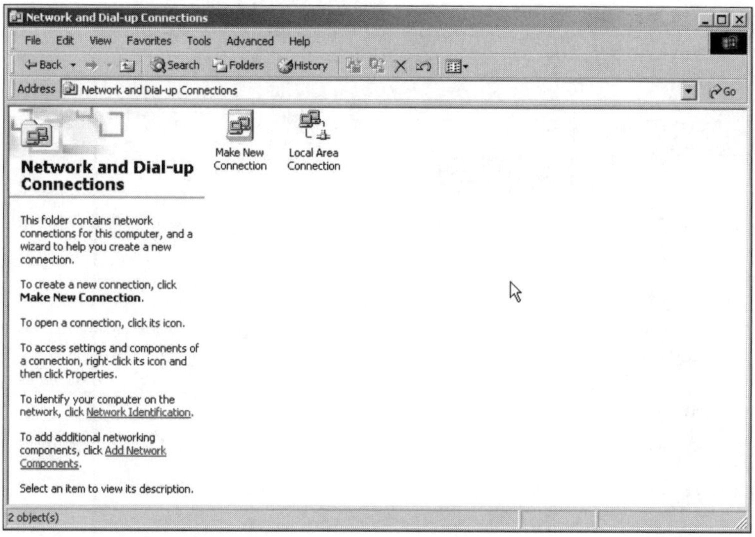

Figure 2.22   The Network and Dial-Up Connections window.

In Windows XP, the Network icon has been changed to the Network Connections icon. It does not offer the dial-up networking function included in the Windows 2000 applet, but it is used to configure and manage LAN and high-speed Internet access connections (such as DSL and cable modem connections). Clicking this icon produces the Network Connections window (featuring the LAN or High-Speed Internet pane), shown in Figure 2.23.

When you create a new connection, you can select from a variety of options, including Connect to the Internet and Connect to the Network at My Workplace. Both of these options have provisions for dial-up modem or broadband connections.

The Network Tasks pane of the Network Connections window provides options for creating, viewing, repairing, renaming, and reconfiguring the displayed connection as well as for disabling a network device.

Right-clicking on the connection produces a shortcut menu that contains the Properties option for the connection. Selecting this option in either operating system version produces the connection's Properties dialog box. The organization of the Windows 2000 Network and Dial-Up Connections and Windows XP Network Connections Properties dialog boxes differs somewhat from the Windows 9x Network applet in Control Panel. The Windows 2000 and XP versions consolidate the Services, Protocols, and Adapters function under a single tab, as illustrated in Figure 2.24.

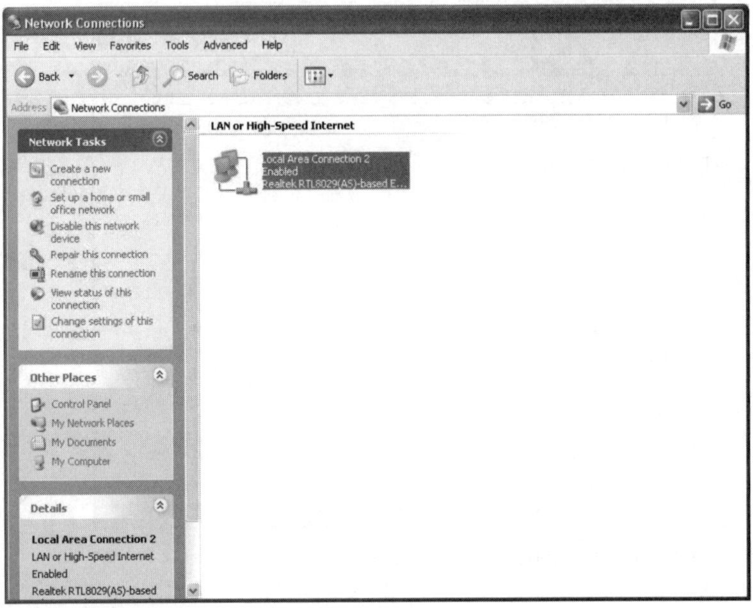

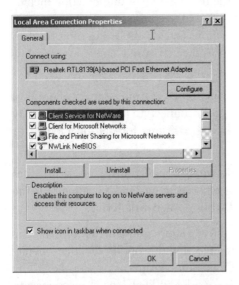

Figure 2.23 Windows XP Network Connections window.

Figure 2.24 Windows 2000/XP Local Area Connections Properties dialog box.

The functions associated with the Windows 2000 and Windows XP Local Area Connections Properties dialog box include

➤ **Services**—Used to add, remove, or configure network services, such as DNS, WINS, and DHCP functions.

➤ **Protocols**—Used to add, remove, or configure network protocols for specific types of network environments.

➤ **Adapters**—Used to add, remove, or configure NICs for operation with the system. This includes loading drivers and assigning system resources to the adapter. This option is not available in Windows XP.

To configure any of these functions for a given component, access the *Local Area Connection Properties* dialog box, highlight the desired component, and click the Install button.

Other functions affecting the Networking and Dial-Up Connections in Windows 2000 and Windows XP include the following:

➤ **Network identification**—Specifies the computer name and the workgroup or domain name to which it belongs. Under TCP/IP, computer names can be up to 63 characters but should be limited to 15 or fewer characters. They can use the numbers 0–9, letters *A–Z* (and *a–z*), as well as hyphens. Using other characters might prevent other nodes from finding your computer or the network. This option is located on the Network Identification tab under the System icon in Control Panel. In Windows XP, the network identification information is only available through the Computer Name tab of the System applet. Under Category view, you must navigate from Control Panel to the Performance and Maintenance option to access the System icon.

➤ **Bindings**—Sets a potential pathway between a given network service, network protocol, and given network adapter. The order of the bindings can affect the efficiency of the system's networking operations. To establish bindings, access the Network and Dial-Up Connections window, click Advanced on its menu bar, and then select the Advanced Settings option from the menu.

The Windows XP Local Area Connections Properties dialog box offers two tabs not available in the Windows 2000 version: *Advanced* and *Authentication*. The Advanced tab is used to enable the Windows XP Internet Connection Firewall (ICF). This feature is embedded in Windows XP so that it can act as an Internet firewall for itself or for a local area network attached to it.

The Authentication tab enables you to configure Authentication protocols for conducting local area and wide area communications across a network. Recall that *authentication* is the process of identifying individuals as who they claim to be. In the dialog box depicted in Figure 2.25, you can select standard protocols associated with particular network types, including Ethernet and 802.1x wireless protocols.

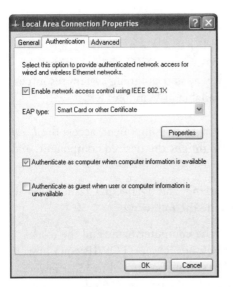

Figure 2.25 Windows XP Authentication tab.

Configuring Windows 2000 and Windows XP Network Shares

In Windows 2000 and Windows XP, the My Network Places applet enables the user to create shortcut icons to network shares on the desktop. A *network share* is an existing shared resource (such as a printer, drive, modem, or folder) located on a remote system. The new icon acts as an alias to link the system to the share point on the remote unit.

Only network shares (shared directories and resources) can be accessed across the network. The sharing function is implemented at the computer that hosts the folder or resource (resources are devices capable of holding or manipulating data).

In Windows 2000, you can institute sharing for resources, such as folders, disk drives, and printers, by right-clicking the device's icon and selecting the Sharing option from the shortcut menu. To establish sharing in Windows XP, right-click the folder or resource and select the Sharing and Security option. These selections produce the Sharing tab of the file's (or folder's) Properties dialog box, as illustrated in Figure 2.26. The presence of a hand symbol under the folder's (or device's) icon indicates that it has been shared.

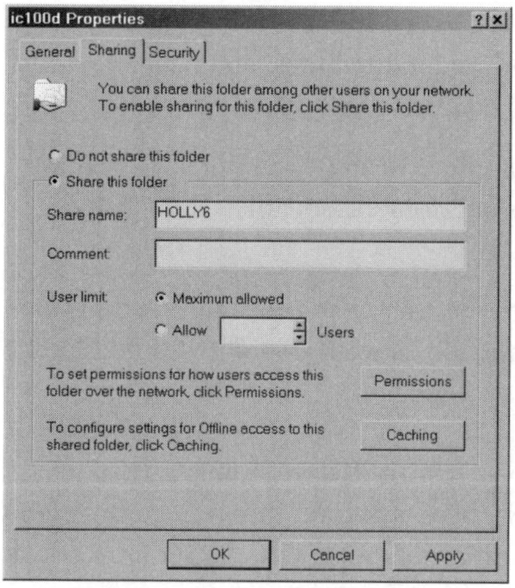

Figure 2.26 The file's or folder's Sharing tab.

To configure a shared folder's Properties, click the Share This Folder radio button and fill in the Share Name text box. Then click the Permissions button to open the folder's Permissions dialog box, where you see the Share Permissions tab, depicted in Figure 2.27.

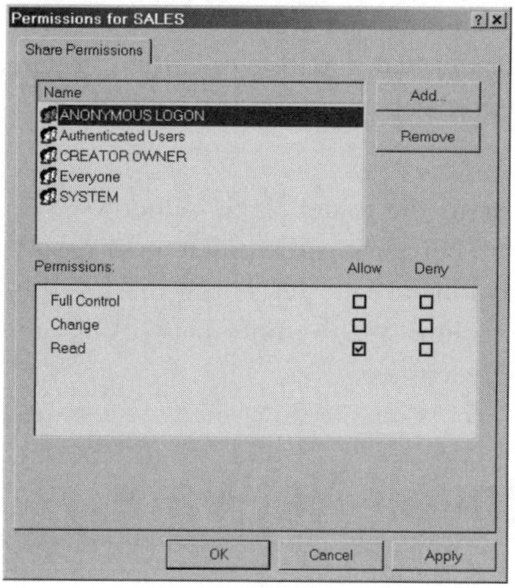

Figure 2.27 The Share Permissions tab.

Standard share permission options in Windows 2000 and Windows XP are as follows:

> ➤ **Read**—This setting enables the user to view file and folder names, run applications, read files, view file and folder attributes, and navigate through the directory tree at levels beneath this folder.

> ➤ **Change**—This setting provides complete Read permissions, as well as the ability to create and delete files and folders, edit files, and change file and folder attributes.

> ➤ **Full Control**—This option enables the user to perform all the functions available through the Change permission as well as modify permissions and take ownership of the folder.

Users might receive these permissions from different sources (that is, as members of different groups that have been assigned different permissions to the folder or resource). When this situation occurs, the different settings combine, and the users receive the highest Allow option setting. However, Deny option settings override any Allow setting.

For example, if a user has Full Control permissions for a certain folder from one group and only Read permissions from another group, the result is Full Control. However, if a Deny permission is assigned for Full Control from another group, all rights are denied for the user even though she has been granted rights from other sources.

To access the shared remote resource, the local operating system must first connect to it. After the connection is established, the local operating system creates a new logical drive on the system to accommodate the new folder in the system.

Share permissions can be assigned only to the folder level. Windows NT, Windows 2000, and Windows XP NTFS permissions are much more robust than share permissions. NTFS permissions can be set at the file level in NTFS systems. However, share permissions are the only network access control option available for non-NTFS partitions.

Networking with Novell NetWare

In a Novell NetWare system, the root directory of the workstation should contain the NETBIOS and IPX.COM files. The NETBIOS file, which is an emulation of IBM's *Network Basic Input/Output System* (*NetBIOS*), represents the basic interface between the operating system and LAN hardware. This function is implemented through ROM ICs, located on the network card. The *Internetwork Packet Exchange* (*IPX*) file passes commands across the network to the file server.

The NetBIOS and IPX protocols must be bound together to navigate the Novell network from a computer using a Windows operating system. You do so by enabling the NetBIOS bindings in the IPX protocol's Properties in the Network Properties window.

The *Open Datalink Interface (ODI)* file is the Novell network shell that communicates between the adapter and the system's applications. Older versions of NetWare used a shell program called NETx. These files should be referenced in the AUTOEXEC.BAT or NET.BAT files.

Installing NetWare Clients and Protocols

For Windows computers to be able to communicate with Novell servers on a network, they must have the client service for NetWare installed and configured. As indicated earlier in this chapter, clients are installed through the Select Network Component Type dialog box, which is located under the connection's Properties.

In Windows 9x and Windows Me systems, you should install the Novell Client for Windows 95 and Windows 98 that is supplied by Novell. This client can be loaded through the Network applet. On the Network tab, click the Add button, select the Client option from the list, click the Add button, and then select the Have Disk option. At this point, you must enter a path to the location on the disk where the Novell client installation files are located.

Similarly, in Windows 2000 and Windows XP systems, you must install the *Client Services for NetWare (CSNW)* option to enable the Windows client to communicate with NetWare servers. CSNW requires that the IPX/SPX protocol be installed on the client. It can be installed manually beforehand, or it is installed automatically when the CSNW client is installed.

There are actually two pieces to the IPX/SPX implementation in Windows: the *NWLink* NetBIOS and NWLink IPX/SPX/NetBIOS Compatible Transport Protocol options. Both are required for interaction with Novell systems. To configure the IPX/SPX protocol, select the NWLink IPX/SPX/NetBIOS Compatible Transport Protocol option from the list in the dialog box and click the Properties button.

In certain instances, you might need to enter an *internal network number* and a *frame type* setting on the General tab of the IPX/SPX Properties dialog box. The network number is used when certain NetWare-specific applications are installed. This number is generally obtained from the NetWare administrator.

The frame type setting is used in Ethernet networks to identify the type of Ethernet packets being used. The *Auto Frame Type Detection* option permits the IPX function to determine what type of frame is actually being used on the network. The default Auto Frame Type Detection setting is normally employed when a single frame format is being used on the network. IPX automatically assigns the frame type to be used. On the other hand, when multiple frame types are being used on the network, the Manual Frame Type Detection option should be used to ensure that the correct type is selected for the network.

Installing Other Network Protocols

Two other protocols are of interest that you can install in a Windows system: *AppleTalk* and *NetBEUI*. AppleTalk is required for Windows computers to communicate with Apple Macs running older Apple operating systems on the network (newer MACs should be using TCP/IP for networking), whereas NetBEUI is required when the network contains computers running older Windows operating systems.

Both of these protocols are available through the Select Network Component Type dialog box. As with the other protocols, you install them simply by clicking the Add button (the Install button in Windows 2000), selecting the Protocol option, clicking the Add button, selecting the desired protocol from the list, and then clicking the OK button.

Wide Area Networking with Windows 9x and Windows Me

The primary method for connecting to the Internet with Windows 9x is through a dial-up networking connection (using a modem). The dial-up communications system in Windows 9x and Windows Me offers many improvements over previous operating systems. Under Windows 9x and Windows Me, applications can cooperatively share the dial-up connections through its *Telephony Application Programming Interface (TAPI)*. This interface provides a universal set of drivers for modems and COM ports to control and arbitrate telephony operations for data, faxes, and voice.

The Windows 9x and Windows Me Internet Connection

To establish a dial-up Internet connection using the Windows 9x or Windows Me operating system, follow these steps:

1. Configure the Windows Dial-up Networking feature.

2. Establish the Windows modem configuration.

3. Set up the ISP dial-up connection information.

4. Establish the server address for the connection (if required by the ISP).

5. Set up Microsoft Internet Explorer (or another browser).

6. Connect to the Internet.

Configuring the Dial-Up Networking Feature

To set up the *Dial-Up Networking* feature to connect to the Internet, double-click the My Computer icon on the desktop, and click the Dial-Up Networking icon. You can also reach this icon through the Start button. Click the Start button, point to Programs, point to Accessories, and click the Dial-Up Networking entry.

If this option has never been set up before, a Welcome to Dial-Up Networking message appears. Click the Next button to advance into the first page of the Make New Connection Wizard, depicted in Figure 2.28. On this page, you should enter a descriptive name for the connection. This option is particularly helpful in quickly identifying different connections if you travel with your computer and have connections set up for different locations.

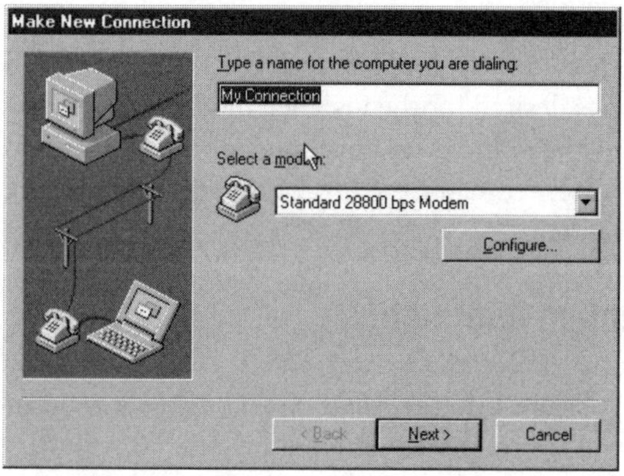

Figure 2.28   The Make New Connection window.

Establishing the Windows 9x and Windows Me Modem Configuration

To establish the Windows 9x and Windows Me modem configuration, click the Configure button and set the maximum speed value to its fastest available setting to enable compression and smoother connection. Next click the Connection tab to see the Modem Preferences information, as illustrated in Figure 2.29.

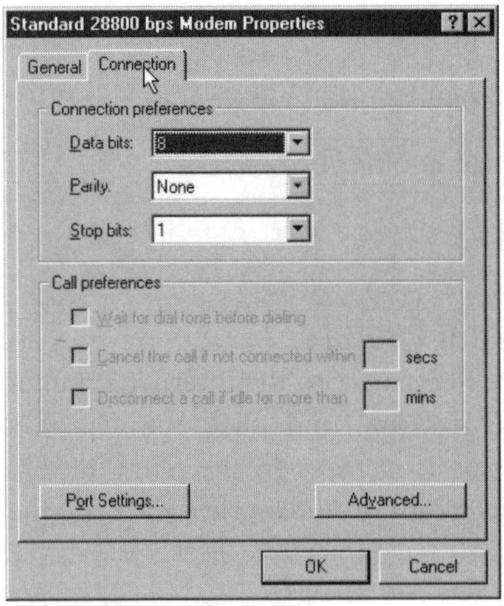

Figure 2.29 The Modem Properties/Connection tab.

Click the Port Settings button and set the Receive Buffer speed setting to 75%. Also, set the Transmit Buffer speed setting to 100%. You must set the Receive Buffer speed below the Transmit Buffer speed; otherwise, the modem tries to receive as fast as it sends and ends up filling the buffer, slowing the operation of the connection.

Click the OK button to return to the Connection tab. Click the Advanced button and add any extra settings desired for the installed modem. For example, an M0 setting should turn the volume on your modem off so that it is quiet when connecting to the Internet. Click the OK button to return to the Modem Properties, Connection tab.

Entering Dial-Up Connection Information

From the Dial-Up Networking applet in Control Panel, double-click the Make New Connection icon to move into the *Make New Connection* window where you can enter dial-up connection information. Click the Next button to advance to the phone number entry window, shown in Figure 2.30.

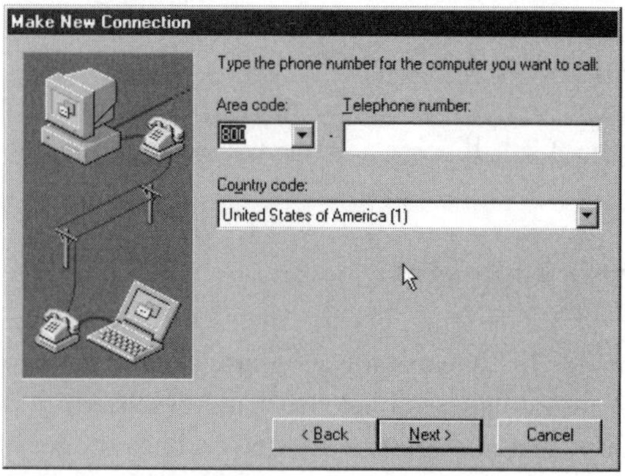

Figure 2.30   Entering the ISP's phone number in the Make New Connection Wizard.

Enter the dial-in phone number of your ISP, area code, and local number. If a dialing prefix is required, such as 9, set up this number as well. If you are using a long-distance number, Windows detects this fact during dialing and automatically enters the appropriate long-distance prefix (that is, a 1 in the United States). Click the Next button to record the information, and then click the Finish button. Then, an icon displays in the Dial-Up Networking window, similar to the one depicted in Figure 2.31.

Figure 2.31   The Dial-Up Networking window.

International Dial-Up

When using the dial-up networking functions outside the United States, several configuration settings must be changed. Most international telephone systems do not feature the same dial-tone/ring characteristics used in the United States. If your modem fails to detect a dial tone in a foreign country, you need to disable the modem's dial-tone detection feature.

To disable the modem's dial-tone detection feature, access the Connections tab under Control Panel, Modems, and then remove the check mark from the Wait for Dial Tone Before Dialing check box. You might also need to increase the cancel call waiting period if connections take a relatively long time from where you are calling. You can do this by increasing the number of seconds in the Cancel the Call If Not Connected setting on the Connections tab.

Establishing IP and Server Addresses

Most ISPs use dynamic IP address assignments for their customers. The DHCP service makes this possible by dynamically assigning IP addresses to the server's clients. This service is available in both the Windows 9x/Me and Windows NT/2000/XP product lines and must be located on both the server and client computers. In Windows 9x, the path to the TCP/IP Properties window is Start, Settings, Control Panel, Network, TCP/IP Properties. In Windows 2000, the path is Start, Settings, Network and Dial-Up Connections, desired connection, Properties, TCP/IP Properties.

The ISP also has one or more name server computers to route traffic onto and off of the Internet, and to reconcile IP addresses to domain names. The users dial in to these computers to establish and conduct their Internet communications. Each name server has a DNS number/name, just as every other Internet computer does. Like IP addresses, the domain server address can be static or dynamic. If the ISP has several servers, the ISP might allow traffic to be routed to the servers with the lightest workload instead of waiting for a particular server to become free.

With some ISPs, it might be necessary to manually enter server addresses and IP information that they supply. Some users require that their IP address not be changed. Therefore, they purchase an IP address from the ISP that is always assigned to them. Of course, this removes an assignable address from the ISP's bank of addresses, but the customer normally pays a great deal more for the constant address. In these situations, it might be necessary to enter the IP address information into the Internet connection's TCP/IP configuration.

Likewise, some ISPs might assign static server addresses that must be entered manually; others assign their server addresses dynamically and, therefore, do not require this information to be entered into the TCP/IP configuration.

In both cases, Windows 9x and Windows Me provide for the local unit to assign values to IP and server addresses, or for the server to assign those values after the connection has been made. In dial-up situations, the ISP typically determines which option is used.

In those situations in which the ISP requires a server and/or IP address to be supplied, simply navigate to the Dial-Up Networking window, right-click the Internet Connection icon, click Properties from the shortcut menu, and then click the Server Types tab, depicted in Figure 2.32.

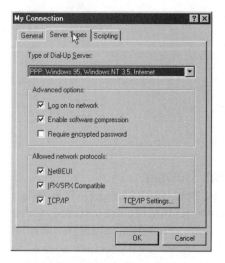

Figure 2.32   The Server Types tab in the My Connection dialog box.

From this tab in the My Connection dialog box, verify the dial-up server type—usually PPP for Windows 9x/Me and Windows NT/2000/XP—and click the TCP/IP Settings button. In the resulting dialog box, set the TCP/IP settings as directed by the ISP's instructions. If specific values are entered in this dialog box, the ISP connects the system to the Internet through a specific server address.

Click the Specify Name Server Addresses button and enter the primary DNS and secondary DNS addresses provided to you by the ISP. The screen should be similar to the one depicted in Figure 2.33.

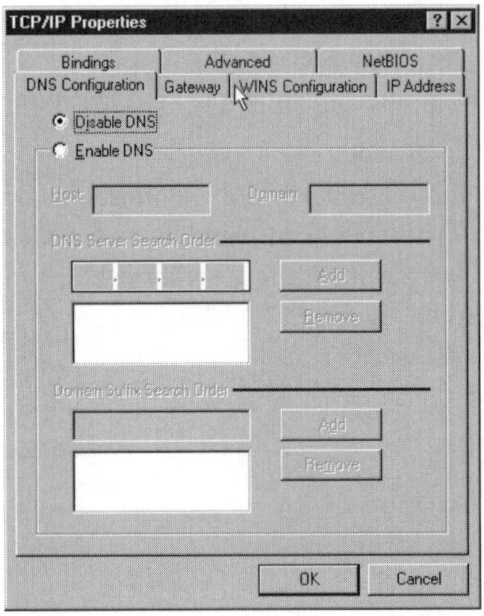

Figure 2.33 Configuring DNS in TCP/IP settings.

Configuring the Internet Explorer Browser

Windows 98, Windows Me, Windows 2000, and Windows XP include a default browser called *Internet Explorer*. Unless a different browser is installed, all of these Windows versions place the Internet Explorer icon on the desktop and automatically use this browser for Internet access. To browse the Internet using Internet Explorer, you must configure it for use. You can do so in three different ways:

➤ From the Internet Explorer Tools menu, click the Internet Options entry.

➤ Right-click the desktop Internet Explorer icon and click Properties.

➤ Click Start, Settings, Control Panel, and then click the Internet Explorer icon.

Selecting one of these options leads to an Internet Options or Internet Properties dialog box. From either dialog box, choose the Connections tab and click the Connect button to bring up the Windows Internet Connection Wizard and access the Get Connected window. Clicking the Next button provides three possible options for setting up the Internet connection and the browser:

➤ I want to choose an Internet service provider and set up an Internet account. (MSN is the default.)

➤ I want a new connection on this computer to my existing Internet account using my phone line or local area network (LAN).

➤ I already have an Internet connection set up on this computer and I do not want to change it.

Connecting to the Internet

To access the Internet in Windows, double-click the icon of the new connection. Enter the username and password supplied by your ISP. Click the Connect button. You should hear the modem dialing at this point. A Connecting To window should appear on the screen, displaying the status of the modem. When it comes up, the Connected To window should minimize to the taskbar. The system is now connected to the Internet.

Setting Up Internet Email

Windows systems that run Internet Explorer versions 4.0 and higher have a built-in email manager called Outlook Express that resides on the desktop taskbar. To set up an email account, open Outlook Express, click Tools on the menu bar, click Account, click the Add button, and then click Mail. On successive screens, you need to enter the following:

➤ Your display name (the name that will be displayed to those receiving emails from you)

➤ Internet Mail Server information (POP3 and SMTP server names) for incoming and outgoing mail (supplied by the service provider who furnishes your email services)

➤ The ISP-supplied Mail Account username and password

At the end of the setup process, you simply click the Finish button to complete the email setup.

Accessing Internet Explorer

After the hardware has been installed and the Internet connection has been arranged, click the desktop Internet Explorer icon to access the Internet. In the Connect To window, click the Connect button. You should hear the modem communications sounds again. The Internet Explorer main window should appear, as depicted in Figure 2.34.

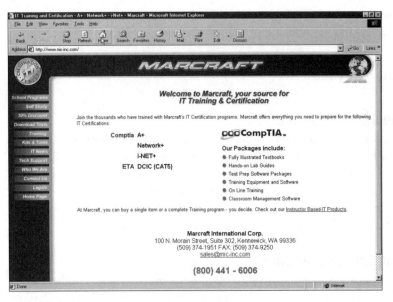

Figure 2.34 Internet Explorer main window.

Wide Area Networking with Windows NT, Windows 2000, and Windows XP

Windows NT Workstations include a TCP/IP network protocol and the Windows NT Workstation Dial-Up Networking component. The Dial-Up Networking component is used to establish a link with the ISP over the public telephone system. This link also can be established over an ISDN line. Windows NT versions from 4.0 forward feature the built-in Internet Explorer web browser and a personal web server.

The Windows 2000 and Windows XP Internet Infrastructure

Windows 2000 replaces the Network Settings utility from the Windows NT 4.0 Control Panel with a New Network and Dial-Up Connections folder, located in the My Computer applet. To create a dial-up connection in Windows 2000, click the Make New Connection icon in the My Computer Network Connections folder.

To create a new connection in Windows XP, you must select Start, My Network Places, View Network Connections, and then click the Create a New Connection option in the Network Tasks pane, as illustrated in Figure 2.35.

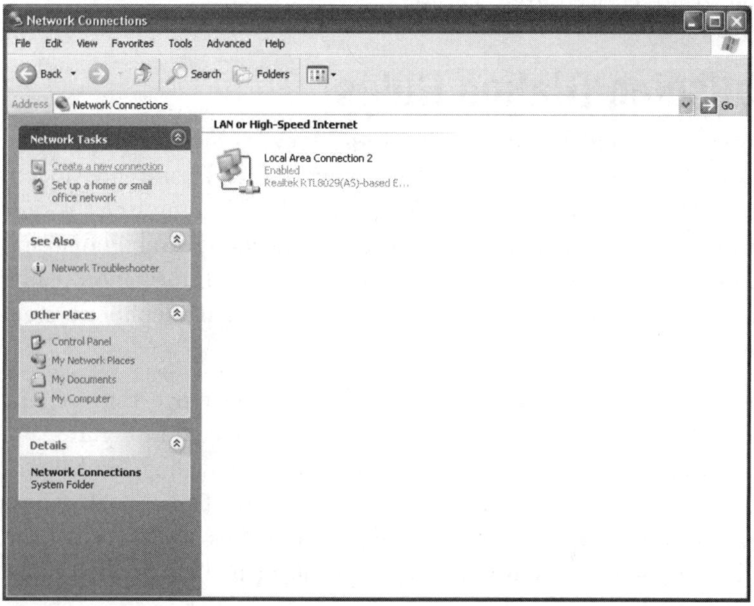

Figure 2.35 Creating a new network connection.

These actions open the Windows 2000 Network Connection Wizard (New Connection Wizard in Windows XP) that guides the connection process. The wizard requires information about the type of connection, modem type, and phone number to be dialed. The connection types offered by the wizard include private networks, virtual private networks, and other computers.

Establishing the Windows 2000 and Windows XP Dial-Up Configuration

Under Windows 2000 and Windows XP, the operating system should detect, or offer to detect, the modem through its plug-and-play facilities. It might also enable you to select the modem drivers manually from a list in Control Panel.

After the modem is detected, or selected, it appears in the Windows 2000 Modem list. You can examine or reconfigure the settings for the modem by selecting it from the list and clicking its Properties tab. In most cases, you should use the device's default configuration settings.

The *Connection Settings* tab from the Windows NT 4.0 Modem Properties dialog box has been replaced by the Advanced tab with space to enter the initialization string received from the ISP.

Establishing Dialing Rules

In Windows 2000 and Windows XP Classic View, you can configure the *Dialing Rules* by selecting Start, Settings, Control Panel, Phone and Modem Options. In Windows XP Category View, the path to Dialing Rules is simply Control Panel, Network and Internet Connections, and Phone and Modem Options. If the connection is new, a Location Information dialog box is displayed, enabling you to supply the area code and telephone system information.

To create a new location, click the New button and move through the General, Area Code Rules, and Calling Card tabs, depicted in Figure 2.36, to add information as required. The default rules for dialing local, long-distance, and international calls are established under the General tab. These rules are based on the country or region identified on this tab. Ways to reach an outside line (such as dialing 8 or 9 to get an outside line in a hotel or office building) are also established here.

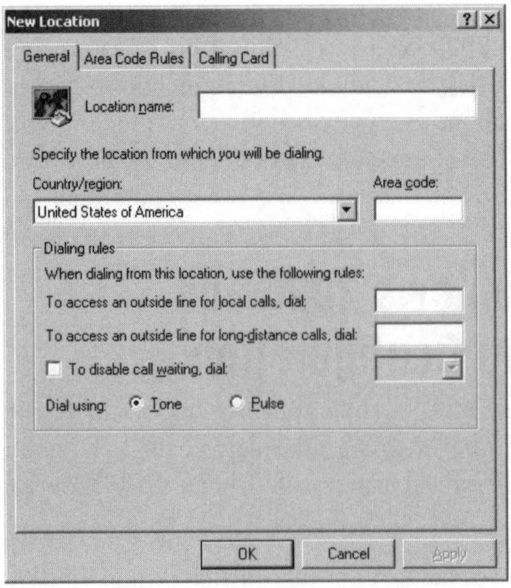

Figure 2.36 The Windows 2000 Phone and Modem Options/New Location dialog box.

Similarly, the information on the Area Code Rules tab modifies the default information located on the General tab. As its name implies, the information on the Calling Card tab pertains to numbers dialed using a specific calling card or long-distance company.

Establishing Dial-Up Internet Connections

The Windows 2000 *Internet Connection Wizard*, depicted in Figure 2.37, provides an efficient way to establish Internet connectivity. In Windows XP, an Internet connection is established through the New Connection Wizard. You can use the Internet Connection Wizard to set up the web browser, the Internet email account, and the newsgroup reader. To create an Internet connection to an existing account with an ISP, you need to know the following:

➤ The username and password

➤ The ISP's dial-in access number

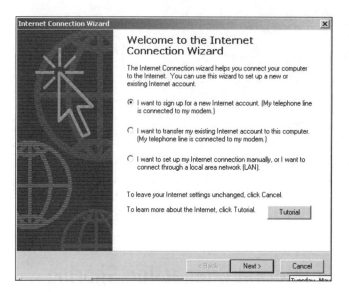

Figure 2.37 The Windows 2000 Internet Connection Wizard.

If the system is equipped with a cable modem or an *Asymmetrical Digital Subscriber Line (ADSL)*, the ISP needs to furnish any additional connection instructions. The cable modem is a device that transmits and receives data through cable television connections. Conversely, ADSL is a special, high-speed modem technology that transmits data over existing telephone lines. The Internet Connection Wizard collects this information and then creates the Internet connection.

To connect to the Internet in Windows 2000, click Start, Programs, Accessories, Communications, and then click the Internet Connection Wizard option. Likewise, to connect to the Internet in Windows XP, you must select the New Connection option from the Accessories, Communications menu. If the connection is new, the Location Information dialog box, depicted in Figure 2.38, along with the dialing rules defined in the preceding section of this chapter, appear. You also need to click the I Want to Sign Up for A New Internet Account option, click the Next button, and follow the wizard's instructions.

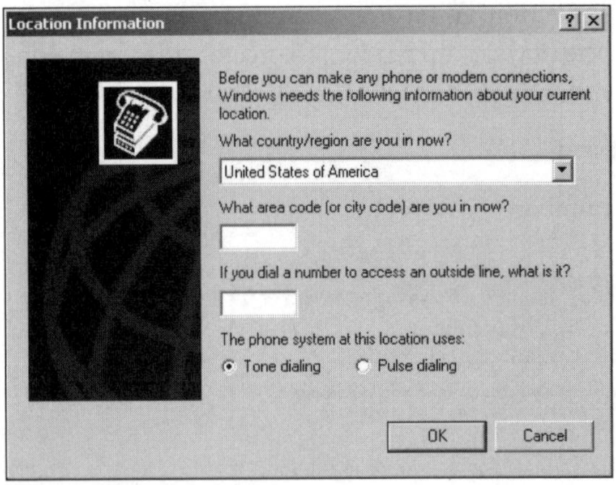

Figure 2.38   The Location Information dialog box.

In a Windows XP system, the New Connection Wizard produces the Network Connection Type dialog box, depicted in Figure 2.39. In this dialog box, you can choose the Connect to the Internet, Connect to the Network at My Workplace, Set Up a Home or Small Office Network, or Set Up an Advanced Connection options.

Establishing Internet Connection Sharing

Windows 2000 and Windows XP make it possible to share resources such as printers, folders, and Internet connections across a network. Sharing an Internet connection allows several computers to be connected to the Internet through a single dial-up connection. These connections can be made individually, or simultaneously, with each user maintaining the ability to use the same services they did when they were connected directly to the Internet.

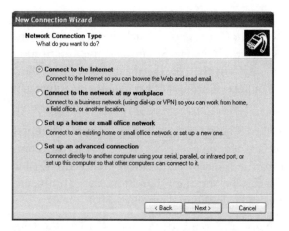

Figure 2.39 Windows XP Network Connection Type dialog box.

To establish *Internet Connection Sharing* (*ICS*) in Windows 2000, you must log on to the computer using an account that has Administrator rights. Afterward, click Start, point to Settings, and then click Network and Dial-Up Connections. Right-click the connection to be shared and select the Properties option. The Connection Properties Sharing tab opens, as shown in Figure 2.40.

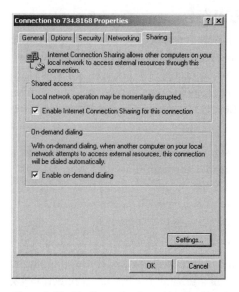

Figure 2.40 The Connection Properties Sharing tab.

To establish ICS in Windows XP, click Start, Control Panel, Network and Internet Connections, and Network Connections. Click the icon of the connection to be shared, and select the Change Settings of the Connection option in the Network Tasks list. On the Advanced tab, select the Allow Other Network Users to Connect Through This Computer's Internet Connection option.

On the Connection Properties Sharing tab, select the Enable Internet Connection Sharing for This Connection check box. If the connecting computer is supposed to dial in to the Internet automatically, click the Enable On-Demand Dialing check box. Clicking the OK button causes protocols, services, interfaces, and routes to be configured automatically.

In Windows XP, access the Network Connections window, select the connection you want to share, and then select the Change Settings of This Connection option from the Network Tasks pane. On the Advanced tab, enable the Allow Other Network Users to Connect Through This Computer's Internet Connection setting. On this tab, you can also enable settings that automatically dial out when another computer on the network tries to access the Internet and that permit other network users to control the shared Internet connection.

The Windows XP Firewall

Windows XP Professional provides a new *Internet Connection Firewall* (*ICF*) feature that is designed to provide protection from outside attacks by preventing unwanted connections from Internet devices. The firewall is used to inspect all traffic going to and coming from the outside network and can be programmed to control traffic flow between the networks based on desirable properties.

The Windows XP ICF service is designed to protect individual computers that are directly connected to the Internet through dial-up, LAN, or high-speed Internet connections. Proper installation and configuration of the ICF service can provide a strong protective barrier between Windows XP Professional and XP Home editions and the outside network.

When combined with the Windows ICS service, the XP firewall can be configured to provide Internet access to multiple computers through a single connection. ICF should be enabled on the shared external connection to secure communication for all internal clients.

Firewalls work by examining the front end (header) of network packets as they are received. Depending on how the firewall is configured, it might look at the header information and permit it to pass through the firewall or block it from going through. By default, the Windows XP ICF service blocks all connection requests initiating from outside its network. It permits only incoming traffic to come through that it recognizes as a response to a request from inside the network. The ICF knows which responses are acceptable because it maintains a table of outgoing connection information for itself and any computers on the local network that are sharing the ICF connection.

However, the ICF function can be configured with filters to enable specific traffic to enter the network. For example, if a service such as a web or FTP service running on the internal network must be made available to external customers, you can configure a filter to open the firewall to let just that service pass through.

Normally, these filters are configured around services recognized by the TCP and UDP networking protocols. These protocols use port numbers to identify specific processes, such as HTTP or FTP. These ports are 16-bit numbers that refer incoming messages to an application that will process them. Many of the port numbers are standardized and are referred to as *well-known ports*. Similarly, their associated applications are called *well-known services*.

Table 2.2 lists several well-known port numbers and their provided services.

Table 2.2 Well-known Ports	
Service	**Well-known Port Number**
FTP	21, 20
Telnet	23
SMTP (mail)	25
HTTP (WWW)	80
POP3 (mail)	110
News	144
HTTP	443
PPTP	1723
IRC	6667

When the firewall examines the incoming packet, it can read the source and destination IP address of the packet and any TCP/UDP port numbers. It uses the IP address and port information in the packet headers to determine whether an incoming packet should be routed into the internal network. If you configure the firewall with the IP address of an internal computer providing FTP services and open ports 20 and 21, the firewall recognizes the IP address and port numbers in the incoming header as valid and routes the packet to that computer. However, all other incoming requests are still blocked.

To enable the Windows XP ICF function, open the Network Connections applet, right-click the connection (dial-up, LAN, or high-speed Internet) that you want to protect, and select the Properties option from the menu. Then, in the Internet Connection Firewall section of the Advanced tab, check the Protect My Computer and Network by Limiting or Preventing Access to This Computer from the Internet check box, and then click the OK button.

On a network that is using ICS, only the outgoing Internet connection should use the ICF feature. The other computers in the internal network should not have their ICF enabled.

Configuring Internet Options

For the most part, no configuration efforts are required to use the Internet Explorer browser. However, several user-selectable options can be established for web browsers. Some of these options are personal preferences, such as colors, fonts, and toolbars. In older browser versions, you could typically find these settings under the Preferences option in a drop-down menu. In newer versions of Internet Explorer, these settings are grouped under the browser's Tools, Internet Options dialog box.

Configuring Security Settings

Various security-related activities involve using your browser and searching the Internet. In Internet Explorer, you can access these functions by selecting Tools, Internet Options and then clicking the Security tab, as depicted in Figure 2.41.

Highlighting the Intranet, Trusted Sites, or Restricted Sites icons enables the Sites button. This button can be used to add or remove sites to each of these different zone classifications. The security settings attached to these different zone types can be modified by clicking the Custom Level button. The Internet icon enables you to establish security settings for all websites that have not been classified as one of the other zone types.

In each zone type, clicking the Custom Level button produces a list of individual controls that can be enabled, disabled, or configured to present a user prompt when the browser encounters related objects. These objects represent web page components that might be encountered by accessing or view-

ing a given website (such as animated scripts, file downloads, and user identification logons).

Figure 2.41   The Security tab in Internet Explorer.

The Reset Custom Settings dialog box features a drop-down list in which
you can establish general levels of security settings for all the items in the
selected zone type's list.

Configuring Script Support

Scripts are executable applications that provide interactive content on websites. They are also capable of retrieving information in response to user
selections. However, the user might not have to do anything to run a script
program; scripts are simply embedded in the website that they access.

You might consider controlling scripts encountered on websites for a couple
of reasons. First, scripts are one of the main sources of virus infections.
Hackers configure scripts to contain viruses that clients might download
unwittingly. Second, scripts also facilitate automatic pop-up windows that
appear without warning on the client's browser. These windows normally
contain unrequested advertisements that tend to annoy users.

You can control the browser's ability to load and run scripts through the
Security tab of its Tools, Internet Options dialog box. The list of individual
web page components that you can control includes different script types,

such as ActiveX and JavaScript. As with the other Security objects, you can configure the browser to enable, disable, or present a user prompt whenever it encounters one of these scripted items.

Configuring Proxy Settings

A *proxy server* is a barrier that prevents outsiders from entering a local area network. All addressing information sent to the Internet uses the IP address of the proxy server. Because the IP address of the workstation that is connecting to the Internet isn't used, an outside intruder has no way of accessing the workstation.

Client access is configured from the web browser of the workstation. To configure a workstation using Internet Explorer for a proxy server, follow these steps:

1. Start Internet Explorer. From the menu bar, click Tools and then Internet Options.

2. Select the Connections tab and click the LAN Setting button. This produces the Local Area Network (LAN) Settings dialog box, similar to the one in Figure 2.42.

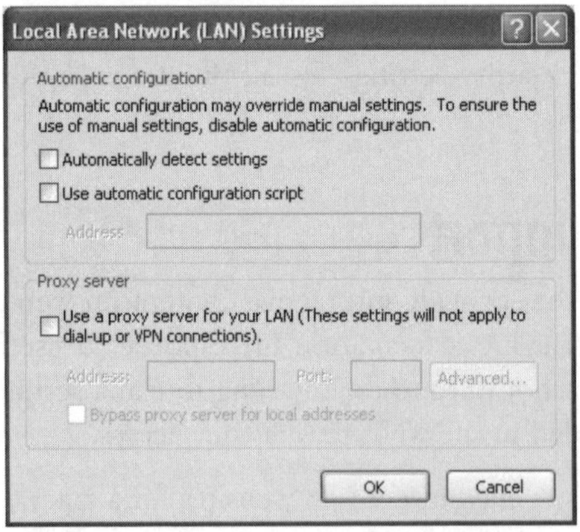

Figure 2.42   Internet Explorer proxy configuration in the Local Area Network (LAN) Settings dialog box.

3. Check the Use a Proxy Server for Your LAN check box, and enter the name of the proxy server in the Address text box. You can enter an IP address in the Address text box instead of the server name.

4. Enter the port number of the server in the Port text box. The port number is usually a well-known port number.

5. Click the Apply button, followed by the OK button.

When fully configured, the proxy server supplies the client with the addresses and port numbers for the Internet services (such as HTTP, FTP, and so on) that are available to it.

You can follow these steps to configure the workstation proxy settings for Netscape Navigator:

1. From the Netscape Navigator menu bar, click Options, and then click Network Preferences. Click the Proxies tab in the Preferences dialog box.

2. Click the Manual Proxy Configuration radio button, and then click the View button.

3. Enter the name or IP address of the proxy server for each service, along with the port number of the service.

4. Click the Apply button, and then click the OK button.

Navigator also permits you to use an automatic proxy configuration for workstations by entering the address where the proxy configuration file is located. Enter the address in the Automatic Proxy Configuration text box of the Preferences dialog box.

Optimizing Windows Performance

Windows operating systems have evolved to the point at which they adapt well to most system settings and changes. Most of these adaptations are automatic in nature. However, some areas of the Windows system can still be optimized by users and administrators. These areas involve the following activities:

➤ Optimizing virtual memory management

➤ Performing disk defragmentation when appropriate

➤ Maintaining files and buffers

➤ Establishing and optimizing various memory caches

➤ Effective temporary file management

Optimizing Windows 9x and Windows Me Systems That Have Legacy Files

In a pure, 32-bit Windows 9x and Windows Me environment, very little memory management is needed. In these systems, new 32-bit virtual device drivers (VxDs) are automatically loaded into extended memory during the bootup process. This eliminates the need for DEVICE= and LOADHIGH commands for devices that have VxDs and Windows 9x or Windows Me application programs. However, when 16-bit device drivers or MS-DOS applications are being used, Windows must create a real-mode MS-DOS environment for them. For this reason, Windows 9x executes a CONFIG.SYS and/or AUTOEXEC.BAT file if it encounters them during the bootup process.

If no MS-DOS based drivers or applications are in the system, the CONFIG.SYS and AUTOEXEC.BAT files are not necessary; however, the Windows 9x and Windows Me version of the IO.SYS file automatically loads the Windows 9x version of the HIMEM.SYS file during bootup. This file must be present for Windows 9x and Windows Me to boot up. Multiple versions of the HIMEM.SYS file are usually found in a Windows 9x or Windows Me system (there could be three or more versions).

If a Windows 9x or Windows Me system has a CONFIG.SYS, AUTOEXEC.BAT, or .INI file that has been held over from a previous operating system, you should be aware that any unneeded commands in these files have the potential to reduce system performance. In particular, the SMARTDRV function from older operating systems inhibits dynamic VCACHE operation and slows the system down. The VCACHE driver establishes and controls a disk cache in an area of RAM as a storage space for information read from the hard disk drive, CD-ROM, and other drives and file operations.

If the system runs slowly, check any CONFIG.SYS and AUTOEXEC.BAT files for SMARTDRV and any other disk cache software settings. Remove these commands from both files to improve performance. Also, remove any Share commands from the AUTOEXEC.BAT file. Likewise, the SYSTEM.INI, WIN.INI, PROTOCOL.INI, CONFIG.SYS, and AUTOEXEC.BAT files can be modified through the System Editor (SysEdit) in Windows 9x. You can access this utility by typing "Sysedit" in the Start, Run dialog box.

Optimizing Virtual Memory in Windows 9x

Windows 9x swap drives do not require contiguous drive space and can be established on compressed drives that use virtual device drivers. The size of the Windows 95 swap file is variable and is dynamically assigned. The Windows 9x swap file is `WIN386.SWP`.

Control of Windows 9x Virtual Memory operations is established through Control Panel, System, Performance tab. Clicking the Virtual Memory button produces the *Virtual Memory Options* dialog box, depicted in Figure 2.43. The default and recommended setting is *Let Windows Manage My Virtual Memory Settings*.

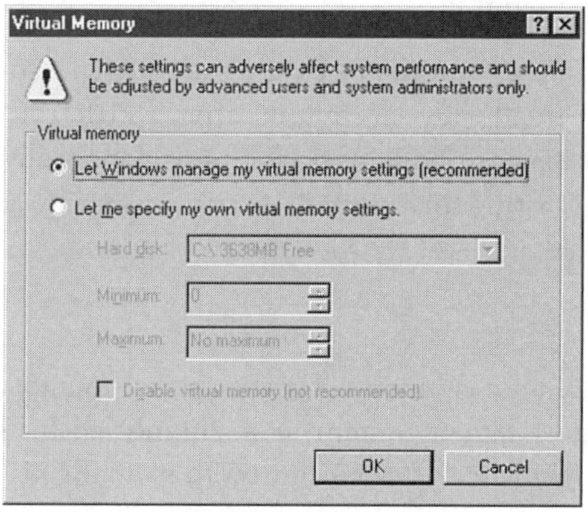

Figure 2.43 The Windows 95 Virtual Memory dialog box.

Optimizing Windows 2000 and Windows XP Systems

As with Windows 9x and Windows Me systems, you can optimize the performance of Windows 2000 and Windows XP machines by defragmenting the system drives, removing unwanted or unused files, and maintaining the operating system's various caches.

Cross-linked files can accumulate and cause the system to slow down. Use the Chkdsk or Scandisk utilities to find and remove or repair cross-linked files that might be using up disk space.

Defragmenting the Drive

The Windows 2000 and Windows XP Disk Defragmenter utility is available through the Administrative Tools, Computer Management console and is used to reposition related files/sectors on a disk drive so that they are located in the most advantageous pattern for being found and read by the system. You can also access the Defrag utility in Windows XP through Start, All

Programs, Accessories, System Tools menu. In a domain network environment, you must have Administrator rights to use the Defrag utility.

Removing Unnecessary Files

The Windows 2000 and Windows XP Disk Cleanup utility can be used to identify optional applications and certain types of temporary files that are not required for operation of the system. The temporary files that you can normally afford to remove from the system to gain needed disk space include Windows, Internet, and multimedia temp files.

Another set of files that are not removed automatically are the cookies associated with Internet usage. These small files can pile up after a little time surfing and take up significant disk space. These must be removed manually. In Windows 2000, you can perform this under the \Documents and Settings\Administrator\Cookies folder.

Optimizing Virtual Memory

In Windows NT, Windows 2000, and Windows XP, the virtual memory functions are located under Control Panel, System icon. Simply click its Advanced tab followed by the Performance Options button to view the dialog box depicted in Figure 2.44.

Figure 2.44 The System Performance Options dialog box.

Clicking the Change button in the dialog box opens the *Virtual Memory* dialog box shown in Figure 2.45. Through this dialog box, you can establish and configure an individual swap file for each drive in the system. By highlighting a drive, you can check its virtual memory capabilities and settings. Entering new values in the dialog boxes and clicking the Set button changes the values for the highlighted drive.

The Windows NT, Windows 2000, and Windows XP pagefiles (named PAGEFILE.SYS) are created when the operating system is installed. This file's default size is typically set at 1.5 times the amount of RAM installed in the system.

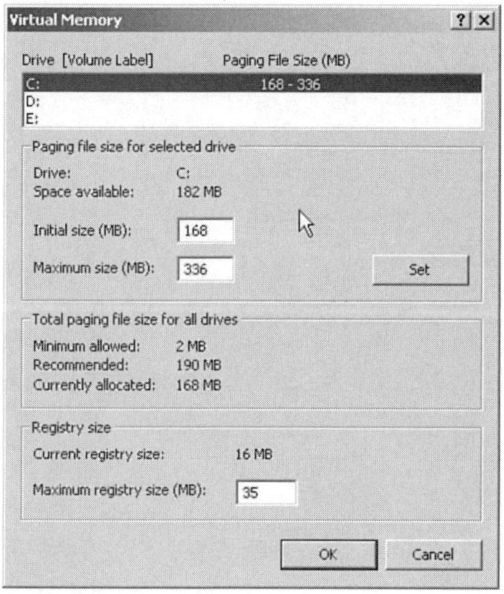

Figure 2.45 The Virtual Memory dialog box.

It is possible to optimize the system's performance by distributing the swap file space between multiple drives. Relocating it away from slower or heavily used drives can also be helpful. You should not place the swap file on mirrored or striped volumes. Also, don't create multiple swap files on logical disks that exist on the same physical drive.

PART II
Troubleshooting

Hardware Troubleshooting Techniques

Introduction

This chapter contains information that applies to identifying and trouble-shooting hardware problems.

Sorting Hardware/Software/ Configuration Problems

One of the first steps in troubleshooting a computer problem (or any other programmable system problem) is to determine whether the problem is due to a hardware failure or to faulty software. In most PCs, you can use a significant event that occurs during the startup process as a key to separate hardware problems from software problems: the single beep that most PCs produce between the end of the power-on self test (POST) and the beginning of the startup process.

Errors that occur, or are displayed, before this beep indicate that a hardware problem of some type exists. Up to this point in the operation of the system, only the BIOS and the basic system hardware have been active. The operating system side of the system does not come into play until after the beep occurs.

If the system produces an error message (such as "The system has detected unstable RAM at location x") or a beep code before the single beep occurs, the system has found a problem with the hardware. In this case, a bad RAM memory device is indicated.

Typically, if the startup process reaches the point at which the system's CMOS configuration information is displayed onscreen, you can safely assume that no hardware configuration conflicts exist in the system's basic components. After this point in the bootup process, the system begins loading drivers for optional devices and additional memory.

If the error occurs after the CMOS screen displays and before the bootup tone, you must clean boot the system and single-step through the remainder of the bootup sequence.

You can still group errors that occur before the beep into two distinct categories:

➤ Configuration errors

➤ Hardware failures

A special category of problems tends to occur when a new hardware option is added to the system, or when the system is used for the very first time. These problems are called *configuration problems*, or *setup problems*. These problems result from mismatches between the system's programmed configuration held in CMOS memory and the actual equipment installed in the system.

It is usually necessary to access the system's CMOS setup utility in the following three situations:

➤ When the system is first constructed.

➤ When it becomes necessary to replace the CMOS backup battery on the system board.

➤ When a new or different option is added to the system (such as memory devices, hard drives, floppy drives, or video display), it might be necessary to access the setup utility to accept the changes that have been implemented.

In most systems, the BIOS and operating system use plug-and-play techniques to detect new hardware that has been installed in the system. These components work together with the device to allocate system resources for the device. In some situations, the PnP logic is not able to resolve all the system's resource needs and a configuration error occurs. In these cases, the user must manually resolve the configuration problem.

When you are installing new hardware or software options, be aware of the possibility of configuration errors occurring. If you encounter configuration (or setup) errors, refer to the installation instructions found in the new component's installation/user documentation.

If you cannot confirm a configuration problem, you most likely have a defective component. The most widely used repair method involves substituting known-good components for suspected bad components. Other alternatives for isolating and correcting a hardware failure that appears before the bootup depend on how much of the system is operable.

Normally, symptoms can be divided into three sections: configuration problems, bootup problems, and operational problems.

The system's configuration settings are normally checked first. It is important to observe the system's symptoms to determine in which part of the system's operation the fault occurs. The error messages described in Table 3.1 are errors that occur and are reported before the single beep tone is produced at the end of the POST routines.

Table 3.1   Common Configuration Error Codes

CONFIGURATION ERROR MESSAGE	MEANING
CMOS System Option Not Set	Failure of CMOS battery or CMOS Checksum test
CMOS Display Mismatch	Failure of display type verification
CMOS Memory Size Mismatch	System configuration and setup failure
Press F1 to Continue	Invalid configuration information
CMOS Time and Date Not Set	Failure of CMOS battery

After the beep tone has been produced in the startup sequence, the system shifts over to the process of booting up and begins looking for and loading the operating system. Errors that occur between the beep and the presentation of the operating system's user interface (command prompt or GUI) generally have three possible sources. These sources are summarized in the following list that includes the typical error messages associated with each source.

➤ Hardware failure (physical problem with the boot drive)

   ➤ General Failure Error Reading Drive x

➤ Corrupted or missing boot files

　➤ Bad or Missing Command Interpreter

　➤ *Nonsystem Disk or Disk Error*

　➤ *Bad File Allocation Table*

➤ Corrupted or missing operating system files

Both configuration problems and bootup problems can be caused by a hardware or operational failure. If the configuration settings are correct, but these symptoms are present, a hardware problem is indicated as the cause of the problem. Conversely, bootup problems are typically associated with the operating system.

Hardware Troubleshooting Tools

The level of troubleshooting most often performed on PC hardware is exchanging *Field Replaceable Units* (*FRUs*). Due to the relative low cost of computer components, it is normally not practical to troubleshoot failed components to the IC level. The cost of using a technician to diagnose the problem further, and repair it, can quickly exceed the cost of the new replacement unit.

However, a few hardware diagnostic tools can be very helpful in isolating defective hardware components. These tools include

➤ Software diagnostic disk

➤ Multimeter

➤ Cable tester

➤ POST card

Software Diagnostic Packages

Several commercially available disk-based diagnostic routines can check the system by running predetermined tests on different areas of its hardware. The diagnostic package evaluates the response from each test and attempts to produce a status report for all of the system's major components. Like the computer's self-tests, these packages produce visual and beep-coded error messages. Figure 3.1 depicts the Main menu of a typical self-booting software diagnostic package.

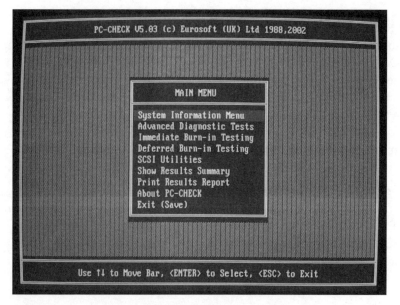

Figure 3.1   A typical software diagnostic main menu.

This menu is the gateway to information about the system's makeup and configuration, as well as the entryway to the program's Advanced Diagnostic Test functions. You can find utilities for performing low-level formats on older hard drive types and for managing small computer system interface (SCSI) devices through this menu. In addition, options to print or show test results are available here, as is the exit point from the program.

The most common software-troubleshooting packages test the system's memory, microprocessor, keyboard, display monitor, and the disk drive's speed. If at least the system's CPU, disk drive, and clock circuits are working, you might be able to use one of these special software-troubleshooting packages to help localize system failures. They can prove especially helpful when trying to track down non-heat-related intermittent problems.

If a diagnostic program indicates that multiple items should be replaced, replace the units one at a time until the unit starts up. Then replace any units removed prior to the one that caused the system to start. This process ensures that there are not multiple bad parts. If you have replaced all the parts, and the unit still does not function properly, the diagnostic software is suspect.

Using a Multimeter in a PC

A number of test instruments can help you isolate computer hardware problems. One of the most basic pieces of electronic troubleshooting equipment is the multimeter. These test instruments are available in both analog and digital readout form and can be used to directly measure electrical values of voltage (V), current in milliamperes (mA) or amperes (A), and resistance in ohms. Therefore, these devices are referred to as VOMs (volt-ohm-milliammeters) for analog types, or DMMs (digital multimeters) for digital types.

Figure 3.2 depicts a digital multimeter. With a little finesse, you can use this device to check diodes, transistors, capacitors, motor windings, relays, and coils. This particular DMM contains facilities built in to the meter to test transistors and diodes. These facilities are in addition to its standard functions of current, voltage, and resistance measurement; however, in computer repair work, only the voltage and resistance functions are used extensively.

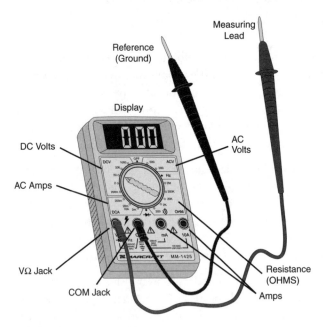

Figure 3.2 A digital multimeter.

The first step in using the multimeter to perform tests is to select the proper function. For the most part, you never need to use the current function of the multimeter when working with computer systems; however, the voltage and resistance functions can be very valuable tools.

In computer troubleshooting, most of the tests are DC voltage readings. These measurements usually involve checking the DC side of the power-supply unit. You can make these readings between ground and one of the expansion-slot pins, or at the system board power-supply connector. It is also common to check the voltage level across a system board capacitor to verify that the system is receiving power. The voltage across most of the capacitors on the system board is 5V (DC). The DC voltages that can normally be expected in a PC-compatible system are +12V, +5V, –5V, and –12V. The actual values for these readings might vary by 5% in either direction.

 It is normal practice to first set the meter to its highest voltage range to be certain that the voltage level being measured does not damage the meter.

The DC voltage function is used to take measurements in live DC circuits. It should be connected in parallel with the device being checked. This could mean connecting the reference lead (black lead) to a ground point and the measuring lead (red lead) to a test point to take a measurement, as illustrated in Figure 3.3.

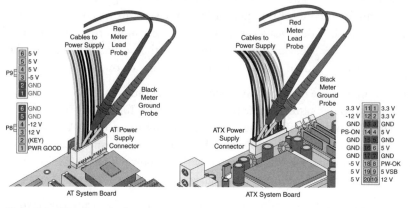

Figure 3.3 DC voltage check.

As an approximate value is detected, you can decrease the range setting to achieve a more accurate reading. Most meters allow for overvoltage protection; however, it is still a good safety practice to decrease the range of the meter after you have achieved an initial value.

The second most popular test is the resistance, or continuity test.

Unlike voltage checks, resistance checks are always made with power removed from the system.

Failure to turn off the power when making resistance checks can cause serious damage to the meter and can pose a potential risk to the technician. Resistance checks require that you electrically isolate the component being tested from the system. For most circuit components, this means desoldering at least one end from the board.

The resistance check is very useful in isolating some types of problems in the system. One of the main uses of the resistance function is to test fuses. You must disconnect at least one end of the fuse from the system. You should set the meter on the 1k ohm resistance setting. If the fuse is good, the meter should read near 0 ohms. If it is bad, the meter reads infinite.

The resistance function also is useful in checking for cables and connectors. By removing the cable from the system and connecting a meter lead to each end, you can check the cable's continuity conductor by conductor to verify its integrity.

You also use the resistance function to test the system's speaker. To check the speaker, simply disconnect the speaker from the system and connect a meter lead to each end. If the speaker is good, the meter should read near 8 ohms (although a smaller speaker might be 4 ohms). If the speaker is defective, the resistance reading should be 0 for shorts or infinite for opens.

Only a couple of situations involve using the AC voltage function for checking microcomputer systems. The primary use of this function is to check the commercial power being applied to the power-supply unit. As with any measurement, it is important to select the correct measurement range; however, the lethal voltage levels associated with the power supply call for additional caution when making such measurements.

The second application for the AC voltage function is to measure ripple voltage from the DC output side of the power-supply unit. This particular operation is very rarely performed in field-service situations.

Cable Testers

The most frequent hardware-related cause of network problems involves bad cabling and connectors. Several specialized, handheld devices designed for testing the various types of data communication cabling are available. These devices range from inexpensive *continuity testers*, to moderately priced *data cabling testers*, to somewhat expensive *time domain reflectometers (TDR)*.

Although inexpensive continuity testers can be used to check for broken cables, data cabling testers are designed to perform a number of different types of tests on twisted-pair and coaxial cables. These wiring testers normally consist of two units—a *master test unit* and a *separate load unit*, as illustrated in Figure 3.4.

The master unit is attached to one end of the cable and the load unit is attached to the other. The master unit sends patterns of test signals through the cable and reads them back from the load unit. Many of these testers feature both RJ-45 and BNC connectors for testing different types of cabling. When testing twisted-pair cabling, these devices can normally detect such problems as broken wires, crossed-over wiring, shorted connections, and improperly paired connections.

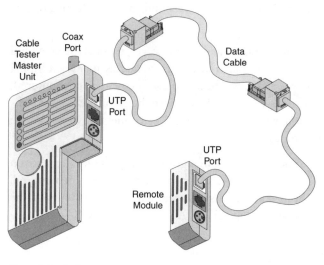

Figure 3.4 Cable tester.

TDRs are sophisticated testers that can be used to pinpoint the distance to a break in a cable. These devices send signals along the cable and wait for them to be reflected. The time between sending the signal and receiving it back is converted into a distance measurement. The TDR function is normally packaged along with the other cable testing functions just described. TDRs used to test fiber-optic cables are known as optical time domain reflectometers (OTDRs).

POST Cards

A POST card is a diagnostic device that plugs into the system's expansion slot and tests the operation of the system as it boots up. These cards can be as simple as interrupt and direct memory access (DMA) channel monitors, or as complex as full-fledged ROM BIOS diagnostic packages that carry out extensive tests on the system.

POST cards are normally used when the system appears to be dead, or when the system cannot read from a floppy or hard drive. The firmware tests on the card replace the normal BIOS functions and send the system into a set of tests. The value of the card lies in the fact that the tests can be carried out without the system resorting to software diagnostics located on the hard disk or in a floppy drive.

The POST routines located in most BIOS chips report two types of errors—*fatal* and *nonfatal*. If the POST encounters a fatal error, it stops the system. The error code posted on the indicator corresponds to the defective operation.

If the POST card encounters a nonfatal error, however, it notes the error and continues through the initialization routine to activate as many additional system resources as possible. When these types of errors are encountered, the POST card must be observed carefully because the error code on its indicator must be coordinated with the timing of the error message or beep code produced by the BIOS routines.

Simple POST cards come with a set of light-emitting diodes (LEDs) on them that produce coded error signals when a problem is encountered. Other cards produce beep codes and seven-segment LED readouts of the error code. Figure 3.5 depicts a typical XT/AT-compatible POST card.

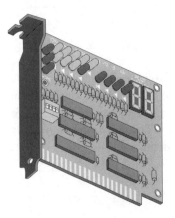

Figure 3.5 A typical POST card.

Troubleshooting Power-Supply Problems

Typical symptoms associated with power-supply failures include the following:

➤ No indicator lights are visible, with no disk drive action and no display on the screen. Nothing works, and the system is dead.

➤ The On/Off indicator lights are visible, but there is no disk drive action and no display on the monitor screen. The system fan might or might not run.

➤ The system produces a continuous beep tone.

Checking Dead Systems

Special consideration must be taken when a system is inoperable. In a totally inoperable system, there are no symptoms to give clues where to begin the isolation process. In addition, it is impossible to use troubleshooting software or other system aids to help isolate the problem.

When the system exhibits no signs of life—including the absence of lights—the best place to start looking for the problem is at the power supply. The operation of this unit affects virtually every part of the system. Also, the absence of any lights working usually indicates that no power is being supplied to the system by the power supply.

1. Check the external connections of the power supply. This is the first step in checking any electrical equipment that shows no signs of life.

2. Confirm that the power supply cord is plugged into a functioning outlet.

3. Verify the position of the On/Off switch.

4. Examine the power cord for good connection at the rear of the unit.

5. Check the setting of the 110/220 switch setting on the outside of the power supply. The normal setting for equipment used in the United States is 110.

6. Check the power at the commercial receptacle using a voltmeter, or by plugging in a lamp (or other 110-volt device) into the outlet.

Before changing any board or connection, always turn the system off first. In an ATX-style system, you should also disconnect the power cable from the power supply. This is necessary because even with the power switch off, some levels of voltages are still applied to the system board in these units.

Other Power-Supply Problems

The absence of the lights and the fan operation indicate that power is not reaching the system and that at least some portion of the power supply is not functional. This type of symptom results from the following two likely possibilities:

1. A portion of the power supply has failed, or is being overloaded. One or more of the basic voltages supplied by the power supply is missing while the others are still present.

2. A key component on the system board has failed, preventing it from processing even though the system has power. A defective capacitor across the power input of the system board can completely prevent it from operating.

The DC voltages that can normally be expected in an ATX PC-compatible system are +3.3V, +12V, +5V, –5V, and –12V. The actual values for these readings might vary by 5% in either direction. The black wires in the power supply/system board connection are the ground reference wires. Figure 3.6 illustrates the correct measurement of voltages at this connector.

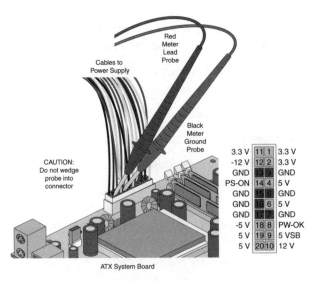

Figure 3.6 Measuring system board voltages.

Troubleshooting the System Board

The microprocessor, RAM modules, ROM BIOS, and CMOS battery are typically replaceable units on the system board. If enough of the system is running to perform tests on these units, you can replace them.

Problems with key system board components produce symptoms similar to those described for a bad power supply. Both the microprocessor and the ROM BIOS can be sources of such problems. You should check both by substitution when dead system symptoms are encountered but the power supply is good.

System Board Symptoms

Typical symptoms associated with system board hardware failures include the following:

➤ The On/Off indicator lights are visible and the display is visible on the monitor screen, but there is no disk drive action and no bootup occurs.

➤ The On/Off indicator lights are visible and the hard drive spins up, but the system appears dead and there is no bootup.

➤ The system locks up during normal operation.

➤ The system produces a beep code with one, two, three, five, seven, or nine beeps (BIOS dependent).

➤ The system produces a beep code of one long and three short beeps (BIOS dependent).

➤ The system does not hold the current date and time.

➤ A DMA Error message displays, indicating a DMA controller failed page register test.

➤ A CMOS Battery Low message displays, indicating failure of the CMOS battery or the CMOS checksum test.

➤ A CMOS Checksum Failure message displays, indicating that the CMOS battery is low or a CMOS checksum test failure.

➤ A 201 error code displays, indicating a RAM failure.

➤ A Parity Check error message displays, indicating a RAM error.

Typical symptoms associated with system board CMOS setup failures include the following:

➤ A CMOS Inoperational message displays, indicating failure of CMOS shutdown register.

➤ A CMOS Memory Size Mismatch message displays, indicating a system configuration and setup failure.

➤ A CMOS Time & Date Not Set message displays, indicating a system configuration and setup failure.

Typical symptoms associated with system board I/O failures include the following:

➤ The speaker doesn't work during operation. The rest of the system works, but no sounds are produced through the speaker.

➤ The keyboard does not function after being replaced with a known-good unit.

Configuration Problems

Configuration problems typically occur when the system is being set up for the first time, or when a new option has been installed. The values stored in CMOS must accurately reflect the configuration of the system; otherwise, an error occurs. Incorrectly set CMOS parameters cause the corresponding hardware to fail. Therefore, check the enabling functions of the advanced CMOS settings as a part of every hardware configuration troubleshooting procedure.

The many configuration options available in a modern BIOS require the user to have a good deal of knowledge about the particular function being configured. In cases in which you have serious configuration circumstances, don't forget that you normally have the option to select default configuration options through the CMOS setup utility.

Typically, if the bootup process reaches the point at which the system's CMOS configuration information is displayed onscreen, you can safely assume that no hardware configuration conflicts exist between the system's basic components. After this point in the bootup process, the system begins loading drivers for optional devices and additional memory.

If errors occur after the CMOS screen has been displayed and before the bootup tone, you must clean boot the system and single-step through the remainder of the bootup sequence to locate the cause of the failure. These techniques are described in detail in Chapter 4, "Operating System Troubleshooting."

Microprocessors

In the event of a microprocessor failure, the system might issue a slow single beep from the speaker along with no display or other I/O operation. This indicates that an internal error has disabled a portion of the processor's internal circuitry (usually the internal cache). Internal problems can also allow the microprocessor to begin processing, but then fail as it attempts additional operations. Such a problem results in the system continuously counting RAM during the bootup process. It might also lock up while counting RAM. In either case, the only way to remedy the problem is to replace the microprocessor.

If the system consistently locks up after being on for a few minutes, this is a good indication that the microprocessor's fan is not running or that some other heat buildup problem is occurring. You also should check the microprocessor if its fan has not been running, but the power is on. This situation might indicate that the microprocessor has been without adequate ventilation and has overheated. When this happens, you must replace the fan unit and the microprocessor. Verify that the new fan works correctly; otherwise, a second microprocessor will be damaged.

Microprocessor Cooling Systems

Microprocessor-based equipment is designed to provide certain performance levels under specified environmental conditions such as operating temperature. Using Pentium class microprocessors, PC systems are designed to maintain the operating temperature of the device in the range of 30 to 40 degrees C.

The ideal operating temperature setting varies between microprocessor types and manufacturers. Also, the location of the CMOS configuration setting varies between different BIOS makers and versions. Some CMOS setup utilities provide a separate Hardware Health configuration screen, whereas others integrate it into the Power Management screen. Many systems include an additional fan control circuit for use with an optional chassis (case) fan. In these cases, the system board features additional BERG connectors for the chassis temperature sensor and fan control cable.

If temperature-related problems like those described in the preceding section occur, you should access the CMOS Hardware Health configuration screen, similar to the one depicted in Figure 3.7, and check the fan speed and processor temperature readings.

If these readings are outside of the designated range, you can enter a different value for the temperature set point. If no fan speed measurement is being shown, check to see if the fan is actually turning. If not, you should turn the system off as soon as possible, check the operation of the fan, and replace it before the microprocessor is damaged.

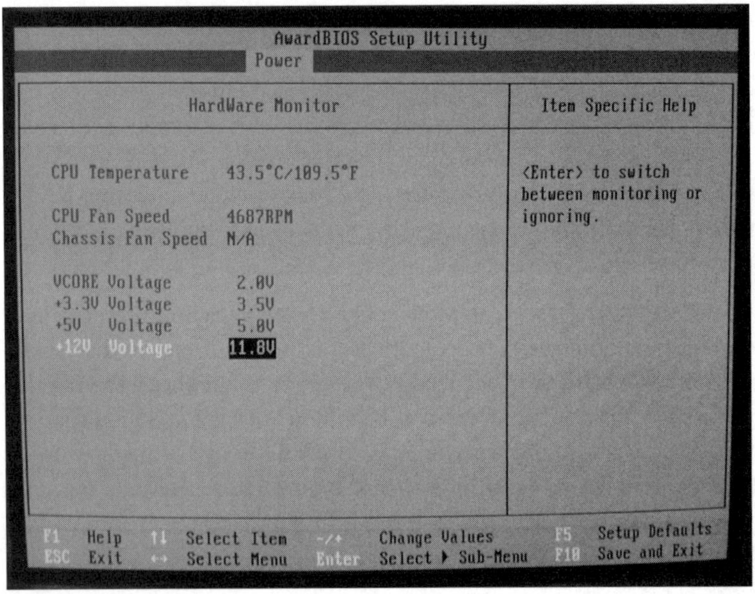

```
                    AwardBIOS Setup Utility
                  │   Power   │

              HardWare Monitor                    Item Specific Help

   CPU Temperature     43.5°C/109.5°F           <Enter> to switch
                                                between monitoring or
   CPU Fan Speed       4687RPM                   ignoring.
   Chassis Fan Speed   N/A

   VCORE Voltage       2.0V
   +3.3V Voltage       3.5V
   +5V   Voltage       5.0V
   +12V  Voltage       11.8V


   F1   Help    ↑↓  Select Item    -/+   Change Values    F5   Setup Defaults
   ESC  Exit    ←→  Select Menu    Enter  Select ▶ Sub-Menu  F10  Save and Exit
```

Figure 3.7   The CMOS Hardware Health configuration screen.

Other alternatives when dealing with thermal problems in a PC include installing an additional chassis fan to help move cooler air through the system unit, changing the microprocessor fan for one that runs faster over a given range of temperatures, and flashing the BIOS to provide different fan control parameters.

Check for missing slot covers that can disrupt airflow in the case and route internal signal cables so that they do not block the flow of air through the case. Likewise, check the case's front cover alignment as well as any upper or side access panels to ensure they are well fitted. If the airflow openings in the front cover are blocked, the system fans cannot properly circulate air though the case.

If the front panel or any of the access doors or covers are not in proper position, they could create alternate airflow paths that disrupt the designed cooling capabilities of the system. In addition to disrupting the designed airflow capabilities of the case, missing or misaligned case panels can permit radio frequency interference (RFI) signals to escape from the case and disrupt the operation of other electronic devices, such as radio receivers and televisions.

RAM

The system board RAM is a serviceable part of the system board. RAM failures basically fall into two major categories and create two different types of failures:

➤ **Soft-memory errors**—Errors caused by infrequent and random glitches in the operation of applications and the system. You can clear these events just by restarting the system.

➤ **Hard-memory errors**—Permanent physical failures that generate NMI errors in the system and require that the memory units be checked by substitution.

Observe the bootup RAM count on the display to verify that it is correct for the amount of physical RAM actually installed in the system. If not, swap RAM devices around to see whether the count changes. Use logical rotation of the RAM devices to locate the defective part. The burn-in tests in most diagnostic packages can prove helpful in locating borderline RAM modules.

You can also swap out RAM modules one at a time to isolate defective modules. When swapping RAM into a system for troubleshooting purposes, take care to ensure that the new RAM is of the correct type for the system and that it meets its bus speed rating. Also, ensure that the replacement RAM is consistent with the installed RAM. Mixing RAM types and speeds can cause the system to lock up and produce hard-memory errors.

ROM

A bad or damaged ROM BIOS typically stops the system completely. When you encounter a dead system board, examine the BIOS chip for physical damage. If these devices overheat, it is typical for them to crack or blow a large piece out of the top of the IC package. Another symptom pointing toward a damaged BIOS involves the bootup sequence automatically moving into the CMOS configuration display, but never returning to the bootup sequence. In any case, you must replace the defective BIOS with a version that matches the chipset used by the system.

In situations in which new devices (for example, microprocessors, RAM devices, hard drives) have been added to the system, there is always a chance that the original BIOS cannot support them. In these situations, the system might or might not function based on which device has been installed and how its presence affects the system. To compensate for these possible problems, always check the websites of the device and the system board manufacturers to obtain the latest BIOS upgrade and support information.

CMOS Batteries

The second condition that causes a configuration problem involves the system board's CMOS backup battery.

If a system refuses to maintain time and date information, the CMOS backup battery or its recharging circuitry is normally faulty. After the backup battery has been replaced, check the contacts of the battery holder for corrosion.

If the battery fails, or if it has been changed, the contents of the CMOS configuration are lost. After replacing the battery, it is always necessary to access the CMOS setup utility to reconfigure the system.

Troubleshooting Keyboard Problems

Most of the circuitry associated with the computer's keyboard is located on the keyboard itself. However, the keyboard interface circuitry is located on the system board. Therefore, the steps required to isolate keyboard problems are usually confined to the keyboard, its connecting cable, and the system board.

Keyboard Symptoms

Typical symptoms associated with keyboard failures include the following:

➤ No characters appear onscreen when entered from the keyboard.

➤ Some keys work, whereas others do not work.

➤ A Keyboard Error—Keyboard Test Failure error appears.

➤ A KB/Interface Error—Keyboard Test Failure error appears.

➤ An error code of *six short beeps* is produced during bootup (BIOS dependent).

➤ The wrong characters are displayed.

➤ An IBM-compatible 301 error code appears.

➤ An Unplugged Keyboard error appears.

➤ A key is stuck.

Basic Keyboard Checks

The keys of the keyboard can wear out over time. This might result in keys that don't make good contact (no character is produced when the key is pressed) or that remain in contact (stick) even when pressure is removed. The stuck key produces an error message when the system detects it; however, it has no way of detecting an open key.

An unplugged keyboard, or one with a bad signal cable, also produces a keyboard error message during startup. Ironically, this condition might produce a configuration error message that says *"Press F1 to continue."*

If the keyboard produces odd characters on the display, check the Windows keyboard settings in Device Manager. Device Manager is located under the System icon (found in Control Panel) in Windows 9x and Windows Me. In Windows 2000, the path is similar—Control Panel, System, Hardware tab. However, in both Windows 2000 and Windows XP, Device Manager is usually accessed through the Computer Management console. If the keyboard is not installed or is incorrect, install the correct keyboard type. Also, be certain that you have the correct language setting specified in the Keyboard Properties dialog box (found by double-clicking the Keyboard icon in Control Panel).

Keyboard Hardware Checks

If you suspect a keyboard hardware problem, isolate the keyboard as the definite source of the problem (a fairly easy task). Because the keyboard is external to the system unit, detachable, and inexpensive, simply exchange it with a known-good keyboard.

If the new keyboard works correctly, remove the back cover from the faulty keyboard and check for the presence of a fuse in the +5V DC supply and check it for continuity. Neither the older five-pin DIN nor the six-pin PS/2 mini-DIN keyboards can be hot-swapped. Disconnecting or plugging in a keyboard that has this type of fuse while power is on can cause the keyboard to fail. If the fuse is present, simply replace it with a fuse of the same type and rating.

If replacing the keyboard does not correct the problem, and no configuration or software reason is apparent, the next step is to troubleshoot the keyboard receiver section of the system board. On most system boards, this ultimately involves replacing the system board.

Troubleshooting Mouse Problems

Most problems with mice are related either to its port connection, the mouse driver, the trackball in a trackball mouse or a trackball unit, and the operation of the mouse buttons.

In newer systems, the mouse is typically connected to the USB port or the dedicated PS/2 mouse port on the back of the unit. In ATX systems, the keyboard and mouse have been given the same six-pin mini-DIN connector and, unfortunately, they do not work interchangeably. Although plugging the mouse into the keyboard connector should not cause any physical damage, it does cause problems with getting the system to work. These connections tend to be color-coded so you can check to ensure the mouse is connected to the green connector.

For PnP-compatible mice, installation and configuration has become a fairly routine process. Connect the mouse to the PS/2 mouse port and let the system autodetect it and install the basic Windows mouse drivers.

However, specialty mice—including USB-connected mice, wireless mice, and infrared mice—along with other pointing devices might require special drivers that are supplied by the manufacturer and loaded from the disk or disc that accompanies the device. Older serial mice used one of the PC's serial ports as their interface. These ports had to be properly configured for the serial mouse to work properly.

When a *trackball mouse* is moved across the table, the trackball picks up dirt or lint, which can hinder the movement of the trackball, typically evident by the cursor periodically freezing and jumping onscreen. On most mice, you can remove the trackball from the mouse by a latching mechanism on its bottom. Twisting the latch counterclockwise enables you to remove the trackball. Then, you can clean dirt out of the mouse.

The other mechanical part of the mouse is its buttons. These items can wear out under normal use. When they do, the mouse should simply be replaced. However, before doing so, check the Properties of the mouse in the operating system to ensure that the button functions have not been altered. It would be a shame to throw away a perfectly good mouse because it had been set up for left-hand use in the operating system.

Mouse Hardware Checks

The hardware check for the mouse involves isolating it from its host port. Simply replace the mouse to test its electronics. If the replacement mouse works, the original mouse is probably defective. If its electronics are not working properly, few options are available for actually servicing a mouse. It might need a cleaning, or a new trackball. However, the low cost of a typical mouse generally makes it a throwaway item if simple cleaning does not fix it.

If the new mouse does not work either, chances are good that the mouse's electronics are working properly. In this case, the mouse driver or the port hardware must be the cause of the problem. If the driver is correct for the mouse, the port hardware and CMOS configuration must be checked.

The system board typically contains all of the port hardware electronics and support so it must be replaced to restore the port/mouse operation at that port. However, if the system board mouse port is defective, another option is to install a mouse that uses a different type of port (for example, use a USB mouse to replace the PS/2 mouse).

Mouse Configuration Checks

When a mouse does not work in a Windows system, restart it and move into safe mode by pressing the F5 function key while the "Starting Windows" message is displayed. This starts the operating system with the most basic mouse driver available. If the mouse does not operate in safe mode, you must check the mouse hardware and the port to which the mouse is connected.

If the mouse works in safe mode, the problem exists with the driver you are trying to use with it. It might be corrupt or it could be having a conflict with some other driver. To check the driver, consult Device Manager. If Device Manager shows a conflict with the mouse, remove the driver and allow the system's PnP process to reinstall it.

If the correct driver for the installed mouse is not available, you must install one from the manufacturer. This typically involves placing the manufacturer's driver disk or disc in the appropriate drive and loading the driver using the Update Driver (requires disk from original equipment manufacturer [OEM]) option on the Device Manager Mouse Properties page. If the OEM driver fails to operate the mouse in Windows, you should contact the mouse manufacturer for an updated Windows driver.

Troubleshooting Video

Figure 3.8 depicts the components associated with the video display. As the figure indicates, in the case of hardware problems, the components involved include the video adapter card, the monitor, and, to a lesser degree, the system board.

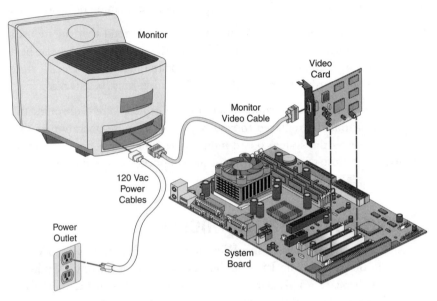

Figure 3.8 Video-related components.

Common symptoms associated with display problems include the following:

➤ There is no display.

➤ The wrong characters are displayed onscreen.

➤ Diagonal lines appear onscreen (no horizontal control).

➤ The display scrolls (no vertical control).

➤ An error code of one long and six short beeps is produced by the system (BIOS dependent).

➤ A CMOS Display Mismatch—Failure to Verify Display Type error displays.

➤ An error code of one long and two short beeps indicates a display adapter problem (BIOS dependent).

➤ Characters are fuzzy.

➤ The monitor displays only a single color.

Video Hardware Checks

The video monitor should come on fairly soon after power has been applied to it. With newer monitors, the monitor is normally only asleep and is awakened through the video adapter card when power is applied to the system. When the system is shut down, the monitor's circuitry senses that no signal is present from the video adapter card and slips into a monitoring mode as long as its power switch is left in the On position.

If the monitor does not wake up early in the system's startup process and present a display, you should assume there is some type of hardware problem—the bootup action and operating system have not been introduced to the system before the single beep tone is produced. However, video problems that occur after the single beep are more likely to be related to operating system configuration settings.

Check the monitor's On/Off switch to see that it is in the On position. Also, check its power cord to see that it is either plugged into the power supply's monitor outlet, or into an active 120V (AC) commercial outlet. In addition, check the monitor's intensity and contrast controls to ensure that they are not turned down.

Determine which of the video-related components is involved. On some monitors, you can do this by just removing the video signal cable from the adapter card. If a raster appears onscreen with the signal cable removed, the problem is probably a system problem, and the monitor is good. If the monitor is an EPA-certified Energy Star–compliant monitor, this test might not work. Monitors that possess this power-saving feature revert to a low-power mode when they do not receive a signal change for a given period of time.

Exchange the monitor for a known-good one of the same type (that is, VGA for VGA). If there is still a video problem, exchange the video controller card with a known-good one of the same type.

Other symptoms that point to the video adapter card include a shaky video display and a high-pitched squeal from the monitor or system unit. If the system still does not perform properly, the source of the problem might be in the system board.

If you can read the contents of the display through the startup process, but then cannot see it after the system boots up, you have an operating system-related video problem. If the Windows video problem prevents you from working with the display, restart the system, press the F8 function key when the "Starting Windows" message appears, and select the Safe Mode option. This should load Windows with the standard 640 × 480 × 16–color VGA driver (the most fundamental driver available for VGA monitors), and should furnish a starting point for installing the correct driver for the monitor being used.

After you have gained access to a usable display, check the installed video drivers. You can access the Windows video information through Device Manager. From this utility, select the Display Adapters entry from the list and double-click the monitor icon that appears as a branch.

The adapter's Properties dialog box should open. The Driver tab reveals the driver file in use. If the video driver listed is not correct, reload the correct driver. Selecting the Resources tab displays the video adapter's register address ranges and the video memory address range, as shown in Figure 3.9. You can manipulate these settings manually by clearing the Use Automatic Settings check box and then clicking the activated Change Settings button. You also can obtain information about the monitor through the System icon.

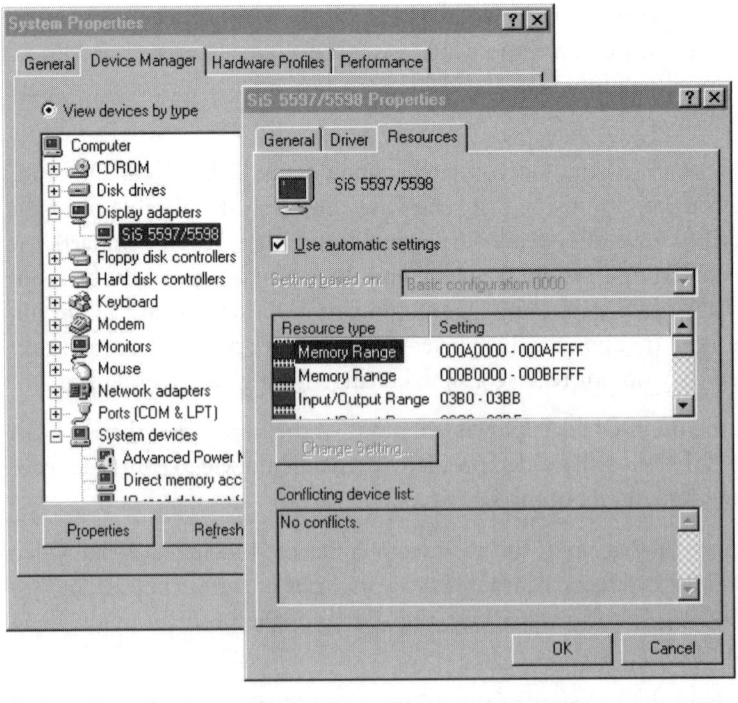

Figure 3.9 Video adapters resources.

You can also gain access to the Windows video information by double-clicking the Display icon found in Control Panel. Of particular interest is the Settings tab. In Windows 95, the Change Display Type button on this tab provides access to both the adapter type and monitor type settings. In Windows 98 and Windows Me, the Advanced button on the Settings tab provides access to both the adapter type and monitor type settings through the Adapter and Monitor tabs.

In Windows 95, the Adapter Type window provides information about the adapter's manufacturer, version number, and current driver files. Clicking the Change button beside this window brings a listing of available drivers from which to select. You also can use the Have Disk button with an OEM disk to install video drivers not included in the list. You also can alter the manner in which the list displays by enabling the Show Compatible Devices or the Show All Devices options.

In Windows 98 and Windows Me, the information about the video adapter card is located on the Adapter tab. Clicking the Change button on this tab produces a wizard that guides the process for changing the drivers for the card. The first option provided by the wizard is to allow Windows to search for the correct driver, or for the user to specify a driver from a list of available drivers. You can also use the Have Disk button to install video drivers from an OEM disk.

If the video problem disappears when lower settings are selected, but reappears when a higher resolution setting is used, refer to the Color Palette box on the Display Properties, Settings tab, and try the minimum color settings. If the problem goes away, contact the Microsoft Download Library (MSDL) service or the adapter card maker for a compatible video driver. If the video problem persists, reinstall Windows. If the video is distorted or rolling, try an alternative video driver from the list.

Some display problems might be caused by incorrectly set front panel display settings. The monitor's front panel controls (either analog or digital) establish parameters for brightness, contrast, screen size and position, and focus. Typical problems associated with these controls include fuzzy characters, poor or missing colors, and incomplete displays.

Actually, there can be several causes of fuzzy characters on the display. The first step in checking out this problem is to reset the display resolution to standard VGA values. If the fuzzy characters remain, check the intensity and contrast controls to see if they are out of adjustment.

Finally, you might need to remove built-up electromagnetic fields from the screen through a process called degaussing. This can be done using a commercial degaussing coil. However, newer monitors have built-in degaussing circuits that can be engaged through their front panel controls. These monitors normally perform a degauss operation each time they are turned on; however, sometimes the user might need to perform this operation.

The front panel controls can also be used to adjust the Red/Green/Blue color mixture for the display. If the monitor is showing poor colors, or only one color, examine the color settings using the front panel controls. If these settings are responsive to change, the problem exists in either the video adapter or the signal cable (broken or bad pin or conductor) or the monitor's color circuitry is deteriorating.

> **You should never remove the outer shell from a CRT video monitor** unless you are trained to work inside the case and it is part of your job. There are very lethal voltage levels (in excess of 25,000 volts) inside the monitor that can remain stored there for some time. Even if the monitor has been unplugged for some time, it can still kill or severely injure you.

Troubleshooting Floppy Disk Drives

Typical symptoms associated with *floppy disk drive* (*FDD*) failures during bootup include the following:

➤ FDD error messages are encountered during the bootup process.

➤ An IBM-compatible 6xx (such as, 601) error code is displayed.

➤ An FDD Controller error message displays, indicating a failure to verify the FDD setup by the system configuration file.

➤ The FDD activity light stays on constantly, indicating that the FDD signal cable is reversed.

Additional FDD error messages commonly encountered during normal system operation include the following:

➤ Disk Drive Read/Write/Seek error messages appear.

➤ The No Boot Record Found message appears, indicating that the system files in the disk's boot sector are missing or have become corrupt.

➤ The system stops working while reading a disk, indicating that the contents of the disk have become contaminated.

➤ The drive displays the same directory listing for every disk inserted in the drive, indicating that the FDD's disk-change detector or signal line is not functional.

A number of things can cause improper floppy disk drive operation or failure. These items include the use of unformatted disks, incorrectly inserted disks, damaged disks, erased disks, loose cables, drive failure, adapter failure, system board failure, or a bad or loose power connector.

Basic FDD Checks

If there is a problem booting the system, insert the bootable floppy disk in the new A drive and turn on the system. If the system does not boot up to the floppy, examine the advanced CMOS setup to check the system's boot order. It might be set so that the FDD is never examined during the bootup sequence.

If the system still does not boot from the floppy, check the disk drive cables for proper connection at both ends. In many systems, the pin-1 designation is difficult to see. Reversing the signal cable causes the FDD activity light to stay on continuously. The reversed signal cable also erases the Master Boot Record (MBR) from the disk, making it nonbootable. Because this is a real possibility, you should always use an expendable backup copy of the boot disk for troubleshooting FDD problems.

 If the system has a second floppy disk drive, turn it off and exchange the drive's connection to the signal cable so that it becomes the A drive. Try to reboot the system using this other floppy disk drive as the A drive.

If there is a problem reading or writing to a particular disk, try the floppy disk in a different computer to determine whether it works in that machine. If not, there is most likely a problem with the format of the disk or the files on the disk. In the case of writing to the disk, you could be dealing with a write-protected disk, but the system normally informs you of this when you attempt to write to it. However, if the other computer can read and write to the disk, you must troubleshoot the floppy drive hardware.

Hardware troubleshooting for floppy disk drives primarily involves exchanging the FDD unit for another one that is working. If necessary, exchange the signal cable with a known-good one. The only other option with most PC-compatible systems is to exchange the system board with a known-good one.

Troubleshooting Hard Disk Drives

Typical symptoms associated with hard disk drive failures include the following:

➤ The front panel indicator lights are visible, and the display is present on the monitor screen, but there is no disk drive action and no bootup.

➤ The computer boots up to a system disk in the A drive, but not to the hard drive, indicating that the system files on the hard disk drive (HDD) are missing or have become corrupt.

➤ The computer does not boot up when turned on.

➤ An IBM-compatible 17xx error code is produced on the display.

➤ No motor sounds are produced by the HDD while the computer is running. (In desktop units, the HDD should generally always run when power is applied to the system—however, this does not apply to all desktops or portables when advanced power-saving features are used.)

➤ A HDD Controller Failure message appears, indicating a failure to verify hard disk setup by system configuration file error.

➤ A C: or D: Fixed Disk Drive error message appears, indicating a hard disk CMOS setup failure.

➤ An Invalid Media Type message appears, indicating the controller cannot find a recognizable track/sector pattern on the drive.

➤ A No Boot Record Found, a Nonsystem Disk or Disk Error, or an Invalid System Disk message appears, indicating that the system boot files are not located in the root directory of the drive.

➤ The video display is active, but the HDD's activity light remains on and no bootup occurs, indicating that the HDD's CMOS configuration information is incorrect.

➤ An Out of Disk Space message appears, indicating that the amount of space on the disk is insufficient to carry out the desired operation.

➤ A Missing Operating System or a Hard Drive Boot Failure message appears, indicating that the disk's MBR is missing or has become corrupt.

➤ A Current Drive No Longer Valid message appears, indicating that the HDD's CMOS configuration information is incorrect or has become corrupt.

HDD Configuration Checks

While booting up the system, observe the BIOS's HDD type information displayed on the monitor. Note the type of HDD that the BIOS recognizes as being installed in the system. Possible error messages associated with HDD configuration problems include the Drive Mismatch Error message and the Invalid Media Type message.

Check the drive to ensure that it is properly terminated. Every drive type requires a termination block somewhere in the interface. For Integrated Drive Electronics (IDE) drives, check the Master/Slave jumper setting to ensure it is set properly for the drive's logical position in the system. Remember that there can only be one master drive selection on each IDE channel. If both drives share an interface and are set to the same selection, neither drive should work.

If you have more than one device attached to a single interface cable, be certain that they are of the same type (for example, all are Enhanced Integrated Drive Electronics [EIDE] devices or all are ATA100 devices). Mixing IDE device types creates a situation in which the system cannot provide the different types of control information each device needs. The drives are incompatible and you might not be able to access either device.

If the drive is a SCSI drive, check to see that its ID has been set correctly and that the SCSI chain has been terminated correctly. Either of these errors results in the system not being able to see the drive. Check the CMOS setup utility to ensure that SCSI support has been enabled along with large SCSI drive support.

Basic HDD Checks

The first task is to determine how extensive the HDD problem is. Place a clean boot disk or an emergency start disk in the A drive and try to boot the system. Then execute a DIR command to access the C drive. If the system can see the contents of the drive, the boot files have been lost or corrupted, but the architecture of the disk is intact.

Modify the DIR command with an /AH or /AS switch (that is, DIR C: /AH or DIR C: /AS) to look in the root directory for the system files and the COMMAND.COM file. It is common to receive a Disk Boot Failure message onscreen if this type of situation occurs.

In Windows 9x and Windows Me systems, if the clean boot disk has a copy of the FDISK program on it, attempt to restore the drive's MBR (including its partition information) by typing the following:

```
A>FDISK /MBR
```

Providing that the hard disk can be accessed with the DIR command, type and enter the following command at the DOS prompt (with the clean boot disk still in the A drive):

```
SYS C:
```

This command copies the IO.SYS, MSDOS.SYS, and COMMAND.COM system files from the boot disk to the hard disk drive. Turn off the system, remove the boot disk from the A drive, and try to reboot the system from the hard drive.

If the system cannot see the drive after booting from the floppy disk, an Invalid Drive message or an Invalid Drive Specification message should be returned in response to any attempt to access the drive. In Windows 9x systems, use the FDISK utility to partition the drive. Next use the FORMAT /S command to make the disk bootable. Any data that was on the drive is lost in the formatting process, but it was already gone because the system could not see the drive.

The process for checking the hard drive on a Windows NT, Windows 2000, or Windows XP computer is similar to the one for checking a Windows 9x-based system. In Windows NT and Windows 2000, the partitioning process is performed through the *Disk Administrator* and *Disk Management* utilities, respectively. These utilities perform all of the basic functions that the FDISK utility does. For instance, both utilities can be used to partition drives and both show you the basic layout of the system's disks.

These disk utilities can also provide advanced functions associated with enterprise (large-scale, business-oriented) computing systems. The Disk Administrator and Disk Management utilities can be used to create both traditional primary and extended partitions for MS-DOS/Windows 9x systems or for Windows NT and Windows 2000 systems. They can also be used to create volumes (partitions that involve space on multiple physical drives).

The Windows 2000 and Windows XP *Disk Management snap-in*, depicted in Figure 3.10, is located under the Computer Management console. To access the Disk Management snap-in, click Start, Settings, Control Panel, Administrative Tools. Double-click the Computer Management icon, and then click the Disk Management entry. Because working with volumes is a major administrative task, you must be logged on as an administrator or as a member of a Windows 2000 Administrators group to carry out this procedure.

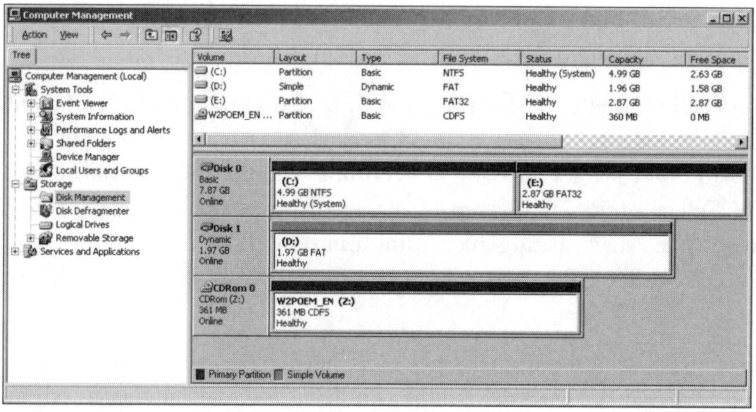

Figure 3.10   Windows 2000 Disk Management snap–in.

Formatting Volumes in Windows 2000 and Windows XP

Formatting a partition or volume prepares the logical structure to accept data by creating the file system in it. If a partition or volume has not been formatted, it does not contain a file system and it cannot be accessed through the operating system or any applications. In the Windows 2000 and Windows XP environment, you can perform many actions to initiate formatting, including the following:

➤ Use the Volume Creation Wizard in the Disk Management utility when the volume is created.

➤ In the Disk Management utility, right-click a volume that has already been created, and then click Format from the shortcut menu.

➤ In Windows Explorer, right-click the desired drive letter, and then click Format from the shortcut menu.

➤ At a command prompt, type the command Format along with the appropriate switches.

> If you format an existing partition or volume, any data residing in the structure is lost. The Windows XP Professional operating system protects its system files by preventing the system and boot partitions from being formatted.

HDD Hardware Checks

If you cannot access the hard disk drive, and its configuration settings are correct, you must troubleshoot the hardware components associated with the hard disk drive. These components include the drive, its signal cable, and the Hard Disk Controller (HDC) on the system board.

Check the HDD signal cable for proper connection at both ends. Exchange the signal cable for a known-good one. Check the Master/Slave jumper settings to ensure they are set correctly. Determine whether the system is using the Cable Select option. This setting enables the system to dynamically assign the master/slave arrangements for multiple IDE drives. Likewise, check the ID configuration settings and terminator installations for SCSI drives.

Although it might seem logical to replace the hard drive unit at this point, it is quite possible that the hard drive might not have any real damage. It might have simply lost track of where it was, and now it cannot find its starting point. In this case, the most attractive option is to reformat the hard disk. This action gives the hard drive a new starting point from which to work. Unfortunately, it also destroys anything that you had stored on the disk.

If the reformatting procedure is not successful, or the system still doesn't boot from the hard drive, replace the hard disk drive unit with a working one.

Troubleshooting CD-ROM Drives

The troubleshooting steps for CD-ROM and DVD drives are nearly identical to those of an HDD system. The connections and data paths are very similar. Basically, three levels of troubleshooting apply to CD-ROM problems. These are the configuration level, the operating system level, and the hardware level.

Basic Checks

In most systems, the CD-ROM and DVD drives share a controller or host adapter with the hard disk drive. Therefore, verify their Master/Slave jumper settings to ensure they are set correctly. Normally, the CD-ROM or DVD drive should be set up as the master on the secondary IDE channel. In this manner, each drive has its own communications channel and does not need to share. If three or four IDE devices are installed in the system, you must determine which devices can share the channels most effectively.

Windows Checks

In the Windows operating systems, you can access the contents of the CD-ROM or DVD through the CD icon in the My Computer applet. The

CD-ROM drive's information is contained in the System Properties dialog box, found by double-clicking the System icon in Control Panel. The Properties of the installed CD-ROM drive are located on the Settings tab. Figure 3.11 shows a typical set of CD-ROM specifications in Windows 9x.

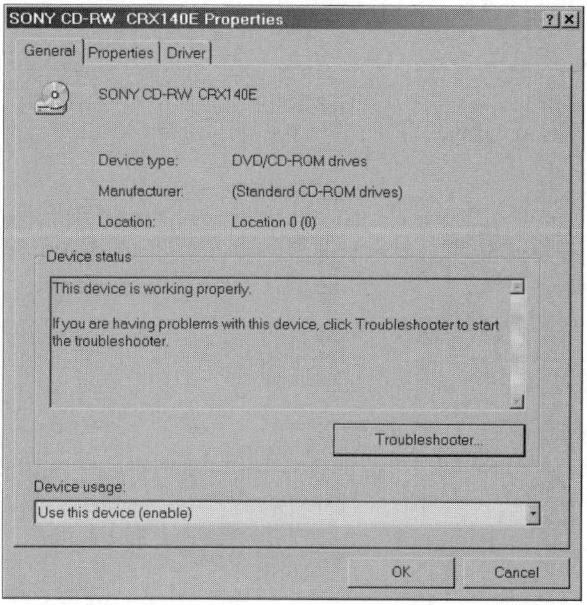

Figure 3.11   CD-ROM specifications in Device Manager.

If the correct drivers are not installed, load them or contact the CD-ROM manufacturer for the correct Windows driver. Check the system for old AUTOEXEC.BAT and CONFIG.SYS files that could contain commands concerning older CD-ROM drives. These commands overrule the Windows CD-ROM configurations and can create problems. Make a copy of the file for backup purposes and remove the MSCDEX lines from the original file.

CD-ROM/DVD Hardware Checks

In many systems, the CD-ROM and DVD drives share a controller or host adapter with the hard disk drive. Therefore, if the hard drive is working and the CD-ROM drive is not, the likelihood that the problem is in the CD-ROM or DVD drive unit is very high.

Before entering the system unit, check for simple user problems:

➤ Is there a CD or DVD in the drive?

➤ Is the label side of the disk facing upward?

➤ Is the disk a CD-ROM or some other type of CD?

If the drive is inoperable and a CD or DVD is locked inside, you should insert a straightened paper clip into the tray-release access hole that's usually located beside the ejection button. This releases the spring-loaded tray and pops out the disc.

If no simple reasons for the problem are apparent, exchange the CD-ROM drive with a known-good one of the same type. If the new drive does not work, check the drive's signal cable for proper connection at both ends. Exchange the signal cable for a known-good one.

Writable Drive Problems

An additional set of problems comes into play when a write or rewrite function is added to the CD-ROM or DVD drive. These problems are concentrated in three basic areas:

➤ The quality of the drive's controller circuitry

➤ The makeup and version of the drive's read/write application interface software

➤ Compatibility with the operating system's multimedia support systems

The quality of the drive is based on the type of controller IC it has. In less expensive drives, the BIOS extension on the drive might not support all of the R/W functions required to coordinate with the application package or the operating system's drivers. Although all newer CD-ROM and DVD drives are ATAPI compatible, they might not have an effective method of controlling Buffer Underrun errors. These errors occur when the system transfers data to the drive faster than the drive can buffer and write it to the disc. The ATAPI compatibility of the chipset ensures that the CD-ROM and DVD read functions work fine, but the nonstandard writing part of the drive might not produce satisfactory results.

Techniques that can be used to minimize buffer underruns include placing the CD-ROM or DVD writer on an IDE channel of its own. This keeps the drive from competing with other drives for the channel's available bandwidth. Also, conducting the write operation on the same drive as the read operation and using reduced write speed options in the R/W software can minimize data flow problems.

In addition, the R/W software for the drive might not be compatible with the operating system version in use, or with the controller chip on the drive. Likewise, the operating system's multimedia enhancement drivers (DirectX in Windows operating systems) might not be compatible with the controller or the R/W application.

Always consult the operating system's hardware and software compatibility lists before buying and installing a CD-RW or DVD-RW drive in a system. This typically means using a more expensive drive, but for now, you do seem to get what you pay for when it comes to rewritable drives.

If the drive has already been purchased, check its documentation for suggestions and check the manufacturer's website for newer R/W applications and driver versions. You might also be able to locate a flash program for the drive's BIOS to upgrade it so that it provides better support for the write function.

Some CD-ROM and DVD R/W applications are simply incompatible with different drive BIOS extension versions or DirectX versions. Check all of the parties involved to find a collection of components that are all compatible with each other.

Troubleshooting Tape Drives

The basic components associated with the tape drive include the tape drive, the signal cable, the power connection, the controller, and the tape drive's operating software. The tape itself can be a source of several problems. Common points to check with the tape include the following:

➤ Is the tape formatted correctly for use with the drive in question?

➤ Is the tape inserted securely in the drive?

➤ Is the tape write-protected?

➤ Is the tape broken or off the reel in the cartridge?

If any jumpers or switches are present on the controller, verify that they are set correctly for the installation. Also, run a diagnostic program to check for resource conflicts that might be preventing the drive from operating (such as interrupt request [IRQ] and base memory addressing).

The software provided with most tape drives includes some error-messaging capabilities. Observe the system and note any tape-related error messages it produces. Consult the user manual for error-message definitions and corrective suggestions. Check for error logs that the software might keep. You can view these logs to determine what errors have been occurring in the system.

Because many tape drives are used in networked and multiuser environments, another problem occurs when you are not properly logged on, or enabled to work with files being backed up or restored. In these situations, the operating system might not allow the tape drive to access secured files, or any files, because the correct clearances have not been met. Consult the network administrator for proper password and security clearances.

Troubleshooting Other Removable Storage Systems

Troubleshooting nontypical removable storage systems is very similar to troubleshooting an external hard drive or tape drive. The system typically consists of an external unit with a plug-in power adapter (anything with a motor in it typically requires an additional power source). These units typically connect to the system through one of its standard I/O port connections. This requires a signal cable that runs between the system and the device. Depending on the exact type of storage device being used, it might have a removable media cartridge or container.

A device driver must be installed for the device to work with the system. This is typically a function of the system's PnP process. The system should detect the external storage and load the driver for it automatically. If the system cannot locate the proper driver, it prompts you to supply the location where the driver can be found. For the most part, external storage systems do not need a support application to be installed. However, you should refer to the device's documentation and follow its installation procedures to determine whether the device can be installed with just a driver.

Check the power supply at the external unit to ensure power is being applied. Most external media devices have power lights to indicate that power is present. Next check the removable media if present, by exchanging it with another cartridge or tape. Next, you should open Device Manager to ensure the device has been recognized there, as well as to check for conflicting device driver information.

If Device Manager cannot see the device after the proper driver has been loaded, and the storage device has power, the final step in checking the system is to check the signal cable by substitution. The only other step typically available is to test the entire storage system on another machine (in most cases, there isn't a second storage system available to use a source of known-good parts).

Troubleshooting Port Problems

Failures of the serial, parallel, and game ports tend to end with poor or no operation of the peripheral. Generally, there are only four possible causes for a problem with a device connected to an I/O port:

➤ The port is defective.

➤ The software is not configured properly for the port (that is, the resource allocation, speed, or protocol settings do not match).

➤ The connecting signal cable is bad.

➤ The attached device is not functional.

Port Problem Symptoms

Typical symptoms associated with serial, parallel, or game port failures include the following:

➤ A 199, 432, or 90x IBM-compatible error code displays on the monitor (printer port).

➤ The printer's Online light is on but no characters are printed when print jobs are sent to the printer.

➤ An 110x IBM-compatible error code displays on the monitor (serial port error).

➤ A Device Not Found error message displays, or you have an unreliable connection.

➤ The input device does not work on the game port.

Basic Port Checks

With newer Pentium systems, you must check the advanced CMOS setup to determine whether the port in question has been enabled and, if so, whether it has been configured correctly. Check the PC board that contains the I/O port circuitry (and its user guide) for configuration information. This normally involves LPT, COM, and IRQ settings. Occasionally, you must set up hexadecimal addressing for the port addresses; however, this is becoming rare as PnP systems improve. For example, a modern parallel port must be enabled and set to the proper protocol type to operate advanced peripherals.

For typical printer operations, the setting can normally be set to Standard Parallel Port (SPP) mode. However, devices that use the port in a bidirectional manner need to be set to Enhanced Parallel Port (EPP) or Enhanced Capabilities Port (ECP) mode for proper operation. In both cases, the protocol must be set properly for the port and the device to carry out communications.

If serial or parallel port problems are occurring, the CMOS configuration window displayed during the startup sequence is the first place to look. Read the port assignments in the bootup window. If the system has not detected the presence of the port hardware at this stage, none of the more advanced levels will find it either. If values for any of the physical ports installed in the system do not appear in this window, check for improper port configuration.

Because the system has not loaded an operating system at the time the configuration window appears, the operating system cannot be a source of port problems at this time. If all configuration settings for the ports appear correct, assume that a hardware problem exists.

Basic Parallel Ports

Run a software diagnostic package to narrow the possible problem causes. This is not normally a problem because port failures generally do not affect the main components of the system. Software diagnostic packages normally require you to place a loopback plug in the parallel port connector to run tests on the port. The loopback plug simulates a printer device by redirecting output signals from the port into port input pins.

You can use a live printer with the port for testing purposes; however, this action elevates the possibility that the printer might inject a problem into the troubleshooting process.

If there is a printer switch box between the computer and the printer, remove the print-sharing equipment, connect the computer directly to the printer, and try to print directly to the device.

Basic Serial Ports

As with parallel ports, diagnostic packages typically ask you to place a serial loopback test plug in the serial port connector to run tests on the port. Use the diagnostic program to determine whether any IRQ or addressing conflicts exist between the serial port and other installed options. The serial loopback plug is physically wired differently from a parallel loopback plug so that it can simulate the operation of a serial device.

You can also attach a live serial device to the port for testing purposes but, like the printer, this elevates the possibility that the port might inject other problems into the troubleshooting process.

Windows Printer Checks

You can reach the I/O port functions in Windows 9x, Windows Me, and Windows 2000 through two avenues. You can access port information through the Start menu (Start, Settings). You also can reach this information through the My Computer icon on the desktop. Printer port information can be viewed through the Printers icon; serial port information is accessed through Device Manager. In Windows XP, the Printers and Faxes folder is located directly on the Start menu.

Windows Parallel Ports

Check to determine whether the Print option from the application's File menu is unavailable (gray). If so, check the My Computer, Printers window for correct parallel port settings. Be certain that the correct printer driver is selected for the printer being used. If no printer (or the wrong printer type) is selected, use the Add Printer Wizard to install and set up the desired printer.

The system's printer configuration information is also available through the Device Manager tab in the System Properties dialog box (found by double-clicking the System icon in Control Panel). Check this location for printer port setting information. Also, check the definition of the printer by double-clicking the Printer icon found in Control Panel.

The Windows operating systems come with embedded tools called *troubleshooters*, one of which is designed to help solve printing problems. To use the Printing Troubleshooter, access the Windows *Help* system through the Start menu and navigate to the Print Troubleshooter (or Printing Troubleshooter in Windows XP). The troubleshooter asks a series of questions about the printing setup. After you have answered all of its questions, the troubleshooter returns a list of recommendations for fixing the problem.

If the conclusions of the troubleshooter do not clear up the problem, try printing a document to a file. This enables you to separate the printing software from the port hardware.

Continue troubleshooting the port by checking the printer driver to ensure that it is the correct driver and version number. Right-click the Printer icon and click Properties from the shortcut menu. Click the Details tab to view the driver's name. Click the About entry under the Device Options tab to verify the driver's version number.

Click the printer port in question (after double-clicking the Printer icon) to open the Print Manager screen. Check the Print Manager for errors that have occurred and that might be holding up the printing of jobs that follow it. If an error is hanging up the print function, highlight the offending job and remove it from the print spool by clicking the Delete Document entry on the Document menu.

Windows 9x and Windows Me Serial Ports

Information on the system's serial ports is contained in three areas in Device Manager. These are the Resources entry, the Driver entry, and the Port Settings entry. The Resources entry displays port address ranges and IRQ assignments. The Driver entry displays the names of the installed device drivers and their locations. The Port Settings entry contains speed and character frame information for the serial ports. The Advanced entry under Port Settings enables you to adjust the transmit and receive buffer speeds for better operation.

Check the Device Manager window for correct serial port settings. Check the correct serial port settings under Windows 9x:

1. Click the Port Settings option to see the setup for the ports. Most serial printers use settings of 9600 Baud, No Parity, 8 Bits, 1 Stop Bit, and Hardware Handshaking (Xon-Xoff).

2. Click the Resources button to determine the IRQ setup for the port.

3. Check the user's manual to document the correct settings for the device using the port in question.

USB Port Checks

Because nearly any type of peripheral device can be added to the PC through a USB port, the range of symptoms associated with a USB device can include all the symptoms listed for peripheral devices in this chapter. Therefore, problems associated with USB ports can be addressed in three general areas:

➤ The USB hardware device

➤ The USB controller

➤ The USB drivers

As with other port types, begin troubleshooting USB port problems by checking the CMOS setup screens to ensure that the USB function is enabled there. If it is enabled in CMOS, check in Device Manager to verify that the USB controller appears there. In Windows 2000, the USB controller should be listed under the Universal Serial Bus Controllers entry, or in the Human Interface Devices entry (using the default Devices by Type setting).

If the USB controller does not appear in Device Manager, or a yellow warning icon appears next to the controller, the system's BIOS might be outdated. Contact the BIOS manufacturer for an updated copy of the BIOS.

If the controller is present in Device Manager, right-click the USB controller entry and click Properties. If any problems exist, a message appears in the device status window, shown in Figure 3.12, describing any problems and suggesting what action to take.

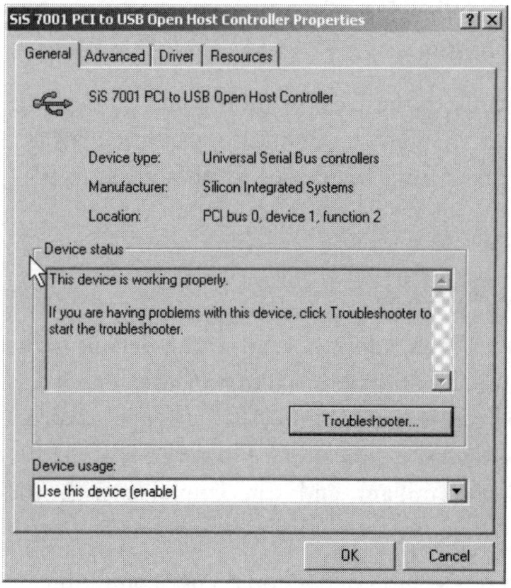

Figure 3.12 The USB Controller Properties dialog box.

If the BIOS and controller settings appear to be correct, the next items to check are the USB port drivers. These ports have a separate entry in Device Manager that you can access by clicking the Universal Serial Bus Controllers option, right-clicking the USB Root Hub entry, and then clicking Properties.

If a USB device does not install itself automatically, you might have conflicting drivers loaded for that device and might need to remove them.

To remove potentially conflicting USB drivers, complete the following steps:

1. Disconnect any USB devices connected to the system and start the system in safe mode.

2. Under Windows 2000, you are asked about which operating system to use. Use the up- and down-arrow keys to highlight Windows 2000 Professional or Windows 2000 Server, and then press Enter.

   If alert messages appear, read each alert and then click the OK button to close it.

3. Open Device Manager, click the desired USB device, and then click the Remove button.

   Your particular USB device might be listed under Universal Serial Bus Controller, Other Devices, Unknown Devices, or a particular device category (such as the Modem entry if the device is a USB modem).

4. Click the Start menu, select the Shut Down option, select the Restart entry, and then click the OK button.

5. Connect the USB device directly to the USB port on your computer. If the system does not autodetect the device, you must install the drivers manually. You might need drivers from the device manufacturer to perform this installation.

IEEE-1394 Adapters and Ports

Because Pentium-based PCs have largely adopted USB as the default high-speed bus, FireWire buses are implemented by installing an adapter card in the system to furnish the physical connection points. Also, there is no direct BIOS support for IEEE-1394 buses in the typical PC. However, IEEE-1394 adapter cards are plug-and-play compliant and can converse with the Windows operating systems.

The FireWire devices that attach to the bus connection do not communicate directly with the system; they work with the controller on the adapter card. Therefore, after the adapter card has been installed, you must troubleshoot it as you would any other adapter card based peripheral. The system should detect the new card when it is installed and load the driver for it automatically. If the system cannot locate the proper driver, it prompts you to supply the location where the driver can be found.

Next, you should open Device Manager to ensure the device has been recognized there and to check for conflicting device driver information (for example, an exclamation point in a yellow circle).

If Device Manager cannot see the device after the proper driver has been loaded, and the attached device has power, the final step is to check the IEEE-1394 cabling and connectors for continuity and good connections. Also verify that the correct FireWire cables are being used (a four-pin device cannot draw power through the FireWire bus). If the device employs its own power supply, verify that power is being applied to it.

If the FireWire bus runs particularly slow, and you have multiple devices attached to the system, you might have a situation in which the slower device in the middle of the chain is slowing everything down. Move the slower device (such as a Camcorder) to the end of the signal chain.

Troubleshooting Infrared Ports

The Infrared Data Association (IrDA) protocols for infrared communications specify communication ranges up to 2 meters (6 feet), but most specifications usually state 1 meter as the maximum range. All IrDA transfers are carried out in half-duplex mode and must have a clear line of sight between the transmitter and receiver. The receiver must be situated within 15 degrees of center with the line of transmission. Therefore, you should test a failing infrared connection by placing the infrared transceivers as close together as possible and straight inline with each other.

The properties of installed IrDA devices can be viewed through their entries in Device Manager. Verify that the *Enable Infrared* communication check box is checked. To engage support for infrared plug-and-play devices, right-click the Infrared icon on the taskbar. Verify that the Enable Plug and Play option is checked. It will only be available if the infrared and searching functions are enabled. If the taskbar icon is not visible, click the Infrared Monitor icon in Control Panel, click the Preferences tab, and select the Display the Infrared Monitor Icon on the Taskbar option.

Right-click the Infrared icon on the taskbar to install software for an infrared device. Verify that the Enable Plug and Play option is checked and verify that the new device is within range.

Windows also provides an *Infrared Monitor* utility that can be used to track the computer's activity. When this utility is running, it alerts you when infrared devices are within range of your computer by placing the Infrared icon on the taskbar. The Infrared Monitor not only notifies you when the computer is communicating with an infrared device, but it also indicates how well it is communicating.

Troubleshooting Modems

A section on troubleshooting modems has to be subdivided into two segments:

➤ External modems

➤ Internal modems

You should check an internal modem using the same basic sequence as any other I/O card. First, check its hardware and software configuration, check the system for conflicts, and check for correct drivers.

Improper software setup is the most common cause of modems not working when they are first installed. Inspect any cabling connections to see that they are connected correctly and functioning properly, and test the modem's hardware by substitution.

If an external modem is being checked, it must be treated as an external peripheral, with the serial port being treated as a separate I/O port.

Modem Symptoms

Typical symptoms associated with modem failures include the following:

➤ There is no response from the modem.

➤ The modem does not dial out.

➤ The modem does not connect after a number has been dialed.

➤ The modem does not transmit after making connection with a remote unit.

➤ The modem does not install properly for operation.

➤ Garbled messages are transmitted.

➤ The modem cannot terminate a communication session.

➤ The modem cannot transfer files.

COM Port Conflicts

Every COM port on a PC requires an IRQ line to signal the processor for attention. In most PC systems, two COM ports share the same IRQ line. The IRQ4 line works for COM1 and COM3, and the IRQ3 line works for

COM2 and COM4. This is common in PC compatibles. The technician must ensure that two devices are not set up to use the same IRQ channel.

If more than one device is connected to the same IRQ line, a conflict occurs because it is not likely that the interrupt handler software can service both devices. Therefore, the first step to take when installing a modem is to check the system to determine how its interrupts and COM ports are allocated.

To install a non-PnP device on a specific COM port (for example, COM2), you must first disable that port in the system's CMOS settings to avoid a device conflict. If not, the system might try to allocate that resource to some other device because it has no way of knowing that the non-PnP device requires it.

Windows Modem Checks

In Windows 9x, you can find the modem configuration information by navigating to Control Panel, Modems. The Modems Properties dialog box has two tabs—the General tab and the Diagnostics tab. The Diagnostics tab, shown in Figure 3.13, provides access to the modem's driver and additional information.

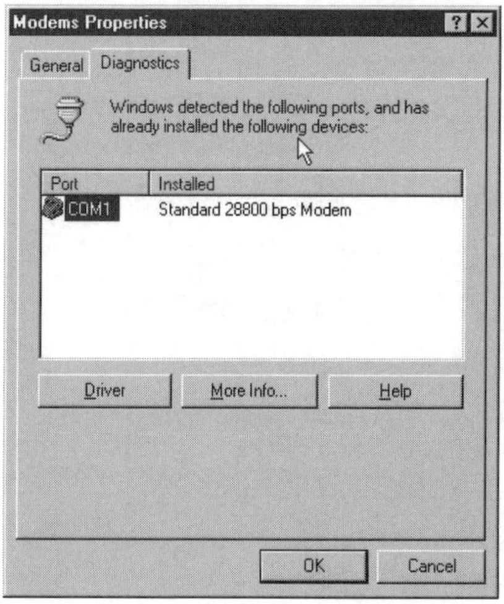

Figure 3.13   The Windows 9x Diagnostics Tab of the Modems Properties dialog box.

In Windows XP, the Diagnostics tab for the modem is available by clicking the Properties button on the Modems tab of the Phone and Modem Options dialog box. The Query Modem button on this tab can be used to perform low-level tests on the modem.

The Hayes **AT** Command Set

The Hayes command set is based on a group of instructions that begin with a pair of attention characters, followed by command words. Because the attention characters are an integral part of every Hayes command, the command set is often referred to as the AT command set.

AT commands are entered at the command line using an ATXn format. The Xn nomenclature identifies the type of command being given (X) and the particular function to be used (n).

Except for the ATA, ATDn, and ATZn commands, the AT sequence can be followed by any number of commands. The ATA command forces the modem to immediately pick up the phone line (even if it does not ring). The Dn commands are dialing instructions, and the Zn commands reset the modem by loading new default initialization information into it. After a command has been entered at the command line, the modem attempts to execute the command and then returns a result code to the screen. Table 3.2 describes the command result codes.

Table 3.2	AT Command Result Codes	
RESULT	CODE	DESCRIPTION
0	OK	The OK code is returned by the modem to acknowledge execution of a command line.
1	CONNECT	The modem sends this result code when line speed is 300 bps.
2	RING	The modem sends this result code when incoming ringing is detected on the line.
3	NO CARRIER	The carrier is not detected within the time limit, or the carrier is lost.
4	ERROR	The modem could not process the command line (entry error).
5	CONNECT 1200	The modem detected a carrier at 1200 bps.
6	NO DIAL TONE	The modem could not detect a dial tone when dialing.
7	BUSY	The modem detected a busy signal.
8	NO ANSWER	The modem never detected silence (@ command only).
9	CONNECT 0600	The modem sends this result code when line speed is 7200 bps.
10	CONNECT 2400	The modem detected a carrier at 2400 bps.
11	CONNECT 4800	Connection is established at 4800 bps.
12	CONNECT 9600	Connection is established at 9600 bps.
13	CONNECT 7200	The modem sends this result code when the line speed is 7200 bps.
14	CONNECT 12000	Connection is established at 12000 bps.
15	CONNECT 14400	Connection is established at 14400 bps.
16	CONNECT 38400	Connection is established at 38400 bps.
17	CONNECT 57600	Connection is established at 57600 bps.
22	CONNECT 75TX/1200RX	The modem sends this result code when establishing a V.23 Originate.
23	CONNECT 1200TX/75RX	The modem sends this result code when establishing a V.23 answer.
24	DELAYED	The modem returns this result code when a call fails to connect and is considered delayed.
32	BLACKLISTED	The modem returns this result code when a call fails to connect and is considered blacklisted.
40	CARRIER 300	The carrier is detected at 300 bps.
44	CARRIER 1200/75	The modem sends this result code when V.23 backward channel carrier is detected.
45	CARRIER 75/1200	The modem sends this result code when V.23 forward channel carrier is detected.
46	CARRIER 1200	The carrier is detected at 1200 bps.
47	CARRIER 2400	The carrier is detected at 2400 bps.
48	CARRIER 4800	The modem sends this result code when either the high or low channel carrier in V.22bis modem has been detected.
49	CARRIER 7200	The carrier is detected at 7200 bps.
50	CARRIER 9600	The carrier is detected at 9600 bps.
51	CARRIER 12000	The carrier is detected at 12000 bps.
52	CARRIER 14400	The carrier is detected at 14400 bps.
66	COMPRESSION: CLASS 5	MNP Class 5 is active CLASS 5.
67	COMPRESSION: V.42bis	COMPRESSION: V.42bis is active V.42bis.
69	COMPRESSION: NONE	No data compression signals NONE.
70	PROTOCOL: NONE	No error correction is enabled.
77	PROTOCOL: LAPM	V.42 LAP-M error correction is enabled.
80	PROTOCOL: ALT	MNP Class 4 error correction is enabled.

Using the **AT** Command Set

At the command line, type ATZ to reset the modem and enter command mode using the Hayes-compatible command set. You should receive a 0, or OK response, if the command was processed. A returned OK code indicates that the modem and the computer are communicating properly.

You can use other AT-compatible commands to check the modem at the command-prompt level. The ATL2 command sets the modem's output volume to medium, to ensure it is not set too low to be heard. If the modem dials, but cannot connect to a remote station, check the modem's Speed and DTR settings. Change the DTR setting by entering AT&Dn.

➤ **n = 0**—The modem ignores the DTR line.

➤ **n = 1**—The modem goes to async command state when the DTR line goes off.

➤ **n = 2**—A DTR off condition switches the modem to the off-hook state and back into command mode.

➤ **n = 3**—When the DTR line switches to off, the modem is initialized.

If the modem connects, but cannot communicate, check the character-framing parameter of the receiving modem, and set the local modem to match. Also, match the terminal emulation of the local unit to that of the remote unit. American National Standards Institute (ANSI) terminal emulation is the most common. Finally, match the file transfer protocol to the other modem.

During a data transfer, both modems monitor the signal level of the carrier to prevent the transfer of false data due to signal deterioration. If the carrier signal strength drops below a predetermined threshold level, or is lost for a given length of time, one or both modems initiate automatic disconnect procedures.

Use the ATDT*70 command to disable call waiting if the transmission is frequently garbled. The +++ command interrupts any activity the modem is engaged in, and brings it to command mode.

Modem Hardware Checks

Modems have the capability to perform three different kinds of self-diagnostic tests:

➤ The local digital loopback test

➤ The local analog loopback test

➤ The remote digital loopback test

If transmission errors occur frequently, you should use the various loopback tests to locate the source of the problem. Begin by running the remote digital loopback test. If the test runs successfully, the problem is likely to be located in the remote computer.

If the test fails, run the local digital loopback test with self-tests. If the test results are positive, the problem might be located in the local computer. On the other hand, you should run the local analog loopback test if the local digital test fails.

If the local analog test fails, the problem is located in the local modem. If the local analog test is successful, and problems are occurring, you should run the local analog test on the remote computer. The outcome of this test should pinpoint the problem to the remote computer or the remote modem.

If the modem is an internal unit, you can test its hardware by exchanging it with a known-good unit. If the telephone line operates correctly with a normal handset, only the modem, its configuration, or the communications software can be causes of problems. If the modem's software and configuration settings appear correct and problems are occurring, the modem hardware is experiencing a problem and it is necessary to exchange the modem card for a known-good one.

With an external modem, you can use the front panel lights as diagnostic tools to monitor its operation. You can monitor the progress and handling of a call, along with any errors that might occur.

Troubleshooting Sound Cards

Most sound cards perform two separate functions. The first is to play sound files; the second is to record them. You might need to troubleshoot problems for either function.

Sound Card Configuration Checks

In the past, sound cards have been notorious for interrupt conflict problems with other devices. Because these conflicts typically exist between peripheral devices, they might not appear during bootup. If the sound card operates correctly except when a printing operation is in progress, for example, an IRQ conflict probably exists between the sound card and the printer port. Similar symptoms would be produced for tape backup operations if the tape drive and the sound card were configured to use the same IRQ channel. Use a software diagnostic program to check the system for interrupt conflicts.

Checking the system for resource conflicts in Windows is relatively easy. Access Control Panel and double-click the System icon. From this point, click Device Manager and select the Sound, Video, and Game Controller option. If the system detects any conflicts, it places an exclamation point within a circle on the selected option.

From Device Manager, choose the proper sound card driver from the list and move into its Resource window. The page's main window displays all the resources the driver is using for the card. The Conflicting Device List window provides information about any conflicting resource that the system has detected in conjunction with the sound card.

If the Windows PnP function is operating properly, you should be able to remove the driver from the system, reboot the computer, and allow the operating system to redetect the sound card and assign new resources to it.

Check to verify that the Multimedia icon is installed in Control Panel and available through the Start, Programs, Accessories path (Start, All Programs, Accessories, Entertainment in Windows XP). Also, check Device Manager to see that the correct audio driver is installed and that its settings match those called for by the sound card manufacturer. If the drivers are missing, or wrong, add them to the system through the Add/Remove Hardware Wizard found in Control Panel.

If the driver is not installed, or is incorrect, add the correct driver from the Available Drivers list. If the correct driver is not available, reinstall it from the card's OEM disk or obtain it from the card's manufacturer.

Sound Card Hardware Checks

These checks include determining that the speakers are plugged into the speaker port. It is not uncommon for the speakers to be mistakenly plugged into the card's MIC (microphone) port. Likewise, if the sound card does not record sound, verify that the microphone is installed in the proper jack (not the speaker jack) and that it is turned on. Check the amount of disk space on the drive to ensure that there is enough to hold the file being produced.

In the case of stereo speaker systems, it is possible to place the speakers on the wrong sides. This produces a problem when you try to adjust the balance between them. Increasing the volume on the right speaker increases the output of the left speaker. The obvious cure for this problem is to physically switch the positions of the speakers.

Troubleshooting Network Cards

Cabling is one of the biggest problems encountered in a network installation. Is it connected? Are all the connections good? Is the cable type correct? Has there been any termination, and if so, has it been done correctly? The most efficient way to test network cable is to use a line tester to check its functionality.

With UTP cabling, simply unplug the cable from the adapter card and plug it into the tester. If coaxial cable is used, you must unplug both ends of the cable from the network, install a terminating resistor at one end of the cable, and plug the other end into the tester. The tester performs the tests required to analyze the cable and connection.

Most network adapter cards come from the manufacturer with an OEM disk or CD-ROM of drivers and diagnostic utilities for that particular card. You can run these diagnostic utilities to verify that the LAN hardware is functioning properly.

However, it might be easier to run the Windows PING utility from the command prompt and attempt to connect to the network. In a LAN environment, you need to know the IP address or the name of a remote computer in the network to which you can direct the PING. Both PING and TRACERT can be used to identify the IP address of a known network address.

 Extensive additional information about **PING**, **TRACERT**, and the other TCP/IP utilities and there usage is provided in Chapter 5, "Important Resources."

Check the activity of the light on the back plate of the LAN card (if available) to determine whether the network is recognizing the network adapter card. If the lights are active, the connection is alive. If not, check the adapter in another node. Check the LAN cabling to ensure it is the correct type and that the connector is properly attached. A LAN cable tester is an excellent device to have in this situation.

Working on Portable Systems

One of the biggest problems for portable computers is heat buildup inside the case. Because conventional power supplies (and their fans) are not included in portable units, separate fans must be designed in portables to carry the heat out of the unit. The closeness of the portable's components and the small amount of free air space inside their cases also adds to heat-related design problems.

The internal PC boards of the portable computer are designed to fit around the nuances of the portable case and its components, rather than to match a standard design with standard spacing and connections. Therefore, inter-changeability of parts with other machines or makers goes by the wayside. The only source of most portable computer parts, with the exception of PC Cards and disk drive units, is the original manufacturer. Even the battery case might be proprietary. If the battery dies, you must hope that the original maker has a supply of that particular model.

Although adding RAM and options to desktop and tower units is a relatively easy and straightforward process, the same tasks in notebook computers can be difficult. In some notebooks, you must disassemble the two halves of the case and remove the keyboard to add RAM modules to the system. In other portables, the hinged display unit must be removed to disassemble the unit. Inside the notebook, you might find several of the components are hidden behind other units. Figure 3.14 demonstrates a relatively simple disassembly process for a notebook unit.

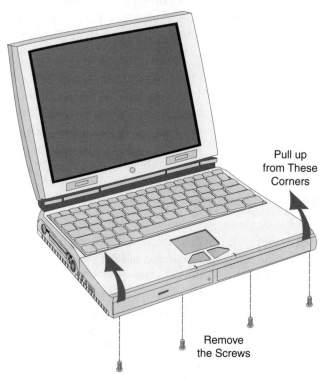

Figure 3.14 Disassembling a notebook computer.

In this example, a panel in front of the keyboard can be removed to gain access to the notebook's internal user-serviceable components. Four screws along the front edge of the unit's lower body must be removed. Afterward, the LCD panel is opened and the front panel of the notebook's chassis is pulled up and away to expose a portion of the unit's interior.

Troubleshooting PCMCIA Problems

One of the mainstays of portable computer products is the credit card-like *PCMCIA cards*, also known as *PC Cards*. The process for troubleshooting PC Cards is nearly identical to troubleshooting other I/O adapter cards.

PCMCIA cards can be plugged into the system at any time and the system should recognize them. In most cases, Windows 9x, Windows Me, Windows 2000, and Windows XP have a copy of the necessary driver software for the PCMCIA adapter being installed and will install it automatically when it detects the adapter. Most Windows operating system versions display messages telling you that they are installing the drivers required. However, Windows 2000 and Windows XP just install the drivers without a notice.

In cases in which the operating system does not have the necessary driver software, it prompts you for a path to the location where the driver can be loaded, when it detects the adapter. PCMCIA manufacturers typically supply drivers for various operating systems on a floppy disk or a CD that comes with the adapter.

To verify that the PC Card device is working, access Device Manager. If there is a problem with the PC Card device, it appears in Device Manager. If the PCMCIA adapter's icon shows an exclamation mark on a yellow background, the card is not functioning properly. Turn the system off and reinsert the device in a different PCMCIA slot. If the same problem appears, three possible sources of problems exist—the card might be faulty, the PC Card controller in the PC might be faulty, or the operating system might not support the device in question.

If the Windows Device Manager displays the PCMCIA socket but no name for the card, the card insertion has been recognized but the socket could not read the device's configuration information from the card. This indicates a problem with the PCMCIA socket installation. To correct this problem, remove the PCMCIA socket listing from Device Manager, reboot the computer, and allow the Windows PnP process to detect the socket and install the appropriate driver for it. If the names of the PCMCIA cards do not appear after the restart, the reinstallation process was not successful.

Therefore, the PCMCIA socket you are using is not supported by the operating system version.

If the names of other PCMCIA cards do appear in the Device Manager, but the card in question does not, it is likely that the card has been damaged. To test the PC Card device, insert a different PC Card device of any type in the slot. If the other card works, it is very likely that the card in question has been damaged.

Troubleshooting Portable Unique Storage

As with other PCMCIA devices, PC Card hard drives are self-contained. Plug them into the PCMCIA slot and the system should detect them (they are hot-swappable). If the system does not detect the card/hard drive, use the troubleshooting steps described for other PCMCIA devices.

Troubleshooting Batteries

If you turn your portable computer on and nothing happens, the first things to check out include the power supply and the battery. If the power supply is plugged in, the computer should start up when the On/Off switch is engaged. However, if the computer is running on battery power and the system does not start up, the battery could be bad or need to be charged.

Verify that the battery doesn't need a recharge by trying to start the system with the AC power adapter plugged in. Check the power indicator in the system display panel. If it is on, power is being supplied to the portable. If the indicator is not on, verify that the power cord is securely connected to a live power source. Check all the power connections to ensure that the AC adapter jack is securely connected to the AC adapter port.

If the portable still doesn't start up, you must troubleshoot the system board. If the system runs from the AC adapter, the battery needs to be recharged or replaced.

Although a dead system is a classic battery/power-supply problem, you might encounter several other battery-related problems with portable computers. These include problems that present the following types of symptoms:

➤ You receive warning messages about the battery not charging.

➤ The computer experiences intermittent system shut downs when operating with only the battery.

➤ The computer does not recognize its network connection when operating with only the battery.

➤ The computer and input devices are slow when operating with only the battery.

➤ The computer loses the time and date information when operating on battery power.

A loose or improperly installed battery can cause these problems. They can also appear when the battery is toward the end of its charge/recharge cycle. Check the installation and attempt to recharge the battery using the portable computer's AC adapter.

The actual life of a laptop computer battery varies from just under one hour to over two hours in each sitting. If you are experiencing battery life cycles that are significantly shorter than this (for example, 10 to 15 minutes), you might have a problem referred to as *battery memory*.

Battery memory is a condition that occurs with some types of batteries in which the battery becomes internally conditioned to run for less time than its designed capacity (for example, if you routinely operate the computer using the battery for an hour and then plug it back in to an AC source, the battery can become conditioned to only run for that amount of time).

To correct battery memory problems, you must fully discharge the battery and then recharge it. To accomplish this, complete the following steps:

1. Turn the portable's Power Management feature off by accessing the Power Management icon in the Windows Control Panel.

2. Restart the computer and access the CMOS setup utility during bootup.

3. Disable the power management functions in the CMOS settings.

4. Start the portable computer using only the battery and allow it to run until it completely discharges the battery and quits.

5. Recharge the battery for at least 12 hours.

6. Repeat this process several times watching for consistently increasing operating times.

Troubleshooting Docking Stations/Port Replicators

Most docking stations offer an internal power supply that can operate the portable and its peripheral attachments: an external parallel port for printers, a serial port for serial devices (mice and modems), USB ports, external VGA/DVI video and full size keyboard connections, and audio connections for external speakers.

In addition, the docking station can host several types of external storage devices, including full-sized FDD/HDD/CD-ROM/DVD drives. Docking stations might also include one or two PCI slots that allow full-sized desktop adapter cards (SCSI or specialized video or LAN card) to be added to the system when it is docked. They might also provide multiple PCMCIA slots that add to the existing PC Card capabilities of the portable it is supporting.

For the most part, these connections are simply physical extensions of the ports provided by the portable. Therefore, if the port works on the portable and doesn't work when connection is made through the docking station, generally something is wrong with the docking station/port replicator. However, many portable computers employ special keystroke combinations (Fn + some other key) to activate external devices, such as a video display monitors or full-size keyboards.

For example, some portables detect that the external video display has been attached. Others use an Fn key combination to switch the display to the external monitor only, and then use another Fn key combination to send the display to both the LCD panel and the external display (that is, internal, external, or both).

If a peripheral device is not working, one of the first steps to take is to refer to the portable's documentation to ensure that the external device has been activated.

For audio problems, verify that the speakers are connected to the correct RCA mini jacks (not the Line IN or Microphone jacks). Check the documentation to ensure the sound output has not been muted using an Fn key combination.

On Windows operating systems, the hardware profile information for the portable computer can be configured differently for docked and undocked situations. When the computer is docked and turned on, its configuration is reset and the *Eject PC* option appears on the Start menu. However, when the computer is not docked, the Eject PC option is automatically removed from the Start menu.

The Windows 2000 and Windows XP Professional operating systems use hardware profiles to determine which drivers to load when the system hardware changes (docked or undocked). It uses the *Docked Profile* to load drivers when the portable computer is docked and the Undocked Profile when the computer starts up without the docking station. These hardware profiles are created by the Windows XP operating system when the computer is docked and undocked if the system is PnP compliant.

If a portable is not PnP compliant, you must manually configure the profile by enabling and disabling various devices present when docked and undocked.

The first check is to verify the power cord connection and docking power supply. Next verify that the portable has been properly inserted in the docking station or port replicator.

If a single docking station connection does not work, bypass the docking station/replicator and try to operate the peripheral directly with the portable unit. Check the power supply for both the docking station and the peripheral device and verify that both are turned on. Reboot the portable while it is attached to the docking station. Then check any signal cables between the docking station and the peripheral.

If the PS/2 mouse connection does not work, verify that it has not been installed in the PS/2 keyboard connector by mistake. Verify that the mouse port is enabled in the CMOS setup utility. Likewise, if you are using a USB or serial mouse, verify that the port is enabled in CMOS and that it is connected to the correct port.

Check the serial port's configuration settings to verify that a proper device driver has been installed for the mouse.

If the portable's touch pad works but the external mouse does not, check the computer's documentation for an Fn key combination requirement for the mouse.

Operating System Troubleshooting

Introduction

Troubleshooting operating system problems involves the same steps as any other logical troubleshooting procedure. The steps are just adapted to fit the structure of the operating system. Analyze the symptoms displayed, isolate the error conditions, correct the problem, and test the repair.

Unless you are installing a new operating system or upgrading a system to a new operating system, you must deal with basically two categories of operating system problems—*startup problems* (those that occur when the system is booting up) and *operational problems* (those that occur during the normal course of operations). By isolating a particular software problem to one of these areas, the troubleshooting process becomes less complex.

Startup problems usually produce conditions that prevent the system hardware and operating system software from starting up and running correctly. Operational problems are problems that occur after the system has booted up and started running.

General Computer Startup Problems

Fortunately, only a few problems can occur during the startup process of a disk-based computer. These problems include the following general categories:

➤ Hardware failures

➤ Configuration problems

➤ Bootup (or operating system startup) problems

➤ Operating system desktop graphical user interface (GUI) won't load

Types of Startup Troubleshooting Tools

All four of the previously listed problem types can result in startup failures. Some prevent any activity from appearing in the system, others produce symptoms that can be tracked to a cause, and yet others produce error messages that can be tracked to a source. When dealing with starting up a disk operating system, the following four items can prove very useful to help you isolate the cause of startup problems:

➤ Error messages and beep codes

➤ Clean boot disks (emergency start disks)

➤ Alternative startup modes (safe mode, single-step, and command prompt only startup procedures)

➤ System log files

The process normally used to sort out startup problems involves the following:

1. Try to reboot the system.

2. Check system log files if available to determine where the process was interrupted.

3. Perform a clean boot with minimal configuration settings to remove nonessential elements from the process.

4. Perform a safe mode startup to start the system in its most basic arrangement.

5. Perform a single-step startup to isolate any driver problems that are preventing bootup from taking place.

Troubleshooting Bootup/Startup Problems

Under Windows operating systems, startup problems can be divided into two subgroups—*bootup problems* and *OS startup problems*. Generally, bootup problems involve the activities that occur between the single beep and the time the Starting Windows message appears on the screen.

Startup problems occur between the appearance of the message and the appearance of the Windows desktop on the display. How you troubleshoot these problems depends somewhat on when these problems actually occur.

 A key troubleshooting point occurs at the single beep in the bootup process of most computers. If the system produces an error message, or a beep-coded error signal, before the single beep, the problem is hardware-related. On the other hand, if the error message or beep code is produced after the single beep occurs, the problem is likely to be associated with starting up the operating system. At this point, the problem becomes primarily a software problem (in particular, an operating system startup problem).

Using Boot/Emergency Disks

If the system startup routine makes it past the beep, but does not arrive at the Starting Windows message, the system is having difficulty with the process of booting up to the most basic part of the operating system on the disk. You can try to restart the system and access one of the safe mode options. However, with these symptoms, you probably need to restart the system using a clean boot disk or an emergency start disk.

Normally, you use a start disk created for the operating system that exists on the disk. These disks are typically created when the operating system is first installed. However, they should be regenerated each time a new hardware item is installed, or when a major configuration change occurs in the system. On the other hand, a simple clean boot disk that has the basic MS-DOS files will start any PC system that has enough subsystems working to start.

If the system boots to the clean boot disk, but does not boot up to the hard drive, and has no configuration or startup file errors, a problem exists in the operating system's boot files. These errors typically return some type of Bad or Missing Command Interpreter message or a Disk Boot Failure message.

You can repair the Missing Command Interpreter error by restoring the boot record and operating system files to the hard disk. To do so, you normally copy or extract the files from the clean boot disk to the hard drive. In a file allocation table (FAT) environment, if the boot disk contains a copy of the FDISK command, you can use the FDISK /MBR command to restore the hard drive's Master Boot Record (MBR), along with its partition information. The command SYS:x (where x is the drive designation) is used to restore the command interpreter.

Using Different Startup Modes

If the system does not start up normally, you must first try to start the system in a minimum configuration to establish a point from which to begin troubleshooting the problem. This should also be attempted if the system makes it past the Starting Windows message before it hangs up. Using minimal startup methods enables you to bypass any unnecessary configuration and normally involves using a clean boot disk or the emergency start disk to start the system.

If the system does start up from the minimal condition, the problem exists in the bypassed files. Restart the system and select a startup mode that single-steps through the configuration and startup file sequence.

A single-step startup procedure enables you to isolate the problem command. If the system crashes while trying to execute a particular command, restart the bootup process and skip the offending command. Repeat the process until the system reaches bootup. Track all offending commands so that you can correct them individually. Check the syntax (spelling, punctuation, and usage) of any offending lines.

General Operational Problems

After the operating system has been started and becomes functional, operational problems come into play. These are problems that occur after the system has booted up and started running. Typical operational problems include the following types of problems and occur under the defined circumstances:

➤ **Memory usage errors**—Occur during normal operation of the system

➤ **Application problems**—Occur when performing normal application and file operations

➤ **Printing problems**—Occur while performing typical printing operations

➤ **Networking problems**—Occur when attempting to perform normal operations across the network

Operational Troubleshooting Tools

The Windows operating systems also include a number of tools and utilities designed to manage and troubleshoot the Windows environment. These tools typically include utilities for managing system configuration settings, device drivers, and system resources. Another set of key tools for solving network problems is the TCP/IP suite of utilities.

Memory Usage Problems

Memory usage problems occur when the operating system, or one of its applications, attempts to access an unallocated memory location. When these memory conflicts occur, the data in the violated memory locations is corrupted and might crash the system. In older Windows versions, these types of problems were labeled General Protection Faults (GPFs) and were generally the product of data protection errors induced by poorly written programs. When these memory conflicts occur, the system might either return an error message or simply stop processing.

Due to the severity of the GPF problems in early Windows versions, Microsoft used memory usage error messages in Windows 9x that say This Application Has Performed an Illegal Operation and Is About to Be Shut Down. When this happens, Windows can take care of the error and permit you to continue operating by simply pressing a specific key combination.

Some memory usage errors are nonfatal and provide an option to ignore the fault and continue working, or to just close the application. These errors are generally caused by Windows applications and can sometimes be tracked to dynamic link library (DLL) files associated with a particular application. Although the application might continue to operate, it is generally not stable enough to continue working on an extended basis. It is recommended that the application be used only long enough to save any existing work.

Windows NT, Windows 2000, and Windows XP all employ a flat memory management scheme that does not use the segmented memory mapping features associated with the Intel microprocessors. Therefore, these operating systems have very few memory usage problems.

General Troubleshooting for Application Problems

In Microsoft systems, if an application is a .BAT, .EXE, or .COM file, it should start when its name is properly entered on the command line, or referenced from a shortcut. If such an application does not start in a command-line environment, you have a few basic possibilities to consider: It has been improperly identified, it is not located where it is supposed to be, or the application program is corrupt.

Check the spelling of the filename and reenter it at the command prompt. Also, verify that the path to the program has been presented correctly and thoroughly. If the path and filename are correct, the application might be corrupt. Reinstall the application and try to start it again.

Applications Will Not Install

Most modern applications autorun when their distribution CD is placed in the drive. The Autorun feature presents a user interface on the display that guides the user through the installation process.

You should check the distribution CD for the presence of the Autorun.inf file. If it is present and no autorun action occurs, you should examine the CD-ROM drive's Properties dialog box to ensure that the Autorun function is enabled.

Some applications do not include the Autorun function as part of their installation scheme and are typically installed through the Add/Remove Programs applet found in Control Panel.

Optional Devices Will Not Operate

The system's basic devices are configured as part of the system's PnP startup process in Windows 9x, Windows Me, Windows 2000, and Windows XP systems; however, this doesn't mean that all of the system's devices are in working order, or that they will remain in working order while the system is on.

Optional devices such as modems, sound cards, and advanced I/O devices might configure properly as part of the PnP process and then fail to operate after the system starts.

As an example, many video cards are capable of displaying very high-resolution screens at high refresh rates. However, some monitors do not have the same capabilities. When you configure the video card with settings that the monitor cannot display, symptoms can range from a simple blank screen to several ghost images being displayed onscreen. After the initial installation, the video drivers are always changed while Windows is operating.

Windows-Related Printing Problems

Check the printer driver using the Print icon from Control Panel to make certain that the correct driver is installed. Substitute the standard VGA driver and try to print a document.

Determine whether the Print option from the application's File menu is unavailable (grayed out). If so, check the Windows Control Panel, Printers window for correct parallel port settings. Be certain that the correct printer driver is selected for the printer being used. If no printer type, or the wrong printer type, is selected, simply set the desired printer as the default printer.

Check for a printer switch box between the computer and the printer. If you find a printer switch box, remove the print sharing equipment, and connect the computer directly to the printer.

General Network Troubleshooting

Because the network is a shared resource, you must be aware of the ramifications of repairs on the network. Normally, you begin troubleshooting a general network problem by determining what has changed since it was running last. If the installation is new, you need to inspect it as a setup problem. Check to determine whether any new hardware or new software has been added. Has any of the cabling been changed? Have any new protocols been installed? Has a network adapter been replaced or moved? If any of these events has occurred, begin by checking them specifically.

If the problem does not appear in, or is not related to, the standalone operation of the unit, you should check the portions of the system that are specific to the network. These elements include the network adapter card, the network-specific portions of the operating system, and the network drop cabling.

Check the activity of the light on the back plate of the LAN card (if available) to determine whether the network is recognizing the network adapter card. If the lights are active, the connection is alive. If not, check the adapter in another node. Check the cabling to ensure it is the correct type and that the connector is properly attached. A LAN cable tester is an excellent device to have in this situation.

Most network operating systems include a number of tools to help test and diagnose network-related problems. One of the major tools for troubleshooting network problems is actually a set of utilities common to the TCP/IP suite.

Network Troubleshooting Tools

When TCP/IP is installed in Windows a number of TCP/IP troubleshooting tools are automatically installed with it. All TCP/IP utilities are controlled by commands entered and run from the command prompt. These TCP/IP tools include the following:

➤ **Address Resolution Protocol (ARP) command**—This utility enables you to modify IP-to-Ethernet address-translation tables.

➤ FTP—This utility enables you to transfer files to and from File Transfer Protocol (FTP) servers.

➤ PING—This utility enables you to verify connections to remote hosts.

➤ NETSTAT—This utility enables you to display the current TCP/IP network connections and protocol statistics. A similar command, called NBTSTAT, performs the same function using NetBIOS over the TCP/IP connection.

➤ **Trace Route (TRACERT)**—This utility enables you to display the route and a hop count taken to a given destination. The route taken to a particular address can be set manually using the ROUTE command.

➤ Pathping—This Windows XP route tracing utility combines many of the functions of the PING and TRACERT commands into a single command. This command sends packets to each router along paths to a final destination and waits for returned packets from each hop along the way. It uses the information from the packets to calculate the percentage of packet loss for given routers or links. This enables administrators to determine which routers or links might be creating network problems.

➤ IPCONFIG—This command-line utility enables you to determine the current TCP/IP configuration (MAC address, IP address, and subnet mask) of the local computer. It also can be used to request a new TCP/IP address from a DHCP server. IPCONFIG is available in Windows 98, Windows Me, Windows 2000, and Windows XP. Windows 95 did not support IPCONFIG.

You can start the IPCONFIG utility using two important option switches: /renew and /release. These switches are used to release and update IP settings received from a DHCP server. The /all switch is used to view the TCP/IP settings for all the adapter cards to which the local station is connected.

➤ WINIPCFG—This GUI version of the IPCONFIG utility is available only in Windows 95 and 98. The various command-line switches available with the IPCONFIG utility are implemented in graphic buttons. Like IPCONFIG, WINIPCFG can be used to release and renew IP addresses leased from a DHCP server.

➤ NSLOOKUP—This Windows 2000 and Windows XP TCP/IP utility can be entered at the command prompt to query Internet (DNS) name servers interactively. It has two modes: *interactive* and *noninteractive*. In interactive mode, the user can query name servers for information about various hosts and domains. Noninteractive mode is used to print just the name and requested information for a host or domain. NSLOOKUP is available only when TCP/IP has been installed.

Although all these utilities are useful in isolating different TCP/IP problems, the most widely used commands are PING and TRACERT.

The PING command sends Internet Control Message Protocol (ICMP) packets to a remote location and then waits for echoed response packets to be returned. The command waits for up to one second for each packet sent and then displays the number of transmitted and received packets. You can use the PING command to test both the name and IP address of the remote unit. A number of switches can be used to set parameters for the PING operation. Figure 4.1 depicts the information displayed by a typical PING operation.

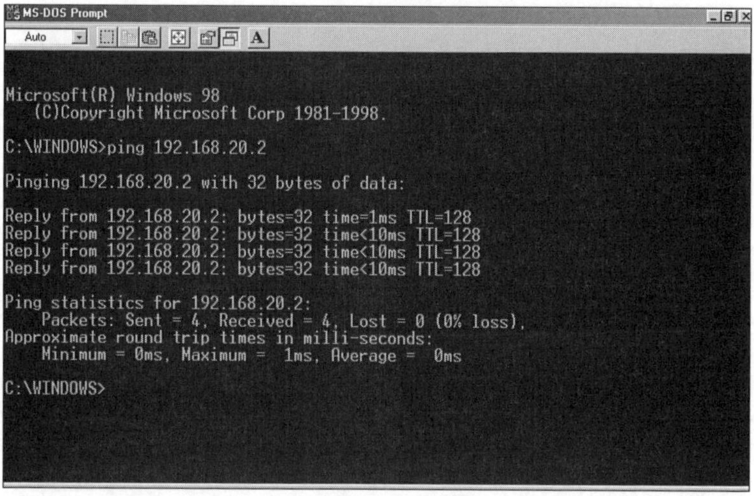

Figure 4.1 A **PING** operation.

Most Internet servers do not respond to ICMP requests created by pinging; however, you can use the PING utility to access www.*somewebsitename*.com. By doing so, you can get a reply that verifies that TCP/IP, DNS, and the gateway are working. The TRACERT utility traces the route taken by ICMP packets sent across the network, as shown in Figure 4.2. Routers along the path return information to the inquiring system, and the utility displays the host name, IP address, and round-trip time for each hop in the path.

Because the TRACERT report shows how much time is spent at each router along the path, it can be used to help determine where network slowdowns are occurring.

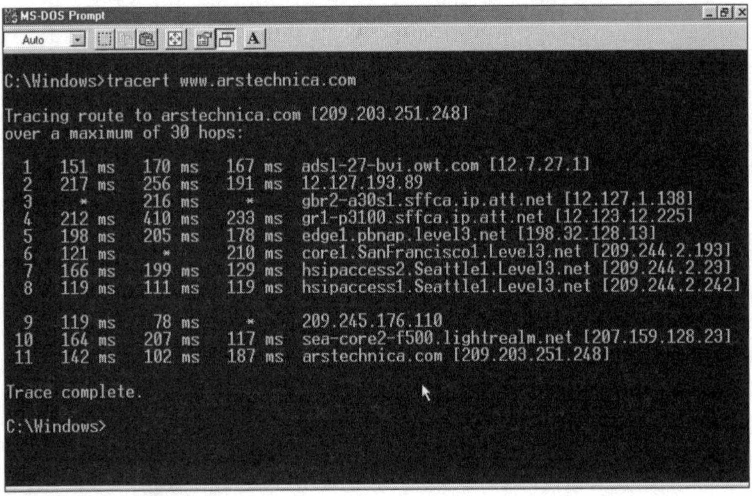

Figure 4.2 A **TRACERT** operation.

Verifying TCP/IP Configurations

Two TCP/IP utilities are particularly important in confirming and troubleshooting a new TCP/IP configuration. These are the IPCONFIG and PING utilities. To verify the configuration of a new TCP/IP installation, begin by running the IPCONFIG utility from the command prompt to verify that the connection has been properly initialized.

Then use the PING utility to test the TCP/IP operations. This is accomplished by pinging different IP addresses in order:

1. PING address 127.0.0.1 to perform a loopback test to verify that TCP/IP has successfully been loaded in the local computer.

2. PING the local adapter's IP address to ensure that it has been initialized.

3. PING the default gateway (router) address to verify that TCP/IP is working on both devices.

4. PING the address of another computer on the same network segment to ensure that the default gateway is functional.

If only one of the PINGed devices does not return a reply, it has a problem. If neither device replies, the local computer might have a problem. Have someone else check your TCP/IP configuration settings to ensure no values have been transposed as they were being entered.

General WAN Troubleshooting

ISPs establish an Internet access account for each user. These accounts are based on the user's account name and password that are asked for each time the user logs on to the account. Forgetting or misspelling either item results in the ISP rejecting access to the Internet.

Most accounts are paid for on a monthly schedule. If the account isn't paid up, the ISP might cancel the account and deny access to the user. In either of these situations, when the user attempts to log on to the account, he is repeatedly asked to enter his account name and password until a predetermined number of failed attempts has been reached.

Dial-Up Problems

Most of the dial-up WAN troubleshooting steps at the local computer level involve the modem. First, the modem hardware should be examined. If the hardware is functional, the operating system's driver and resource configuration settings must be checked.

The most common dial-up communication error is the Disconnected message. This message occurs for a number of reasons, including a noisy phone line or random transmission errors. You can normally overcome this type of error by just retrying the connection. Other typical error messages include the following:

➤ **No Dial Tone**—This error indicates a bad or improper phone line connection, such as the phone line plugged into the modem's line jack rather than the phone jack.

➤ **Port in Use**—This error indicates a busy signal or an improper configuration parameter.

➤ **Can't Find Modem**—This error indicates that the PnP process did not detect the modem, or that the modem has not been correctly configured to communicate with the system.

If the system cannot find the modem, reboot it so that Windows can attempt to redetect the modem. If rebooting does not detect the modem, check any hardware configuration settings for the modem and compare them to the settings in Device Manager. These values can be checked through the Modem's Properties dialog box in Control Panel; however, the Device Manager must be used to make changes to these settings.

Normally, each user receives a packet of information from their ISP when the service was purchased. These documents normally contain all the ISP-specific configuration information needed to set up the user's site. This information should be consulted when installing, and configuring, any Internet-related software.

Logon Problems

Logon problems are a common type of problem that can occur during start-up (even though they are not actually startup problems) or when trying to access different applications and utilities. Basically, in network and internet-worked computer environments, users cannot log on to systems and applications unless they have the proper authorization to do so. These problems tend to be very common in secure environments, such as local and wide area networks.

The most common logon problem is a forgotten or invalid username and password. Invalid usernames and passwords typically result from poor typing, or from having the Caps Lock function turned on. Users can also be prevented from logging on due to network station or time restrictions imposed by administrators. You should check with the network administrator to see whether the user's rights to the system have been restricted.

In the Internet environment, the *Internet service provider* (*ISP*) is responsible for establishing Internet access accounts for each user. These accounts are based on the user's account name and password, which are asked for each time the user logs on to the account. Forgetting or misspelling either item results in the ISP rejecting access to the Internet.

Most accounts are paid for on a monthly schedule. If the account isn't paid up, the ISP might cancel the account and deny access to the user. In either of these situations, if the user attempts to log on to the account, he is repeatedly asked to enter his account name and password until a predetermined number of failed attempts has been reached.

Dealing with Viruses

Computer viruses are destructive programs designed to replicate and spread on their own. Viruses are created to sneak into personal computers. Sometimes, these programs take control of a machine to leave a humorous message, and sometimes, they destroy data. After they infiltrate one machine, they can spread into other computers through infected disks that friends and co-workers pass around, or through local and wide area network connections.

Because viruses tend to operate in the background, it is sometimes difficult to realize that the computer has been infected. Typical virus symptoms include the following:

➤ Hard disk controller failures occur.

➤ Disks continue to be full even when files have been deleted.

➤ The system cannot read write-protected disks.

➤ The hard disk stops booting and files are corrupted.

➤ The system boots to floppy disk, but does not access the HDD.

➤ An *Invalid Drive Specification* message usually displays when attempting to access the C: drive.

➤ CMOS settings continually revert to default even though the system board battery is good.

➤ Files change size for no apparent reason.

➤ System operation slows down noticeably.

➤ A blank screen appears when booting (flashing cursor).

➤ Windows crashes.

➤ The hard drive is set to MS-DOS compatibility and 32-bit file access suddenly stops working.

➤ Network data transfers and print jobs slow down dramatically.

The most common means of virus protection involves installing a virus-scanning program that checks disks and files before using them in the computer. If the computer is a standalone unit, it might be nonproductive to have the antivirus software run each time the system is booted up. It is much more practical to have the program only check floppy disks and CDs and DVDs because these are the only entry points into this type of computer environment.

A networked or online computer has more opportunity to contract a virus than a standalone unit because viruses can enter the unit over the network or through the modem. In these cases, setting the software to run at each boot-up is more desirable. Most modern antivirus software includes utilities to check files downloaded to the computer through dial-up connections, such as from the Internet.

Windows 9x and Windows Me Startup Problems

If problems occur during the startup of the Windows 9x or Windows Me system, these systems typically respond by producing some type of error message. Understanding what types of events cause these messages greatly improves your ability to efficiently identify and repair startup problems in either of these systems. Typical Windows 9x startup error messages include the following:

➤ HIMEM.SYS Not Loaded

➤ Swap File Corrupt

➤ Damaged or Missing Core Files

➤ Bad or Missing COMMAND.COM

➤ Unable to Initialize Display Adapter

➤ Device Referenced in WIN.INI Could Not Be Found

➤ Device Referenced in SYSTEM.INI Could Not Be Found

These and other Windows 9x-related startup messages indicate the presence of problems that must be corrected before the system can boot up and run correctly.

Troubleshooting Windows 9x Startup Problems

There is a generic process for isolating the cause of Windows 9x startup problems. This process is as follows:

1. Use the emergency start disk to gain access to the system and the hard drive.

2. If necessary, repair the system files and command interpreter files. Refer to the "Using Boot/Emergency Disks" section earlier in this book for methods of repairing these files using the FDISK /MBR and SYS commands.

3. Attempt to boot up into safe mode to see if the problem is driver-related.

4. Reboot the system into the step-by-step confirmation startup mode to isolate configuration and driver problems. Continue single-stepping through the startup process until all offending steps have been identified and corrected.

5. Review the Windows 9x log files for problem steps.

HIMEM.SYS Problems

In the case of the HIMEM.SYS error, use the System Editor to check the syntax and correctness of the entry in the CONFIG.SYS file, if present. With Windows 9x, the HIMEM.SYS statement must be present in the \Windows directory and must be the correct version for the operating system to run.

Check the HIMEM.SYS file to ensure it is the correct version and in the correct location. For example, there might be as many as three different versions of the HIMEM.SYS file present in a system that has been upgraded from Windows 9x.

Initializing the Display Adapter

The Unable to Initialize Display Adapter error message indicates that errors are occurring during the hardware-detection phase of the Windows 9x PnP bootup routine. These errors normally occur when the Windows 9x PnP function cannot detect the hardware component, or because it cannot reconcile the adapter's needs to the available system resources.

However, do not assume that PnP is in effect and working simply because Windows 9x is running. The system's BIOS and the peripheral devices must also be PnP-compliant for the autodetection function to work.

You should be able to sort out problems that occur during the detection phase by starting the system in step-by-step confirmation mode (pressing F8 during the bootup) and then single-stepping through the driver loading process to sort out the display driver/hardware problem. You must use the Add New Hardware Wizard (found in Control Panel) to install device drivers when the PnP detection function does not work correctly.

Windows 9x and Windows Me Boot Problems

Key Windows 9x and Windows Me files prevent the system from starting up if they become corrupted. These files include those associated with the MBR, the boot sector, the FATs, and the Windows core files. The following list details some of the Windows 9x and Windows Me boot problems you might encounter:

➤ Errors that occur between the single beep marking the end of the *power-on self test* (*POST*) and the appearance of the Starting Windows 9x message on the screen are associated with the boot sector.

➤ Problems that show up between the Starting Windows message and the appearance of the desktop involve the Windows core files.

If the IO.SYS file is corrupted in Windows 9x, the system hangs up before the Starting Windows message appears and produces a System Disk Invalid error message onscreen.

If the MSDOS.SYS file is missing or corrupt, Windows displays a blue screen with an Invalid VxD Dynamic Link message and fails to start up. Other MSDOS.SYS-related problems relate to the Registry, the Extended Memory Manager (XMS), and the Installable File System Manager (IFSMGR). These problems produce errors that appear during startup and are caused by syntax errors in the [Paths] section of the file. You should check these entries if Windows 9x does not start properly.

Likewise, a COMMAND.COM problem produces an error message onscreen and fails to start up Windows. You can repair a missing COMMAND.COM by using the command-line COPY and SYS commands. These commands copy the COMMAND.COM and system files from the clean boot disk to the hard drive. As mentioned earlier, if the boot disk contains a copy of the FDISK command, you can use the FDISK/MBR command to restore the hard drive's MBR, along with its partition information.

To correct these problems, start the system using the emergency start disk. At the command prompt, type SYS C: to copy the IO.SYS, MSDOS.SYS, and COMMAND.COM files onto the hard disk. You can use the MS-DOS Attribute command to verify that the hidden system files have been successfully copied to the disk (that is, type Attrib -r -s -h C:\IO.SYS and Attrib -r -s -h C:\MSDOS.SYS at the command prompt to make them visible and to remove their read-only and system status).

The COMMAND.COM file can also be restored from the command line, or through Windows Explorer. To restore the COMMAND.COM file from the command line, start the system from the startup disk and use the Copy command to transfer the file manually. The COMMAND.COM file can also be dragged from the startup disk to the root directory of the hard drive using the Windows 9x My Computer or Windows Explorer functions. As with the manual copy procedure, the COMMAND.COM file's Read-only, System, and Hidden attributes must be removed so that the COMMAND.COM file can be manipulated within the system.

Missing Windows Core File Problems

To locate and correct the missing core file problem cited earlier, check for corrupted files on the disk drive. To accomplish this, start the system in safe mode using the Command Prompt Only option. When the command prompt appears, move to the Windows \Command directory and run the ScanDisk utility. If ScanDisk detects corrupted files, you must replace them. The ScanDisk utility can locate and fix several types of problems on the hard drive. These problems include corrupted FATs, long filenames, lost clusters and cross-linked files, tree structure problems, and bad sectors on the drive.

The ScanDisk version used with a Windows 9x system must be the one specifically designed for that operating system (that is, a Windows 95 ScanDisk version should not be used on a Windows 98 system). Other versions might not work correctly and could result in data loss. When using ScanDisk to isolate startup problems, the Windows 9x version used should be the version that is located on the particular computer's emergency start disk and runs from the command prompt.

You can use the Windows 9x setup function to verify or repair damaged Windows operating system files. To accomplish this, run the setup utility and select the Verify option when presented by the setup procedure. You can then repair damaged system files without running a complete reinstall operation.

If corrupted Windows 9x files are found in the system, it is not possible to simply copy new ones onto the drive from the CD. Instead, you must run setup using the distribution CD and the *Validate/Restore option*.

You also can run the EXTRACT.EXE command from the Windows Command directory to extract selected compressed cabinet (.CAB) files from the Windows distribution CD. The preferable method is the setup option. In most cases, however, it is simpler to reinstall Windows than to search for individual files and structures.

Swap File Problems

The Windows 9x swap file is controlled through the System icon in Control Panel. From this point, enter the Performance page and click its Virtual Memory button. Typically, the *Let Windows Manage Virtual Memory* option should be selected. If the system locks up and does not start, the swap file might have become corrupt, or the Virtual Memory setting might have been changed to Disabled. In either case, you must reinstall Windows 9x to correct the problem.

Initialization File Problems

The device or driver files referenced in the *Missing INI Files* error messages should be checked to ensure that they have been properly identified and that their location and path are correct. If they are not, use the System Editor to make the necessary changes by installing the specified device driver in the designated .INI file. If the path and syntax are correct for the indicated files, you should reload the .INI file from the emergency start disk.

Errors in the CONFIG.SYS and AUTOEXEC.BAT files produces the Error in CONFIG.SYS Line XX or Error in AUTOEXEC.BAT Line XX messages. The line specified by the XX in the error message contains a syntax (spelling, punctuation, or usage) error that prevents it from running. yntax errors can also produce an Unrecognized Command in CONFIG.SYS message. These errors are caused by missing or corrupt files referenced in the CONFIG.SYS or AUTOEXEC.BAT files. To correct these errors, use one of the system's text editors, such as Sysedit, to correct the designated line in the file, reload the indicated file with a known-good copy, and restart the computer.

Windows 9x and Windows Me Troubleshooting Tools

Microsoft Windows 9x and Windows Me operating systems include an extensive set of system troubleshooting tools. These tools include several safe mode startup options, a trio of system log files, and an extensive interactive troubleshooting Help file system.

Windows 9x also includes three important tools that can be used when a Windows 9x system is having startup problems: the emergency start (clean boot) disk, *safe modes*, and the step-by-step startup sequence. With Windows 9x, the clean boot disk is referred to as an *emergency start disk*.

An expanded built-in Troubleshooting menu is also located in the Windows 9x and Windows Me Help functions. All these items have been included to assist in the location and correction of Windows-related problems.

Although Windows Me minimizes the user's access to the command-prompt functions, it also includes a number of new self-repairing capabilities that perform some of the technician's repair functions automatically. In particular, Windows Me introduced the *System Restore* utility that enables technicians to reset the computer's configuration settings to a previously known good condition. This feature has appeared in the newer Windows operating system versions.

Windows 9x Safe Mode

If Windows 9x determines that a problem has occurred that prevented the system from starting, it attempts to restart the system in *safe mode*. This mode bypasses several startup files to provide access to the system's configuration files. You can access safe mode in Windows 9x by pressing the F5 function key when the *Starting Windows 9x* message is displayed onscreen.

As Figure 4.3 illustrates, Windows 9x has six safe mode startup options: Normal, Logged, Safe Mode, Step-by-Step Confirmation, Command Prompt Only, and Safe Mode Command Prompt Only. Each option is customized for specific situations and disables selected portions of the system to prevent them from interfering with the startup process.

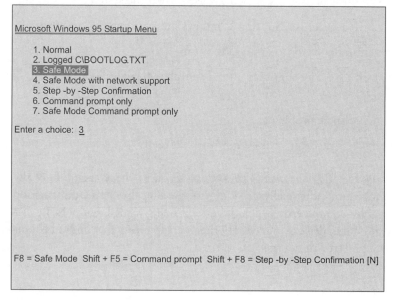

```
Microsoft Windows 95 Startup Menu

   1. Normal
   2. Logged C\BOOTLOG.TXT
   3. Safe Mode
   4. Safe Mode with network support
   5. Step -by -Step Confirmation
   6. Command prompt only
   7. Safe Mode Command prompt only

Enter a choice: 3




F8 = Safe Mode  Shift + F5 = Command prompt  Shift + F8 = Step -by -Step Confirmation [N]
```

Figure 4.3 The Startup menu.

The special function keys available during the Windows 9x startup are:

➤ **F5**—Safe mode

➤ **F6**—Safe mode with network support

➤ **F8**—Step-by-step confirmation mode

➤ **Shift+F5**—Safe mode command prompt only

In safe mode, the minimal device drivers (keyboard, mouse, and standard-mode video graphics adapter [VGA] drivers) are active to start the system. The CD-ROM drive, however, is not active in safe mode.

When using the *Step-by-Step Confirmation* option, the system displays each startup command line by line and waits for a confirmation from the keyboard before moving ahead. This way, an offending startup command can be isolated and avoided so that it can be replaced or removed.

NOTE | Windows 98 does not officially support the Safe Mode with Network Support option; however, you can access this safe mode version by pressing the F6 function key during Windows startup.

Using Safe Mode

The standard safe mode startup, initiated by pressing the F5 key when the Starting Windows message is present, is used when the system:

➤ Does not start after the Starting Windows message appears onscreen

➤ Stalls repeatedly or for long periods of time

➤ Cannot print to a local printer after a complete troubleshooting sequence

➤ Has video display problems

➤ Slows down noticeably or does not work correctly

The *Step-by-Step Confirmation* option enables you to check each line of the startup procedure individually. In doing so, the Step-by-Step Confirmation option enables you to verify which drivers are being loaded, temporarily disable any offending drivers, and check other startup errors that might be indicated through error messages.

The Step-by-Step Confirmation option is obtained by pressing the F8 function key at the Startup menu and should be employed when the system

➤ Fails while loading the startup files

➤ Needs to load real-mode drivers

➤ Displays a Registry Failure error message

The Safe Mode with Network Support option is used in networked environments when the system

➤ Stops responding when a remote network is accessed

➤ Cannot print to a remote printer

➤ Stalls during startup and cannot be started using a normal safe mode startup

Command Prompt Modes

Other startup options might also be available from the menu, depending on the configuration of the system. Some options start the system and bring it to an MS-DOS-like command prompt. Selecting the *Command Prompt Only* option causes the system to boot up to the command line, using the startup files and the Registry.

If this option does not start the system, reboot the computer and select the *Safe Mode Command Prompt Only* option from the Startup menu. This option performs the same function as pressing the Shift and F5 keys simultaneously (Shift+F5) during the bootup process. The system starts in safe mode with minimal drivers (while not executing any of the startup files) and produces the command-line prompt.

The *Safe Mode Command Prompt Only* option loads only COMMAND.COM and the disk-compression utility files (DriveSpace or DoubleSpace), if present. This option should be chosen when the system fails to start in safe mode. You can enter this mode directly during the startup process by pressing the Shift and F5 keys simultaneously (Shift+F5) when the *Starting Windows* message is onscreen.

The Safe Mode Command Prompt Only option can be used to

➤ Employ command-line switches, such as WIN /d:x

➤ Employ command-line tools, such as MS-DOS editors

➤ Avoid loading HIMEM.SYS or IFSHLP.SYS

A *Safe Mode Without Compression* option appears only in systems using compressed drives. In operation, it is similar to the *Command Prompt Only* option, with the exception that no compression drivers are loaded. The following list provides reasons for selecting the Safe Mode Without Compression option:

➤ The system stops responding when a compressed drive is accessed.

➤ A Corrupt CVF (Compressed Volume File) error appears during startup.

➤ Safe Mode and Safe Mode Command Prompt Only options fail to start the system.

WIN Switches

When Windows 9x or Windows Me refuses to start up, a number of options are available for starting it from the command prompt. After gaining access to the system using a boot disk, you should attempt to start Windows by typing the WIN command at the command prompt.

Using WIN Switches

The Windows 9x and Windows Me operating systems can be started from the command prompt using the command WIN, followed by one or more switch options. For example, starting Windows 9x or Windows Me from the command prompt using the /D switch is often helpful in isolating different areas of the operating system as possible problem sources (that is, WIN /D). You can modify the /D switch to start Windows in a number of different configurations:

➤ Using a /D:F switch disables 32-bit disk access.

➤ The :M and :N variations start Windows in safe mode, or safe mode with network support.

➤ An :S modifier inhibits Windows from using address space between hexadecimal addresses F0000h and FFFFFh.

➤ The :V variation prevents Windows from controlling disk transfers. Instead, hard disk drive (HDD) interrupt requests are handled by the BIOS.

➤ The :X switch prevents Windows from using the area of memory between hexadecimal addresses A000h and FFFFh.

You can obtain a full listing of the WIN switches by typing WIN /? at the command prompt.

The WIN /B switch causes Windows to start in Logged mode and to produce a BOOTLOG.TXT file during startup. This option enables you to determine whether specific device drivers are stalling the system. You also can select Logged mode by pressing the F8 key while the *Starting Windows 9x* message is onscreen. After selecting the Logged option, restart the system using the Safe Mode Command Prompt Only option. Then use a text editor to examine the contents of the BOOTLOG.TXT file and determine which driver has failed to load.

You can use a question mark as a switch with the WIN command (that is, WIN /?) to show a listing of all the switches associated with the command. You can use these switches to start Windows with various portions of the operating system disabled. If the system runs with a particular section disabled, at least some portion of the problem can be linked to that area.

Creating a Windows 95 Emergency Start Disk

In the event that Windows 95 becomes nonfunctional, you need to use the *emergency start disk* to gain access to the system so that you can restore it to proper operation. The Windows 9x emergency start disk boots up the system only to the command prompt. From this point, you need to be familiar with command-line operations so that you can employ tools and utilities that will get the system up and running again.

During the Windows setup operation, the software provides an option for creating an emergency start disk. This option should be used for every Windows 9x installation. The setup routine copies the operating system files to the disk along with utilities for troubleshooting startup problems. The disk can then be used to boot up the system in safe mode and display a command-line prompt. The emergency start disk can also be used to replace lost or damaged system files on the hard disk.

An emergency start disk can also be created through the Add/Remove Programs icon in Control Panel. This option is normally used to create a new startup disk after new hardware has been installed or when configuration information has been changed.

In addition to creating a startup floppy disk, Windows 95 transfers a number of diagnostic files to the disk, including the following:

➤ IO.SYS

➤ MSDOS.SYS

➤ COMMAND.COM

➤ SCANDISK.EXE

➤ SYS.COM

➤ FDISK.EXE

➤ FORMAT.COM

➤ SCANDISK.INI

➤ EDIT.COM

➤ REGEDIT.EXE

➤ ATTRIB.EXE

Because the Windows 95 system settings are basically contained in the two Registry files SYSTEM.DAT and USER.DAT, it is not uncommon to back them up on the emergency start disk. This operation is performed with the Export function of the Regedit utility. The Export function can be used to save a selected branch or the entire Registry as a REG text file.

In addition to the .DAT Registry files, you might want to include copies of any CONFIG.SYS, AUTOEXEC.BAT, WIN.INI, SYSTEM.INI, and CD-ROM driver files on the emergency start disk. These files can be quite useful for maintaining compatibility with installed hardware and software applications. The CD-ROM driver (that is, MSCDEX.EXE) should be included to provide CD-ROM support for access to the utilities on the Windows distribution CD.

The Registry backup file can be used to restore the Registry to the system after a crash. This procedure involves using the Regedit *Import* function to restore the Registry for use. This function can be performed using the Windows-based version, or it can be conducted from the command line using the real-mode version located on the emergency start disk.

The REGEDIT /C command should not be used except for cases in which the Registry is heavily corrupted. It must have a complete image of the Registry to be used in this manner. Also, realize that Windows 9x backs up the Registry files each time it is started. Several iterations of the Registry files should exist that could be renamed and copied over the existing Registry files to repair them.

The Windows 98 Emergency Start Disk

The Windows 98 emergency start disk can be created during the installation process or by accessing the Startup Disk tab in the Add/Remove Programs window of Control Panel.

In addition to the system files required to start the system in a minimal, real-mode condition, the Windows 98 emergency start disk provides a number of diagnostic programs and a trio of real-mode CD-ROM drivers (MSCDEX.EXE for Integrated Drive Electronics [IDE] drives and BTDCDROM.SYS and ASPICD.SYS for small computer system interface [SCSI] drives) to enable the CD-ROM drive to operate in safe mode.

The Windows 98 emergency start disk includes real-mode SCSI CD-ROM support, provides a RAMDrive, and features an Extract command (EXT.EXE) to work with EXTRACT.EXE. The Extract command is used to pull necessary files from the cabinet (.CAB) files on the Windows 98 distribution CD.

Using the Windows 98 Startup Disk

If the system does not make it to the Startup menu, you must boot the system with the startup disk and begin checking the operating system on the boot drive. When the system is booted from a Windows 98 startup disk, a menu such as the following displays:

1. Start the computer with CD-ROM support.

2. Start the computer without CD-ROM support.

3. View the Help file.

If the CD-ROM support option is selected, the system executes the portion of the CONFIG.SYS file that loads the CD-ROM driver, and sets up a 2MB RAM drive. Use the startup disk to boot the system and gain access to the operating system's files. After gaining access to the system, you can use the built-in troubleshooting aids on the Windows 9x startup disk to isolate the cause of the problem.

System Configuration Troubleshooting Tools

In addition to the clean boot, safe mode, and log file functions previously described, the Windows 98 contains a wealth of other troubleshooting tools that you can use to isolate and correct problems. These utilities include the Device Manger, the System Configuration Utility (MSCONFIG.EXE), the Automatic Skip Driver Agent (ASD.EXE), and the Version Conflict Manager (VCMUI.EXE).

Device Manger

The *Device Manager* utility, depicted in Figure 4.4, provides a graphical representation of the devices configured in the system. This interface can be used to identify installed ports, update device drivers, and change I/O settings. It can also be used to manually isolate hardware and configuration conflicts. The problem device can be examined to see where the conflict is occurring. In Windows 9x, the Device Manager can be accessed through the Start, Settings, Control Panel, System path.

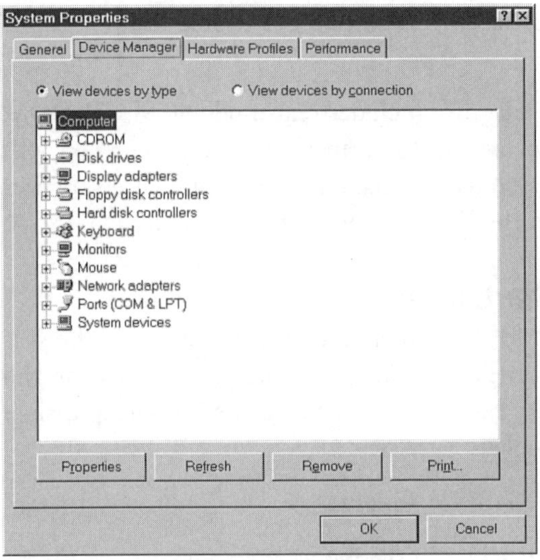

Figure 4.4 The Windows 9x Device Manager.

The Device Manager displays an exclamation point (!) inside a yellow circle whenever a device is experiencing a direct hardware conflict with another device. Similarly, when a red X appears at the device's icon, the device has been disabled due to a user selection conflict.

If a conflict is suspected, click on the offending device in the listing, verify that the selected device is the current device, and then click the User Selection Conflict tab to examine its Conflicting devices list. Verify that the device has not been installed twice.

The Device Manager contains a set of buttons that permit its various functions to be accessed. These buttons include Properties, Refresh, Remove, and Print.

Typical Device Manager Properties pages provide tabs that can be used to access General information, device Settings, device Drivers information, and device Resources requirements and usage. Each device might have some or all of these tabs available depending on what type of device it is and its requirements.

The information on the tabs can be used to change the properties associated with the selected device. This often becomes necessary when resource conflicts occur in a system that has legacy devices installed. The Device Manager can be used to identify possible causes of these IRQ, DMA, I/O, and memory settings conflicts.

System Configuration Utility (MSCONFIG.EXE)

The *System Configuration Utility* enables you to examine the system's configuration through a check box system. By turning different configuration settings on and off, you can isolate and correct problem settings by a process of elimination. You can access this utility through the System Information screen. From the Tools menu, select the System Configuration Utility. This tool is especially useful in controlling which programs are automatically loaded at startup.

When the System Configuration Utility is accessed, its main dialog box opens, as displayed in Figure 4.5. The screen is divided into six tabs that correspond to the files that run during the startup process. The information under the General tab enables you to select the type of startup.

For most troubleshooting efforts, the Diagnostic Startup option is selected first to provide a clean environment. When the Selective Startup option is chosen, complete sections of the bootup sequence can be disabled. After an offending section has been isolated, you can use the individual tabs to enter that section and selectively disable individual lines within the file.

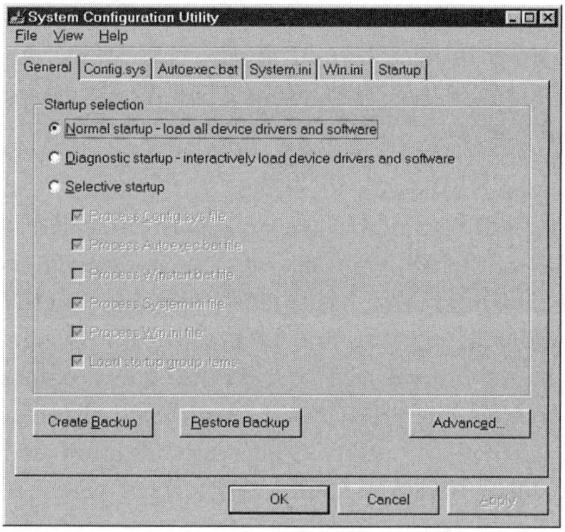

Figure 4.5　System Configuration Utility.

If a startup problem disappears when the system is started using any of the safe modes, use the System Configuration Utility to isolate the conflicting items. Of course, you might need to enter this command from the command line.

Select the Diagnostic Startup option to interactively load device drivers and software options from the General tab screen. When the Startup menu appears, select the *Step-by-Step* option. Begin by starting the system with only the CONFIG.SYS and AUTOEXEC.BAT files disabled.

If the system starts, move into those tabs and step through those files, one line at a time, using the Selective Startup option. The step-by-step process is used to systematically enable or disable items until all the problem items are identified. If an entry is marked with a Microsoft Windows logo, it is employed when the Selective Startup option is disabled.

If the problem does not go away, you can use the Advanced button from the General tab to inspect lower-level configuration settings, such as real-mode disk accesses and VGA standard video settings.

You also can start the Device Manager from the MSCONFIG View option. This allows the protected-mode device drivers to be inspected. The MSINFO-Problem Devices section also should be examined to check for possible problem-causing devices.

Other items to check include missing or corrupted system files (using the System File Checker utility), corrupted Registry entries (using the Registry Checker), viruses (using a virus checker program), and hardware conflicts using the CMOS Configuration screens.

The Automatic Skip Driver Agent (ASD.EXE)

In cases in which the configuration problem is more severe, you can use the *Automatic Skip Driver Agent*. This utility senses and skips configuration steps that prevent Windows 98 from starting.

When a potential problem setting has been identified in the CONFIG.SYS, AUTOEXEC.BAT, or Registry, use the ASD utility to automatically isolate and disable the suspect line. Simply select the ASD option from the Tools menu in System Information. Select the operation that has failed by marking it in the Hardware Troubleshooting Agent dialog box, and then select the Details option. This action should cause the *Enumerating a Device* dialog box to provide recommendations for correcting any problems. This normally involves replacing the driver disabled by the ASD utility. This series of automated tests basically replaces the manual isolation method performed with the Step-by-Step Startup option.

The Version Conflict Manager (VCMUI.EXE)

The *Version Conflict Manager* automatically installs Windows 98 drivers over other drivers that it finds, even if these drivers are newer. The System Configuration Utility (described in a previous section) is located in the Windows\System path, whereas the other two utilities are found under the \Windows directory.

The System File Checker Utility (SFC.EXE)

The *System File Checker utility* (SFC.EXE) checks the system files for changed, deleted, or possibly corrupt files. If it finds such files, it attempts to extract the original versions of the files from Windows files. You can find this utility in the Windows\System folder; however, you can simply click the System File Checker entry in the System Information Tools menu to activate it.

Registry Checker Utilities (SCANREG.EXE and SCANREGW.EXE)

Windows 98 and Windows Me also include a pair of Registry checker utilities (SCANREG.EXE and SCANREGW.EXE) to scan, fix, back up, and restore Registry files. The SCANREG file is a command-line program, whereas SCANREGW is a Windows-based version. The command-line version is located in the Windows\Command path, whereas the Windows version is just in the \Windows directory.

The Windows 98 system can contain up to five backup copies of the Registry structure. If the system fails to start up after installing some new software or hardware component, run the Registry Checker utility using the /Restore option (ScanReg /Restore) to return the Registry to its previous condition. Just type "ScanReg /Restore" at the MS-DOS prompt to view a list of available backup copies. Generally, the most recent version should be selected for use. These tools are discussed in greater detail later in this chapter.

Windows 9x and Windows Me Operational Problems

If the Windows 9x or Windows Me operating system starts up properly, only a limited number of things can go wrong afterward. The disk drive can run out of space, files can become corrupt, or the system can lock up due to software exception errors. When these problems occur, the system can either return an error message or simply stop processing.

Drive Space and Memory Problems

If the system produces an Out of Memory error in Windows 9x, it is very unlikely that the system is running out of RAM, unless you are running MS-DOS-based applications. In Windows 9x, this error indicates that the system is running out of memory space altogether—RAM and virtual memory.

The *System Information utility* in the Start, Programs, Accessories, System Tools path can be used to view the disk drive's space parameters. You also can check the drive's used/available space information by performing a CheckDisk operation on it.

Run the Windows *System Monitor* utility to observe system memory usage and determine the nature of the error. If you are running MS-DOS-based applications, you can optimize the system's use of conventional memory by running the old DOS MEMMAKER utility from the \Tools\Oldmsdos directory on the Windows distribution CD.

You can view the system's swap file settings through the Control Panel, System, Performance, Virtual Memory option, or through the System Information utility (Start, Programs, Accessories, System Tools, System Information). Any lost clusters taking up space on the drive can be identified and eliminated using the ScanDisk utility. A heavily used, heavily fragmented hard drive can affect the system's virtual memory and produce memory shortages as well. Run the Defrag utility to optimize the storage patterns on the drive.

If the system is running a FAT16 drive, you can free up additional space by converting it to a FAT32 drive using the CVT1.EXE command of the Drive Converter (FAT32) utility. The smaller sector clustering arrangement available through FAT32 frees up wasted space on the drive. The drawbacks of performing this upgrade are that you have some risk of losing data if a failure occurs in the conversion process, and that larger files have slightly slower read/write times than they did under FAT16.

If these corrective actions do not clear the memory error, you need to remove unnecessary files from the drive, or install a larger drive. If the system still runs out of hard disk space, remember that there might be up to five backup copies of the Registry on the drive. These copies are a product of using the SCANREGW utility to check out the Registry structure for corruption. Each backup is up to 2MB in size and can be removed to free up additional disk drive space.

Applications Will Not Install

When an application will not install in a Windows 9x or Windows Me system, you should check the application's distribution CD for an autorun file. If this file is present and the CD does not autostart, examine the CD-ROM drive's Properties to see that the Autorun option is enabled. In Windows 9x and Windows Me, the Autorun feature is a function of the Registry and is not generally available to the user.

If the distribution media does not include an autorun file, the application needs to be installed using the Add/Remove Programs utility in Control Panel.

Stalled Applications

If the system locks up, or an application stalls, it is often possible to regain access to the Close Program dialog box by pressing the Ctrl+Alt+Del key combination. When the Close Program dialog box appears, you can close the offending application and continue operating the system without rebooting.

As an example, in Windows 9x, the Windows Explorer shell (EXPLORER.EXE) might crash and leave the system without a Start button or taskbar. To recover from this condition, use the Ctrl+Alt+Del combination to access the Close Program dialog box and shut the system down in a proper manner.

Pressing the Ctrl+Alt+Del combination again immediately shuts down the operating system and any unsaved data in other open applications.

The Alt+F4 key combination can also be used to close active windows. Pressing this key combination in an application stops the application and moves to the next active application in the task list. If the Alt+F4 combination is pressed when no applications are active, the Shut Down Windows menu appears on the display. This enables you to shut down or restart the system in an orderly fashion.

If the application repeatedly locks the system up, you must reinstall the application and check its configuration settings. The Dr. Watson utility also proves very useful in detecting application faults. When activated, Dr. Watson intercepts the software actions, detects the failure, identifies the application, and provides a detailed description of the failure. The information is automatically transferred to the disk drive and stored in the \Windows\Drwatson*.WLG file. You can view and print the information stored in the file from a word processor.

If an MS-DOS-based program is running and the system locks up, you must restore Windows 9x. To accomplish this, attempt to restart the system from a cold boot. If the system starts in Windows 9x, check the Properties of the DOS application. This information can be obtained by locating the program through the My Computer or Windows Explorer interfaces, right-clicking its filename, and selecting the Properties option from the shortcut menu.

From the Properties dialog box, select the Programs tab and then click the Advanced button to view the file's settings, as shown in Figure 4.6. If the application is not already set for MS-DOS-mode operation, click the box to select it. Also select the Prevent MS-DOS-Based Programs from Detecting Windows option. Return to the failing application to see whether it runs correctly in this environment.

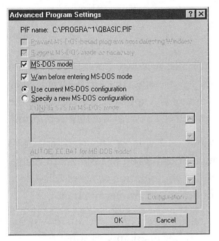

Figure 4.6   MS-DOS program properties.

Windows 98 occasionally produces an error message that says you are running out of resources. This message indicates that the operating system believes that it has exhausted all the system's real and virtual memory. Although the message tells you to correct the problem by shutting down applications, and it provides an endless series of application shutdown dialog boxes, this process almost never works. Even shutting the applications down through the Close Program dialog box does not restore the system. Therefore, you should shut down the system and restart it. This action normally clears the problem.

Troubleshooting Windows 9x Application Problems

If an application does not start in Windows 9x, you have four basic possibilities to consider: The application is missing; part or all of the application is corrupted; the application's executable file is incorrectly identified; or its attributes are locked.

As with other GUI-based environments, Windows 9x applications hide behind icons. The properties of each application's icon must correctly identify the filename and path of the application's executable file; otherwise, Windows cannot start it. Likewise, when a folder or file accessed by the icon, or by the shortcut from the Windows 9x Start menu, is moved, renamed, or removed, Windows again cannot find it when asked to start the application.

Check the application's Properties to verify that the filename, path, and syntax are correct. An application's Properties can be accessed by right-clicking the application's desktop icon, as well as by right-clicking its entry in the Start menu, in the My Computer window, or in Windows Explorer.

Most applications require Registry entries to run. If these entries are missing or corrupt, the application does not start. In addition, Windows 9x and Windows Me retains the DLL structure of its Windows 3.x predecessor under the \Windows\System directory. Corrupted or conflicting DLL files prevent applications from starting. To recover from these types of errors, you must reinstall the application.

In some cases, the best method of correcting an application problem is to use the Add/Remove Programs utility to remove the failing application and then to reinstall it.

Optional Devices Will Not Operate in Windows 9x or Windows Me

Recall that optional devices such as modems, sound cards, and advanced I/O devices might configure properly as part of the PnP process and then fail to operate after the system starts.

To correct these problems in Windows 9x, start the system in safe mode. Windows loads a basic VGA video driver, enabling you to then change the display properties of the video card.

Similarly, adding input devices, such as a new mouse or joystick, can create problems where the new device does not work under the Windows environment. In both the Windows 9x and Windows Me operating systems, several tools can be used to identify and isolate hardware-related problems. These tools include the Device Manager (located under the System icon in Control Panel), the Hardware Troubleshooter procedures (located under the Help entry of the Start menu), and the various hardware-related icons in Control Panel.

Troubleshooting Windows 9x and Windows Me Printing Problems

If a printer is not producing anything in a Windows 9x or Windows Me environment, even though print jobs have been sent to it, check the print spooler to see whether any particular type of error has occurred. To view documents waiting to be printed, double-click the desired printer's icon.

Return to the Printer folder, right-click the Printer icon, click Properties, and then select Details. From this point, select Spool Settings, and select the Print Directly to the Printer option. If the print job goes through, a spooler problem exists. If not, the hardware and printer driver are suspect.

To check spooler problems, examine the system for adequate hard disk space and memory. If the Enhanced Metafile (EMF) Spooling option is selected, disable it, clear the spooler, and try to print.

To check the printer driver, right-click on the Printer icon, select the Properties option, and click the Details option. Reload or upgrade the driver if necessary. You can also stop the spooler service and restart it to see if the problem clears.

If the printer operation stalls during the printing operation, some critical condition must have been reached to stop the printing process (for example, the system was running but stopped). Restart the system in safe mode and try to print again. If the system still does not print, delete backed-up spool files (SPL and TMP) in the System\Spool\Printers directory.

Windows 9x and Windows Me Networking Problems

In Windows 9x or Windows Me, run the Add New Hardware Wizard and allow it to detect the network hardware. This should point out any hardware-related network problems. However, you might also want to click the Network icon in Control Panel to review the *network interface card* (*NIC*) settings. Use the *Detected Config* option from the adapter's Resources tab if the NIC settings are not known.

If the network adapter is installed and the cabling is connected correctly, the operating system's network support must be checked. The most obvious items to check are those found in the Properties dialog box of the Network Neighborhood window. Possible reasons for not being able to log on to the network include the following:

➤ Incorrect Services Settings (Check the Configuration tab)

➤ Incorrect Protocol Settings (Check the Configuration tab)

➤ Incorrect Adapter Settings (Check the Configuration tab)

➤ Incorrect Primary Network Logon Settings (Check the Configuration tab)

➤ Missing Computer Name (Check the Identification tab)

➤ Missing Workgroup Name (Check the Identification tab)

Begin the troubleshooting process by checking the system for resource conflicts that might involve the network adapter card. You can obtain this information by accessing the Device Manager. If a conflict exists, an exclamation point (!) should appear beside the network adapter card in the listing. If Windows thinks the card is working properly, the Device Manager displays a normal listing.

If a conflict is detected, move into the network adapter's Properties dialog box and check the adapter's resources against those indicated by the card's diagnostic utility. The conflict must be resolved between the network adapter and whatever device is using its resources.

If the adapter resources are okay, the next step depends on the type of symptom being encountered:

➤ Can any units be seen on the network?

➤ Can other units be seen but not used?

If the network cannot be seen in Network Neighborhood, or the network cannot be browsed from this utility, the network protocols and drivers should be checked. Network adapters and protocols are checked through the Network icon in Control Panel. Check the protocols listed in the Configuration tab's Installed Components window. Compare these to those listed on working units in the workgroup. Each machine must have all the clients and protocols other machines are using; otherwise, it is not possible to browse the network. The local computer and the Entire Network icon should be present, but the other units are not visible.

If you can browse the network but cannot access or use certain resources in remote locations, sharing is not turned on in the remote unit, or the local unit does not have proper access rights to that resource. To use the remote resource across the network, the system's File and Print functions must be turned on, and its Share function must be enabled. Turning on the File and Print functions places the local resources in the network's Browse listing.

This does not enable the Share function, however. The Share function is established by supplying the system with a valid share name. In addition, the computer must be running Client for Microsoft Networks for File and Print to be available on a Microsoft network. If this client service is not installed, the File and Print functions are unavailable for use (dimmed or grayed out). The Client for Microsoft Networks services component must be installed in the *Select Network Component Type* screen.

Troubleshooting Windows 9x and Windows Me Network Printing Problems

When printing cannot be carried out across the network, verify that the local computer and the network printer are set up for remote printing. This involves sharing the printer with the network users. The local computer that the printer is connected to is referred to as the print server and should appear in the Windows 9x Network Neighborhood window of the remote computer. If the local computer cannot see files and printers at the print server station, file and print sharing might not be enabled there.

In Windows 9x and Windows Me, file and printer sharing can be accomplished at the print server in a number of ways. First, double-click the printer's icon in the My Computer window, or in Windows Explorer. Single click on the desired Printer, click on the File menu, and select the Properties option from the drop-down list. From the Printer Properties page, click the Sharing tab, select the Share As option, and then choose the desired configuration settings.

The second method employs a right-click on the printer's icon, followed by selecting the Share option in the context menu, enabling the Share As option and then choosing the desired configuration. The final method is similar except that you right-click the printer's icon, click Properties and Sharing, and then set up the configuration.

If the local print server operation is working correctly, verify the operation of the network by attempting to perform other network functions, such as transferring a file from the remote unit to the print server. In Windows 9x and Windows Me, open the Printer folder (found in Control Panel) and select the Properties entry in the drop-down File menu. Check the information under the Details and Sharing tabs.

If other network functions are operational, verify the printer operation of the local computer. If possible, connect a printer directly to the local unit and set up its print driver to print to the local printer port. If the file prints to the local printer, a network/printer driver problem still exists. Reload the printer driver and check the network print path. The correct format for the UNC network path name is:

```
\\computer_name\shared_device_name
```

Windows 9x and Windows Me Dial-Up Problems

In Windows 9x, you can find the modem configuration information in Control Panel under the *Modems* icon. This icon has two tabs: the General tab and the Diagnostics tab.

The Properties button on the General tab provides *Port* and *Maximum Speed* settings in the resulting dialog box. Also, on this resulting dialog box you will see the Connection tab, which provides character-framing information, as illustrated in Figure 4.7. The Connection tab's Advanced button provides *Error and Flow Control* settings, as well as *Modulation Type*.

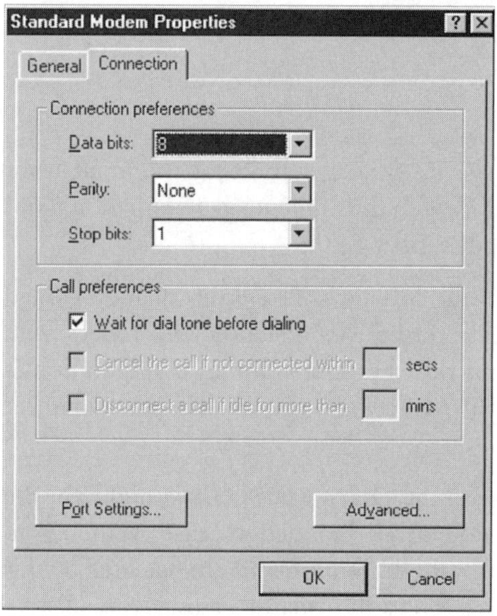

Figure 4.7   The Connection tab.

The Diagnostics tab, depicted in Figure 4.8, provides access to the modem's driver and additional information. The PnP feature reads the modem card and returns its information to the screen, as demonstrated in the depiction.

Reboot the system to determine whether the system can detect the modem. If not, check the modem's configuration settings in the Device Manager.

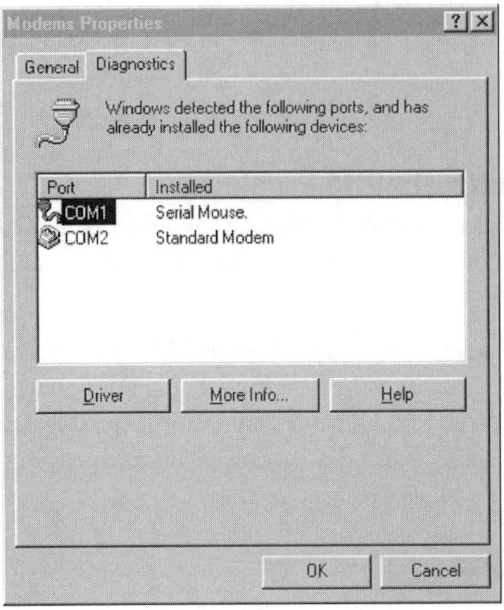

Figure 4.8 The Diagnostics tab.

If the modem is present, use the Device Manager to check the modem for resource conflicts. If there is a conflict with the modem, an exclamation point (!) should appear alongside the modem listing.

If you detect a conflict, move into the Modems, Properties dialog box and check the modem's resources. Also, record the Connection Preferences from the Connection tab and be certain the character-framing configuration is correct. The conflict must be resolved between the modem and whatever device is using its resources.

If no conflict is indicated, move into the Diagnostics tab and highlight the installed device. Click the More Info button. This action causes Windows to communicate with the modem hardware. If no problems are detected by this test, Windows 9x displays the modem's port information, along with a listing of the AT commands that it used to test the hardware. If an error is detected during the Windows testing, an error message displays onscreen. These messages are similar to those previously listed.

If the modem tests are okay, check the username and password settings. This can be accomplished through the My Computer, Dial-Up Networking path, or through the Start, Programs, Accessories, Communications, Dial-Up Networking path in Windows 98.

In the Dial-Up Networking window, right-click the desired connection icon, and click the Properties option from the shortcut menu. Check the phone number and modem type on the General tab. Next move into the Server Types tab and check the Type of Dial-Up Server Installed check box. For Windows Internet dial-up service, this is typically a "PPP, Internet, Windows NT, Windows 98" connection. Also, disable the NetBEUI and IPX/SPX settings from the tab and be certain that the TCP/IP setting is enabled.

In many business and travel settings you might need to specify a number, such as an 8 or a 9, which must be dialed first to obtain an outside line. If this value is not configured correctly for the facility you are calling from, the connection will fail.

Windows NT, Windows 2000, and Windows XP Startup Problems

For Windows 2000 and Windows XP, you can build on the operating system troubleshooting methodology previously discussed in the generic and Windows 9x and Windows Me sections. As with these other operating systems, if Windows 2000 or Windows XP fails to boot, the first troubleshooting step is to determine whether the computer is failing before or after the operating system takes control. If the startup process makes it to the beep that indicates the end of the POST, but you do not see the operating system's Boot Selection menu, the problem is probably one of the following:

➤ System partition

➤ Master Boot Record

➤ Partition boot sector

These types of problems are usually the result of hard disk media failures or a virus, and must be repaired before the operating system will function. Typical symptoms associated with hard disk media failures include the following:

➤ A blue screen or Stop message appears.

➤ Bootup stops after the POST.

➤ The Boot Selection menu is never reached.

➤ An error message is produced.

Windows 2000 and Windows XP might display a number of different error messages related to these problems, including the following:

➤ Missing Operating System

➤ Disk Read Error

➤ Invalid Partition Table

➤ Hard Disk Error (or Absent/Failed)

➤ Insert System Disk

➤ Error Loading Operating System

➤ Inaccessible Boot Device

The Error Loading Operating System message from the previous list indicates that the system partition was located, but could not start the operating system. The system partition on that drive could be missing or misidentified.

In Windows NT, the Disk Administrator utility is used to manage partitions on the system's disks. In Windows 2000 and Windows XP, this function is performed through the Disk Management utility.

Windows XP Professional includes a command-line utility called DISKPART.EXE that can be used to manage disks, volumes, and partitions from the command prompt. This utility enables you to create scripts for managing primary and extended partitions, as well as logical disks and different types of volumes.

The BOOT.INI or NTLDR files also could be missing or have become corrupted. If you receive a message indicating that a Kernel File Is Missing, or that the NTLDR Could Not Be Found, the partition boot sector is okay, but the NTLDR file is probably corrupt. Use the ATTRIB command-line utility to change the attributes. Copy the file over from the startup disk to the root folder. All the startup files, including NTLDR, BOOT.INI, NTDETECT, and NTOSKRNL, can be restored from the ERD.

The Missing Operating System and Invalid Partition Table errors indicate a problem with the MBR. In Windows 2000 and Windows XP, you can use the copy command in the Recovery Console to replace the MBR if the console has been installed beforehand. In Windows 2000, the *emergency repair process* can be used to repair the boot sector.

The Inaccessible Boot Device blue screen error occurs when applications, such as those furnished with CD-ROM recording packages, are removed from a Windows 2000 Professional system and it cannot find boot information that has been referenced through the Registry (that is, the application has written information directly into the Registry that the system is supposed to use for booting from CD-ROMs and it is no longer there).

One method of repairing this error involves using the *Recovery Console* to replace the system hive with an old copy that does not have the rewritten value in it. Other options include disabling the CD-ROM service and copying the system hive from a similar (parallel) system. All of these operations involve altering the system's Registry and, therefore, can seriously affect the system. Before performing any of these options, you should consult the Microsoft online Knowledge Base.

Windows 2000 and Windows XP Network Startup Problems

For network clients, such as Windows 2000 and Windows XP systems, one additional startup phase can produce errors. This is the *network logon phase* (which is automatic in client/server network environments).

1. **Check physical connectivity**—For failures during this portion of the startup procedure, the troubleshooting process should start by checking for physical connectivity issues. Observe the link light on the rear of the network adapter. If the light does not show activity, check the properties of the network adapter and its physical connection to the network cable.

2. **Check the Event Viewer for errors**—During this portion of the operating system startup, the desktop should appear on the screen. However, several communication services are still being loaded into the system behind the scenes. Failure to load one of these services (or the device that supports them) results in a Device or Service Has Failed to Start error message being displayed on the screen.

   In most cases, when this type of error occurs, you should still have a desktop display from which to work. However, the system is working in a standalone fashion. In Windows 2000 or Windows XP systems, you should access the Event Viewer utility and expand the System node to view the event log of system events looking for failures, such as

   ➤ Error loading the networking services

   ➤ Duplicate IP address

   ➤ DHCP server unavailable

   These errors point to particular types of errors that can be checked and corrected. Even if no desktop is available, you can restart the system in safe mode and access the Event Viewer and use these logs to isolate the cause of the error.

3. **Verify the TCP/IP configuration**—Use the IPCONFIG /ALL command to verify the TCP/IP configuration. Also, check the TCP/IP configuration under the Support tab of the connection status. Items to check closely include

➤ Incorrect or duplicate IP addresses

➤ Incorrect or missing subnet masks

➤ Incorrect or missing default gateways, DNS, or WINS server addresses

4. **Run the network connectivity tester**—In both Windows 2000 and Windows XP, you can run the network connectivity tester from the command line. The Netdiag.exe utility (also called *Network Connectivity Tester* in Windows XP) is a simple-to-use command-line tool that performs an array of tests on the network. It also provides a report about the status and functionality of network clients. All of the network tests are performed by default. Different switches can be used to limit the number and type of tests to be performed.

The network connectivity tester must be installed from the \SUPPORT\TOOLS folder of the Windows XP distribution CD. It is not part of the normal Windows installation.

5. In Windows XP, you can also use the *Network Diagnostics* tool located in the *Help and Support Center*. This tool (not to be confused with the Netdiag.exe command-line tool available in Windows 2000) provides a view of the network's hardware and software configuration.

In the Help and Support Center, select the Use Tools to View Your Computer Information and Diagnose Problems option from the Pick a Task menu. Then select the Network Diagnostics option from the list. The system conducts tests on the system and reports the results of the tests.

Windows NT, Windows 2000, and Windows XP Startup Troubleshooting Tools

Windows NT 4.0, Windows 2000, and Windows XP provide a wealth of tools for recovering from a startup problem, including the following:

➤ Windows NT 4.0 Startup Options

➤ Windows 2000 and Windows XP safe mode options

➤ Windows 2000 and Windows XP Recovery console

➤ Windows 2000 Emergency Repair Disk

➤ Windows XP System Restore function

➤ Windows XP Automated System Recovery

➤ Windows XP Driver Roll Back option

The following sections describe these tools and their use in detail.

Alternative Windows NT 4.0 Startup Modes

Unlike the Windows 9x and Windows Me products, Windows NT 4.0 provides very few options when it starts up. The user is normally offered two options. The system displays a selection menu of which operating system to boot from, along with an option to start the system in VGA mode. The menu listing is based on what NTLDR finds in the BOOT.INI file. If the VGA option is selected, the system starts up as normal, with the exception that it loads only the standard VGA driver to drive the display.

The second option presented is the Last Known Good Hardware Configuration option. Selecting this option causes the system to start up using the configuration information that it recorded the last time a user successfully logged on to the system. These options appear on the screen for a few seconds after the operating system selection is made. You must press the spacebar while the option is displayed on the screen to select this startup mode. If no selection is made, the system continues with a normal startup as previously outlined, using the existing hardware configuration information.

Alternative Windows 2000 and Windows XP Startup Modes

The Windows 2000 and Windows XP operating systems incorporate a number of Windows 9x–like startup options that can be engaged to get the system up and running in a given state to provide a starting point for troubleshooting operations. The Windows 2000 *Advanced Options Menu*, shown in Figure 4.9, contains several options that can be of assistance when you are troubleshooting startup failures. To display this menu, press F8 at the beginning of the Windows 2000 startup process.

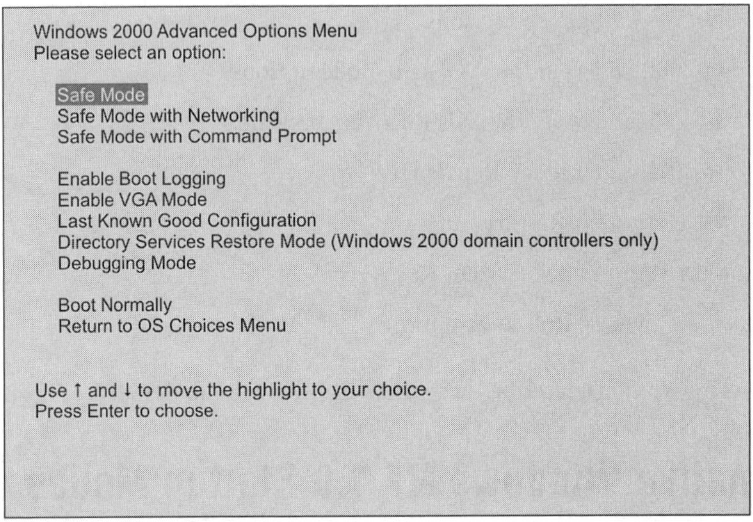

```
Windows 2000 Advanced Options Menu
Please select an option:

   Safe Mode
   Safe Mode with Networking
   Safe Mode with Command Prompt

   Enable Boot Logging
   Enable VGA Mode
   Last Known Good Configuration
   Directory Services Restore Mode (Windows 2000 domain controllers only)
   Debugging Mode

   Boot Normally
   Return to OS Choices Menu


Use ↑ and ↓ to move the highlight to your choice.
Press Enter to choose.
```

Figure 4.9 The Advanced Options menu.

The *Windows 2000 Advanced Options menu* basically provides the same safe mode options as the Windows 9x operating systems (that is, Boot Normally, Safe Mode, Safe Mode with Networking, and Safe Mode with Command Prompt). The Windows 2000 Advanced Options menu also provides a number of Windows NT–like options:

➤ **Enable Boot Logging**—This option creates a log file called NTBTLOG.TXT in the root folder. This log is similar to the BOOTLOG.TXT file described earlier in that it contains a listing of all the drivers and services that the system attempts to load during startup and can be useful when you are trying to determine which service or driver is causing the system to fail.

➤ **Enable VGA Mode**—When selected, this option boots the system normally but uses only the standard VGA driver. If you have configured the display incorrectly and are unable to see the desktop, booting into VGA mode enables you to reconfigure those settings.

➤ **Last Known Good Configuration**—This option starts Windows 2000 or Windows XP using the settings that existed the last time a successful user logon occurred. All system setting changes made since the last successful startup are lost. This option is particularly useful if you have added or reconfigured a device driver that is causing the system to fail.

➤ **Debugging Mode**—This option starts Windows 2000 or Windows XP in a kernel debug mode that enables special debugger utilities to access the kernel for troubleshooting and analysis.

Windows NT and Windows 2000 Emergency Disks

For Windows NT and Windows 2000, you should have two different types of troubleshooting-related disks on hand:

➤ Windows setup disks

➤ Emergency Repair Disks (ERDs)

Setup disks are the equivalent of the Windows 9x startup disk. Windows NT 4.0 generates a three-disk set, and Windows 2000 creates a four-disk set. Unlike the Windows 9x startup disk, the setup disks do not bring the system to a command prompt. Instead, they initiate the Windows setup process.

Both Windows NT 4.0 and Windows 2000 provide for an *Emergency Repair Disk (ERD)* to be produced. The ERD is different from the setup disks in that it is intended for use with an operational system when it crashes. It is not a bootable disk and must be used with the setup disks or the Windows distribution CD.

Whereas the setup disks are uniform for a given version of Windows NT, the ERD is specific to the machine from which it is created. It contains a copy of the *Security Accounts Manager (SAM)* in Windows NT and the Registry in Windows 2000. When dealing with the NT ERD, you need to manually copy the Registry files to the disk.

Windows NT and Windows 2000 Setup Disks

The Windows NT setup disks load a miniature file system into the system, initialize its drives, and start the installation process. All Windows NT setup disks are the same for all machines running that version of the operating system. To create setup disks under Windows NT 4.0, you must insert the Windows NT distribution CD in the system and type WINNT /ox at the command prompt.

Under Windows 2000, you must place the distribution CD in the drive and launch the *MakeBootDisk* utility to create the four disk images for its Windows 2000 setup disks. You can also create setup disks from the command prompt using the MAKEBT32.EXE file for Windows 2000. You also can make these disks by first selecting Start, Run, Browse, CD-ROM. Then, from the CD, select the BOOTDISK option, followed by the MAKEBT32.EXE command.

You can also create a Windows XP boot disk by formatting a floppy from a working Windows XP system. Then, you should copy the Ntldr, Ntdetect.com and Boot.ini files to the floppy. If the files Bootsect.dos or Ntbootdd.sys are present in the system, you should also copy these files to the floppy. However, these files are installation specific and might not work correctly on a machine other than the one used to create the floppy. This floppy can be used to boot the system and permit you to circumvent corrupt file problems on the system partition.

Windows NT 4.0 ERD

During the installation process, Windows NT setup asks whether you want to create an Emergency Repair Disk. You can also create an ERD later using the *Repair Disk* program (RDISK.EXE). To do so, select the Run option from the Start menu, enter the CMD command in the Run dialog box, and then type RDISK at the command prompt.

When Windows NT is installed, the setup routine stores Registry information in the \system32\config folder and creates a \repair folder to hold key files.

Windows 2000 ERD

The Windows 2000 setup routine prompts you to create an ERD during the installation process. The ERD can also be created using the Windows 2000 Backup utility, which you can access by selecting Start, Programs, Accessories, System Tools. The Windows 2000 ERD contains configuration information specific to the computer that is required during the emergency repair process.

Performing an Emergency Repair

The ERD provides another troubleshooting tool that can be used when safe mode and the Recovery Console do not enable you to repair the system. If you have already created an ERD, you can start the system with the Windows 2000 Setup CD or the setup floppy disks, and then use the ERD to restore core system files. The *emergency repair process* enables you to do the following:

➤ Repair the boot sector.

➤ Replace the system files.

➤ Repair the startup files.

The emergency repair process is designed to repair the operating system only, and cannot be of assistance in repairing application or data problems. To perform an emergency repair, follow these steps:

1. Boot the system from the Window 2000 CD. If the system does not boot from a CD, you must boot with the Setup Boot Disk (the first of four setup floppy disks that are required). You create the setup floppy disks with MAKEBOOT.EXE, which is in the \BOOTDISK folder in the Windows 2000 CD root directory.

2. When the text-mode portion of setup begins, follow the initial prompts. When you reach the Welcome to Setup screen, as shown in Figure 4.10, press the R key to repair the Windows 2000 installation.

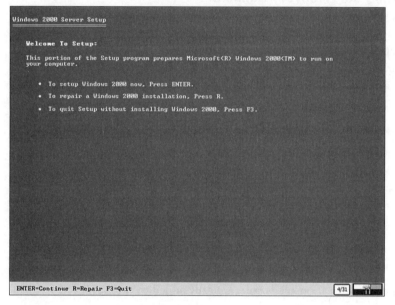

Figure 4.10   The Welcome to Setup screen.

3. When prompted, choose the Emergency Repair Process by pressing R.

4. When prompted, press F for Fast Repair.

5. Follow the instructions and insert the ERD into the floppy disk drive when prompted.

Windows 2000 and Windows XP Recovery Console

The *Recovery Console* available in Windows 2000 and Windows XP is a command-line interface that provides you with access to the hard disks and many command-line utilities when the operating system does not boot (that is, after the Last Known Good Configuration and safe mode options have been tried).

The Recovery Console can access all volumes on the drive, regardless of their file system type. However, if you have not added the Recovery Console option prior to a failure, you cannot employ it and need to use the Windows 2000 setup disks or the Windows 2000 or Windows XP distribution CD instead.

Installing the Recovery Console

The Recovery Console can be permanently installed on a system and be made accessible from the Advanced Options menu. You can start the Recovery Console at any time by booting from the Windows 2000 setup disks or the Windows 2000 or Windows XP distribution CDs, choosing to repair an installation, and selecting Recovery Console from the repair options.

To install the Recovery Console on a computer, follow these steps:

1. Put the Windows 2000 or Windows XP distribution CD in the CD-ROM drive, or connect to an installation share on the network (for example, the path on a Windows XP CD for installing the Recovery Console is D:\I386\WINNT32, where D:\ is the CD-ROM).

2. Run the winnt32 /cmdcons command. Windows 2000 and Windows XP setup starts up, as illustrated in Figure 4.11, and installs the Recovery Console.

3. The Recovery Console is automatically added to the Advanced Options menu.

Figure 4.11   Installing the Recovery Console using **Winnt32 /cmdcons**.

Using the Recovery Console

You can use the Recovery Console to perform tasks such as the following:

► Copy files from a floppy disk, CD, or another hard disk to the hard disk used for bootup, enabling you to replace or remove files that might be affecting the boot process. Because of the security features built in to Windows 2000 and Windows XP, you are granted only limited access to certain files on the hard drive. You cannot copy files from the hard drive to a floppy or other storage device under these conditions.

➤ Control the startup state of services, enabling you to disable a service that could potentially be causing the operating system to crash.

➤ Add, remove, and format volumes on the hard disk.

➤ Repair the Master Boot Record (MBR) or boot sector of a hard disk or volume.

➤ Restore the Registry.

You can use the Recovery Console to restore the Windows 2000 or Windows XP Registries. Every time you back up the System State data with Windows 2000 or Windows XP Backup, a copy of the Registry is placed in the \Repair\RegBack folder. If you use the copy command to move the entire contents of this folder (or only particular files) to \system_root\System32\Config (which is the folder where the working copy of the Registry is stored), you can restore the Registry to the condition it was in the last time you performed a System State data backup.

You can also accomplish this task through the Windows 2000 Backup/Restore function. You can access this function by selecting Start, Programs, System Tools, Backup. In Windows XP, the path is Start, All Programs, System Tools, Backup. You should create a copy of the files located in \System32\Config prior to restoring the other files from backup. This way, you can restore the Registry to its original condition if necessary.

Starting the Recovery Console

The Recovery Console can be started from the Repair option on the Windows 2000 setup disks or distribution CD. You can also use the Windows XP CD for Windows XP systems. To do so

1. Start the system with the distribution CD in the drive, and choose the option to Repair the installation (press the R key).

2. Enter the administrator's password to access the Recovery Console.

The password protection for the Recovery Console permits only two incorrect attempts by default. On the third incorrect attempt, the system stops accepting further entries for a predetermined amount of time (referred to as *lockout time*).

3. When prompted, choose the folder that contains the Windows 2000 or Windows XP installation that you are trying to repair.

4. Log on as the local Administrator and use the Recovery Console commands to perform the tasks described previously.

Recovery Console Commands

The commands that can be used with the Recovery Console include most of the MS-DOS–based commands for command-line navigation, creating, removing, and renaming directories. The include such standards as DIR, DEL, RD (RMDIR), MD (MKDIR), CD (CHDIR), and REN (RENAME). After you log on to the system, you can type HELP at the command line to obtain a list of available commands.

Other key Recovery Console commands you can use include CHKDSK, DISABLE, DISKPART, ENABLE, EXPAND, FIXBOOT, FIXMBR, FORMAT, LISTSVC, MAP, SET, SYSTEM_ROOT, and TYPE.

You can enter the CHKDSK command to run the Check Disk utility that examines the contents of the disk for faults and lost clusters.

Entering LISTSVC at the command prompt produces a listing of all the services and drivers available on the system. You can use the DISABLE and ENABLE commands to disable or enable selected Windows system services or drivers to determine whether it is causing the system startup to fail. If the system starts up after disabling a particular driver, you can focus on repairing that service or driver.

Likewise, the MAP command displays a drive letter listing of all the physical devices. The SET command is used to set the Recovery Console environment variables, while the SYSTEM_ROOT establishes the current directory to system_root.

Several disk-related commands are available through the Recovery Console. The DISKPART utility can be used to create and manage partitions on a drive, whereas the FIXBOOT and FIXMBR commands are used to repair defective master boot records and boot sectors. The FORMAT command formats the disk for use with the operating system.

You can use the EXPAND command to expand compressed files and you can use the TYPE command to display a test file on the screen.

One of the major Windows Me and Windows XP Recovery Console commands is Bootcfg. This command can be used to change the configuration of the BOOT.INI file or to recover from bootup problems. The Bootcfg file is only available for use through these Recovery Consoles.

Altering **BOOT.INI**

The BOOT.INI file in Windows NT, Windows 2000, and Windows XP systems is a special, hidden, read-only boot text file that is used to generate the Advanced Boot Options menu during the Windows NT, Windows 2000, and Windows XP startup process. The system reads this file during the bootup process and places the Advanced Boot Options menu on the screen to permit the user to select different bootup options. If no selection is made within a specified time frame, the bootup process continues in default mode.

The default values of the BOOT.INI file are generated automatically by the system when the Windows NT, Windows 2000, or Windows XP operating system is installed. You can access this file using a text editor. Before doing this, you must change its attributes so that it becomes visible and so that you can open it. You can do this by using My Computer, Windows Explorer, or the Attrib command.

The **BOOT.INI** File

The settings in the BOOT.INI file are used to select an operating system to boot to. It supports the starting of different Windows NT versions as well as provides for starting one non-NT operating system.

The BOOT.INI file contains two sections of text that can be read and modified. This enables technicians and administrators to configure the system so that the Advanced Boot Options menu displays the different operating system options available.

The following sample BOOT.INI file shows these two sections—the boot loader section and the operating system section—and features a dual-boot option:

```
[boot loader]timeout=30default=multi(0)disk(0)rdisk(0)partition(1)WINDOWS
[operating system] multi(0)disk(0)rdisk(0)partition(1)WINDOWS=
"Microsoft Windows XP Professional" /fastdetect
multi(0)disk(0)rdisk(0)partition(2)WINNT="Microsoft Windows 2000
Professional" /fastdetectC:\="Windows 98"
```

The *timeout=* value sets the time allowed for a boot option to be selected before the default setting is used. The default operating system selection is keyed to the information listed after the "default=" statement.

The *operating system* section contains a definition for each installed operating system. These definitions employ arc pathnames to direct the Ntldr file to the boot record of the selected operating system. Each definition also contains the text that will be displayed in the Advanced Boot Options menu, as well as any optional parameters.

The *multi* value defines the type of disk drive controller the system will look for (multi=IDE and scsi=SCSI adapter). The numeric value associated with this setting (called the *instance*) indicates which controller or channel should be used. The value in the example is 0 and indicates the first IDE controller.

The *disk* value indicates the instance of the hard drive that will be booted to. This value is always 0 for IDE drives, but can be altered to use different drives in a SCSI system.

The *rdisk* value indicates the instance of the hard disk on the adapter (or the SCSI logical unit number). A 0 is used for the first IDE drive or the first SCSI disk.

Likewise, the *partition* parameter indicates the partition number. The final entry indicates the */system_root* path to where the operating system is installed. This value is often \WINDOWS, WINNT, or WINNT.SRV—indicating the folder where the files are located.

You can manipulate these values to cause the system to use different options to start up. For example, changing the values of rdisk to 1 causes the system to seek the boot volume on the second drive of the first IDE controller. Likewise, changing the partition number to 3 causes the system to look to the third partition of the indicated adapter and disk.

BOOT.INI Switches

Many switches are available for use with the BOOT.INI entries in the menu to change the bootup process. Some of the switches that are particularly interesting for troubleshooting purposes are as follows:

➤ /BASEVIDEO forces the computer to start up using the Standard VGA driver.

➤ /DEBUG starts the system in debug mode, as described in the "Alternative Windows 2000 and Windows XP Startup Modes" section earlier in this chapter.

➤ MAXMEM:n can be used to specify the maximum amount of RAM with which the system starts up.

➤ /SOS displays the different drive names as they are loaded (similar to the step-by-step startup option in safe mode).

Using Device Manager

Hardware and configuration conflicts also can be isolated manually using the Windows 9x Device Manager from the System icon in Control Panel. This utility is basically an easy-to-use interface for the Windows 9x and Windows 2000 Registries.

You can use the Device Manager, depicted in Figure 4.12, to identify installed ports, update device drivers, and change I/O settings. From this window, the problem device can be examined to see where the conflict is occurring.

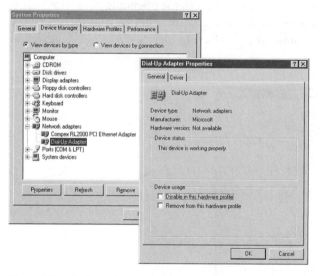

Figure 4.12 The Device Manager's display.

Two radio buttons on the Device Manager page can be used to alter the way it displays the devices installed in the system. Clicking the left button (the page's default setting), displays the system's devices alphabetically by device type. The rightmost radio button shows the devices by their connection to the system. As with the Registry and Policy Editors, the presence of plus (+) and (ms) signs in the nodes of the devices indicates expandable and collapsible information branches at those nodes.

The Device Manager displays an exclamation point (!) inside a yellow circle whenever a device is experiencing a direct hardware conflict with another device. The nature of the problem is described in the device's Properties dialog box. Similarly, when a red X appears at the device's icon, the device has been disabled due to a user selection conflict.

This situation can occur when a user wants to disable a selected device without removing it. For example, a user who travels and uses a notebook computer might want to temporarily disable device drivers for options that aren't used in travel. This can be accomplished through the Disable in This

Hardware Profile option in Device Manager. This keeps the driver from loading up until it is reactivated.

Clicking the Properties button at the bottom of the Device Manager screen produces the selected device's Properties dialog box. The three tabs at the top of the page provide access to the device's general information, driver specifications, and system resource assignments.

When a device conflict is suspected, just click the offending device in the listing, verify that the selected device is the current device, and then click the Resources tab to examine the conflicting device's list, as depicted in Figure 4.13.

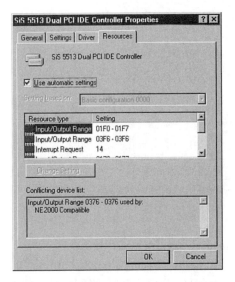

Figure 4.13 The Device Manager Resources dialog box.

To change the resources allocated to a device, click the resource to be changed, remove the check mark from the Use Automatic Settings box, click the Change Setting button, and scroll through the resource options. Take care when changing resource settings. The Resource Settings window displays all the available resources in the system, even those that are already spoken for by another device. You must know which resources are acceptable for a given type of device and which ones are already in use.

To determine what resources the system already has in use, click the Computer icon at the top of the Device Manager display. The Computer Properties page, depicted in Figure 4.14, provides ways to view and reserve system resources.

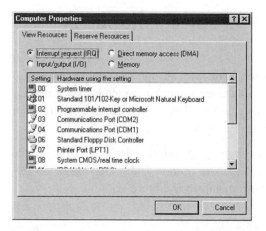

Figure 4.14 The Device Manager Computer Properties dialog box.

Through this page, you can click radio buttons to display the system's usage of four key resources: IRQ channels, DMA channels, I/O addresses, and memory addresses. The Reserve Resources page is used to set aside key resources to avoid conflicts with the PnP configuration operations. If a resource is reserved and Windows detects it as already in use, a warning dialog box displays onscreen and asks for a confirmation.

Normal causes for conflict include devices sharing IRQ settings, I/O address settings, DMA channels, or base memory settings. The most common conflicts are those dealing with the IRQ channels. Nonessential peripherals, such as sound and network adapters, are most likely to produce this type of conflict.

When a device conflict is reported through the Conflicting Device list on the Resource tab, record the current settings for each device, refer to the documentation for each device to determine what other settings might be used, and change the settings for the most flexible device. If either device continues to exhibit problems, reset the configurations to their original positions and change the settings for the other device.

Verify that the device has not been installed twice. When this occurs, it is normally impossible to determine which driver is correct. Therefore, it is necessary to remove both drivers and allow the PnP process to redetect the device. If multiple drivers are present for a given device, remove the drivers that are not specific to the particular device installed in the system.

Using the Windows XP Driver Rollback Feature

The Windows XP operating system includes an option that can be used to revert to an older device driver whenever a driver upgrade causes problems with a device. This feature is called *Driver Rollback* and can be implemented through the Windows XP Device Manager.

To roll back the driver, simply right-click on the device in the Device Manager listing and select the Properties option. Click the Driver tab followed by the *Roll Back Driver* button, shown in Figure 4.15.

Figure 4.15   Device Manager/Roll Back Driver option.

Windows XP System Restore

The Windows XP System Restore utility enables administrators to roll back the Windows XP Professional operating system to a previous operational state and configuration—without affecting any of the user's personal data. This feature extends the Last Known Good Configuration option by allowing the system to be rolled back to predetermined restore points.

Restore points are records of information that are created at specific intervals and when certain events occur. Some restore points are created automatically on a 24-hour/daily basis. Others are created when significant events occur, such as when you upgrade the system hardware or software, when you perform a recovery operation, or when a new driver is loaded. However, restore points can also be created manually as a method of preserving the current state of the operating system prior to performing management activities. Such activities include

➤ When you are updating a driver and it appears to cause problems with the system that rolling back the driver does not resolve

➤ When you are installing a new software program and it creates problems with the system that uninstalling the software does not resolve

➤ Any time you need to get back to a point at which you know the system was functioning correctly

You should actually create a restore point any time that you are making changes to the system that might make it unstable or that might disable it.

To access the System Restore Wizard through the *Help and Support* option (found on the Start menu), click the *Performance and Maintenance* option from its menu, click the Using System Restore to Undo Changes entry, and click the *Run the System Restore Wizard* option.

Using Windows XP System Restore

To activate the Windows XP System Restore Wizard, select Start, All Programs, Accessories, System Tools, System Restore. The Welcome screen is displayed, as shown in Figure 4.16.

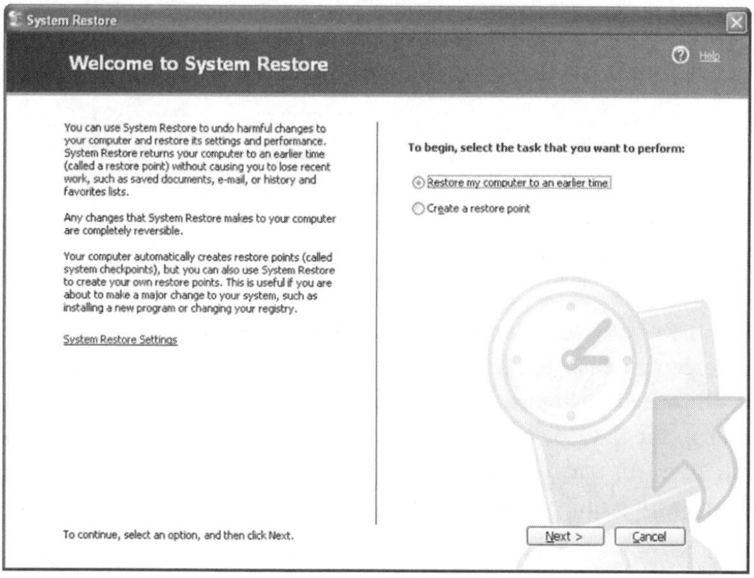

Figure 4.16 System Restore Welcome screen.

You must be a member of the Administrators group to use the System Restore feature.

To manually create restore points, simply select the *Create a Restore Point* option from the Welcome to System Restore screen (the Create a Restore Point option can also be accessed through the Help and Support Center option on the Start menu). Click the Next button and enter the name for the restore point in the Restore Point Description text box, as illustrated in Figure 4.17. The System Restore utility automatically adds this name, along with the time and date, to the restore point list. Click the Create button to finish the process.

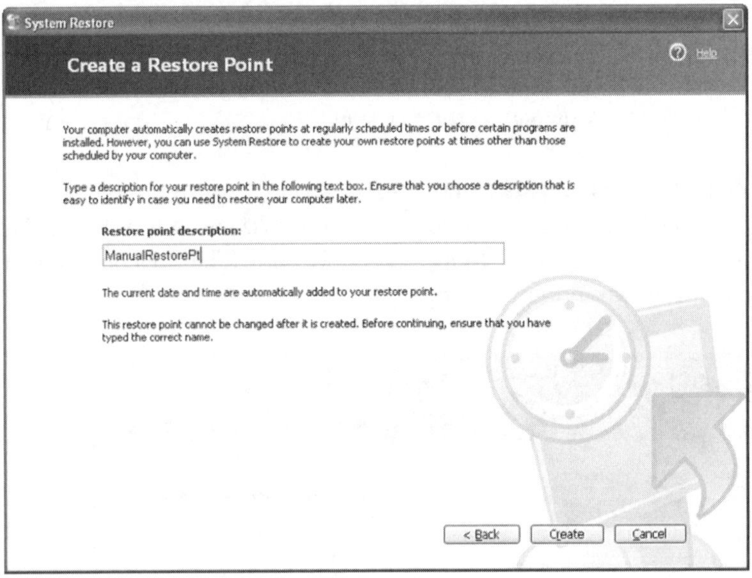

Figure 4.17 Creating a restore point.

Selecting the Restore My Computer to an Earlier Time option from the Welcome screen enables you to select a restore point from a calendar and a listing, as illustrated in Figure 4.18. Unless you simply need a restore point from earlier in the day, select the date on the calendar that you want to roll the system back to, and if there are multiple restore points for that day, choose the restore point you want to use.

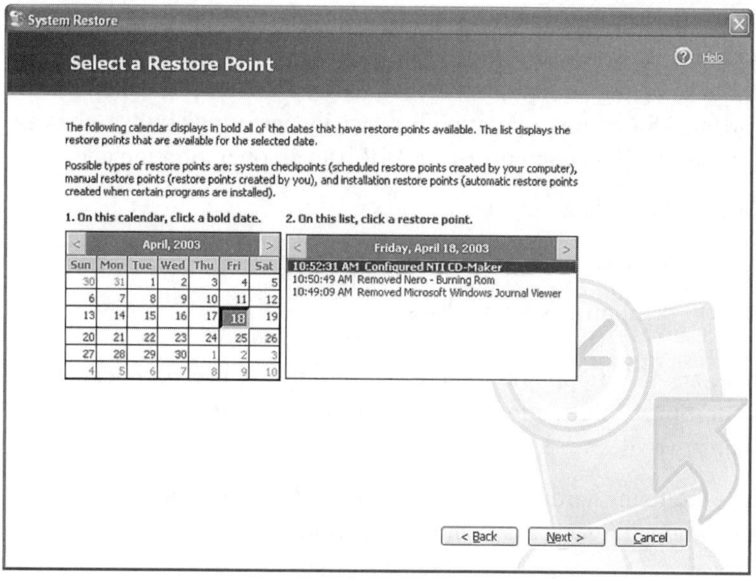

Figure 4.18 The Select a Restore Point screen.

After you confirm the restore point, the system conducts the rollback and restarts the system automatically. You can use the Undo option (Undo My Last Restoration) if the restore operation does not solve the problem or the problem is worse.

To access the System Restore Wizard through the Help and Support option on the Start menu, select the Performance and Maintenance option from its menu, click the Using System Restore to Undo Changes entry, and click the Run the System Restore Wizard option. You can also access the System Restore utility from Help and Support by selecting the Undo Changes to Your Computer with System Restore option. This is on the first page of the Help and Support menu and is somewhat easier to access.

Windows XP Automated System Recovery

In the Windows XP operating system, the ERD has been replaced with an emergency startup tool called the *Automated System Recovery (ASR)*. The ASR tool can be used to back up and restore the System State information, along with all the files stored on the system volume. As with the Windows NT and Windows 2000 Emergency Repair Disk, the ASR feature is considered to be the last resort to use when you have been unable to recover the system using other methods, including safe mode, Last Known Good Configuration, and Recovery Console.

The ASR utility is a function of the NTBackup.exe backup utility. As with other backup options, ASR is a two-part system: *backup and restore operations*. ASR backups should be performed periodically to keep them up to date. On the other hand, an ASR restore operation is normally performed only in the case of a system failure. The contents of an ASR backup operation include

➤ The System State data

➤ The system services

➤ The system components for all disks

In addition, an ASR floppy disk is created during the backup operation; it contains additional information required for the ASR restore process. This disk contains two files:

➤ Asr.sif—Contains hard disk, partition, and volume configuration information along with general system information

➤ Asrpnp.sif—Contains PnP device configuration data

Conducting ASR Backups

You perform ASR backup operations through the Windows XP Backup utility as follows:

1. Access the Windows XP Backup utility and click the Next button on the Backup and Restore Wizard Welcome screen.

2. From the Welcome screen, switch to Advanced mode.

3. Click the Automated System Recovery Wizard button, as shown in Figure 4.19, and click the Next button.

4. Select a backup media type, specify the backup name, and click the Finish button to complete the ASR backup operation.

You should not place the ASR backup on the system or boot volume when specifying a location for the backup. The system volume is reformatted during an ASR restore, and depending on the condition of the system, the boot volume might be reformatted as well. You should also be aware that performing a restore operation from network shares is not an option with ASR. You must use local devices, such as another hard disk, a CD-ROM, or a tape drive to hold the ASR backup.

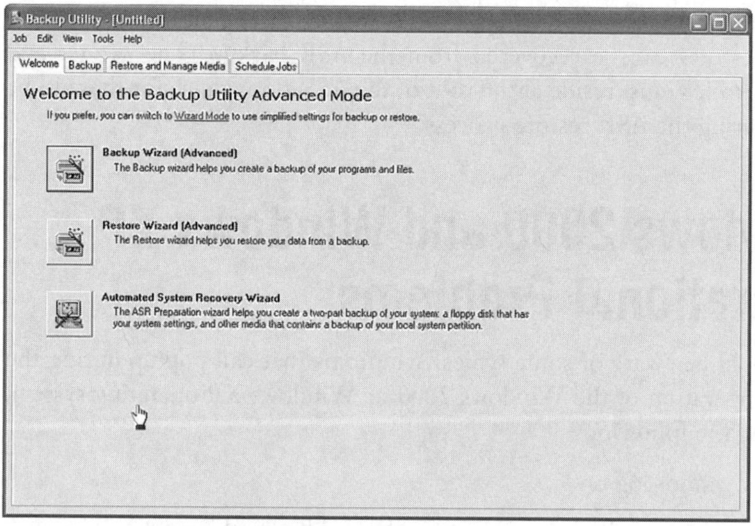

Figure 4.19   Launching the ASR Wizard.

NOTE

If the ASR backups are being used as a method of system restore, be certain that they are performed on a regular schedule.

ASR Restore Operations

The ASR restore process is launched from Windows XP Professional Setup as a part of the operating system install process (that is, the operating system is reinstalled, and then the ASR backup information is used to complete the restoration of the system).

The following three items are required to conduct the ASR restore operation:

➤ The Windows XP distribution CD

➤ The ASR floppy disk

➤ The ASR backup

You should be certain that you have access to these items prior to launching an ASR restore operation.

To perform an ASR restore, boot the system using the Windows XP Professional CD and press the F2 function key when the Welcome to Setup screen is displayed. The ASR process should automatically start at this point. Then, when prompted, insert the ASR floppy disk and simply follow the onscreen prompts.

In the event that the ASR floppy disk is lost or damaged, the Asr.sif and Asrpnp.sif files can be recovered from the ASR backup. The Asf.inf and Asrpnp.inf files must reside at the root of the ASR floppy disk for them to be found during the ASR restore process.

Windows 2000 and Windows XP Operational Problems

You should be aware of some typical symptoms that can pop up during the normal operation of the Windows 2000 or Windows XP operating system, including the following:

➤ A user cannot log on.

➤ You cannot recover an item that was deleted by another user.

➤ You cannot recover any deleted items.

➤ The video adapter supports higher resolution than the monitor does.

➤ You cannot find key files using Windows utilities.

When Windows 2000 or Windows XP is first installed, the only usable account is the Administrator account—the Guest account is disabled by default. An administrator must create any additional user accounts. Each user account is given a password and a username.

If a user cannot log on, check her password. The password is case sensitive, so verify that the Caps Lock key is not an issue. If you forget the Administrator password and have not created any other accounts with Administrator privileges, you must reinstall Windows 2000 or Windows XP.

You cannot recover an item that has been deleted by another user because the Recycle Bin is maintained on a user-by-user basis. If one user deletes something, only that user can recover it. You must log on as the user who deleted the item. Files and folders deleted from a floppy disk or network drive are permanently deleted and cannot be recovered. After the Recycle Bin fills to capacity, any newly deleted file or folder causes older deleted items to be automatically removed from the Recycle Bin.

Optional Devices Will Not Operate in Windows 2000 or Windows XP

As with Windows 9x and Windows Me, there are times when optional devices such as modems, sound cards, and advanced I/O devices might configure properly as part of the PnP process and then fail to operate after the system starts.

In a Windows NT, Windows 2000, or Windows XP system, you should select the VGA Mode option to gain access to the video configuration by loading a standard VGA driver.

Windows XP offers Device Driver Rollback, System Restore, and Disable This Device options that can be used to replace a failing or older driver (other than a printer driver) that might be the source of a problem. The Device Driver Rollback option reinstalls the driver that was being used previous to the current driver and restores any driver settings that were updated when the driver was installed.

The System Restore feature can be used to restore the system and its applications to a previous operating configuration that was known to be working correctly at a specific point. You would resort to this method of changing the device driver in Windows XP if the Device Driver Rollback option does not repair the system.

The Disable This Device option should be used when you believe that a specific device is causing a system problem. This option simply disables the device and its drivers so that you can verify that it is the actual cause of whatever problem the system is experiencing.

Windows 2000 and Windows XP Application Problems

Windows 2000 and Windows XP can suffer the same types of application problems described for the Windows 9x and Windows Me versions:

➤ Incorrect application properties (filename, path, and syntax)

➤ Missing or corrupt Registry entries

➤ Conflicting DLL files

As with Windows 9x or Windows Me systems, check the application's Properties to verify that the filename, path, and syntax are correct. An application's Properties can be accessed by right-clicking the application's desktop icon, as well as by right-clicking its entry in the Start menu, in the My Computer window, or in Windows Explorer.

The Windows Application Installer in both Windows 2000 and Windows XP provides better DLL handling than previous Windows versions. In previous versions of Windows, applications copied similar versions of shared DLL files, and other support files, into the \Windows folder. When a new application overwrites a particular DLL file that another application requires for proper operation, a problem is likely to occur with the original software package.

The Windows 2000/XP *Application Installer* enables applications to check the system before introducing new DLLs to the system. Software designers who want their products to carry the Windows 2000 or Windows XP logo must write code that does not place proprietary support files in the \Windows directory—including DLL files. Instead, the DLL files are located in the application's folder.

Windows Installer-compatible applications can repair themselves if they become corrupted. When the application is started, the operating system checks the properties of its key files. If a key file is missing, or appears to be damaged, it invokes the Installer and prompts the user to insert the application distribution CD. After the CD is inserted, the Installer automatically reinstalls the file in question.

Problems with Windows NT, Windows 2000, and Windows XP Files, Folders, and Printers

Because Windows NT, Windows 2000, and Windows XP are typically used in client/server networks, some typical administrative problems associated with files, folders, and printers can pop up during normal operations. These problems include such things as

➤ Users cannot gain access to folders.

➤ Users complain that they can see files in a folder, but cannot access any of the files.

➤ Users cannot make changes to files inside a folder.

➤ Users cannot set NTFS permissions on files or folders.

In the Windows NT, Windows 2000, and Windows XP environment, a user might not have permissions that enable him to access different files and folders. This is an administrative decision and can only be overcome by an administrator establishing permission levels that permit access.

When users complain that they can see files in a folder, but cannot access any of the files, they might have been assigned the List permission at the folder level. The List permission enables users only to view the contents of the folder, denying them all other permissions, including Read and Execute.

For users who have Read permission for a folder, but can still make changes to files inside the folder, their file permissions must be set to Full Control, Write, or Modify. These permissions are set directly to the file and override the folder permissions of Read. You can correct this by changing the permissions on the individual files or at the folder level and allow the permissions to propagate to files within the folder.

With users who complain that they cannot set any NTFS permissions, the first item to check is that the file or folder is on an NTFS partition. FAT16 and FAT32 have no security options that can be assigned. If the partition is NTFS, the user must have Full Control permission to set any security permissions to a file or folder.

Locating Hidden Files

By default, Windows 2000 and Windows XP hide known filename extensions. If you cannot see filename extensions, open Windows Explorer, click Tools, click Folder Options, click the View tab, and deselect the Hide File Extensions for Known Files option.

Likewise, Windows 2000 and Windows XP by default do not display hidden or system files in Windows Explorer. To see hidden or system files, open Windows Explorer, click Tools, click Folder Options, click the View tab, and select the Show Hidden Files and Folders option.

Applications Will Not Install

Most applications will autorun when their distribution CD is placed in the drive. If the Autorun feature in Windows 2000 or Windows XP is disabled in the drive's Properties dialog box, the automatic interface does not start and the installation is not performed.

If an application is not on the Windows 2000 *Application Compatibility Toolkit (ACT)*, the software equivalent of the *Hardware Compatibility List (HCL)* listing, the application might not install on the system or operate properly. This toolkit can be downloaded from the Microsoft Upgrade web page.

Windows 2000 and Windows XP Operational Troubleshooting Tools

The Windows 2000 and Windows XP operating system versions have taken a different approach to system administration and preventive maintenance by concentrating many of the system's administration tools in a single location, under the *Administrative Tools* icon in Control Panel.

The tools are combined in the Windows 2000 and Windows XP *Computer Management Console*. You can access the Management Console by right-clicking the My Computer icon and selecting the Manage option from the pop-up menu. The resulting console includes three primary *Microsoft Management Consoles* (*MMCs*):

➤ System tools

➤ Storage

➤ Services and applications

Two of the main tools involved in solving Windows 2000 or Windows XP operational problems are the Event Viewer and the Task Manager utilities.

Windows 2000 and Windows XP Event Viewer

In Windows 2000 and Windows XP, significant events (such as system, application, and security events) are routinely monitored and stored. These events can be viewed through the Event Viewer utility, shown in Figure 4.20. To access this tool, select Control Panel, Administrative Tools, Computer Management.

System events include items such as successful and failed Windows component startups, as well as successful loading of device drivers. Likewise, application events include information about how the system's applications are performing. Not all Windows applications generate events that the Event Viewer logs. Security events are produced by user actions, such as logons and logoffs, file and folder accesses, and creation of new Active Directory accounts.

Three default event logs track and record the events just mentioned. The system log records events generated by the operating system and its components. The application log tracks events generated by high-end applications.

Likewise, the security log contains information generated by audit policies that have been enacted in the operating system. If no audit policies are configured, the security log remains empty.

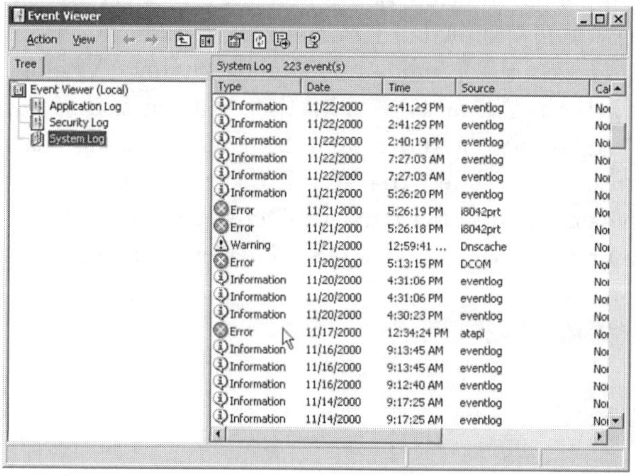

Figure 4.20   Windows 2000 Event Viewer.

In addition to the default logs, some special systems such as domain controllers and DNS systems have specialized logs to track events specifically related to the function of the system.

The Event Viewer produces three categories of system and application events:

➤ **Information events**—Events that indicate an application, service, or driver has loaded successfully. These events require no intervention.

➤ **Warning events**—Events that have no immediate impact, but that could have future significance. These events should be investigated.

➤ **Error events**—Events that indicate an application, service, or driver has failed to load successfully. These events require immediate intervention.

Figure 4.20 depicts the Windows 2000 Event Viewer displaying these types of events. Notice that the information events are denoted by a small "i" in a cloud, whereas warning and error events are identified by an exclamation mark (!) and an X, respectively.

Windows NT, Windows 2000, and Windows XP Task Manager

In Windows NT, Windows 2000, and Windows XP, the Close Program dialog box is referred to as the *Task Manager*. This utility can be used to determine which applications in the system are running or stopped, as well as which resources are being used. You can also determine the general micro-processor and memory usage levels.

When an application hangs up in these operating systems, you can access the Windows Task Manager window, shown in Figure 4.21, and remove it from the list of tasks. You can access the Windows 2000 and Windows XP Task Manager by pressing Ctrl+Alt+Del or Ctrl+Shift+Esc. You can also access the Task Manager by right-clicking the system tray and selecting Task Manager from the context menu. The Ctrl+Shift+Esc key sequence moves directly into Task Manager, whereas the Ctrl+Alt+Del selection opens the Windows Security menu screen, which offers Task Manager as an option.

Figure 4.21 The Windows Task Manager.

To use the Task Manager, select the application from the Applications tab and click the End Task button. If prompted, click the End Task button again to confirm the selection. The Processes tab provides information that can be helpful in tracking down problems associated with slow system operation. The Performance tab provides a graphical summary of the system's CPU and memory usage.

Windows 2000 and Windows XP System Information

The Windows 2000 and Windows XP *System Information* utility provides five subfolders of information about the system, as illustrated in the right pane of Figure 4.22. These folders include a system summary, a list of hardware resources being used, a list of I/O components in the system, a description of the system's current software environment, and a description of Microsoft Internet Explorer.

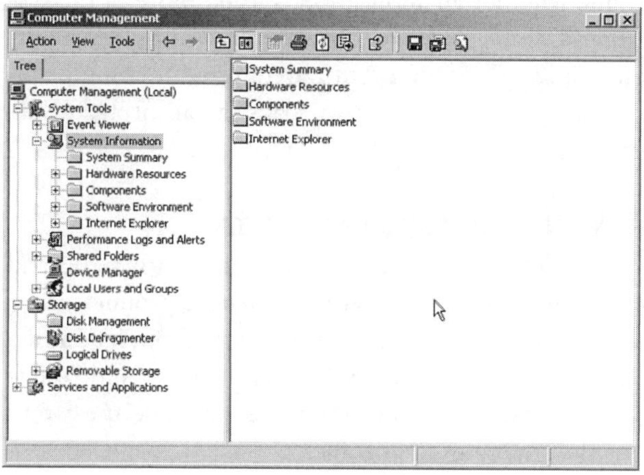

Figure 4.22 The System Information tool.

As with the Windows 98 and Windows Me System Information tool, the Windows 2000 and Windows XP version can be used to enable remote service providers to inspect the system's information across a LAN environment. To save system information to a file, right-click the System Information entry and select the Save As option from the resulting menu. Saving this information enables you to document events and conditions when errors occur. You can use the results of different system information files to compare situations and perhaps determine what changes might have occurred to cause the problem.

Applying Task Manager to Application Problems

In Windows 2000 and Windows XP, the *Task Manager* can be used to monitor the condition and operation of application programs and key Windows operating system services and components. In these operating systems, the Task Manager is available at any time and can be accessed by pressing the Ctrl+Alt+Del key combination.

When the Task Manager appears, the Applications tab is shown by default. The tab displays the applications that are currently running in the system along with a description of their status (for example, Running or Not Running). When an application is present in this window and shows a Not Running status, it has stalled and you should remove it. You can use this tab to remove these applications from the active system by highlighting the task and clicking the End Task button.

If the system is running slow, you should consult the Processes tab of the Task Manager to determine whether an application is using more of the system's resources than it should. If the memory usage number for a given application consistently grows, the application might have a programming problem known as a memory leak. Over time, memory leaks can absorb all of the system's free memory and crash the system.

Applying Event Viewer to Application Problems

Although Blue Screen Stop errors are primarily associated with setup and configuration problems involving new hardware or software products, they can happen at any time. When they occur during the normal operation of a Windows NT, Windows 2000, or Windows XP system, you should restart the system and see if it reoccurs. When the system restarts, use the Event Viewer utility to look for the source of the problem.

The Windows 2000 and Windows XP application logs can be used to examine the operation of the higher-end applications and some operating system services. The contents of this log can be examined through the Event Viewer utility to determine what conditions the system logged leading up to a failure, such as an application failing to start or stalling. The Event Viewer shows whether the application or service ran correctly. It might also indicate present conditions that you should take note of before they become failures.

Another indicator of application-related problems is the appearance of an Event Log Is Full error message. The event logs have a specified maximum file size that they can become before they are considered full. By default, the event logs are set to overwrite any log data that is more than seven days old if they become full. Therefore, if events are occurring so quickly that the logs fill up before the default time, this indicates that an excessive number of system errors (events) are occurring. You should examine the full event log to determine what activity is accounting for so many loggable events.

In the case of failure events, the system normally generates a user alert through a pop-up dialog box on the screen. The information in the box indicates the nature of the problem and refers you to the Event Viewer for details. The Event Viewer is available through the Start, Programs, Administrative Tools, Event Viewer path.

Using Dr. Watson

The main tool for isolating and correcting GPFs is the Dr. Watson utility provided in all Windows versions. It is used to trace problems that appear under certain conditions, such as starting or using a certain application. When Dr. Watson is started, it runs in the background with only an icon appearing on the taskbar to signify that it is present. For a GPF that cannot be directly attributed to the Windows operating system, an application program might be the source of the problem and the Dr. Watson utility should be set up to run in the background as the system operates.

As the system operates, the Dr. Watson utility monitors the code moving through the system and logs its key events in the DRWATSON.LOG file. When a system error occurs, the Dr. Watson log contains a listing of the events that were going on up to the time of the failure. This log provides programmers with a detailed listing of the events that led up to the failure. The information is automatically stored in the log file so that it can be provided to software developers, or to Microsoft, so that they can debug their software and produce patches for it. In many cases, the program describes the nature of the error and possibly suggests a fix.

The Dr. Watson utility is not located in any of the Windows 98, Windows Me, Windows 2000, or Windows XP menus. To use it, you must execute the program by clicking Start, clicking Run, typing the name drwatson in the dialog box, and then clicking OK to start the log file. This causes the Dr. Watson icon to appear on the taskbar. Dr. Watson also can be started through the Tools menu in the System Information screen. This option is located in the Start, Programs, Accessories, System Tools path.

Troubleshooting Windows 2000 and Windows XP Printing Problems

As with Windows 9x or Windows Me systems, if a printer is not producing anything in a Windows 2000 or Windows XP environment, even though print jobs have been sent to it, check the print spooler to determine whether any particular type of error has occurred.

The local printer troubleshooting process in Windows 2000 and Windows XP involves the following steps:

1. **Check the queue**—Verify that the print jobs are reaching the queue. Double-click the specific Printer icon and examine the list of jobs waiting to be printed. If the jobs are making it to the queue, check the operation of the printer. Check the simple things such as the On/Off switch, paper, cabling, and error codes. Also, check to see that the proper printer is being selected as the target for the jobs. If these items

are correct, cycle the printer on and off to see if the condition resets. Finally, recycle the host computer to see if the problem disappears.

2. **Check the spooler**—If the jobs are making it to the printer and the physical printer seems to be working correctly, select the Print Directly to the Printer option to determine whether a job is stuck in the spooler. Also disable EMF spooling by clearing the Enable Advanced Printing Features check box on the Advanced tab of the printer's Properties. If a job is stuck, stop and start the Print Spooler service through the Services option in Computer Management.

You should also check the amount of disk space available for the Print Spooler's stored jobs. If the amount of disk (or volume) space is too small to store the jobs while they are waiting for the printer, you will receive error messages and the document will not print. To correct this situation, you can either free up additional space on the drive, or move the spool directory to another drive.

3. **Check the printer driver**—Often, a corrupt or incorrect driver causes the printer to produce garbled print. In Windows XP, access the Advanced tab of the printer's Properties to check and update the driver. Attempt to print from another application to determine whether the application is having a problem. If the second application produces correct output, reinstall the failing application.

Troubleshooting Windows 2000- and Windows XP-Related Network Printing Problems

Windows 2000 and Windows XP machines are typically used in domain-based client server environments in which administrators set permissions and limit access and usage of resources such as printers.

In addition to the normal network-related problems discussed in the General and Windows 9x and Windows Me Network Printing Problem sections, you must verify that the permission levels for the user is correct to allow printing to go on. Check the Sharing tab of the printer's Properties page.

Similarly, if a print job is visible in the spooler but does not print, the printer availability hours might be set for times other than when the print job was submitted.

Troubleshooting Windows 2000 and Windows XP Blue Screen Errors

In the normal course of operation, Windows NT, Windows 2000, or Windows XP can encounter situations that cause it to stop and display a blue screen on the display. Collectively, these errors are referred to as *Stop errors* and basically occur whenever Windows NT, Windows 2000, and Windows XP operating systems detect a condition from which they cannot recover. The system stops responding, and a screen of information with a blue or black background display, as illustrated in Figure 4.23, appears. Stop errors are also known as *Blue Screen errors*, or simply as the *Blue Screen of Death (BSOD)*.

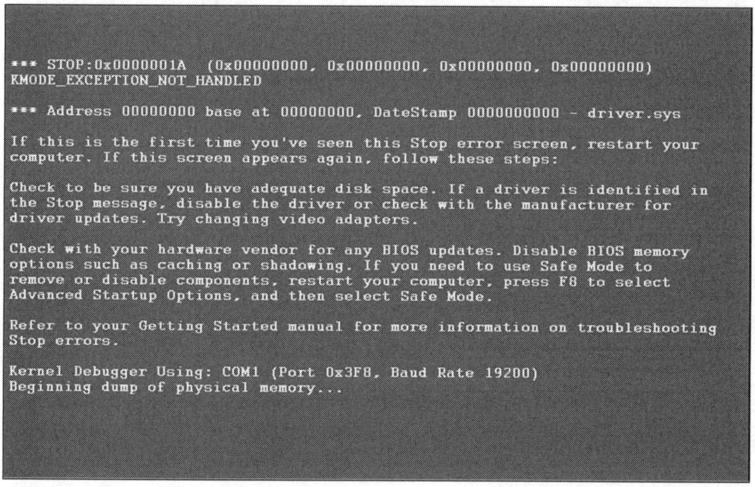

```
*** STOP:0x0000001A  (0x00000000, 0x00000000, 0x00000000, 0x00000000)
KMODE_EXCEPTION_NOT_HANDLED

*** Address 00000000 base at 00000000, DateStamp 00000000 - driver.sys

If this is the first time you've seen this Stop error screen, restart your
computer. If this screen appears again, follow these steps:

Check to be sure you have adequate disk space. If a driver is identified in
the Stop message, disable the driver or check with the manufacturer for
driver updates. Try changing video adapters.

Check with your hardware vendor for any BIOS updates. Disable BIOS memory
options such as caching or shadowing. If you need to use Safe Mode to
remove or disable components, restart your computer, press F8 to select
Advanced Startup Options, and then select Safe Mode.

Refer to your Getting Started manual for more information on troubleshooting
Stop errors.

Kernel Debugger Using: COM1 (Port 0x3F8, Baud Rate 19200)
Beginning dump of physical memory...
```

Figure 4.23 Stop error or Blue Screen error.

Although Stop errors occur most frequently after new hardware devices (or their device drivers) have been installed, they can also occur when the system is running low on disk space. In addition, they can occur without apparent reasons on systems that have been running for some time without a problem.

When a Stop error occurs, you can perform the following activities to gather additional information about what caused the error so that you can troubleshoot and repair it:

➤ Restart the system to determine whether the error repeats itself. In many cases, a temporary condition in the system can cause a stop error to occur. In these cases, simply restarting the system corrects the condition.

➤ If new hardware devices or updated drivers have been installed in the system, verify that they have been installed correctly and that they are the most current version of its device drivers. Check the Windows HCL to verify that any newly installed hardware and device drivers are compatible with the operating system version.

➤ Remove any newly installed hardware and restart the system. If the operating system starts up, use the Event Viewer utility to view any error messages generated before the Stop error occurred.

➤ Restart the system in *safe mode*. If the system starts up, remove any newly installed drivers or applications that could possibly be causing the Stop error.

➤ Attempt to restart the system using the *Last Known Good Configuration* boot option. This resets the system and provides an opportunity to install the new hardware device again.

➤ Access the Windows Components window of the Add/Remove Software applet and be certain that the latest available service pack for the operating system has been installed.

➤ Access the Microsoft Support Center or TechNet website, and search for information about the particular Stop error number you are encountering.

➤ Access the CMOS setup utility, and disable any memory caching or shadowing options that have been established.

➤ Restart the system using a software diagnostic utility, and check the system for memory errors.

➤ Check the system for viruses.

Windows 2000 and Windows XP Networking Problems

Because Windows NT, Windows 2000, and Windows XP systems are typically involved in client/server networks, the types of problems encountered are somewhat different than those found in Windows 9x network environments. Typical networking problems that can occur during normal Windows 2000 and Windows XP operations include the following:

➤ The user cannot see any other computers on the local network.

➤ The user cannot see other computers on different networks.

➤ The clients cannot see the DHCP server, but do have an IP address.

➤ The clients cannot obtain an IP address from a DHCP server that is on the other side of a router.

A major cause of connectivity problems is the physical layer. Check to see that the computer is physically connected to the network and that the status light is glowing (normally green). The presence of the light indicates that the NIC sees network traffic.

If a client cannot see any other computers on the network, improper IP addressing might be occurring. This is one of the most common problems associated with TCP/IP. Users must have a valid IP address and subnet to communicate with other computers. If the IP address is incorrect or invalid, or conflicts with that of another computer on the network, you can see your local computer, but you cannot see others on the network.

One reason for an incorrect IP address is that the local system in a TCP/IP network is looking for a DHCP server that is not present. In some LANs, the DHCP server is used to dynamically assign IP addresses to its clients on the network. In large networks, each segment of the network requires its own DHCP server to assign IP addresses for that segment. If the DHCP server is missing or not functioning, none of the clients in that segment can see the network.

Likewise, if a DHCP client computer is installed in a network segment that does not use DHCP, it needs to be reconfigured manually with a static IP address. The DHCP settings are administered through the TCP/IP Properties dialog box. This dialog box is located under the Start, Settings, Networking and Dial-Up Connections option. From this point, open the desired local area or dial-up connection and click the Properties button.

Begin by checking the TCP/IP Properties under the Network icon. Next check the current TCP/IP settings by using the IPCONFIG/ALL (or the WINIPCFG) command-line utility. They offer a starting point for troubleshooting. Afterward, use the PING utility to send test packets to other local computers you have found. The results of this action indicate whether the network is working.

If users can see other local computers on a TCP/IP network, but cannot see remote systems on other networks, you might have routing problems. Determine whether the address for the default gateway (router) listed in the TCP/IP properties is valid.

Use the NET VIEW command to determine whether the remote computer is available. If the user is relying on the My Network Places feature to see other computers, a delay in updating the Browse list might cause remote systems to not be listed. The NET VIEW command directly communicates with the remote systems and displays available shares.

If the clients have an IP address of 169.254.xxx.xxx, it is because they cannot communicate with the DHCP server. Windows 98, Windows Me, Windows 2000, and Windows XP automatically assign the client computer an IP address in the 169.254 range, if it cannot be assigned an address from a DHCP server.

Many routers do not pass the broadcast traffic generated by DHCP clients. If clients cannot obtain an IP address from a DHCP server that is located on the other side of a router, the network administrator must enable the forwarding of DHCP packets, or place a DHCP server on each side of the router.

Windows 2000 and Windows XP Dial-Up Problems

In Windows 2000 and Windows XP systems, the *Phone and Modem* tabs are Dialing Rules, Modems, and Advanced. Under these operating systems, the Properties button on the Modems tab provides access to all of the settings listed for the Windows 9x and Me dialog boxes and tabs.

As with Windows 9x and Windows Me systems, reboot the system to determine whether it can detect the modem. If not, check the modem's configuration settings in the Windows 2000 or Windows XP Device Manager. If the modem is present, use the Device Manager to check the modem for resource conflicts. If you detect a conflict, move into the Modem's Properties dialog box and check its resources. The conflict must be resolved between the modem and whatever device is using its resources.

Return to the Phone and Modem applet and examine the modem Properties.

Troubleshooting Internet Connection Sharing

Windows 2000 and Windows XP enable networked computers to share a single connection to the Internet. This feature is known as Internet Connection Sharing (ICS) and must be configured on the connection host and the client computers in the network. ICS is configured on the host computer through the Advanced tab of its Local Area Connection properties. On this tab, check the Allow Other Network Users to Connect Through This Computer's INTERNET Connection check box.

Each client computer must be configured to automatically obtain an IP address. The ICS service dynamically assigns the client computers an IP configuration using an IP address in the range of 192.168.0.x, with a subnet mask of 255.255.255.0. It also produces a default gateway address of 192.168.0.1 and a DNS server address of 192.168.0.1.

If the ICS function is not working:

1. Verify that the ICS host computer is configured to share its Internet connection. Also be certain that the ICS host is not enabled to automatically obtain an IP address.

2. Check the clients' IP configuration settings to ensure they are within the ranges listed in the previous paragraph. The x value in the IP address must be between 2 and 254.

3. If the clients' IP addresses are 169.254.0.0, the ICS function is not supplying the IP address. This address is the default for the APIPA function. From the command prompt, run the IPCONF /RENEW command to determine whether an appropriate address can be obtained. If not, you should examine the physical connections for the network and be certain that the ICS function is enabled properly.

4. Check the ICS host's connection to the Internet. If the clients are receiving the proper IP configurations but cannot connect to the Internet, the problem most likely involves the host to ISP connectivity.

5. Check the network for other DHCP services that might be conflicting with the ICS function (such as a wireless router configured to provide DHCP services).

PART III
Technical Data

5 Important Resources

Important Resources

Introduction

This chapter contains information and references useful in everyday computer administration and troubleshooting situations.

The first sections deal with working from the command prompt in both Microsoft and Linux systems. Key information in these sections includes common commands used for navigation and troubleshooting as well as command-line utilities.

The midsection of this chapter is dedicated to cabling associated with PC peripheral and networking systems. This information includes information about different cable specifications and wiring pinouts for constructing common cable types.

The final sections of this chapter provide resource listing for obtaining help and technical information and for contacting key manufacturers and support services in the PC business.

Using the Windows Command Line

At times, you might need to reduce the operation of the PC to its most basic components. These times are normally associated with the system being broken. In many cases, whatever is broken affects the graphical nature of the Windows operating systems. Therefore, the graphical portions of the operating system are usually the first things to go when the system breaks down.

Both the Windows 9x/Me and Windows NT/2000/XP lines of operating systems provide an MS-DOS-like command-line interface that works independently of their GUIs.

The command line is the space immediately following the command line's drive letter prompt on the screen. All command-line functions and actions are typed into the space immediately to the right of the prompt. These commands are executed by pressing the Enter key on the keyboard. The command prompt for using the C hard disk drive as the active directory is displayed in Figure 5.1.

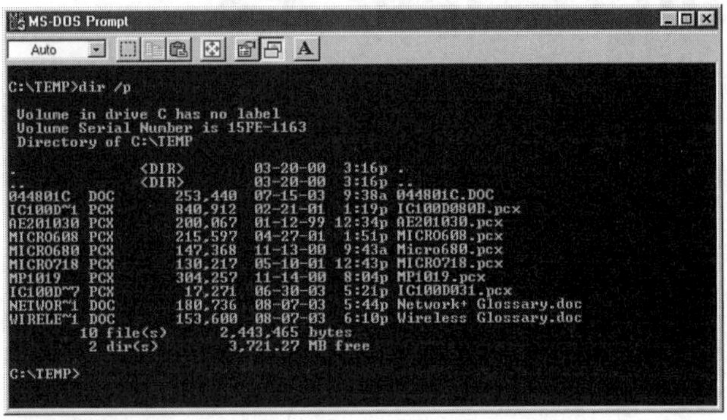

Figure 5.1 The command prompt.

Accessing the Windows Command Prompt

Access to the command prompt interface is provided through different paths in the different operating systems. Therefore, you must know how to reach the interface in each operating system. To access the MS-DOS emulator in Windows 9x or Windows NT 4.0, select the Run option from the Start menu, and type the word COMMAND in the Run dialog box. To access this function in Windows 2000 or Windows XP, enter CMD (or COMMAND) in the dialog box. This produces the command-line prompt.

Working from the Command Line

All command-line functions can be entered and executed from the command prompt. Application programs can also be started from this prompt. In a Microsoft environment, these programs can be discerned by their filename extensions. Files with .COM, .EXE, or .BAT extensions can be started directly from the prompt. The .COM and .EXE file extensions are reserved by Microsoft operating systems and can only be generated by programs that can correctly configure them.

Programs with other types of extensions must be associated with one of these three file types to be operated. The user can operate application software packages, such as graphical user interfaces, word processors, business packages, data communications packages, and user programming languages.

The user can also enter operating system batch commands on the command line to perform different functions. The format for using command-line statements in a Microsoft command-line environment is as follows:

COMMAND (space) SOURCE location (space) DESTINATION location

The previous example is used for command-line operations that involve a source and a final destination, such as moving a file from one place to another.

COMMAND (space) location

This example illustrates how single-location operations, such as formatting a partition on a particular disk drive, are specified.

This final example applies to commands that occur in a default location, such as obtaining a listing of the files on the current disk drive.

COMMAND

You can modify the performance of various commands by placing one or more software *switches* at the end of the basic command. A switch is added to the command by adding a space, a forward slash (/), and the designator for the switch (such as /a, /all, or /renew):

COMMAND (space) option /switch

Common MS-DOS command switches include **/P** for page, **/W** for wide format, and **/S** for system. Different switches are used to modify different command functions. You can obtain definitions for switches that can be added to a given command by typing **/?** after the command.

Microsoft Drives and Disks

Microsoft operating systems reserve the letters A: and B: for the first and second floppy drives in the system. Multiple hard disk, CD-ROM, and DVD drive units can be installed along with the floppy drives.

Likewise, Microsoft operating systems recognize the first logical hard drive in the system as the C drive. Disk Management utilities can be used to partition a single physical hard disk drive into two or more volumes that the system recognizes as logical drives C, D, and so on.

In the case of networked systems, logical drive letters can be extended to define up to drive Z. These drives are actually hard drives located in remote computers. The operating system in the local machine treats them as additional logical drives (for example, F:, G:, and so on). Under Windows 2000 and Windows XP, logical drives can be given names and the 26-drive limit imposed by the alphabet is done away with.

Drive and Disk-Level Command Operations

The following command-line functions pertain to drive and disk-level operations. They must be typed at the command prompt, and they carry out the instruction along with any drive modifiers given.

➤ FORMAT—This command is used to prepare a new disk for use with an operating system. Actual data locations are marked off on the disk for the tracks and sectors, and bad sectors are marked. In addition, a file directory is established on the disk. New disks must be formatted before they can be used.

➤ C:\>FORMAT A—This command creates the tracks, sectors, and file system structure on the specified disk (in this case, the A: floppy drive).

➤ C:\>FORMAT A:/S—This command causes three system files (boot files—IO.SYS, MSDOS.SYS, and COMMAND.COM) to be copied into the root directory of the disk after it has been formatted.

➤ SETVER—This command sets the OS version number that the system reports to an application. Programs designed for previous OS versions might not operate correctly under newer versions unless the version has been set correctly:

```
C:> SETVER C:
```

This entry causes all the files on the C drive to be listed in the operating system version table.

➤ VER—This command displays the current operating system version onscreen.

Directory-Level Functions

The following commands are used for directory-based operations. The format for using them is identical to that for the drive and disk-related commands discussed earlier.

The root directory of a Microsoft FAT16 root directory is limited to 512 entries. If you receive an Unable to Create <"New Folder"> error message, you might have exceeded this limit.

➤ DIR—The directory command gives a listing of the files on the disk that is in the drive indicated by the drive specifier.

C:\>DIR or DIR C—If DIR is used without any drive specifier, the contents of the drive indicated by the prompt are displayed. The command might also be used with modifiers to alter the way in which the directory is displayed. The C:\>DIR/W command displays the entire directory at one time across the width of the display, whereas the command C:\>DIR/P displays the contents of the directory one page at a time.

➤ MKDIR (MD)—The make directory command creates a new directory in an indicated spot in the directory tree structure.

C:\>MD C:\DOS\XXX—This example creates a new subdirectory named XXX in the path that includes the ROOT directory (C:\) and the DOS subdirectory.

➤ CHDIR (CD)—The change directory command changes the location of the active directory to a position specified with the command.

C:\>CD C:\DOS—This example changes the working directory from the C: root directory to the C:\DOS directory.

➤ RMDIR (RD)—The remove directory command erases the directory specified in the command. You cannot remove a directory until it is empty, and you cannot remove a directory if it is currently active.

C:\>RD C:\DOS\forms—This example removes the DOS subdirectory "forms," provided it was empty.

➤ PROMPT—The Prompt command changes the appearance of the command prompt.

C:\>PROMPT PG—This example causes the form of the prompt to change from simply C: to C:\ and causes the complete path from the main directory to the current directory to be displayed at the DOS prompt (that is, C:\>DOS).

➤ TREE—The Tree command lists all of the directory and subdirectory names on a specified disk.

C:\>TREE C—This example displays a graphical representation of the organization of the C hard drive.

➤ DELTREE—The Deltree command removes a selected directory and all the files and subdirectories below it.

C:\>DELTREE C:\DOS\DRIVER\MOUSE—This example deletes the subdirectory "Mouse" and any subdirectories it might have.

File-Level Commands

The following commands are used to carry out file-level operations. The format for using them is identical to the drive and disk-related and directory-related commands discussed earlier. However, the command must include the filename and its extension at the end of the directory path. Depending on the operation, the complete path might be required, or a default to the currently active drive is assumed.

➤ COPY—The file copy command copies a specified file from one place (disk or directory) to another.

C:\>COPY A:filename.ext B—This command is used if the file is to have the same name in its new location; the second filename specifier can be omitted.

    C:\>COPY A:filename.ext B:filename.ext

➤ XCOPY—This command copies all the files in a directory, along with any subdirectories and their files. This command is particularly useful in copying files and directories between disks with different formats (for example, from a 1.2-MB disk to a 1.44-MB disk):

    C:\>XCOPY A: B: /s

This command copies all of the files and directories from the disk in drive A: (except hidden and system files) to the disk in drive B:. The /s switch instructs the XCOPY command to copy directories and subdirectories.

➤ DEL or ERASE—This command allows the user to remove unwanted files from the disk when typed in at the command prompt:

    C:\>DEL filename.ext
    C:\>ERASE B:filename.ext

A great deal of care should be taken when using this command. If a file is erased accidentally, it might not be retrievable.

➤ REN—This command enables the user to change the name or extension of a filename:

```
C:\>REN A:filename.ext newname.ext
C:\>COPY A:filename.ext B:newname.ext
```

Using this command does not change the contents of the file, only its name. The original filename (but not the file) is deleted. If you want to retain the original file and filename, a copy command, using different filenames, can be used.

If the filename is supposed to be changed during the copy operation, the command should be typed as follows:

```
C:\>FC A:filename.ext B:newname.ext
```

➤ ATTRIB—This command changes file attributes, such as Read-only (+R or –R), Archive (+A or –A), System (+S or –S), and Hidden (+H or –H). The + and – signs are used to add or subtract the attribute from the file.

```
C:\>ATTRIB +R C:\DOS\memos.doc
```

This command sets the file MEMOS.DOC as a read-only file. Read-only attributes protect the file from accidentally being overwritten. Similarly, one of the main reasons for giving a file a Hidden attribute is to prevent it from accidentally being erased. The System attribute is reserved for use by the operating system and marks the file as a system file.

Command-Line Shortcuts

When using filenames in command-line operations, the filename appears at the end of the directory path in the source and destination locations. The * notation is called a *wildcard* and allows operations to be performed with only partial source or destination information. Using the notation as *.* tells the software to perform the designated command on any file found on the disk using any filename and extension.

A question mark (?) can be used as a wildcard to represent a single character in a filename or extension. Multiple question marks can be used to represent multiple characters for example, QuarterlyReport2.* or QuarterlyReport?.xls. In the first example, the system returns all occurrences of QuarterlyReport2, with or without any filename extension. However, in the second example, the system returns all occurrences of QuarterlyReport that are followed by a single letter and a .xls extension.

User Account Maintenance in Windows

It is possible to manage network user accounts from the command line using the NET.EXE command. This includes adding, deleting, and disabling accounts. To add an account using the NET command, use the following command syntax:

```
Net user username\password /add
```

where *username* is the name of the account and *password* is the password set by the administrator on the account.

To make an account inaccessible, you can set it to not active using the NET command. The procedure for this operation is as follows:

```
Net user username /active:no
```

Deleting a user account is very similar to adding one. However, no password is required.

```
Net user username /delete
```

Typically, deleting a user account is less desirable than disabling it. Use the active option to disable user accounts from the command prompt.

Networking

One of the most versatile command-line utilities for networking is the NET.EXE command. It can be modified to perform a number of key administrative and troubleshooting functions from the command prompt.

You can use NET.EXE to map a drive letter to a UNC path by executing the following command:

```
Net use drive_letter: \\server_name\share_name
```

where *drive_letter* is the letter to which you want to map, and *server_name**share_name* is the UNC path to the shared folder.

For example, the syntax for mapping drive H: to \\Computer2\folder1 is as follows:

```
Net use h:\\Computer2\folder1
```

Common syntax errors in using the **NET.EXE** command include omitting the colon after the drive letter and not leaving a space between the colon and the UNC path.

Disconnecting Mapped Drives

You can also use the NET command to disconnect a mapped drive when it is no longer needed. This action removes the mapping to the shared folder, but does not delete any data in the shared folder. You can use the following procedure to disconnect a mapped drive:

```
Net use assigned_drive_letter /delete
```

Finding Shared Folders

You can use the NET command to obtain a listing of the shared folders available on a server by executing the following command:

```
Net view \\Server_name
```

where *Server_name* is the name of the server that holds the shared folders.

Controlling Services

You can also use the NET command to turn services running in the system on and off. This is accomplished through the Net Start and Net Stop options. For example, you use the following command to start the Windows print spooler.

```
Net start spooler
```

Likewise, you use the following command to stop the Windows Messenger service.

```
Net stop messenger
```

Windows Command-Line Utilities

Because technicians must frequently work from the command line, many of the tools that they use must also be available from the command prompt. The following list describes most of the major tools associated with maintaining and repairing the system's hard disk drives:

➤ SCANDISK—A hard disk checking utility that inspects the data on a specified disk for errors and corruption. It is used to find and possibly repair cluster chains that make up files which have become disconnected from each other.

➤ DEFRAG—A disk drive utility that organizes disjointed information on hard disk drives into more efficient patterns to speed up the access and read times associated with finding and reading data from the drive.

➤ FDISK—An MS-DOS/Windows 9x disk partitioning utility used to establish logical structures on a hard disk drive.

Other operating system tools are available that enable administrators and technicians to manage files and memory usage in the PC system. Three such tools are

➤ EDIT—A command that opens the operating system's default MS-DOS text editor package. This editor can be used to alter and repair text-based files, including CONFIG.SYS, AUTOEXEC.BAT, and various .INI files.

➤ SCANREG—A Windows 9x RegistryChecker utility that scans, fixes, backs up, and restores Registry files.

➤ MEM—A command-line utility used to display the amount of used and free memory in a system.

Some command-line functions can be combined into *batch programs* (as they are in the AUTOEXEC.BAT program described in earlier chapters) to carry out different operations.

➤ ECHO—A batch-processing command that can be used to display character string messages on the screen

➤ SET—A batch-processing command that can be used to set two different character strings as equal to each other

Linux Commands and Utilities

Linux employs a variety of commands that can be entered at the command prompt to directly control the operation of the system. These commands can be organized into groups that relate to directory-level operations, file-level operations, and directory/file operations.

The format for writing Linux commands is dictated by the type of activity that each is designed to perform. The basic format for writing Linux commands is as follows:

```
Prompt Command /Path/Argument
Command Output
```

where *Path* is the relative position of the file or device to be acted upon—with respect to the root directory—and *Argument* is composed of parameters that more fully define the actions of the command.

As an example

```
$ ls
```

or

```
$ ls /dev/floppy/files
```

The first command simply causes Linux to list the contents of the current directory on the display. The second example causes the contents of the directory located at /dev/floppy/files to be displayed.

As with the DOS command line, the Linux command structure includes various types of commands. Some types of commands need no modifications to run (such as the previous ls example). Other commands require some user-supplied specifications (such as the previous ls /path/destination example). Yet other Linux commands require both a source and destination to be specified—such as a Linux copy (cp) operation—to carry out the command.

Most Unix commands can be used with one or more options (similar to Microsoft command switches) that modify the argument. These options are normally preceded by a hyphen. (For example, the /-a option causes the command to include hidden files.)

Some Linux commands can also be grouped together and executed as a batch from a single command-line entry. This is accomplished by separating the command sequences with a semicolon, as follows:

```
$ls /dev/floppy/files ; cat newfile
```

This pair of commands lists the contents of the directory at /dev/floppy/files and displays (concatenates) the contents of the file newfile, in that order.

Although regular system users can execute most commands, some commands can only be executed by the *root user*. You must also remember that everything in Linux, including the commands and their arguments, is case sensitive. Therefore, the commands must be entered just as they were created.

The Linux command prompt can also be used from within Linux windowing systems. In these cases, the windowing system must provide a command shell or an X-terminal window.

Linux Paths

When referring to the organizational structure of a Linux partition, the root directory is represented by a forward slash (reversed from the backslashes used in Microsoft systems). Likewise, successive directory levels in a path statement are separated by forward slashes.

The complete, or absolute, pathname always begins with the forward slash of the root directory and includes all of the subdirectories leading to the specified directory or file. In some cases, it might be more convenient to use a relative pathname that employs the current directory as the starting point for a path. Although an absolute pathname must begin with a forward slash, a relative pathname cannot.

When a user logs on to a Linux system, she is automatically placed in her *home directory*. Each user who has been granted access to the system has been provided with a personal home directory. This is the default location for the creation and storage of the user's personal files. Generally, only the user and the system administrator have access to this directory. At the time of logon, the user's home directory is also her working directory, or current working directory.

In many Linux shells, the user can specify his home directory by placing a tilde (~) character in the path. This same character can also be used to refer to another user's home directory. Using this method, the command interpreter changes the example path *~Charles/files* to */home/Charles/files*. The tilde simply provides a shortcut for navigating through the system.

Directory-Level Linux Commands

As with the Microsoft disk organization, Linux provides a number of commands that can be used to manipulate its directory structure. The following Linux command-line options are used for directory-level operations:

➤ pwd **(print working directory)**—Provides the user with the complete pathname of the current working directory.

```
pwd
```

pwd causes the line */bin/usr* to be displayed if the user is currently working in the */bin/usr* directory.

➤ cd **(change directory)**—Changes the location of the current working directory to the user's home directory, or a directory specified with the command.

```
cd
cd directory
```

cd */user* changes the working directory from the root directory to the */user* directory.

➤ `ls` **(list)**—Provides a listing of the files on the disk that is in the designated directory.

`ls directory`

`ls /-a` (include hidden files in list) causes the system to display all of the files from the specified location, including those that are marked as hidden.

`ls /-1` (list with file information) adds descriptive information about the files, such as size and modification date, to be displayed. Adding an `R` (for recursive) to the `-1` modifier causes the system to list the subdirectories of the specified directory.

➤ `mkdir` **(make directory)**—Creates a new directory in an indicated spot in the directory tree structure.

`mkdir path directory`

`mkdir /usr/bin/myfiles` creates a new subdirectory named *myfiles* in the path that includes the root, usr, and bin directories.

➤ `rmdir` **(remove directory)**—Erases the directory specified in the command. You cannot remove a directory until it is empty and you cannot remove the directory if it is currently active.

`rmdir directories`

`rmdir /bin/myfiles` removes the subdirectory *myfiles*, provided it is empty.

File-Level Linux Commands

Unix filenames can contain special characters and punctuation marks that are not permitted in the MS-DOS 8+3 filename system. These special characters include such items as hyphens, periods, and underscores (but not the forward slash [/]). As an example, a filename of `document.new.type` is perfectly legal under Linux.

Beginning a filename with a period marks it as a hidden file that can only be viewed with commands and tools that show hidden files.

Recall that filenames in Linux can be up to 256 characters in length. Also, Unix is a *case-sensitive* system, so filenames with upper- and lowercase characters must be typed exactly as they are created.

Linux makes use of wildcard characters to replace an undefined pattern of characters. An asterisk (*) can be employed to replace any number of characters in a file or directory name. If the asterisk is used alone, it replaces all possible filenames. Likewise, if it is employed as part of a filename, it replaces the missing character with every possible substitution.

However, the asterisk can also be used to locate every file containing a given letter. (For example, ls *a* lists every file that contains the letter "*a*" in its filename.) The * wildcard does not match filenames that begin with a period because these files are treated as hidden files by the system.

A question mark (?) is used to replace a single character in a file or directory name. However, multiple question marks can be used to replace a given number of characters in a filename (for example, the command ls h??e lists each four-letter filename that begins with "h" and ends with "e").

Some of the most common file-level Linux commands include

➤ Cat (**concatenate**)—This command prints the contents of a specified file. It can also be used to print out direct input (text from the keyboard) to a direct output device (such as a video display).

```
cat files
```

or

```
cat
text string
```

```
cat
answer the phone
```

This example displays the text "answer the phone" on the display when entered.

➤ More (**more**)—This command is used to view the contents of a file that is longer than the screen display can present at one time. The *spacebar* is used to move forward one page, whereas the *b* key is used to move backward one page. The *q* key is used to exit the display and return to the command line.

```
/filename/more
```

/usr/papers /more prints the file papers to the screen on a page at a time basis.

➤ rm (**remove**)—This command enables the user to remove unwanted files from the disk when entered at the command line:

```
rm filename
```

A great deal of care should be taken when using this command. If a file is erased accidentally, it might not be retrievable.

➤ rm /R **(recursive remove)**—The /R modification of the remove command removes a selected directory and all the files and subdirectories below it.

```
rm /R directory
```

➤ cp **(copy)**—This command copies a specified file from one place (disk or directory) to another while leaving the original copy in place. This command roughly approximates the XCOPY and XCOPY32 commands from Microsoft systems.

```
cp /files/destination
```

cp /charlesfile1/charles is used to copy the file *charlesfile1* from the current working directory to the *charles* directory.

➤ Chmod **(change access mode)**—This command changes file permissions through their access mode for specified files. Modifying the command with an /R switch changes the mode of the subdirectories and files beneath a specified directory.

```
Chmod mode files
```

➤ mv **(move)**—This command relocates a specified file from one location (disk or directory) to another without leaving the original copy in place.

```
mv file destination
```

This command can also be used to rename a file or a directory.

```
mv oldfile newfile
```

or

```
mv olddirectory newdirectory
```

➤ find **(find)**—This command searches through specified paths for files with names matching a prescribed character pattern.

```
Find path - name pattern - print
```

➤ lpr **(line printer)**—This command sends specified files to the print queue.

```
Lpr files
```

➤ `lpq` **(display line printer queue)**—This command prints the entries currently in the printer queue.

`lpq`

➤ `lprm` **(quit line printer)**—This command sends specified files to the print queue.

`Lprm job`

User Account Maintenance

Typically, three different classes of users exist in a Linux environment:

➤ **Super user (or root user)**—The administrator who has all privileges to a system

➤ **Regular user**—A user who has accounts on machines and uses his packages to accomplish nonadministrative tasks

➤ **System user**—A process that runs on the computer and requires access to all the files and other processes in the system

Access levels to files and directories can be established through the `chmod x+/- nnn` command. `x` represents the owner (o), group (g), other user (u), or all users (a). The `+` and `-` signs are used to add or prevent permissions from being added to a file. The `nnn` argument to the command is used to assign the access levels of the owner, group, and others. Only file owners can change the permission settings of a file. Some examples of assigning file permissions include

➤ `chmod a+r file1`—Provides all users Read permission to the file named *file1*

➤ `chmod +r file1`—Assumes an "a" condition and provides all users Read permission to the file named *file1*

➤ `chmod og-x file1`—Removes Execute permission from everyone except the owner and the users in the file's group

➤ `chmod u+rwx file1`—Applies Read, Write, and Execute permissions to other users of *file1*

➤ `chmod o-rwx file1`—Removes Read, Write, and Execute permissions from everyone except the owner

In many Linux distributions, a graphical interface is now included for system administrators to manage groups and users. For example, in a Red Hat Linux system, the GUI tool for managing groups and users is the *Users and Groups* item in the *System Settings* menu.

Linux Networking Tools

The Linux network-support architecture provides transport protocols, an Internet protocol, and device drivers for network devices. The Linux networking functions are normally established during the installation process. The installation routine presents the Network Configuration dialog box that can be used to configure networking functions if the system is connected to a LAN.

If a network interface must be added, or replaced, after the installation process has been conducted, you can accomplish the installation in two possible ways—through the linuxconf utility or through the desktop's Control Panel.

To set up a LAN connection using linuxconf, type linuxconf at the prompt. This produces the linuxconf tree menu. Navigate to the Config/Networking/ Client tasks/Basic Host Information level.

Control Panel also enables you to install and configure LAN adapters using only a few mouse clicks. The LAN configuration process begins by configuring the *kerneld* daemon to load drivers for the new network interface being installed.

The Red Hat Linux package employs a daemon called kerneld that automatically loads hardware support into memory when needed. Although it can load some elements without explicit instructions, when it comes to LAN cards, it must be instructed as to which LAN card is being used and about any special configuration requirements that it might require. This is established through the *kernel configurator* option.

Administering Linux Services

You can use multiple administrative tools under Linux to control services. These utilities can be used to start, stop, restart, or reorder services at different runlevels. All of these tools work with an initialization script in /etc/rc.d/init.d. The commands used in this script can be as simple as Start, Stop, Restart, or Reload.

The most basic approach is to manually start or stop services. This involves entering the service's location and name on the command line along with the appropriate keyword:

```
# etc/rc.d/init.d/servicename start
```

where etc/rc.d/init.d/ is the location of the script, *servicename* is the name of the service to be manipulated, and *start* is the keyword.

Another script that can be used to manually start or stop a service is the *Service* command. It is used as follows:

```
# Service servicename start
```

Chkconfig is a text-based command-line tool that is used to administer system services and their different runlevels. The format for using chkconfig to turn on a service is as follows:

```
# chkconfig -level X service on (or off)
```

The chkconfig command does not actually turn services on or off; it simply changes a script that does, in turn, control the services when it is run.

A graphical interface can be used to access the chkconfig tool. This is the *ntsysv* interface. It offers older, block graphic interface images that work with the Tab key and the spacebar. In the ntsysv interface, you can scroll through the system services and use the spacebar to toggle service conditions.

Different Linux distributions provide better GUI-based service management tools. For example, Red Hat Linux provides the Service Configuration tool under the System Settings, Services menu. Likewise, the KDE desktop offers the *ksysv* or *SysV-init* editor. In this editor, you drag and drop services from an Available Services panel into a runlevel panel where it should be started or stopped.

Linux Hard Drive Utilities

FDISK is the traditional Linux partitioning tool. Like the Microsoft DISK utility, the Linux version requires that the user have some knowledge of the drive that is being partitioned. Conversely, the Linux *disk druid* is an install-time Disk Management utility that can create and delete disk partitions, as well as manage mount points for each partition in the system.

In many places, the disk druid has been replaced by the *GNUparted* (or simply parted) command utility. This utility can be used to create, delete, move, copy, or resize ext2 or FAT32 partitions.

You can create a file system (the equivalent of formatting a drive in a Microsoft environment) using variations of the mkfs (make file system) command. For example, you can create the following different types of file systems using the indicated command variation:

➤ mkfs.ext2—The ext2 file system

➤ mkfs.dos—The MS-DOS file system

➤ mkfs.vfat—The FAT32 file system

Other commands for creating file systems in Linux include

➤ mke2fs *device*—For creating the ext2 or ext3 file system on a specified device

➤ mkfs.ext3—For creating the ext3 file system

The Linux directory tree structure can be distributed across multiple partitions or disks. The directories and partitions are linked to each other through the process of *mounting*. Each partition, or disk, being added to the structure has a directory in the main structure, known as its *mount point*. This directory marks the beginning of its storage area. All of the mount points for the Linux file system are stored in a table at etc/fstab.

Drive mounting selections are usually taken care of during the operating system installation process. However, they can also be performed from the Linux command line, using the mount command. The format for using this command is as follows:

```
mount device name mount point
```

(For example, mount /dev/cdrom /mnt/cdrom.)

Linux TCP/IP Utilities
The TCP/IP network utility suite is pretty much the same for Linux as it is for Microsoft operating systems. The one noticeable difference is that there is no IPCONFIG utility. Instead, Linux uses a similar utility called IFCONFIG.

Linux Text Editors
Nearly every distribution (version) of the Linux operating system includes the *vi text editor*. This editor is a command set–driven editor that is easy to use and very powerful. The editor operates in viewing mode (in which you can move through the file and examine it) and editing mode (in which changes are made to the file—this is where the commands come in). Some of the most basic vi commands include

➤ $ vi file.txt—This command starts the editor and brings up the indicated text file.

➤ i—This single-letter command can be used to begin inserting text at the cursor.

➤ a—This command can be used to append text to the file at the cursor.

➤ esc—This key is used to exit the insert or append mode and return to the viewing mode.

➤ x—This command deletes a character.

➤ dd—This command deletes a line.

➤ :q—This command is used to quit.

➤ :q!—This command is used to quit without saving.

➤ :w—This command is used to save a file (write).

Another popular Linux text editor is the *Emacs* editor found in many Linux distributions. Emacs is an editing environment that can be used to create large-scale programs. It also features email, calendar, and electronic appointment features. Like the vi editor, Emacs is command driven and typically uses commands that are a combination of the Ctrl key and some other key. For example:

➤ $ emacs file.txt—This command starts the Emacs editor and brings up the indicated text file.

➤ Ctrl+d—This command deletes a character.

➤ Ctrl+k—This command deletes a line.

➤ Ctrl+x, Ctrl+s—This command saves a file.

➤ Ctrl+x, Ctrl+w—This command allows you to use the Save As feature (saving a file with a new name in a new location).

➤ Ctrl+x, Ctrl+c—This command is used to quit.

➤ Ctrl+x, Ctrl+u—This command is used to undo the most recent change.

I/O Buses and Cabling

Many different types of cables are used with PC systems to attach peripheral equipment to the main system. In many cases, it might be necessary to provide or construct a cable to implement or troubleshoot a peripheral device. The following sections deal with communication media and connector classifications and specifications for the different PC I/O buses and ports.

Twisted-Pair Cabling

One of the specifications associated with the *Physical* layer of the OSI model is the *EIA/TIA-568* specification for network wiring. This standard applies to the use of *unshielded twisted pair* (*UTP*) cable for different networking applications. It also categorizes different grades of cable along with connector, distance, and installation specifications to produce the EIA/TIA UTP wiring *category (CAT) ratings* for the industry (for example, CAT3 and CAT5 cabling).

Table 5.1 lists the industry's various CAT cable ratings that apply to UTP data communications cabling. CAT5 cabling is currently the most widely used specification for data communication wiring.

Table 5.1	UTP Cable Category Ratings		
CATEGORY	MAXIMUM BANDWIDTH	WIRING TYPES	APPLICATIONS
3	16 MHz	100 Ω UTP; Rated Category 3	10 Mbps Ethernet; 4 Mbps Token Ring
4	20 MHz	100 Ω UTP; Rated Category 4	10 Mbps Ethernet; 16 Mbps Token Ring
5	100 MHz	100 Ω UTP; Rated Category 5	100 Mbps TPDDI; 155 Mbps ATM
5E	160 MHz	100 Ω UTP; Rated Category 5E	1.2 Gbps 1000Base-T High-Speed ATM
6	250 MHz	100 Ω UTP; Rated Category 6	1.2 Gbps 1000Base-T High-Speed ATM and beyond
7 Proposed	600–862 MHz	100 Ω UTP; Rated Category 7	1.2 Gbps 1000Base-T High-Speed ATM and beyond

The connector and color-coded connection schemes specified for four-pair, EIA/TIA 568-A and 568-B CAT5 UTP network cabling configurations is illustrated in Figure 5.2. In both cases, the UTP cabling is terminated in an 8-pin RJ-45 plug. The color code for attaching the connector to the cable is also provided in the figure.

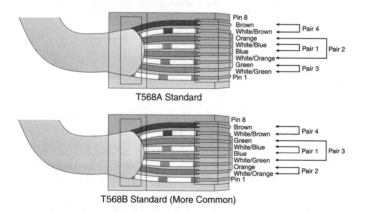

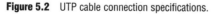

Figure 5.2   UTP cable connection specifications.

UTP LAN connections are made through modular RJ-45 registered jacks and plugs. RJ-45 connectors are very similar in appearance to the RJ-11 connectors used with telephones and modems. However, the RJ-45 connectors are considerably larger than the RJ-11 connectors.

Some Ethernet adapters include 15-pin sockets that enable special systems, such as fiber-optic cabling, to be interfaced to them. Other cards provide specialized ST connectors for fiber-optic connections.

CAT5 Crossover Cables

The CAT5 wiring scenarios presented in the previous section are normally wired in a *straight-through cable* arrangement (that is, pin 1 at both ends of the cable wired together, as are all the other connections). However, you must be aware that not all CAT5 cables are wired this way.

A CAT5 *crossover cable* is a good tool to have for troubleshooting NICs and hubs. These cables can also be used to connect two computers together without a hub or other network connectivity device. They might also be required to connect two hubs together.

Figure 5.3 depicts the wiring specification for such a crossover cable. Notice that the wire pairs remain constant with the earlier straight-through CAT5 wiring examples. The only difference with the crossover cable is that the Transmit pair of one end (TX+ and TX–) is crossed over to match the Receive pair (RX+ and RX–) at the other end.

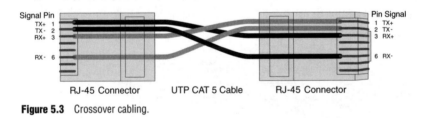

Figure 5.3 Crossover cabling.

Cabling from a NIC to a hub or router is normally performed with a straight-through cable. Crossover cables are typically used for connecting two hubs together. Hubs typically have markings on their ports to indicate whether a straight-through or crossover cable is required. The markings that are used to identify straight-through and crossover cables are

➤ **MDI (Media Dependent Interface)**—This connection requires an external crossover (either the cable or the other hub must perform the crossover function).

> **MIDX (Media Independent Interface Crossover)**—This type of connection can be switched so that the port performs the crossover function. This allows a straight-through cable to be used to make the connection when engaged.

If there is no marking on the port, it is generally assumed that the hub performs the crossover. However, you should always check the hub documentation to verify this arrangement.

Ethernet Cabling Standards and Specifications

The Ethernet specification is based on a bus topology. This topology has been implemented across several different network media types, including

> Coaxial cable

> Twisted-pair copper cable

> Fiber-optic cable

> Wireless RF

Coaxial Ethernet Specifications

The original Ethernet scheme was classified as a 10-Mbps transmission protocol. The maximum length specified for Ethernet is 1.55 miles (2.5km), with a maximum segment length between nodes of 500 meters. This type of LAN is referred to as a 10BASE-5 LAN by the IEEE organization.

The XXBaseYY IEEE nomenclature designates that the maximum data rate across the LAN is 10Mbps, that it is a baseband LAN (versus broadband), and that its maximum segment length is 500 meters. One exception to this method is the 10BASE-2 implementation. The maximum segment length for this specification is 185 meters (almost 200 meters).

Coaxial Ethernet connections can be made through 50-ohm RG-8 *ThickNet* coaxial cable (10BASE-5) or *ThinNet* coaxial cable (10BASE-2). The 10BASE-2 Ethernet LAN uses thinner, industry-standard RG-58 coaxial cable, and has a maximum segment length of 185 meters.

Both coaxial connection methods require that a terminating resistor be installed at each end of the transmission line. Ethernet systems use 52-ohm terminators.

Twisted-Pair Ethernet Specifications

The UTP specifications are based on telephone cable and are normally used to connect a small number of PCs together. The twisted pairing of the cables uses magnetic-field principles to minimize induced noise in the lines. The original UTP LAN specification (10BASE-T) had a transmission rate that was stated as 1Mbps. Using UTP cable, a LAN containing up to 64 nodes can be constructed with the maximum distance between nodes set at 100 meters. Newer Ethernet implementations are producing LAN speeds of up to 1Gbps (1,000Mbps) using UTP copper cabling.

For these networks, the IEEE adopted 10BASE-T, 100BASE-T, and 100BASE-TX designations, indicating that they operate on twisted-pair cabling and depend on its specifications for the maximum segment length. The 100BASE designation is referred to as Fast Ethernet. The TX version of the Fast Ethernet specification employs two pairs of twisted cable to conduct high-speed, full-duplex transmissions. The cables used with the TX version can be Cat5 UTP or shielded twisted pair (STP). There is also a 100BASE-FX Fast Ethernet designation that indicates the network is using fiber-optic cabling.

Network cards capable of supporting both transmission rates are classified as 10/100 Ethernet cards. The recommended maximum length of a 10/100BASE-T segment is 100 meters (actually, the maximum segment length of any Ethernet connection designated with a T is 100 meters).

The latest Ethernet designations for copper cabling are the 1000BASE-T Gigabit Ethernet specification that delivers 1 Gigabit (1,000 Mbps) data transfers over Category 5 UTP cable and the 1000BASE-CX specification that provides the same Gigabit transfer rate over two pairs of STP cable.

Fiber-Optic Ethernet Specifications

The IEEE organization has created several fiber-optic variations of the Ethernet protocol. They classify these variations under the IEEE-803 standard. These standards are referenced as the 10/100BASE-F specification. Variations of this standard include

➤ **10BASE-FP**—This specification is used for passive star networks running at 10Mbps. It employs a special hub that uses mirrors to channel the light signals to the desired node.

➤ **10BASE-FL**—This specification is used between devices on the network. It operates in full-duplex mode and runs at 10Mbps. Cable lengths under this specification can range up to 2 kilometers.

> ➤ **100BASE-FX**—This specification is identical to the 10BASE-FL specification with the exception that it runs at 100Mbps. This particular version of the specification is referred to as Fast Ethernet because it can easily run at the 100-Mbps rate.

> ➤ **1000BASE–LX**—This Gigabit Ethernet specification is delivered over two multimode or single-mode optical fiber cables using longwave laser techniques.

> ➤ **1000BASE-SX**—This Gigabit Ethernet specification is delivered over two multimode or single-mode optical fiber cables using shortwave laser techniques.

Table 5.2 summarizes the different Ethernet specifications. Other CSMA/CD-based protocols exist in the market. Some are actually Ethernet compatible. However, these systems might, or might not, achieve the performance levels of a true Ethernet system. Some might actually perform better.

Table 5.2   Ethernet Specifications

CLASSIFICATION	CONDUCTOR	MAX. SEGMENT LENGTH	NODES	MAX. LENGTH	TRANS. RATE
10Base2	RG-58	185 m	30/1024	250 m	10 Mbps
10Base5	RG-8	500 m	100/1024	2.5 km	10 Mbps
10Base-T	UTP/STP	100 m/200 m	2/1024	2.5 km	10 Mbps
100Base-T	UTP	100 m	2/1024	2.5 km	100 Mbps
100Base-FX	FO	412 m	1024	5 km	100 Mbps
1000Base-T	UTP	100 m	1024	-	1000 Mbps
1000Base-SX	FO (multimode)	275 m-550 m	1024	-	1000 Mbps
1000Base-LX	FO (single mode)	500 m-550 m-5 km	1024	-	1000 Mbps

Wireless Ethernet Specifications

Wireless networking standards fall under the designation of *802.11x*. Current standard versions include 802.11a, b, g, and i. These are sometimes referred to as wireless Ethernet standards; however, true Ethernet protocols are classified under IEEE-802.3 standards.

The IEEE 802.11b (also known as *802.11 High Rate* or *Wi-Fi*) wireless standard has gained wide acceptance as the preferred wireless networking technology for both business and home network applications. Most current wireless LANs are based on this specification and operate at transfer rates in the range of 11Mbps, with fallback operations at 5.5Mbps, 2Mbps, and 1Mbps. This version of the 802.11 specification provides Ethernet-like functionality.

Typically, the effective range of the 802.11b signal is from 100 to 300 meters. However, these signals require a direct line of site to achieve the stated distances and can be affected by intervening objects, such as walls and trees. The practical range for 802.11b is 150 feet.

Other 802.11 wireless specifications include

➤ **802.11**—The original wireless LAN specification that furnishes 1- or 2-Mbps data rates using Frequency Hopping Spread Spectrum (FHSS) or Direct Sequence Spread Spectrum (DSSS) signaling techniques in the 2.4-GHZ frequency range.

➤ **802.11a**—An upgraded 802.11 specification that provides up to 54-Mbps data rates in the 5.2-GHz frequency range. The practical range for 802.11a signals is less than the 802.11b specification (225 feet, with direct line of site).

➤ **802.11g**—A newly completed wireless specification that delivers data transfer rates in excess of up to 54Mbps in the 2.4-GHz band. The practical distance for 802.11g signals is the same as the 802.11b specification.

➤ **802.11x**—A group of pending 802.11 WLAN update standards being developed to support the general 802.11 specification. These include Quality of Service (802.11e), Access Point Interoperability (802.11f), Interference (802.11h), and Security (802.11i).

Wireless Security

To minimize the risk of security compromise on a wireless LAN, the IEEE 802.11b standard provides a security feature called *Wired Equivalent Privacy* (*WEP*). This standard provides a method for encrypting data transmissions and authenticating each computer on the network.

WEP is implemented through the configuration setup programs for the wireless access points and network cards. You can select from two levels of WEP encryptions, including 64-bit and 128-bit encryption levels. Some utilities refer to these as 40-bit and 104-bit schemes (24 bits are actually used for header information instead of encryption purposes).

WEP has shown several security shortfalls. The wireless industry has developed the *Wi-Fi Protected Access* (*WPA*) standard to improve on the security features of WEP. WPA offers two major improvements over WEP—improved data encryption (using Temporal Key Integrity Protocol [TKIP]) and *user authentication* (using the Extensible Authentication Protocol [EAP]). The WPA specification will be replaced by the IEEE's 802.11i standard when it is complete and accepted.

Wireless Installation Considerations

The radio frequency (RF) signal strength at wireless LAN clients can be negatively affected by signals bouncing off walls and objects in an indoor environment. The radio waves can arrive from multiple directions and, in some cases, can cancel or severely reduce the signal strength between portable users. This effect, called *multipath*, is eliminated by analyzing the signals with test instruments or moving the nodes to different locations. Most access points include software-based, signal-strength analysis tools as part of their support package. These tools can be used to test for signal strength after the computer has been installed and brought online.

Microwave radio emissions from other devices using the unlicensed 2.4-GHz radio spectrum are also a source of electromagnetic interference. The WLAN adapter cards and the access point should be installed in such a way that they provide the maximum exposure for the antenna to maximize signal strength.

Wireless networking relies on spread spectrum transmission techniques to communicate. In some instances, it is necessary to spread the channel settings of the access points in situations in which multiple access points are in use. Wireless networking divides the 2.4-GHz frequency range (between 2.0GHz and 2.474GHz) into 11 overlapping 22-MHz channels. Because they overlap, the channels must be spread out when using more than one access point. Typical settings for 802.11b and 802.11g systems are channels 1, 6, and 11.

Because FHSS wireless moves between different bands of frequency within the allocated frequency range for wireless networking, it is necessary to use a manufacturer-supplied chart to configure the proper settings for multiple wireless access points to operate in a single location.

Telephone Cabling

The telephone cabling inside residence and office buildings is typically CAT3 cabling. The CAT3 cabling is made up of three pairs of conductors. The wire pairs are made up of a tip and a ring wire. These terms are used for polarity purposes and are carried over from old RCA telephone plugs and jacks. These plugs had an electrical contact point at the tip of the plug and another through a ring around the shaft of the plug. The voltage applied to the tip wire is 0Vdc, whereas the ring voltage is –48Vdc (this voltage level is specific to the phone line at the company office [CO]—it is less at a residence or business location due to voltage drop of 5Vdc to 12Vdc along the transmission line).

Table 5.3 lists tip and ring pairing for different types of cabling used to handle analog voice communications. The polarity of these wires is very important in DSL installations.

Table 5.3 Tip and Ring Wiring

	TIP	RING
Residential Cabling		
Pair 1	Green	Red
Pair 2	Black	Yellow
Pair 3	White	Blue
RJ-11 Plugs and Jacks		
Pair 1	3	4
Pair 2	5	2
Pair 3	1	6
Business Cabling		
Pair 1	White/Blue Band	Blue/White Band
Pair 2	White/Orange Band	Orange/White Band
Pair 3	White/Green Band	Green/White Band
Pair 4	White/Brown band	Brown/White Band
RJ-45 Plugs and Jacks		
Pair 1	5	4
Pair 2	3	6
Pair 3	1	2
Pair 4	7	8

These color codes here are for the *Universal Service Order Code* (*USOC*) specifications for telephone connections and should not be confused with 568A or 568B data cabling codes depicted earlier in this chapter. This distinction becomes very important when wiring from an Ethernet LAN system and a telephone system are combined.

In both the USOC and 568B wiring scenarios, pins 4 and 5 (the blue wire pair) are the same. Therefore, a single line USOC telephone can be used with this circuitry. If the USOC connection involves two pair, the color codes do not match up (the green pair runs into the orange pair).

However, comparing the USOC and 568A wiring schemes, the blue pair and the orange pair match up with each other. This arrangement permits one- and two-line phone systems to be used with the 568A wiring.

Serial Cable Pinout Descriptions

Since the advent of the PC AT, the system's first serial port has typically been implemented in a 9-pin D-shell male connector on the computer. Figure 5.4 depicts a typical 9-pin to 25-pin connection scheme. Notice the crossover wiring technique employed for the TXD/RXD lines displayed in this example. This type of connection became popular with the 9-pin PC AT serial port.

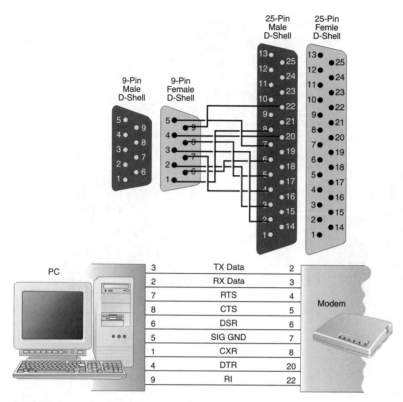

Figure 5.4 A 9-pin to 25-pin RS-232 cable.

In cases in which the serial ports are located close enough to each other, a *null modem* connection can be implemented that allows the two serial ports to communicate directly without using modems. A typical null modem connection scheme is illustrated in Figure 5.5.

The RS-232 standard also establishes acceptable voltage levels for the signals on its pins. These levels are generally converted to and from standard digital logic level signals that can produce a maximum baud rate of 20,000 baud over distances of less than 50 feet. This is the recommended maximum length of an RS-232 cable. The RS-232C version extends this length to 100 feet.

All serial cables are not created equal. Incorrect serial cabling can be a major problem when attaching third-party communication equipment to the computer. Read the serial device's documentation carefully to be certain the correct pins are being connected together.

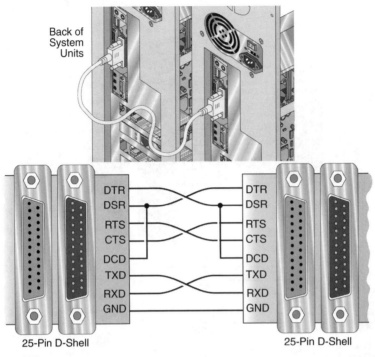

Figure 5.5 A null modem cable.

SCSI Cables and Connectors

The SCSI standard has been implemented using a number of different cable types. In PC-compatible systems, the SCSI interface uses a 50-pin signal cable arrangement. Internally, the cable is a 50-pin flat ribbon cable. However, 50-pin shielded cables, with Centronic connectors, are used for external SCSI connections. The 50-pin SCSI connections are referred to as A-cables.

Advanced SCSI specifications have created additional cabling specifications. A 50-conductor alternative cable using 50-pin D-shell connectors has been added to the A-cable specification for SCSI-2 devices.

A second cable type, referred to as B-cable, was added to the SCSI-2 specification to provide 16- and 32-bit parallel data transfers. However, this arrangement employed multiple connectors at each end of the cable and never received widespread acceptance in the market.

A revised 68-pin P-cable format, using D-shell connectors, was introduced to support 16-bit transfers in the SCSI-3 specification. A 68-pin Q-cable version was also adopted in SCSI for 32-bit transfers. The P and Q cables must be used in parallel to conduct 32-bit transfers.

For some PS/2 models, IBM used a special 60-pin Centronics-like connector for their SCSI connections. The version of the SCSI interface used in the Apple Macintosh employs a variation of the standard that features a proprietary miniature 25-pin D-shell connector.

These cabling variations create a hardware incompatibility between different SCSI devices. Likewise, some SCSI devices just will not work with each other due to software incompatibilities.

In addition, SCSI devices can be classified as internal or external devices. An internal SCSI device has no power supply of its own and, therefore, must be connected to one of the system's options power connectors. On the other hand, external SCSI devices come with built-in or plug-in power supplies that need to be connected to a commercial AC outlet. Therefore, when choosing a SCSI device, always inquire about compatibility between it and any other SCSI devices installed in the system.

Figure 5.6 depicts a 25-pin D-shell, a 50-pin Centronics, and a 68-pin Centronics-type SCSI connectors used for external connections. Inside the computer, the SCSI specification employs 50-pin and 68-pin ribbon cables with BERG pin connectors.

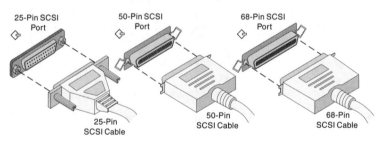

Figure 5.6 SCSI connectors.

SCSI Signaling

You should also be aware that two types of signaling are used with SCSI interfaces—*single-ended* (*SE*) and *differential*. Single-ended signaling transmits signals in a straightforward manner in which the information is applied to a signal line and referenced to ground.

Differential signaling applies reciprocal versions of the same signal to two wires in the cable and compares them at the other end of the cable. This differential signal technique provides exceptional noise rejection properties and enables the signal to be transmitted much further (from 3 or 6 meters using SE, but up to 25 meters using differential) before it significantly deteriorates.

For this reason, a single-ended interface uses half as many active conductors in the cable as differential cables do. The other conductors in the SE cable are used to provide grounds for the individual signal cables. In a differential cable, the ground conductors are used to carry the differential portion of the signal. Single-ended and differential SCSI cables are available for A, P, and Q applications. Because they are electrically different, confusing them with each other is problematic (for example, using a differential cable to connect single-ended devices together could damage the devices because of the missing ground capabilities).

For this reason, the industry has adopted different symbols, as illustrated in Figure 5.7, to identify SE and differential cables and devices. These symbols are placed on the connectors of the cables and ports so that they should not be confused with each other. Fortunately, most PC applications use single-ended connections. Therefore, you are unlikely to run into differential cables or devices.

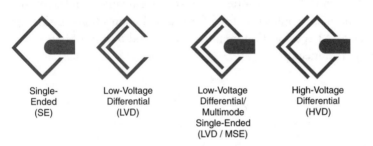

Single-
Ended
(SE)

Low-Voltage
Differential
(LVD)

Low-Voltage
Differential/
Multimode
Single-Ended
(LVD / MSE)

High-Voltage
Differential
(HVD)

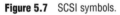

Figure 5.7 SCSI symbols.

Two different differential signal specifications have been used in the SCSI environment:

➤ **High Voltage Differential (HVD)**—The high differential refers to the +5Vdc and 0Vdc signal levels used to represent data bits. These voltage levels were implemented with the original SCSI-1 bus and have been included with all of the specifications up to the Wide Ultra SCSI version.

➤ **Low Voltage Differential (LVD)**—This is similar to the move in microprocessors to reduce the core voltage to 3.3V to make them run faster and consume less power. LVD interfaces operate on 3-volt logic levels instead of the older TTL-compatible 5-volt levels.

Unlike the earlier HVD interfaces that were incompatible with SE devices, LVD SCSI devices actually operate in what is known as *multimode* (that is, they can shift back and forth between traditional SE mode and LVD mode). The LVD is backward compatible with single-ended SCSI. However, connecting one single-ended peripheral to a multimode LVD bus causes the entire bus to switch to the single-ended mode for protection. With the switch, the single-ended limitations on data throughput and cable length come into play.

LVD mode was not defined in the original SCSI standards. If all devices on the bus support LVD, operations at up to 12 meters is possible at full speed. However, if any device on the bus is singled-ended only, the entire bus switches to single-ended mode and the distance is reduced back to the 3- or 6-meter range.

To add a single-ended peripheral to an LVD bus and preserve the data throughput and cable length of the LVD, you can add a SCSI expander called an LVD-to-SE or LVD/MSE-to-LVD/MSE converter. This converter divides the SCSI domain into two bus segments. One segment can operate at the LVD data throughput rate and cable length, while the other segment uses the single-ended data throughput and cable-length ratings. Most LVD controllers employ a single-ended connector for connecting to slower tape drives so that they can preserve the speed and cable length of the LVD segment.

SCSI Addressing

The original SCSI specification permits up to eight SCSI devices to be connected together. The SCSI port can be daisy-chained to allow up to six external peripherals to be connected to the system. To connect multiple SCSI devices to a SCSI host, all the devices, except the last one, must have two SCSI connectors: one for SCSI-In and the other for SCSI-Out. It does not matter which connector is used for which function. If the device has only one SCSI connector, however, it must be connected to the end of the chain.

It is possible to use multiple SCSI host adapters within a single system to increase the number of devices that can be used.

Each SCSI device in a chain must have a unique ID number assigned to it. Even though there are a total of eight possible SCSI ID numbers for each controller, only six are available for use with external devices. Most SCSI host adapter cards are set to SCSI-7 by default from their manufacturers.

Historically, manufacturers have classified the first internal hard drive as SCSI-0. In other cases, most notably IBM, the manufacturer routinely uses ID 2 for the first SCSI hard drive and ID 6 for the host adapter. In most newer systems, it typically doesn't matter which devices are set to which ID settings; however, if two SCSI devices in a system are set to the same ID number, one or both of them appears invisible to the system. The priority levels assigned to SCSI devices are determined by their ID number, with the highest numbered device receiving the highest priority.

SCSI Termination

The SCSI daisy chain must be terminated with a resistor network pack at both ends. Single-connector SCSI devices are normally terminated internally. If not, a SCSI terminator cable (containing a built-in resistor pack) must be installed at the end of the chain. SCSI termination is a major cause of SCSI-related problems. Poor terminations cause a variety of different system problems, including the following:

➤ Failed system startups

➤ Hard drive crashes

➤ Random system failures

Several different types of termination are commonly used with SCSI buses. In general, the slower bus specifications are less particular in the termination method required, whereas the faster buses require better termination techniques. The different types of termination commonly used with SCSI systems include

➤ **Passive termination**—This is the simplest and least reliable method of termination. It employs nonactive resisters to terminate the bus. Passive termination is fine for short, low-speed SCSI-1 buses; however, it is not suitable for faster SCSI buses.

➤ **Active termination**—Adding active elements such as voltage regulators to the resistors used in passive termination provides for more reliable and consistent termination of the bus. Active termination is the minimum requirement for any of the faster, single-ended SCSI buses.

➤ **Forced perfect termination (FPT)**—FPT is a more advanced form of active termination, in which the diode clamps are added to the circuitry to force the termination to the correct voltage. This virtually eliminates any signal reflections or other problems, and provides for the best form of termination of a single-ended SCSI bus.

Newer SCSI buses that employ LVD signaling require special types of terminators. In addition, special LVD/SE terminators are designed for use with *multimode LVD* devices that can function in either LVD or SE modes. When the bus is in single-ended mode, they behave like active terminators. LVDs are currently more popular than HVDs because LVDs can support the Wide Ultra 2 SCSI, so the bandwidth is effectively doubled from 80MBps to 160MBps.

Newer SCSI technologies provide for automatic cable termination. Many of the latest internal SCSI cables provide the termination function on the cable itself. The terminator is permanently applied at the end of the cable. For this reason, you should always verify the type of SCSI cables and components you are using before installation. This helps to ensure that your SCSI installation process moves along as effortlessly as possible.

In these systems, after a SCSI component has been installed, the system queries the device to detect modifications to the SCSI configuration. It then provides termination as required to enable the system to operate properly. In addition, these intelligent systems can also assign SCSI IDs as required. Even in these systems, you can still manually select ID numbers for the devices. In many cases, this is the best option because it enables you to document each SCSI component's ID for future reference.

Table 5.4 contrasts the specifications of the SCSI and IDE interfaces.

Table 5.4   SCSI/IDE Specifications

INTERFACE	BUS SIZE	# DEVICES	ASYNC. SPEED	SYNC. SPEED
IDE (ATA-1)	16 bits	2	4 MB/s	3.3/5.2/8.3 MB/s
EIDE (ATA-2)	16 bits	2	4 MB/s	11/16 MB/s
SCSI (SCSI-1)	8 bits	7	2 MB/s	5 MB/s
Wide SCSI (SCSI-2)	8/16 bits	15	2 MB/s	5 MB/s
Fast SCSI (SCSI-2)	8/16 bits	7	2 MB/s	5/10 MB/s
Wide Fast SCSI (SCSI-2)	8/16 bits	15	2 MB/s	10/20 MB/s
Ultra SCSI	8 bits	7	2 MB/s	10/20 MB/s
Wide Ultra SCSI (SCSI-3)	16 bits	15	2 MB/s	10/20/40 MB/s
Ultra2 SCSI	8 bits	7	2 MB/s	10/20/40 MB/s
Wide Ultra2 SCSI	16 bits	15	2 MB/s	10/20/40/80 MB/s
Wide Ultra3 SCSI	16 bits	15	2 MB/s	10/20/40/160 MB/s
Ultra320 SCSI	16 bits	15	2 MB/s	10/20/40/320 MB/s

Universal Serial Bus

The *universal serial bus* (*USB*) provides a fast, flexible method of attaching up to 127 peripheral devices to the computer. USB is an improved port connection format designed to replace the PC's traditional serial- and parallel-port connections.

USB peripherals can be daisy-chained, or networked together, using connection hubs that enable the bus to branch out through additional port connections.

USB devices can be hot-swapped or hot plugged (added to or removed from the system while it is powered up and fully operational). The PnP capabilities of the system detect the presence (or absence) of the device and configure it for operation.

USB Cabling and Connectors

USB transfers are conducted over a four-wire cable. The signal travels over a pair of twisted wires (D+ and D–) in a 90-ohm cable. The differential signal and twisted-pair wiring provide minimum signal deterioration over distances and high noise immunity.

The Vbus is the +5V (DC) power cord. The interface provides power to the peripheral attached to it. The root hub provides power directly from the host system to those devices directly connected to it. Hubs also supply power to the devices connected to them. Even though the interface supplies power to the USB devices, they are permitted to have their own power sources if necessary.

The USB specification defines two types of plugs: series-A and series-B. Series-A connectors are used for devices in which the USB cable connection is permanently attached to devices at one end. Conversely, the series-B plugs and jacks are designed for devices that require detachable cabling. Both are four-contact plugs and sockets embedded in plastic connectors, as shown in Figure 5.8.

The sockets can be implemented in vertical, right angle, and panel-mount variations. The icon used to represent a USB connector is depicted at the centers of the A and B "plug connectors."

FireWire

Apple Computer, Inc., and Texas Instruments worked together with the IEEE (Institute of Electrical and Electronics Engineers) to produce the FireWire (or IEEE-1394) specification to bring together the PC with the consumer products market. This bus specification offers a very fast option for connecting consumer electronics devices, such as camcorders and DVDs, to the computer system.

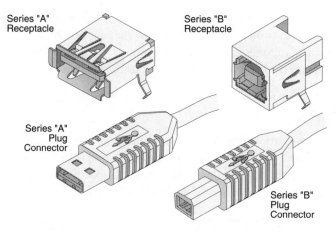

Figure 5.8 USB connectors.

FireWire is also capable of using a special, high-speed *isochronous transfer* mode to support data transfer rates up to 400Mbps. This actually makes the FireWire bus superior to the USB bus. Its high-speed capabilities make FireWire well suited for handling components, such as video and audio devices, which require real-time, high-speed data transfer rates.

A single IEEE-1394 connection can connect up 63 devices to a single port; however, up to 1,023 FireWire buses can be interconnected. PCs usually employ a PCI expansion card to provide the FireWire interface. Whereas audio/visual (A/V) equipment typically employs four-pin 1394 connectors, computers normally use a six-pin connector, with a four-pin to six-pin converter.

Figure 5.9 depicts the FireWire connector and plug most commonly used with PCs.

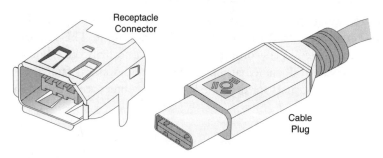

Figure 5.9 FireWire connector and plug.

The IEEE-1394 cable is composed of two twisted-pair conductors similar to those used in local area networks. Like USB, FireWire supports both PnP and hot-swapping of components and provides power to the peripheral devices through one pair of the twisted conductors in the interface cable.

Infrared Ports

The Infrared Data Association (IrDA) has produced a wireless peripheral connection standard based on infrared light technology, similar to that used in consumer remote control devices. The IrDA standard specifies four protocols that are used with different types of devices:

➤ **IrLPT**—The protocol used with character printers to provide a wireless interface between the computer and the printer

➤ **IrDA-SIR**—The standard infrared protocol used to provide a standard serial port interface with transfer rates ranging up to 115kbps

➤ **IrDA-FIR**—The fast infrared protocol used to provide a high-speed serial port interface with transfer rates ranging up to 4Mbps

➤ **IrTran-P**—The protocol used to provide a digital image transfer standard for communications with digital image capture devices

These protocols specify communication ranges up to 2 meters (6 feet), but most specifications usually state 1 meter as the maximum range. All IrDA transfers are carried out in half-duplex mode and must have a clear line of sight between the transmitter and receiver. The receiver must be situated within 15 degrees of center with the line of transmission.

Common Router Default Settings

When you are setting up new routers in a network environment, you need to perform an initial logon to the router to start configuring it. This requires the default username and password. These items can normally be found in the router's installation documentation. However, traditional default usernames and password settings for different brands of routers are included in Table 5.5.

Table 5.5	Manufacturer Default Router Usernames and Passwords	
Router	**Username**	**Password**
Linksys	no username	admin
Cisco	cisco	cisco
Netgear	admin	admin
SMC	no username	admin
Proxim	public	public

IP Addresses

Three standard classes of IP addresses are supported for LANs: Class A, Class B, and Class C. These addresses occur in four-octet fields using the format XXX.YYY.ZZZ.AAA. Each address consists of four 8-bit fields separated by dots (referred to as dotted decimal notation).

➤ **Class-A addresses**—Reserved for large networks and use the last 24 bits (the last three octets or fields) of the address for the host address. The first octet always begins with a 0, followed by a seven-bit number. Therefore, valid Class-A addresses range between 001.x.x.x and 126.x.x.x. This permits a Class-A network to support 126 different networks with nearly 17 million hosts (nodes) per network.

➤ **Class-B addresses**—Assigned to medium-sized networks. The first two octets can range between 128.x.x.x and 191.254.0.0. The last two octets contain the host addresses. This enables Class-B networks to include up to 16,384 different networks with approximately 65,534 hosts per network.

➤ **Class-C addresses**—Normally used with smaller LANs. In a Class-C address, only the final octet is used for host addresses. The first three octets can range between 192.x.x.x and 223.254.254.0. Therefore, the Class-C address can support approximately 2 million networks with 254 hosts each.

The 127.x.x.x address range is a special block of addresses reserved for testing network systems. The U.S. government owns some of these addresses for testing the Internet backbone. The 127.0.0.1 address is reserved for testing the bus on the local system.

Subnets

Sections of the network can be grouped together into *subnets* that share a range of IP addresses. These groups are referred to as *intranets*. An intranet requires that each segment have a protective gateway to act as an entry and exit point for the segment. In most cases, the gateway is a device called a router. A router is an intelligent device that receives data and directs it toward a designated IP address.

Some networks employ a *firewall* as a gateway to the outside. A firewall is a combination of hardware and software components that provide a protective barrier between networks with different security levels. Administrators configure the firewall so that it will only pass data to and from designated IP addresses and TCP/IP ports.

Subnets are created by masking off (hiding) the network address portion of the IP address on the units within the subnet. This, in effect, limits the mobility of the data to those nodes within the subnet because they can reconcile only addresses from within their masked range. Three common reasons to create a subnet are as follows:

➤ **To isolate one segment of the network from all the others**—
Suppose, for example, that a large organization has 1,000 computers, all of which are connected to the network. Without segmentation, data from all 1,000 units would run through every other network node. The effect of this would be that everyone else on the network would have access to all the data on the network, and the operation of the network would be slowed considerably by the uncontrolled traffic.

➤ **To efficiently use IP addresses**—Because the IP addressing scheme is defined as a 32-bit code, only a limited number of possible addresses are available. Although 126 networks with 17 million customers might seem like a lot, in the scheme of a worldwide network system, that's not many addresses to go around.

➤ **To utilize a single IP address across physically divided locations**—
For example, subnetting a Class-C address between remotely located areas of a campus would permit half of the 253 possible addresses to be allocated to one campus location, and the other half to be allocated to hosts at the second location. In this manner, both locations can operate using a single Class-C address.

Private IP Classes

Because the Internet is basically a huge TCP/IP network in which no two computers connected to it can have the same address, networks connected to the Internet must follow a specific IP addressing scheme assigned by an Internet service provider (ISP). However, any IP addressing scheme can be used as long as your network is not connected to the Internet. This is referred to as a *private network*.

When configuring a private network, you must design an IP addressing scheme to use across the network. Although, technically, you could use any IP addressing scheme you want in a private network without consulting an ISP, special ranges of network addresses in each IP class have been reserved for use with private networks. These are reserved addresses that are not registered to anyone on the Internet.

If you are configuring a private network, you should use one of these address options rather than creating a random addressing scheme. The total number of clients on the network typically dictates which IP addressing class you should use. The following list of private network IP addresses can be used:

➤ An IP address of 10.0.0.0, with the subnet mask of 255.0.0.0

➤ An IP address of 169.254.0.0, with the subnet mask of 255.255.255.0 (the Microsoft AIPA default)

➤ An IP address of 172.(16–32).0.0, with the subnet mask of 255.240.0.0

➤ An IP address of 192.168.0.0, with the subnet mask of 255.255.0.0

In addition, remember that all *hosts* must have the same network ID and subnet mask and that no two computers on your network can have the same IP address when you are establishing a private IP addressing scheme.

Well-known TCP/UDP Ports

Port identifiers are used in TCP/UDP messages to refer to high-layer applications running on network computers. The port identifier and IP address together form a *socket*, and the end-to-end communication between two hosts is uniquely identified on the Internet by the source port, source address, destination port, and destination address.

Port numbers are always specified as a 16-bit number. Port numbers in the range 0–1023 are called *well-known ports*. These port numbers are assigned to the server side of an application.

Port numbers in the range 1024–49151 are called *registered ports*, and these are numbers that have been publicly defined as a convenience for the Internet community to avoid vendor conflicts. Server or client applications can use the port numbers in this range.

The remaining port numbers, those in the range 49152–65535, are called *dynamic* and/or *private ports* and can be used freely by any client or server.

Some well-known port numbers are listed in Table 5.6.

Table 5.6 Well-known Port Numbers

PORT #	COMMON PROTOCOL	SERVICE	PORT #	COMMON PROTOCOL	SERVICE
7	TCP	echo	80	TCP	http
9	TCP	discard	110	TCP	pop3
13	TCP	daytime	111	TCP	sunrpc
19	TCP	chargen	119	TCP	nntp
20	TCP	ftp-control	123	UDP	ntp
21	TCP	ftp-data	137	UDP	netbios-ns
23	TCP	telnet	138	UDP	netbios-dgm
25	TCP	smtp	139	TCP	netbios-ssn
37	TCP	time	143	TCP	imap
43	TCP	whois	161	UDP	snmp
53	TCP/UDP	dns	162	UDP	snmp-trap
67	UDP	bootps	179	TCP	bgp
68	UDP	bootpc	443	TCP	https (http/ssl)
69	UDP	tftp	520	UDP	rip
70	TCP	gopher	1080	TCP	socks
79	TCP	finger	33434	UDP	traceroute

Some additional TCP port numbers associated with remote services include 135—messenger for remote procedure calls, 3389—terminal server, and 5631 and 5632—PCAnywhere. (With these types of remote access and control products, it is common to change the port numbers over to obscure numbers to keep others from guessing them.)

Standard PC Resource Usage

The most frequent operation that occurs in a personal computer involves the movement of information from one location to another. Controlling the movement of data through the system involves allocating system resources (that is, interrupt request channels, I/O addresses, and direct memory access channels) to the system's different hardware devices.

In some situations, you must be able to determine what system resources are required for the device, what resources are available in the system, and how they might be allocated to successfully install hardware components in a PC.

Interrupts

Each device in a PC-compatible system that is capable of interrupting the microprocessor must be assigned its own unique IRQ number. The system uses this number to identify which device is in need of service.

Two varieties of interrupts are used in microcomputers:

> **Maskable interrupts** (in the form of interrupt request [IRQ] channels)—Interrupts that the system microprocessor can ignore under certain conditions.

> **Nonmaskable interrupts (NMI)**—Very serious interrupts to which the system microprocessor must always respond. NMI conditions normally result in the system being shut down.

Two serious system board–based conditions can cause an *NMI error*. The first condition occurs when an active *IO Channel Check* (*IOCHCK*) signal is received from an adapter card located in one of the system board's expansion slots. The other event is the occurrence of a *Parity Check* (*PCK*) error in the system's DRAM memory. Because these errors indicate that information from I/O devices or memory cannot be trusted, the NMI signal causes the system to shut down without storing any of the potentially bad data.

Table 5.7 shows the designations for the various interrupt levels in the system.

Table 5.7	System Interrupt Levels		
INTERRUPT	DESCRIPTION	INTERRUPT	DESCRIPTION
NMI	I/O CHANNEL CHECK OR PARITY CHECK ERROR		
	INTC1		INTC2
IRQ0	TIMER/COUNTER ALARM	IRQ8	REAL TIME CLOCK
IRQ1	KEYBOARD BUFFER FULL	IRQ9	SPARE
IRQ2	CASCADE FROM INTC2	IRQ10	SPARE
IRQ3	SERIAL PORT 2	IRQ11	SPARE
IRQ4	SERIAL PORT 1	IRQ12	SPARE PS/2 MOUSE
IRQ5	PARALLEL PORT 2	IRQ13	COPROCESSOR
IRQ6	FDD CONTROLLER	IRQ14	PRIMARY IDE CTRL
IRQ7	PARALLEL PORT 1	IRQ15	SECONDARY IDE CTRL

Each IRQ input is assigned a priority level. With this in mind, it is not difficult to see that the priority orders for IRQs in an AT-compatible machine begin with IRQ0 as the highest, followed by IRQ1, IRQ8 through IRQ15, and, finally, IRQ3 through IRQ7.

PCI Interrupts

PCI system boards bring four flexible *PCI interrupt* lines (INTa through INTd, or INT1 through INT4) to the system. Adapter cards in the PCI slots can use these lines to activate up to four different interrupts that are mapped to the system's IRQ channels (typically IRQ9 through IRQ12). You can see these interrupts described in the PnP and PCI Configuration screen of the CMOS setup utility. In Windows-based systems, the operating system can manipulate the use of the PCI interrupts and steer them to different IRQ lines so that there is never a conflict between devices sharing them.

Direct Memory Access

Direct memory access (DMA) operations are very similar to interrupt-driven I/O operations, except that the controller does not ask the system microprocessor to stop what it is doing to manage the I/O operation. Instead, the DMA controller asks the microprocessor to get out of the way so that it can control the system and handle the I/O transfer.

Table 5.8 describes the default PC DMA channel designations.

Table 5.8	DMA Channel Designations		
CHANNEL	FUNCTION	CONTROLLER	PAGE REGISTER ADDRESS
CH0	SPARE	1	0087
CH1	SDLC (NETWORK)	1	0083
CH2	FDD CONTROLLER	1	0082
CH3	SPARE	1	0081
CH4	CASCADE TO CNTR 1	2	
CH5	SPARE	2	008B
CH6	SPARE	2	0089
CH7	SPARE	2	008A

PC Address Allocations

In the PC system, you have two types of addresses to contend with—those that refer to locations in the systems memory map (that is, RAM and ROM addresses) and those that apply to I/O device locations.

The various I/O port addresses listed in Table 5.9 are used in the PC-compatible system. When dealing with PC-compatibles, you have two forms of I/O to contend with—the system board's onboard I/O systems (System) and the peripheral devices that interact with the system through its expansion slots or port connectors (I/O).

Table 5.10 provides an abbreviated listing of the standard PC memory map.

Table 5.9   I/O Port Addresses

HEX ADDRESS	DEVICE	USAGE
000–01F	DMA Controller (South Bridge)	System
020–03F	Interrupt Controller (South Bridge)	System
040–05F	Timer/Counter (South Bridge)	System
060–06F	Keyboard Controller	System
070–07F	Real-Time Clock, NMI Mask (South Bridge)	System
080–09F	DMA Page Register (South Bridge)	System
0A0–0BF	Interrupt Controller (South Bridge)	System
0F0	Clear Math Coprocessor Busy	System
0F1	Reset Math Coprocessor	System
0F8–0FF	Math Coprocessor	System
170–177	Second IDE Controller	I/O
1F0–1F7	First IDE Controller	I/O
200–207	Game Port	I/O
278–27F	Parallel Printer Port #2	I/O
2F8–2FF	Serial Port #2	I/O
378–37F	Parallel Printer Port #1	I/O
3B0–3BF	MGA/first Printer Port	I/O
3D0–3DF	CGA	I/O
3F0–3F7	FDD Controller	I/O
3F8–3FF	Serial Port #1	I/O
FF80–FF9F	USB Controller	I/O

Table 5.10   System Memory Map

ADDRESS	FUNCTION
0–3FF	Interrupt Vectors
400–47F	ROM BIOS RAM
480–5FF	BASIC and Special System Function RAM
600–9FFFF	Program Memory
A0000–BFFFF	VGA/EGA Display Memory
B0000–B7FFF	Monochrome Display Adapter Memory
B8000–BFFFF	Color Graphics Adapter Memory
C0000–C7FFF	VGA/SVGA BIOS
C8000–CBFFF	EIDE/SCSI ROM (also older HDD Types)
D0000–D7FFF	Spare ROM
D0000–DFFFF	LAN Adapter ROM
E0000–E7FFF	Spare ROM
E8000–EFFFF	Spare ROM
F0000–EFFFF	Spare ROM
F4000–EFFFF	Spare ROM
F8000–EFFFF	Spare ROM
FC000–FDFFF	ROM BIOS
FE000–FFFFF	ROM BIOS

Support Sources

The computer industry involves so many facets and changes so rapidly that it is impossible for a support person to stay current with the entire industry for very long. In the following sections, support information is grouped into five basic headings—Information Resources, Third-Party Utility Websites, Product Support Websites, FTP Utility Site Listings, and Manufacturer Support Phone Numbers.

Information Resources

One of the best tools that a technician can have is access to resources from which he can acquire timely and accurate information required for whatever task he is performing.

Windows Troubleshooting Help Files

Windows 9*x*, Windows NT 4.0, Windows 2000, and Windows XP come with built-in troubleshooting Help file systems. This feature includes troubleshooting assistance for a number of different Windows problems. The Windows 9x, Windows 2000, and Windows XP Troubleshooters are much more expansive than the Windows NT Troubleshooters. In all three systems, the Troubleshooter utilities can be accessed from the Start menu, or from the Help menu entry on the toolbar.

Selecting the Help (or Help and Support in Windows XP) entry from the Start menu produces the main Help window, depicted in Figure 5.10. The local Help screens are manipulated by making a selection from the electronic Contents list. In the Troubleshooting entry, just follow the questions and suggestion schemes provided.

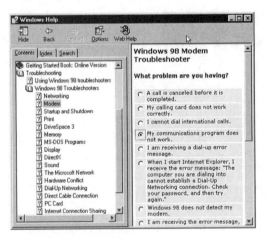

Figure 5.10 Windows 98 Help window.

The Windows Troubleshooters are a special type of help that is available in Windows 9x, Windows 2000, and Windows XP. These utilities enable you to pinpoint problems and identify solutions to those problems. Troubleshooters ask a series of questions and then provide you with detailed troubleshooting information based on your responses to those questions. You can access the troubleshooters in many ways, including through context-sensitive Help, through the Help (or Help and Support) option on the Start menu, and through the Device Manager.

Windows 2000 Resource Kits

The Windows 95, Windows 98, Windows NT 4.0, Windows 2000, and Windows XP *Resource Kits* provide thousands of pages of in-depth, technical information on these Windows operating systems, as well as hundreds of additional utilities that you can use to enhance deployment, maintenance, and troubleshooting of your Windows network. The Resource Kit is an excellent printed reference for Windows 2000, and also comes with searchable electronic versions.

Two different versions of the Resource Kit are available for each NT operating system: one for Windows NT Workstation and one for Windows NT Server (as well as one for Windows 2000 Professional and one for Windows 2000 Server). The Resource Kits are published by Microsoft Press and are available from major book retailers.

Internet Help

You can activate the Windows 98, Windows 2000, and Windows XP *online Help* functions by selecting a topic from the menu and then clicking the Web Help button. Afterward, you must click the Support Online option at the lower-right of the Help window. This action brings up the Internet Sign-In dialog box, if the system is not already logged on to the Internet. After signing in, the Microsoft technical support page appears, as depicted in Figure 5.11.

Microsoft online *Product Support Services* can provide a wealth of information about Microsoft products, including their operating systems. The URL for Product Support Services is www.Microsoft.com/support. Features of Microsoft Product Support include the following:

➤ *Microsoft Knowledge Base*, which is a searchable database of information and self-help tools. The Knowledge Base is used by Microsoft Technical Support to support their customers and is made available to you free of charge.

➤ *Download Center*, which enables you to search all available downloads for any Microsoft product, including service packs, patches, and updates.

➤ *Facts by Product*, which enables you to browse for information by product, and includes a list of most frequently asked questions about each product.

➤ Listing of support phone numbers, which can be used to access live assistance. A charge applies for phone support.

➤ *Online Support Requests*, which permits you to submit questions to Microsoft support personnel. A charge applies for online support.

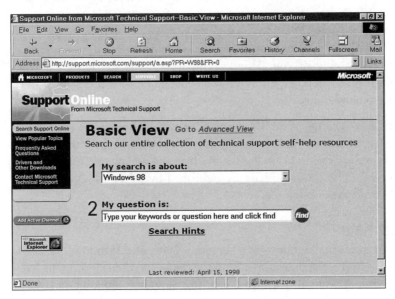

Figure 5.11 Microsoft Online Help window.

Microsoft TechNet

The Microsoft *TechNet* website is designed to support IT professionals. The URL for this site is www.Microsoft.com/technet. This is an excellent site for getting the latest information about Windows 2000 or Windows XP (and all other Microsoft products and technologies).

TechNet features include the following:

➤ Search capabilities for the Technical Information database and the Knowledge Base

➤ A What's New section that highlights new issues every month

➤ Access to the Product Support Services website

➤ Information categorized by product to help you troubleshoot, maintain, and deploy software

➤ Chats, user groups, and Feedback Central for communicating with your peers and with Microsoft

Microsoft also provides a TechNet subscription service. For an annual fee, the Technical Information database, Knowledge Base, service packs, patches, fixes, software utilities, product enhancements, Resource Kits, beta versions of future Microsoft products, training information, and many other useful items are shipped to you each month in CD-ROM format. A TechNet subscription can be purchased at the TechNet website.

Online Information Resources

A great deal of PC support information is available through the Internet. The following list provides web addresses for obtaining information about various PC topics:

➤ **http://webopedia.com**—An excellent online dictionary and search engine for computer and Internet technology definitions.

➤ **http://www.sandpile.org**—An extensive source of searchable technical information covering the x86 processor line.

➤ **http://www.amptron.com/html/bios.html**—The BIOS support site for updating BIOS versions.

➤ **http://www.pctechguide.com**—A good source for technical explanations of different hardware components and specifications.

➤ **http://www.pcguide.com**—One of the Internet's premier sites for detailed PC reference information.

➤ **http://www.scsita.org**—The SCSI trade association's official website. A great source of up-to-date SCSI products and information.

➤ **http://www.computer.howstuffworks.com**—A huge searchable collection of explanations about how different computer components and technologies work.

➤ **http://www.tomshardware.com**—A collection of news and articles about different PC products. A good source of new PC product information.

➤ **http://www.fapo.com**—A source of advanced IEEE-1284 parallel port and high-speed I/O connectivity information.

➤ **http://www.pcsupport.about.com**—A collection of links to many third-party PC utilities.

➤ **http://www.suggestafix.com**—A forum-based discussion of operating systems, FDISK and partitions, general computing, Internet and security, as well as a number of off-topic discussion areas.

➤ **http://www.techadvice.com/tech/index.htm**—A searchable collection of information and a troubleshooting source for PC hardware components.

➤ **http://www.modemsite.com**—An extensive collection of information about modems, including technical data, driver downloads, and troubleshooting information.

➤ **http://www.sysopt.com**—A source of industry forums, articles and product reviews, benchmarks, and reviews.

➤ **http://www.zerosurge.com**—A source of surge suppressor information. The site has a good explanation of surge suppression and related information.

➤ **http://www.cablesnmor.com**—An extensive source of PC cabling information with pictures of a wide variety of cables and connectors.

➤ **http://www.tufftest.com**—A provider of PC diagnostic products. Note the free download for the "Lite" version of their diagnostic tool.

➤ **http://www.dslcenter.com**—A source of information on Digital Subscriber Line (DSL) technology.

➤ **http://www.**cable-modems.org—A tutorial and information about cable modems.

➤ **http://www.winsupersite.com**—A source of information for evaluating upcoming Microsoft Windows platform technologies.

➤ **http://www.windows.about.com/cs/dualboot**—A source of dual-booting information and directions.

➤ **http://www.seattlewireless.com**—A site with extensive and up-to-date wireless networking information.

Third-Party Utility Websites

In addition to having resources for acquiring information, the technician also needs access to software and tools that might be required to perform different tasks. One of the biggest problems encountered in the field involves finding the correct driver for different I/O devices and systems. The following list offers several sources for obtaining device drivers for a wide variety of devices.

The list also includes sites for obtaining a number of troubleshooting and security utilities.

➤ **http://www.download.com**—A site that offers downloadable drivers and utilities for a variety of applications.

➤ **http://www.driverguide.com**—A massive membership-based database archive of drivers and resources.

➤ **http://www.windrivers.com**—A leading online source for device drivers, antivirus updates, and security patches.

➤ **http://www.drivershq.com**—An active driver matchup process that examines your machine and selects the most up-to-date driver available for your system. Membership-driven site.

➤ **http://www.driverzone.com**—An extensive driver download library. Also includes FCC device lookup service.

➤ **http://www.tucows.com**—A large download site for Windows, Mac, and Linux systems, including applications, utilities, and games.

➤ **http://www.symantec.com**—A premier antivirus and security products provider. Provides current information on virus and worm threats. Also, includes free downloads and scanning options.

➤ **http://www.sarc.com**—A Symantec antivirus resource center. Provides up-to-date advisories and tools for current virus threats.

➤ **http://www.mcafee.com**—A premier antivirus and security products provider. Provides current information on virus and worm threats.

➤ **http://www.windsortech.com**—A provider of diagnostic software products for troubleshooting desktop PCs.

➤ **http://www.bios-drivers.com/**—A site that provides BIOS updates for various BIOS makers.

➤ **http://www.cert.org**—An Internet security expertise site, located at the Software Engineering Institute, a federally funded research and development center operated by Carnegie Mellon University.

➤ **http://www.winzip.com**—A compression utility site.

Product Support Websites

Nearly every hardware manufacturer and software producer offers support for their products through the Internet. The following list provides website contact points for the major hardware and software vendors in the PC industry:

- ► **http://www.ami.com**—Extensive BIOS information. Includes motherboard identification process and BIOS updating information and utilities.

- ► **http://www.phoenix.com/en/home/**—Phoenix and Award BIOS manufacturer home page.

- ► **http://www.support.microsoft.com**—Microsoft Help and Support site for researching Windows operating system problems and options.

- ► **http://www.intel.com/sites/support/**—Intel support site. Offers searchable technical information as well as software, drivers, BIOS, and other utilities downloads.

- ► **http://www.amd.com**—Microprocessor support site with technical specifications and application information covering AMD processors.

- ► **http://www.kingston.com**—Memory support site. Includes computer, flash, and camera memory devices.

- ► **http://www.usb.org**—Official USB website. Includes technical information about the USB bus, along with advanced specification news.

- ► **http://www.apple.com/support**—Apple Computer's support website.

- ► **http://solutions.brother.com**—Support website for Brother printers and products.

- ► **http://www.usa.canon.com/html/conCprTSIndex.jsp**—The Canon support website for Canon printers, copiers, and other products.

- ► **http://www.epson.com/cgi-bin/Store/support/SupportIndex.jsp**—Epson printer driver and support center.

- ► **http://www.xerox.com**—Xerox main website. Click Support and Drivers to access their support center.

- ► **http://www.lexmark.com**—Lexmark printer main website. Click Technical Support for their technical support or Drivers and Downloads to access their driver support center.

- ► **http://www.ibm.com/support/us/**—Main technical support web page for IBM products. Click Search Technical Support for technical service, or click Downloads and Drivers to search for PC drivers, software fixes, and updates.

- ► **http://www.cisco.com/en/US/support/index.html**—Cisco support index. The main entrance to Cisco product support, technology support, tools, and downloads.

➤ **http://welcome.hp.com/country/us/en/support.html**—Hewlett Packard support center. Offers downloadable drivers and software as well as troubleshooting information and support.

➤ **http://www.support.dell.com**—Main support page for Dell Computer products.

➤ **http://support.gateway.com/support/default.asp**—Gateway Computer main support page. Offers support on a range of Gateway products.

➤ **http://support.dlink.com/**—Support site for D-Link networking products. Includes downloads, drivers, knowledge base, manuals, and technical support for their products.

➤ **http://www.linksys.com/support/default.asp**—Support site for Linksys networking products. Includes downloads, drivers, knowledge base, manuals, and technical support for their products.

FTP Utility Site Listings

Some FTP client utilities include

➤ **http://www.ipswitch.com**—Site for obtaining FTP client, messaging, and network monitoring software.

➤ **http://www.cuteftp.com**—Downloadable evaluation version of an FTP client.

➤ **ftp://ftp.microsoft.com**—Microsoft official FTP site. This site contains service packs and downloadable software updates.

FTP Commands

The FTP environment is a command-line environment. So, you should be familiar with some FTP commands. These include

➤ Open—Used to open a connection with another computer

➤ Close—Used to terminate the connection with another computer

➤ Put—Used to copy a local file to the remote machine

➤ Mput—Used to copy multiple files from the local machine to the remote machine (with user prompts before transferring each file)

➤ Get—Used to copy a remote file to the local machine

➤ Mget—Used to copy multiple files from the remote machine to the local machine (with user prompts before transferring each file)

➤ Ls—Used to list the names of the files in the current remote directory

➤ Mkdir—Used to make a new directory within the current remote directory

➤ Help—Can be used to request a list of all available FTP commands

➤ ?—Used to obtain help and information about the FTP commands

FTP sites exist on the Internet in two basic formats: *private* and *public*. To access most private sites, you must connect to the site and input a username and password designated by the FTP host. Most public FTP sites employ *anonymous authentication* for access to the site. Anonymous authentication is an interaction that occurs between the local browser and FTP host without involving the remote user (that is, no username or password is required to gain access). Most organizations support anonymous access because when you authenticate against an FTP server, you are sending your username and password as clear text.

Manufacturer Support Phone Numbers

In this field, you can never have enough telephone numbers to access help—no matter the condition of the computer or network on which you are working. This section provides a collection of the most widely used manufacturer service numbers we could find.

➤ **IBM (US)**—1-800-IBM-SERV (1-800-426-7378; PCs and notebooks)

➤ **Intel (US)**—1-916-377-7000 (Microprocessors), 1-800-404-2284 (system boards; this is a "Pay per incident" number)

➤ **Microsoft (US)**—1-866-PC SAFETY for free virus and security patch related support in the United States and Canada

➤ **Hewlett Packard (US)**—1-800-HP invent (1-800-474-6836) or 1-800-OK Compaq (1-800-652-6672; for Compaq products)

➤ **Dell Computers**—1-800-624-9896 (General), 1-800-624-9897 (Home office), 1-877-773-3355 (Small/Medium business)

➤ **Gateway Computers**—1-800-369-1409 (Home office), 1-888-888-1094 (Business), or 1-800-211-4952 (Education)

➤ **Cisco Systems (US)**—1-800-553-2447 or 1-408-526-7209

➤ **Linksys (US)**—1-800-326-7114

Index

How can we make this index more useful? Email us at indexes@quepublishing.com

D

I-J

K-L

kernald daemon, 329
keyboards, troubleshooting, 194-196
kingston.com Web site, 364
ksysv editor, 330

LANs (local area networks), connections
    configuring
        Windows 9x, 133-140
        Windows Me, 136-140
    connections, setting up, 329
laptops. *See* portable computers
launching applications, 124-125
LBA (logical block addressing), 44
LEDS (light-emitting diodes), 186
legacy files, 170
lexmark.com Web site, 364
light-emitting diodes (LEDs), 186
Linksys (US), phone numbers, 366
linksys.com Web site, 365
Linux
    command-line
        batch commands, 323
        command formats, 322
        directory-level commands, 324-325
        file-level commands, 325-332
        paths, 323-324
        root users, 323
    file permissions, 328
    file systems, creating, 330
    filenames, 325
    home directories, 324
    user accounts, maintaining, 328
linuxconf utility, LAN (local area network) con-
    nections, 329
Local Area Connections Properties dialog box,
    144-145
local area networks (LANs), connections, 329
local area networks. *See* LANs
local printers, installing (Windows 2000/XP),
    128-130
local upgrades, 110-112
logical block addressing (LBA), 44
logical drive letters, 316
logons, WANs (wide-area networks), 244
logs, application, 302
loopback plugs (ports), 214-215
LVD (Low Voltage Differential), 344

M

Make New Connection Wizard, 151
MakeBootDisk utility, 277
manually configurations, microprocessors, 20-21
manufacturers, phone numbers, 366
mapped drives, disconnecting, 321
maskable interrupts (PCs), 355

Master Boot Record (MBR), erasing, 203
master drives, installing, 40
Master File Table (MFT), 45
master test units (data cabling testers), 185
MBR (Master Boot Record), erasing, 203
mcafee.com Web site, 363
MDI (Media Dependent Interface), 334
Media Independent Interface Crossover (MIDX),
    335
MEM tool, 322
memory. *See also* RAM
    bandwidth, 35
    battery memory (portable computers), 230
    buffers, 33
    data throughput, 35
    devices, detecting, 35
    register, 33
    ROM, troubleshooting, 193-194
    speed mismatch, troubleshooting, 116
    Split Bank configurations, 37
    troubleshooting
        operating systems, 237
        Windows 9x/Me, 262
    upgrading, 30
        optimization, 36-38
        SDRAM (synchronous DRAM), 31-32
        speed, 34-36
        SRAM (Static RAM), 32-33
        system board documentation, 31
    virtual, optimizing Windows 9x, 170
memory modules, 29-30
MFT (Master File Table), 45
microprocessors
    BIOS, upgrading, 26
    buses, 20
    compatibility, 21, 25
    configuring, 19-21
    core voltage, 24
    installing, 16-17, 25-26
    operating temperatures, 191
    POST (power-on self test), 22
    SEC (Single Edge Cartridges), 17
    slot specifications, 26-28
    speed/clocking ratings, 21
    troubleshooting, 191-193
    upgrading, 21-25
    ZIF (zero-insertion-force) sockets, 16
Microsoft
    disks/drives (Windows command-line), 315
    software, registering, 100
Microsoft (US), phone numbers, 366
Microsoft Download Library (MSDL), 201
Microsoft FTP Web site, 365
Microsoft Management Consoles (MMCs), 298
Microsoft Product Support Services, 359-360
Microsoft TechNet, 360-361
MIDX (Media Independent Interface Crossover),
    335
milliamperes (mA), measuring current, 182

How can we make this index more useful? Email us at indexes@quepublishing.com

parallel printer cables, 66
parallel printer ports, 72
Parity Check (PCK), 355
Parity Check error, 189
parity RAM, 33
partition boot records, 43
partition tables, 43
partitioning, 43
 active, dual-booting operating systems, 114
 drives, 206
 LBA (logical block addressing), 44
 mounting (Linux), 331
 physical drives, 42-44
passive termination (SCSI cables), 346
passwords
 logon problems (WANs), 244
 Recovery Console, 281
 Windows 2000/XP, 294
patches, 104-105
Pathping utility, 240
paths
 Linux command-line, 323-324
 upgrade (microprocessors), 22
PC resources, allocating, 354-357
pcguide.com Web site, 361
PCI interrupts, 356
PCK (Parity Check), 355
PCMCIA cards, troubleshooting, 228-229
pcsupport.about.com Web site, 361
pctechguide.com Web site, 361
Pentium microprocessors, SEC (Single Edge Cartridges), 17
peripherals
 adapter card-based
  installing, 54-56, 61-62
  upgrading, 62-64
 installing, 64
  digital cameras, 70-71
  FireWire, 68
  IrDA (Infrared Data Association), 69-70
  ports, 65-67, 72-73
  USB (Universal Serial Bus), 68
 upgrading, 71-72
permissions
 Linux files, 328
 share, 147-148
phoenix.com Web site, 364
PING utility, 240-242
pins, serial cables, 340-341
pipeline SRAM (Static RAM), 33
Plastic Pin Grid Array (PPGA), 28
plastic standoffs (system boards), 10
Point-to-Point Protocol over Ethernet (PPPoE), modem connections, 61
Port in Use error, 243
port replicators, portable computers, 230-232
portable computers, troubleshooting, 226
 batteries, 229-230
 docking stations, 230-232

PCMCIA cards, 228-229
port replicators, 230-232
ports
 ECP (Enhanced Capabilities Port), 67
 EPP (Enhanced Parallel Port), 67
 implementing, 72-73
 installing, 65-67
 modems, troubleshooting, 220-221
 parallel (printers), 72
 SPP (Standard Parallel Port), 72
 TCP/UDP (IP addresses), 353-354
 troubleshooting, 213-219
 well-known, 165
POST (power-on self test), 248
 determining problems, 177
 microprocessors, 22
POST cards, 186
power supply
 troubleshooting, 187-188
 upgrading, 80-82
power-on self test (POST), 248
 determining problems, 177
 microprocessors, 22
PPGA (Plastic Pin Grid Array), 28
PPPoE (Point-to-Point Protocol over Ethernet), modem connections, 61
primary partitions, 43
print servers, 127
Print Troubleshooter, 215
printer sharing, enabling (Windows 9x/Me), 268
printers
 ECP (Enhanced Capabilities Port) mode, 214
 EPP (Enhanced Parallel Port) mode, 214
 installing, 215
  properties, 131-132
  Windows 9x, 126-128
  Windows 2000, 128-130
  Windows Me, 126-128
  Windows XP, 128-130
 network, troubleshooting (Windows 9x/Me), 268-269
 parallel cables, 66
 parallel ports, 72
 ports, troubleshooting, 215-219
 SPP (Standard Parallel Port) mode, 214
 troubleshooters, 215
 troubleshooting, 132, 296-297
printing, troubleshooting
 Windows 9x/Me, 266
 Windows 2000, 303-304
 Windows XP, 303-304
 operating systems, 239
private FTP sites, 366
private IP classes, 353
private networks, 353
private ports (TCP/UDP ports), 354

Q-R

S

How can we make this index more useful? Email us at indexes@quepublishing.com

T

How can we make this index more useful? Email us at indexes@quepublishing.com

How can we make this index more useful? Email us at indexes@quepublishing.com

X-Z